Dialogue in Early South Asian Religions
Hindu, Buddhist, and Jain Traditions

Edited by

BRIAN BLACK
Lancaster University, UK

LAURIE PATTON
Duke University, USA

ASHGATE

Published by
Ashgate Publishing Limited
Wey Court East
Union Road
Farnham
Surrey, GU9 7PT
England

Ashgate Publishing Company
110 Cherry Street
Suite 3-1
Burlington, VT 05401-3818
USA

www.ashgate.com

British Library Cataloguing in Publication Data
A catalogue record for this book is available from the British Library.

The Library of Congress has cataloged the printed edition as follows:
Dialogue in early South Asian religions : Hindu, Buddhist, and Jain traditions / edited by Brian Black and Laurie Patton.
pages cm. – (Dialogues in South Asian traditions: religion, philosophy, literature, and history)
Includes index.
ISBN 978-1-4094-4012-3 (hardcover) – ISBN 978-1-4094-4013-0 (pbk.) – ISBN 978-1-4094-4014-7 (ebook) – ISBN 978-1-4724-0051-2 (epub) 1. South Asia – Religion. 2. Sacred books – History and criticism. 3. Religious literature – History and criticism. 4. Dialogue – Religious aspects. 5. Hinduism. 6. Buddhism. 7. Jainism. I. Black, Brian, 1970– editor. II. Patton, Laurie L., 1961– editor.
BL1055.D53 2015
294–dc23

2014035199

ISBN 9781409440123 (hbk)
ISBN 9781409440130 (pbk)
ISBN 9781409440147 (ebk – PDF)
ISBN 9781472400512 (ebk – ePUB)

MIX
Paper from responsible sources
FSC www.fsc.org FSC® C013985

Printed in the United Kingdom by Henry Ling Limited, at the Dorset Press, Dorchester, DT1 1HD

Contents

Contributors

Naomi Appleton teaches and researches Asian religions in the School of Divinity at the University of Edinburgh, specializing in the ways in which story is used to construct, communicate and challenge religious ideas and practices in early South Asia. She is the author of *Jātaka Stories in Theravāda Buddhism* (Ashgate, 2010) and *Narrating Karma and Rebirth: Buddhist and Jain Multi-life Stories* (Cambridge University Press, 2014), as well as a number of articles on religious narrative in South and Southeast Asia. She is currently working with Dr James Hegarty of Cardiff University on a project entitled 'The Story of Story in Early South Asia: Character and Genre across Buddhist, Jain and Hindu Traditions'.

Brian Black is Lecturer in Religious Studies in the Department of Politics, Philosophy and Religion at Lancaster University. His research interests include Indian religions, comparative philosophy, the use of dialogue in Indian religious and philosophical texts, and Hindu and Buddhist ethics. He is author of the book *The Character of the Self in Ancient India: Priests, Kings, and Women in the Early Upaniṣads* (SUNY Press, 2007); he is co-editor (with Simon Brodbeck) of the book *Gender and Narrative in the* Mahābhārata (Routledge, 2007); and he is co-editor (with Laurie Patton) of the book series *Dialogues in South Asian Traditions: Religion, Philosophy, Literature and History* (Ashgate).

Lisa Wessman Crothers is Assistant Professor of Religion at Wooster College in Wooster, Ohio. Her research interests include kingship in ancient India, rhetoric and ideology in Indian Buddhist and Brahmanical narratives, and scripture as literature. She is the author of, among other essays, 'Duryodhana's Pride and Perception: The Dynamics of Distrust in the Moment of Counsel at the Kaurava Court,' in *The Mahābhārata: What is not here is nowhere else*, edited by T.S. Rukmani (New Delhi: Munshiram Manoharlal Publishers, 2005). She is currently working on a book manuscript about the role of the advisor and moments of advice-giving in early Indian traditions.

Anna Aurelia Esposito is Assistant Professor to the Chair of Indology in the Department of Cultural Studies of East- and South-Asia at the University of Würzburg. She studied Indology and Cultural Anthropology in Würzburg, Heidelberg, and Tübingen, where she obtained her MA by producing a critical edition and translation of the one-act play *Dūtavākya* attributed to Bhāsa (1998). After her dissertation – a critical edition of the drama *Cārudatta* with translation and a study of the South Indian drama Prakrits (2003) – she moved the focus of her research to Jaina Prakrit and literature. She is currently working on a project granted by the German Research Foundation about the transmission of religious and moral contents in Jain narrative literature.

Jonathan Geen received his doctorate at McMaster University (Hamilton, Ontario, Canada) in 2001 under Phyllis Granoff. He has taught at McMaster University, Butler University, and the University of Rochester, and is currently Associate Professor of Religious Studies at King's University College at Western University (London, Ontario, Canada). Much of his academic work has focused upon the textual interactions between Hinduism and Jainism, particularly as manifested in epic and mythological texts.

Alf Hiltebeital is Professor of Religion at George Washington University. The focus of his research is the great epics of India (specifically the Sanskrit epics of *Mahābhārata* and *Rāmāyaṇa*), regional folk epics, and the cult of the goddess Draupadī. He has authored, edited, and translated 11 books and dozens of articles on these topics. Hiltebeitel has been the director of the Human Sciences Program at George Washington University and is Editor in Chief of Oxford Bibliographies Online.

Michael Nichols is the William Johnston Jr. Assistant Professor of Religious Studies at Saint Joseph's College, Indiana. His research focuses on the dialogic interaction and evolution of Indian mythic narrative traditions, particularly between early Buddhism and Hinduism. His current project is a study of the development and varied meanings of the Buddhist figure Mara.

Andrew J. Nicholson is Associate Professor of Hinduism and Indian Intellectual History at the State University of New York at Stony Brook. His research interests include the history and historiography of Indian philosophy, intra- and inter-religious dialogue in South Asia, and comparative philosophy. He has written two books, *Unifying Hinduism: Philosophy and Identity in Indian Intellectual History* (Columbia University Press, 2010) and *Lord Śiva's Song: The Īśvara Gītā* (SUNY Press, 2014).

Douglas Osto is a Senior Lecturer and Programme Coordinator for the Religious Studies Programme at Massey University in Palmerston North, New Zealand. He is the author of *Power, Wealth and Women in Indian Mahāyāna Buddhism: The Gaṇḍavyūha-sūtra* (Routledge, 2008). His research interests include Indian Mahāyāna Buddhism, South Asian religions and philosophies, and the contemporary practice of Buddhism.

Laurie Patton is Durden Professor of Religions and the Dean of Arts & Sciences at Duke University, Durham, NC. She is the author or editor of nine books and fifty articles on South Asian religion and culture, particularly early Indian ritual, poetics and sacrifice, as well as comparative mythology. She has also translated the *Bhagavad Gita* for the Penguin Classics Series (2008), and has published two books of poetry (2003; 2011). She is currently at work on two book manuscripts: the first on religious studies and its public spheres, and the second a large-scale ethnography of women and Sanskrit in twenty-first century India.

Elizabeth M. Rohlman is Associate Professor in the Department of Classics and Religion at the University of Calgary in Canada. She is an historian of religion whose research examines the role of narrative literature in articulating and constructing religious identity in pre-modern South Asia. Her forthcoming book is entitled *Telling the Stories of Geography: Compositional Process and Communal Identity in the* Sarasvatī Purāṇa. Her current research includes a literary study of the *Mārkaṇḍeya Purāṇa* and an exploration of the *jati purāṇas* of Gujarat.

Acknowledgements

This book is a result of a project spanning several years, called the Sammukham Project. Convened by Brian Black and Laurie Patton, the Saummukham project held workshops in Chicago in 2008 and Montreal in 2009, during which scholars of South Asian religions came together to discuss the themes of the dialogical that occur in their work. The conversations have resulted in the book series 'Dialogues in Indian Traditions: Religion, Philosophy, Literature, and History', as well as this edited volume within the series. All of the scholars who presented there have shaped our thinking in key ways, and together they form a foundation for what we hope will be a broad, sustained commitment to the study of dialogue and pluralism in India. We wish to thank Seth Ligo and Anil Mundra for their patient and committed help preparing this manuscript in 2013–14. We would also like to thank our respective families, Sophie Barker, the staff at Ashgate, and Valerie Roebuck who helped us find the cover image.

Note on Transliteration and Citation

Every effort has been made to be consistent in the style of reference and transliteration of the several Indian languages in this volume. However, authors may differ slightly in their citation of individual texts and names.

Introduction

Brian Black and Laurie Patton

The Issues at Stake

The *Kauṣītakī Upaniṣad* begins with a scene about the transmission of a sacred teaching. The young brahmin Śvetaketu, on the recommendation of his father Uddālaka Āruṇi, goes to perform a Vedic ritual for King Citra Gāṅgyāyani. The king asks him if he knows the paths to the other world. Śvetaketu replies that he does not know this teaching and then returns to his father to ask how he should reply. Uddālaka Āruṇi, though, does not know this teaching either, so he goes to the king himself to learn. The respected brahmin then approaches King Citra with firewood in hand and announces himself as the king's student. Citra delivers a teaching about death and rebirth, describing the journey after life to the worlds of different gods. Finally, the king's discourse unfolds into another dialogue, this one between a person who has reached the world of Brahmā and the god Brahmā.

This opening scene of the *Kauṣītakī Upaniṣad* contains a number of aspects of dialogue that this book will develop further. The first is that we are introduced to dialogue both inside and outside the text. Within the text, this *upaniṣad* places its content within a dialogical context, presenting its teachings as emerging from a conversation. According to tradition, the genre of Upaniṣad is transmitted orally from teacher to student from one generation to the next. Keeping this in mind, we can see the dialogue in the text as a self-conscious mirror of the text's own transmission. As several chapters in the book discuss, South Asian religious and philosophical literature is often framed as a dialogue between teacher and student, with the dialogue form acting as one way that texts explore the orality of their own transmissions. And in that exploration, the texts also give keys to the ways they might be interpreted.

A second feature of this opening scene of the *Kauṣītakī Upaniṣad* is that it is intertextual, as this scene appears in two other Upaniṣads (*Bṛhadāraṇyaka Upaniṣad* 6.2; *Chāndogya Upaniṣad* 5.3–10). In each of its three versions there are variations concerning the interactions of the characters, as well as concerning the content of the teaching.[1] It is not clear if the *Kauṣītakī Upaniṣad* is referring directly to one or both of the other versions, but in comparing this version against the others we can catch a glimpse of the different agendas of these three Upaniṣads. As we will see in some of the chapters of this book, dialogues in some texts sometimes explicitly refer to dialogues in other texts, invoking their authority, while also taking the formal features of the dialogue in new directions.

A third aspect of dialogue examined in this book is that it can serve as a way of exploring relationships across traditions. While this scene from the *Kauṣītakī Upaniṣad* addresses the *varṇa* relationship between the Brahmins Śvetaketu and Uddālaka Āruṇi on the one hand, and King Citra Gāṅgyāyani on the other, a Buddhist version of this scene

---

[1] Patrick Olivelle (trans. and ed.), *The Early Upaniṣads: Annotated Text and Translation* (New York, 1998).

explores the relationship between Buddhists and Brahmins.[2] As a number of chapters in this book suggest, dialogue is both a shared literary feature across texts of different religious traditions and an effective literary means for exploring interactions amongst them. Dialogue mediates difference, but scholars have not yet fully examined exactly how, why, and when that mediation occurs. The essays in this book are an attempt to close that gap.

This book will explore these three themes, as well as others, across religious and philosophical texts from the Hindu, Buddhist and Jain traditions. As we will see, dialogue is an important compositional feature as far back as the *Ṛg Veda* and the Upaniṣads, and becomes a central device in terms of framing and structuring texts in the *Mahābhārata*, *Rāmāyaṇa* and Purāṇas. In the Buddhist tradition, dialogue features prominently in early literature such as the Nikāyas and the Jātakas, but continues to be important in the *Prajñāpāramitā* literature and other Mahāyāna sources. In the Jain tradition, dialogue is used extensively in canonical texts such as the *Rāyapaseṇiya* and the *Vivāgasuyaṃ*, and continues to be a dominant textual feature in the *Vasudevahiṇḍi*, as well as in Hemacandra's *Sthavirāvalīcaritra*.

One word among the many that stand for dialogue in early India, *saṃvāda*, might give us an idea of the semantic range and textual usages of dialogue. One of the earliest occurrences of the term is in the *Ṛg Veda*, where the poet asks Mitra and Varuṇa to defend him from the one 'who has no pleasure in questioning, nor in repeated calling, nor in dialogue'.[3] The Brāhmaṇas can use the term to mean 'bargain' (*Śatapatha Brāhmaṇa* 9.5.2.16). It is used in the Upaniṣads themselves to name certain dialogues between teacher and pupil within their own tradition. The Dharma Sūtras (*Baudhāyana Dharmasūtra* 2.2.79) use it to mean conversation, discussion or dialogue, which are the word's more common meanings. In the *Yuddhakāṇḍa* of the *Rāmāyaṇa*, *saṃvāda* means an 'account', 'incident' or 'story' (6.125.8A). The *Mahābhārata* continues in this semantic range, only with the added connotation of dispute, ironically enough, in the *Śanti Parvan* (12.235.14). In Mīmāṃsā, it means the opposite – 'agreement' or 'accord' (cf. Śabara 1.3.11; 1.4.22. So too in the *Tantravārttika* 1.2.22; 1.2.47) and in the Jain texts of the *Prabandhacintāmaṇi* (52.4) *saṃvāda* seemed to function as a discrete, if not strictly bounded literary technique. *Saṃvāda* is frequently used in reference to the *Bhagavad Gītā*, where it is described as a *saṃvāda* between Nara and Narayana, as well as Arjuna and Kṛṣṇa (BG 18.74.76). The term is used by the *anukrāmaṇi*s and other late Vedic texts to describe certain Vedic hymns. Throughout the *Mahābhārata* (*Adi Parvan* 1.2.45; 1.2.125 and *passim*) it is used to name certain dialogues, such as the harmonious exchange between Draupadī and Kṛṣṇa's wife, Satyabhāma.

The texts discussed in this book use many different terms for dialogue in addition to *saṃvāda*. And the possibilities for its interpretation are equally rich and varied. As we will see throughout this book, dialogue can take various forms, from being completely implicit, where the speakers must be inferred, to being explicitly the speaking parts of longer narratives. Dialogues can frame entire texts in their own right, or they can be embedded within texts of other literary prose and poetic styles. Throughout its various forms, dialogue has a variety of purposes and effects, yet it also has numerous recurring uses both across textual genres and across religious traditions. While dialogue has been commented upon sporadically in academic studies about South Asian religious and philosophical sources, it

---

[2] Brian Black, 'Ambaṭṭha and Śvetaketu: Narrative Connections between the Upaniṣads and Early Buddhism', *Journal of the American Academy of Religion* 79/1 (2011): 136–61.

[3] *ny yaḥ sampṛche na purnar havītave na saṃvādāya ramate* RV 8.101.4ab.

has tended to be quite specific and has only rarely been the primary focus of investigation more broadly across the boundaries of methods, genres and traditions.[4] The shared usages of dialogue across religious and philosophical traditions are ripe for analysis, as are the differential usages. By bringing together a number of scholars working with sources across Hindu, Buddhist and Jain traditions, this book is an initial attempt to bring attention to the many roles of dialogue in South Asian religious and philosophical literature.

The Shape of the Book

While most of the chapters in this book address more than one way that dialogue shapes texts and conveys meanings, we have divided the book into three parts, each of which explores a distinct aspect of dialogue. Part I, 'Dialogues Inside and Outside the Texts', examines how dialogue provides an internal commentary on the transmission of the text, as well as looking at how the conversational participants inside the text can indicate audiences outside the text. One theme we find throughout the chapters of Part I is the relationship between a text and its community of reception. Part II, 'Texts in Dialogue', looks closely at the use of dialogue to establish relationships between a text and other texts within its own tradition. Part III, 'Moving Between Traditions', focuses on the shared uses of dialogue between texts, particularly across the Brahmanical, Buddhist and Jain traditions, as well as how the literary use of dialogue reflects engagement between traditions. All of the chapters in this Part pay close attention to the interactions between the interlocutors and how these interactions play out possible 'real-world' rivalries across traditions.

---

[4] In addition to the more philological debates about dialogue in the nineteenth and twentieth centuries, best summarized by Paul Horscht, *Die vedische Gatha-und Sloka-Literatur* (Bern, 1966), we should also mention F.B.J. Kuiper's classic 'The Ancient Aryan Verbal Contest', *Indo-Iranian Journal* 4/4 (1960): 217–81. More recently, see George Thompson, 'The Brahmodya and Vedic Discourse', *Journal of the American Oriental Society* 117/1 (Jan. – Mar. 1997): 13–37; Laurie Patton, 'Samvada: A Literary Resource for Conflict Negotiation in Classical India', in *Evam: Forum on Indian Representations* 3/1–2 (Delhi, 2004, pp. 177–90); and Laurie Patton, 'How do you Conduct Yourself? Dialogical Gender in the *Mahābhārata*', in Simon Brodbeck and Brian Black (eds), *Gender and Narrative in the Mahabharata: New Essays* (London, 2007, pp. 97–109); Tamar Reich, 'The Sacrifice of Battle and the Battle of Yoga, or How to Word-Away a Discontented Wife', in Laurie L. Patton (ed.), *Notes from a Mandala: Essays in the History of Indian Religions* (Newark, NJ, 2010, pp. 182–99); Christopher Z. Minkowski, 'Janamejaya's *Sattra* and Ritual Structure', *Journal of the American Oriental Society* 109/3 (1989): 401–20; and Christopher Z. Minksowski, 'Snakes, *sattras* and the *Mahābhārata*', in Arvind Sharma (ed.), *Essays on the Mahābhārata* (Leiden, 1991, pp. 384–400). Brian Black has focused much of his early work on this theme: 'Ambaṭṭha and Śvetaketu: Narrative Connections between the Upaniṣads and Early Buddhism', *Journal of the American Academy of Religion* 79/1 (2011): 136–61); 'Rivals and Benefactors: Encounters between Buddhists and Brahmins in the Nikāyas', *Religions of South Asia* 3/1 (2009): 25–43 and *The Character of the Self in Ancient India: Priests, Kings, and Women in the Early Upanishads* (Albany, 2007). Not exclusively on dialogue but still relevant are two additional recent works: Adam Bowles, *Dharma, Disorder and The Political in Ancient India: The Āpaddharmaparvan of the Mahābhārata* (Leiden, 2007) and James Hegarty, *Religion, Narrative and Public Imagination in South Asia: Past and Place in the Sanskrit Mahābhārata* (New York and London, 2012). For the issue of philosophical dialogue, addressed by Nicholson in this volume, see Daya Krishna et al. (eds), *Samvada, a Dialogue between Two Philosophical Traditions* (Delhi, 1991); and Esther Solomon, *Indian Dialectics: Methods of Philosophical Discussion* (Ahmedabad, 1976).

While these three Parts are not the only way that the chapters in this book could be arranged, they represent a starting point for distinguishing the multiple, yet overlapping uses of dialogue in South Asian religious and philosophical literature. They also provide us with an opportunity to put the chapters in this book into a dialogue with each other, enabling us to bring out some of the shared and distinguishing features of dialogue from one text to another and from one tradition to another. While it remains to be seen whether dialogue could be understood as a genre in its own right in South Asian religious and philosophical traditions, its frequency from the very earliest texts suggests that it deserves more critical comparative attention than it has previously received.

Dialogues Inside and Outside the Texts

We begin with Laurie Patton's chapter, which discusses dialogue in the *Ṛg Veda*. Most of the hymns of the *Ṛg Veda* are praises addressed to gods. As we imagine such hymns performed in a ritual context, we might see them as dialogues with deities – as ritual poets speaking directly to the gods. In addition to the oral and rhetorical dimensions of these praises as performed in a ritual context, a number of the hymns are composed in the form of a dialogue. Patton mentions the dialogues between Agastya and Lopāmudrā (RV 10.79), Saramā and the Paṇis (RV 10.108), and Indra and Agni (RV 10.124). We might imagine such hymns as scripted performances with different speaking parts enacted by different speakers on the ritual ground.

Patton's chapter focuses on *Ṛg Veda* 7.103, known as the Frog Hymn. In contrast with the other dialogues she mentions, this hymn does not contain named speakers engaged in a verbal encounter, but is more of a reflection on dialogue. As Patton suggests, *Ṛg Veda* 7.103 can be read 'as a poetic commentary on the nature of Vedic dialogue and the development of voice' (p. 25). Indeed, many of the themes related to dialogue that are raised in the Frog Hymn are present in the other dialogues examined in this book.

Ṛg Veda 7.103 begins with an explanation of what starts a dialogue. As the hymn recounts, the frogs have raised their voices, enlivened by Parjanya, the god of rain. In other words, this hymn presents dialogue as inspired by the gods. We might see connections here with dialogues that appear in devotional texts, such as the *Rāmāyana* (see Chapter 2) and Purāṇas (see Chapter 6), where dialogue can be seen as a practice of *bhakti* – that one way of praising a god was through dialogue. Two of the chapters of this book (Chapters 6 and 7) will discuss a specific type of dialogue, called *gītā*, which is a conversation between a supreme god and a devotee.

While the god Parjanya does not speak in *Ṛg Veda* 7.103, we can assume he is listening. Moreover, as we think of Parjanya as a participant in this dialogue, we encounter another crucial aspect of dialogue that is addressed in *Ṛg Veda* 7.103, which is explored throughout many of the chapters in this book. We are referring here to the way that dialogues can address an audience outside the text. In addition to addressing Parjanya, Patton suggests that *Ṛg Veda* 7.103 is self-consciously aware of its own oral transmission, both bringing attention to it and as commenting upon its dialogical context. The other chapters in Part I will develop this theme further, as they explore how dialogues within the text can address specific audiences and communities.

Another crucial aspect of *Ṛg Veda* 7.103 is the explicit connection between dialogue and ritual. In this hymn dialogue is encountered almost exclusively in terms of its ritual context. Not only does voice emerge through ritual, but words are considered to have power and efficacy when articulated in a ritual context. As the hymn makes explicit, the croaks of the frogs bring rain. Patton links her discussion of this hymn with her previous work on metonymy, which she characterizes as a ritual agency in ancient India in which ritual performers would set up possible 'associated worlds' between the words they spoke and the physical surroundings of the ritual.[5] In terms of the strong connection between dialogue and ritual, we might also think of the work of Christopher Minkowski,[6] who argues that in texts such as the *Mahābhārata*, the dialogical structure of multiple embedding is based on the structure of Vedic ritual. While in texts such as the *Ṛg Veda*, the Upaniṣads and the *Mahābhārata* we can see strong connections between dialogue and ritual, in other texts, especially those belonging to the Buddhist and Jain traditions, we see other organizational principles at work in terms of the way dialogue is structured.

It is not until verse three of *Ṛg Veda* 7.103 when there emerges a dialogue between the frogs. As Patton describes it, this verse describes 'the beginning of actual dialogue between two characters, where one frog approaches and speaks to another' (p. 30). *Ṛg Veda* 7.103, as Patton points out, is reflective upon the repetition involved in dialogue. This is made explicit through the reference to echoing the voices of the other, like the student repeats after his teacher (p. 27). As we will see in the other chapters of Part I, a number of the dialogues that frame texts are between teachers and students, thereby setting up the entire text as a teaching.

But while the student–teacher exchange might be the ideal type of dialogue in this hymn and in many other textual contexts, *Ṛg Veda* 7.103 also explores the diversity of dialogue. The hymn accomplishes this, Patton argues, by comparing 'the frogs' speech to another form of speech; a likening of the frogs' conversations with another form of conversation' (p. 30). Also, through simile the hymn explores the different types of voices that arise from different animals. 'One lows like a cow; one bleats like a goat; one is dappled; one is green. They have the same name, but different shapes. As they are speaking, they fashion their voice in many ways.' As Patton points out, 'the voices are in harmony, even though they have different parts' (p. 31). Further on, the hymn refers to these different voices as having 'enriched us'. As Patton reflects, the multiplicity of voices is 'orchestrated and collaborative'. Indeed, like some of the other dialogues explored in this book, we see an interest in how different speakers speak differently (see Chapter 8) and an acknowledgement of the diversity of voices (see Chapter 11).

Finally, Patton discusses how the frogs 'build upon each other to provide a progressively thicker description of dialogue itself' (p. 26), reflecting that 'the hymn could be read as a contemplation of the growth of dialogue' (p. 31). At the beginning of the hymn, the frogs' voices are enlivened, but unformed; but as the hymn progresses, they speak out and then begin to speak to each other through repetition and in unison, until finally their individual voices emerge in harmony. As Patton describes it: 'the frogs are literally "raising their voice", verse by verse' (p. 35). In this way, the verses build upon each other, as the hymn, which begins with the frogs, becomes increasingly about Brahmins chanting in a ritual setting. Here we see the hymn explore the temporality of dialogue, conveying that dialogue does not merely entail the inclusion of more than one voice, but that each time different voices come together, their interaction moves through time and different dynamics emerge through their exchanges.

---

[5] See Laurie L. Patton, *Bringing the Gods to Mind: Mantra and Ritual in Early Indian Sacrifice* (Berkeley, CA, 2005).

[6] Minkowski, 'Janamejaya's *Sattra* and Ritual Structure'.

In Chapter 2, Alf Hiltebeitel offers a creative comparison of the use of dialogue in the *Mahābhārata* and the *Rāmāyaṇa*, two texts which have complex dialogical structures. In the *Mahābhārata*, the main story is embedded within three 'braided' frame stories. Among these three are the two well-known dialogues between Ugraśravas and Śaunaka during a 12-year *sattra* in the Naimiṣa Forest, and between Vaiśaṃpāyana and Janamejaya at the king's snake sacrifice. Hiltebeitel also adds the dialogue between Vyāsa, the author of the text, and his five disciples. Although this is not a dialogue that is depicted in the text, this transmission constitutes the text's first telling and, as Hiltebeitel suggests, 'presumes a dialogical situation at Vyāsa's hermitage' (p. 44). Moreover, Vyāsa's transmission of the text to his students 'tacitly' frames the *Mahābhārata*'s other two frames. In addition to these three dialogues that frame the text as a whole, Hiltebeitel also brings attention to 'two other lengthy interior dialogues': the conversation between Saṃjaya and Dhṛtarāṣṭra, which frames the entire account of the war and the post-war dialogue between king Yudhiṣṭhira and Bhīṣma, the wise Kuru patriarch. Hiltebeitel explores how the dialogues that frame the text are braided together, with Vyāsa not only appearing in what Hiltebeitel calls the 'outermost frame', but also in every other layer of transmission. In Hiltebeitel's view, the net effect of this complexly interwoven dialogical structure 'is to set up mirrors, puzzles, and echoes between subtales and the main story – and between subtales themselves – and to reinforce such echoes through back-and-forth framings and multiple tellings to numerous auditors' (p. 38).

In contrast to the *Mahābhārata*, the *Rāmāyaṇa* has a single-frame story, but, as Hiltebeitel suggests, this frame 'can also be said to have three dialogical strands or even tiers' (p. 62). The single frame story contains two dialogues that are presented as sequential, rather than one embedded within the other; the first is between Nārada and Vālmīki, the second between Vālmīki and the god Brahmā. There is also a presumed 'ongoing dialogical situation at Vālmīki's *āśrāma*' (p. 64) where Rāma's twin sons Kuśa and Lava address the *Rāmāyaṇa* to him. As Hiltebeitel observes, Rāma's role as a listener is also made explicit throughout the text, as he is 'usually the main hearer of stories', with the 'net effect' putting Rāma into an imaginable 'interior dialogue with himself' (p. 38). In exploring the idea that the *Rāmāyaṇa* can be read as Rāma's internal dialogue, Hiltebeitel differentiates between dialogue and apostrophe, suggesting that apostrophe is used 'to lift dialogue "out of context" to address the reader: that is, to engage the epics' target audience' (p. 37). Hiltebeitel suggests that Vālmīki's 'new move' towards apostrophe is a way of conveying the *Rāmāyaṇa*'s devotion towards the god Rāma. Yet at the same time, apostrophe characterizes Rāma in ways that are distinctly human. Hiltebeitel argues that both 'dialogue in the *Mahābhārata* and apostrophe in the *Rāmāyaṇa* would have been innovative means to create new dialogical communities of those engaged in these texts' (p. 37).

The dialogues that frame the *Mahābhārata* have been discussed on multiple occasions, while Hiltebeitel's chapter indicates that the dialogues introducing the *Rāmāyaṇa* are also complexly woven into the text's structure. In Chapter 3, Anna Aurelia Esposito's discussion of the use of frame dialogues in Jain literature brings attention to similarly complex dialogical framing structures in other texts and traditions. As she observes, both the *Rāyapaseṇiya* and the *Vivāgasuyaṃ* – two texts from the canonical scriptures of the Śvetāmbaras – are examples of texts that use dialogue to frame a number of embedded stories. In the *Vivāgasuyaṃ* the frame dialogue is between Mahāvīra and Iṃdabhūti, with the different chapters of the text following a similar pattern: Iṃdabhūti 'sees some extraordinary things happen and questions his master Mahāvīra about it. Mahāvīra explains the actual incident and tells Iṃdabhūti all about the former and future births of the persons involved' (p. 87). Similar to the Jātaka tales in the Buddhist tradition (as discussed by Appleton in Chapter 4), this framing dialogue allows Mahāvīra to display his advanced knowledge about rebirth. Esposito points out that the dialogue between Mahāvīra is embedded within a dialogue between Mahāvīra's pupil Suhamma and his pupil Jambu. This 'double dialogue' is also present in the *Nāyādhammakahāo*, as well as other sections of the Śvetāmbara canon. Here we see that the canon brings attention to Mahāvīra's authority, while also using its double dialogue structure to portray a lineage, thus reflecting upon how knowledge is transmitted within the Jain tradition.

Esposito further discusses how Jain narrative literature continued to use dialogues to frame texts, but developed this technique in more complex ways, particularly as a 'means to connect the various stories with each other' (p. 89). Similar to the *Mahābhārata*, the *Vasudevahiṇḍī* uses several narrative frames, 'thus presenting the narrative as a series of embedded conversations from different times and places' (p. 89).[7] Making similar points to those of Hiltebeitel, Esposito argues that one of the ways dialogue is employed in the *Vasudevahiṇḍī* is to engage the text's target audience. Narrative texts such as the *Vasudevahiṇḍī* not only continue to frame teachings in dialogues, but use the same double dialogue in which Suhamma and Mahāvīra are the narrators. On one level, these dialogues 'imitate the canonical texts by using the same narrative framing' (p. 96), yet a significant difference is that their dialogue partners change from ascetics to kings, indicating a 'shift in Jain narrative literature from the sphere of spirituality to a more worldly realm' (p. 89). Esposito further observes that the content of the stories 'are of a more secular kind ... more suitable for the new target audience consisting of laymen and laywomen instead of monks and nuns' (p. 89).

In addition to engaging an audience, Esposito shows how the complex organization of the text conveys a philosophical message. Similar to Hiltebeitel's argument that the *Rāmāyaṇa* uses dialogue to convey a devotional teaching, while the *Mahābhārata* sets up mirrors and puzzles, Esposito shows how the complex dialogical structure demonstrates profound theological ideas: 'dialogues can serve as a kind of illustration and recreation of the complex and incomprehensible nature of the world' (p. 79). Esposito suggests that the intricate structure of the *Vasudevahiṇḍī* mirrors the complex content of the teachings, which deal with the nature of karma. As Esposito explains, the 'reader is deliberately abandoned in the wilderness of dialogues ... lost not only in this thicket of stories, but also in the complex and incomprehensible nature of the world, recreated by these inscrutable narrations' (p. 91).

In Chapter 4, Naomi Appleton discusses the use of dialogue in the Jātaka literature. Jātakas are stories of the Buddha's previous lives that appear in a number of texts throughout the Buddhist tradition. Appleton looks specifically at the *Jātakatthavaṇṇanā*, which as she points out, is the only *jātaka* collection that frames each of the stories within the teaching career of the Buddha. The *Jātakatthavaṇṇanā*, as Appleton explains, 'would therefore appear to be unique in that it exclusively contains *jātaka* stories and places these in a dialogical frame involving the Buddha and a variety of interlocutors' (p. 100).

One of the functions of the *Jātakatthavaṇṇanā* was 'as a repository of narrative. Many stories were collected together into the text, and established as authentically Buddhist by being placed in the teaching career of the Buddha' (p. 101). But in addition to being a way of

[7] Unlike the *Mahābhārata*'s main story, which is at the second level of dialogue, the main story of the *Vasudevahiṇḍī* is recounted at the fourth level of dialogue. In all, the *Vasudevahiṇḍī* contains nine levels of dialogue, as compared with the *Mahābhārata*, which goes up to seven dialogues deep (see Hegarty, *Religion, Narrative and Public Imagination in South Asia* and Minkowski, 'Janamejaya's *Sattra* and Ritual Structure').

including the material, the dialogue form highlights the Buddha's role as the narrator, with Appleton observing that 'the Buddha was the source of all the narratives and the worldly wisdom contained within them' (p. 101). This is not only true because the Buddha tells the stories, but also because the stories themselves are so wide-ranging that the Buddha is thus depicted as having universal knowledge. Each tale unfolds as the Buddha remembering incidents from one of his numerous previous lives, with his 'ability to recount his own past and that of other people' establishing him 'as a great spiritual leader, with supernormal vision into the way the universe operates' (p. 109). We see here similarities with Esposito's observations about Mahāvīra in the canon of the Śvetāmbaras, where 'dialogue can function as legitimation, as proof of the absolute and undoubtable truth of contents' (p. 79).

As with the *Mahābhārata* and the *Vasudevahiṇḍī*, the dialogues that frame the Jātakas also bring attention to the text's own transmission and potential audience. The primary audience of most of the Jātakas, as Appleton points out, consists of monks, who are auditors in 80 per cent of the stories. But some *jātaka*s address other audiences, including various laypeople, such as kings, merchants, Brahmins and even gods. As Appleton observes, the audience represented inside the texts challenges the widespread assumption that the Jātakas were primarily for a lay audience, as the frame dialogues 'are often specifically aimed at illustrating or solving *monastic* problems, particularly the difficulty of leaving behind (and resisting the temptation of returning to) one's wife' (p. 105). By bringing attention to the audience, Appleton illustrates that the *jātaka* tales are not 'just about the Buddha, but also all those people who had the great fortune of meeting him and hearing his stories' (p. 108).

As we have seen, there are a number of recurring themes throughout the chapters in Part I, including dialogue as a reflection upon a text's own transmission, as an expression of a text's teaching, and as a way of addressing a text's potential audience. Another theme addressed by the chapters in Part I is the gendered dimensions of dialogue. As we have seen, *Ṛg Veda* 7.103 mentions dialogues between father and son, and teacher and student, seemingly limiting its exploration of dialogue to those containing male participants. Yet the other texts discussed in Part I contain at least some dialogues with female interlocutors. Hiltebeitel makes a comparison between the dialogue between Draupadī and Satyabhāmā in the *Mahābhārata* and the conversation between Sītā and Anasūyā in the *Rāmāyaṇa*, observing that these two instances are rare occasions where we see dialogues between female interlocutors, with each exchange taking us 'momentarily outside the mainly men's world of the main epic stories' (p. 66). In both cases, as Hiltebeitel describes, 'the interlocutor's interest lies in asking her about some personal or even private dimension of her marital situation' (p. 66). Hiltebeitel then turns to dialogues between Sītā and Rāma, arguing that Sītā 'gives voice' to the 'double divine-human dimension of Rāma's portrayal' (p. 70). In other words, Hiltebeiltel argues, Sītā plays a significant role in bringing out some of the devotional aspects of the *Rāmāyaṇa*'s teachings.

Similarly, Esposito brings attention to a number of cases where dialogues in Jain sources include female interlocutors. In addition to instances where laywomen participate in dialogues, the *Nāyādhammakahāo* features Mallī, a beautiful princess, who is the nineteenth *tīrthaṃkara*. In this verbal encounter, Mallī 'enlightens her six suitors about the disgusting constitution of the body and the vanity of love's pleasures' (pp. 83–4). As Esposito writes: 'Although female speakers appear considerably less often than their male counterparts, they have – at least in the tradition of the Śvetāmbaras – usually the same speaking authority as male speakers. This is reflected by the existence of a female *tīrthaṃkara*, Mallī' (p. 86).

Appleton also comments on the participation of female interlocutors in the *Jātakatthavaṇṇanā*, pointing out that despite the emphasis on a monastic audience, there 'is no explicit mention of a nun being told a *jātaka* story' (p. 106). This male bias is in keeping with other extant Theravādin texts, as the Buddha is never depicted as talking to an individual nun in any of the four Nikāyas. But whereas nuns are not mentioned as primary members of the audience, there are a few *jātaka*s 'that are said to have been told to laywomen' (p. 107).

Texts in Dialogue

While a unifying theme in Part I is dialogue as a way of engaging audiences outside the text, all the chapters in Part II look at dialogue as a way of engaging other texts. Here we are thinking in terms of texts invoking the authority of particular dialogues in earlier sources and of the dialogue style itself, of developing distinct dialogical genres, and of sharing similar organizational structures.

In Chapter 5, Douglas Osto examines some of the intertextual dimensions of Buddhist sources by discussing the dialogues in the Prajñapāramitā Sūtras in relation to dialogues that appear in earlier canonical literature. As Osto shows, one of the ways that the Prajñapāramitā Sūtras engage with earlier Buddhist dialogues is by featuring characters such as the Buddha, Śāriputra and Subhūti: 'By employing characters from the mainstream tradition, the Prajñapāramitā Sūtras attempt to borrow the authority of these characters, use their traditional personas as a means of critiquing the views of earlier schools, and present its new philosophical message as if it were part of the original teachings of the Buddha' (p. 125). Whereas other Mahāyāna literature often include *bodhisattva*s as teachers, the Prajñapāramitā texts are far more likely to present its teachings as delivered by a character from the mainstream Buddhist tradition. The Prajñapāramitā Sūtras also differ from other Mahāyāna literature in terms of how they characterize the Buddha. Whereas in a number of Mahāyāna *sūtra*s the Buddha does not have a significant speaking role and is depicted entering a trance or performing miracles, in the Prajñapāramitā Sūtras he 'teaches the perfection of wisdom in discourses and enters into dialogues and lively debates with his disciples and *bodhisattva*s' (p. 126). Osto reflects: 'This type of dialogical Buddha is more in line with the literary Buddha of mainstream sources such as the Pāli Canon' (p. 126).

Other recurring characters are Śāriputra and Subhūti. In the Nikāyas Śāriputra is one of the Buddha's foremost disciples, known for his 'special proficiency in the Abhidhamma' (p. 126). As the Prajñapāramitā Sūtras often present new ideas, especially the teaching of emptiness, in contradistinction to the Abhidharma, Śāriputra is repeatedly depicted as lacking in wisdom, as 'he embodies the very view these *sūtra*s so rigorously attack' (p. 126). Like Śāriputra, Subhūti is a character from earlier Buddhist sources. But whereas he was a rather minor character in older texts, in the Prajñapāramitā Sūtras he plays a prominent role, featuring as 'the main interlocutor in the *Aṣṭasahśrikā*, the *Pañcaviṃśati*, and the *Diamond Sūtra*s' (p. 126).

In addition to bringing attention to the main characters in the dialogues of the Prajñapāramitā Sūtras, Osto looks at how dialogue conveys a sense of orality. As we have seen, dialogues in texts such as the Upaniṣads and Nikāyas might be seen as reflecting their own oral transmission. Here, however, Osto sees dialogue more as a literary trope, a way of masking its written composition.[8] The earliest Buddhist sources were accepted to be the spoken recollections of Ānanda, recounted to the Buddhist community at the first Buddhist

---

[8] Elsewhere, Alf Hiltebeitel, *Rethinking the Mahābhārata: A Reader's Guide to the Education of the Dharma King* (Chicago, 2001), p. 4, has made similar arguments about dialogue in the *Mahābhārata*.

council. His opening phrase 'thus I have heard' 'became the authenticating marks of a text as *sūtra*, endowing it with all the authority of the 'Buddha's words'' (*buddhavacana*). All Mahāyāna *sūtra*s also begin with the opening formula, 'thus I have heard', as a way to present themselves as authoritative Buddhist texts. As Osto reflects: 'This strategy is significant in that it employs speech acts and preserves the dialogical style of the oral discourses found in the earlier mainstream traditions' (pp. 132–3). Osto further suggests that one of the reasons why the Prajñapāramitā Sūtras present themselves in rather traditional ways is because their central teachings are quite radical. In other words, the Prajñapāramitā Sūtras might have been trying 'to cushion the blow of their radical philosophical innovation – namely the doctrine of "emptiness"' (p. 129).

Whereas Osto explores a number of ways in which the Prajñapāramitā Sūtras can be read against the backdrop of earlier Buddhist dialogues, in Chapter 6 Elizabeth Rohlman sees similar intertextual uses of dialogue in the *Sarasvatī Purāṇa*. Pointing out that this medieval Gujarati text uses the same frame narrative as that of the *Skanda Purāṇa*, Rohlman argues that the *Sarasvatī Purāṇa* uses this frame to draw 'on other textual and theological traditions to create intertextual discourse' (p. 138). In addition to the frame narrative, the *Sarasvatī Purāṇa* also retells the story of Kapila from the *Bhāgavata Purāṇa*. Rohlman argues that the *Sarasvatī Purāṇa* refashions the *Kapila Gītā* 'into a *bhakti* revelation more compatible with the Vaiṣṇava traditions of late medieval Gujarat' (p. 138). In the *Sarasvatī Purāṇa*, Kapila, who is an *avatāra* of Viṣṇu, is cast as the teacher, while his mother Devahūti is the student. Rohlman maintains that 'the discourse between Kapila and Devahūti facilitates a metaphorical dialogue between texts' (p. 149).

Rohlman further explains that the Gītā is a specific type of dialogue that includes 'a direct didactic exchange between a god and a devotee' (p. 139). Like the *Bhagavad Gītā*, the most famous example of the genre, other Gītās are also 'embedded within epic and purāṇic literature, but often circulate as independent texts' (p. 141). Drawing on the work of Mackenzie Brown, Rohlman points out that 'the essential distinction of Gītā literature is one of perspective: whereas Purāṇas and Māhātmyas are told from the perspective of the devotee, the Gītā is related from the perspective of the deity' (p. 142). By refashioning a Gītā from another text, the Gītā in the *Sarasvatī Purāṇa* works on two levels: 'as a discourse between god and devotee and as a discourse between regional and pan-Indic textual and theological traditions' (p. 139).

But while dialogue is generally acknowledged to be a formal feature of the Gītā genre, Rohlman suggests that dialogue is equally integral to the genre of Purāṇa. While the Purāṇas are traditionally defined in terms of the *pañcalakṣaṇa*, or the 'five 'marks' or topics that all *purāṇas* are supposed to address' (p. 139), the 'the only formal quality that is universal to all purāṇic literature is the manner in which these theological teachings are presented, as a dialogue between a guru and his student' (p. 140). Rohlman sees the guru–student dialogue as a 'didactic format' that 'is prominent throughout Indic traditions and that stretches back at least to the Upaniṣads' (p. 140). In this way, the literary style of the texts reinforces the importance of a proper lineage of knowledge. In addition to emphasizing the *param-parā* – the lineage from teacher to student –, the dialogue form also creates a textual lineage, as many of 'the gurus and sages who narrate the *purāṇas* .... allude to other texts, especially the *Mahābhārata*' (p. 141). In these ways, 'dialogue represents not only the means by which knowledge is acquired but also the source of its authority' (p. 141).

Also paying close attention to the relationship between dialogue and genre, in Chapter 7 Andrew Nicholson looks at three types of philosophical dialogue: Gītā, polemic and doxography. All three genres are dialogical in character, but, as Nicholson shows, they portray dialogue very differently, with the Gītā including named speakers and with polemic and doxology containing dialogues in more oblique ways.

As we have seen in Rohlman's chapter, the Gītā is a form of dialogue that involves a deity and a devotee. But while Gītās are defined by their devotional character, they also tend to be quite philosophical in content, containing teachings associated with the Sāṃkhya, Yoga and Vedānta schools of Indian philosophy. While the *Bhagavad Gītā* is the most famous example, Nicholson brings attention to a number of other texts of this genre. The *Anugītā*, for example, is not merely 'a watered down repetition' of the *Bhagavad Gītā*, but it 'claims the authority of Kṛṣṇa's teaching in order to displace it, to portray a world in which renunciation, not dispassionate action, is the best way of life' (p. 156). As Nicholson suggests, this tendency is shared among other Gītās, which 'claim the authority associated with the *Bhagavad Gītā* while simultaneously subverting parts of the *Bhagavad Gītā*'s message' (p. 156).

Next, Nicholson looks at the genre of polemic, arguing that these texts base their method of analysis on the Mīmāṃsā school of Vedic exegesis. As Nicholson explains, these philosophical commentaries usually divide their works into five sections: (1) topic; (2) doubt; (3) prima facie view; (4) response; and (5) final decision. This formalized structure, which is 'based on Indian theoreticians' ideas of what a conversation between a teacher and pupil does or should look like' (p. 159), is 'an immediately recognizable genre of text' (p. 159). Yet unlike most of the dialogues discussed in other chapters of this book, Nicholson points out that in the polemic the interlocutors are not presented as characters and the opponent is rarely named. Although the polemic has often been compared to a Socratic dialogue, Nicholson observes that unlike the dialogues of Plato which often end without an established conclusion, the Indian polemics contain the formal requirement that each section ends with a final decision. Summing up, Nicholson describes the polemic as a 'systematic method of argumentation for establishing one's own conclusions and overturning those of one's opponents, who are always inevitably vanquished in order for the final decision (*nirṇaya*) to appear. It is a kind of machine for debate, and unapologetically dogmatic' (p. 160).

The third genre of philosophical dialogue explored by Nicholson is doxography, which refers to the compendia or compilations of philosophical views. Although these texts are widely consulted for their philosophical content, few scholars have examined their form. Noting similarities with the structure of the *Maṇimēkalai*, a sixth-century Tamil text about a temple dancer who becomes a Buddhist philosopher, Nicholson suggests that doxologies might have evolved out of 'narratives recounting dialogues between a single spiritual seeker and his or her various teachers' (p. 162). The last section of the *Maṇimēkalai*, which contains 'a lengthy compendium of the teachings of the various philosophical systems, culminating with a discussion of Buddhist logic' (p. 163), has 'numerous characteristics in common with later Sanskrit doxography' (p. 163). It begins, for example, with a 'typology of the schools according to the number of means of valid knowledge' and then lists the views of six schools. Another similarity is that the *Maṇimēkalai* presents the rival philosophical positions in terms of a hierarchy, proceeding 'dialectically from lower doctrines to the highest truth' (p. 164). In this way, rival positions are 'depicted as worthwhile only insofar as they point towards Buddhist truths' (p. 164). As Nicholson observes, the dialectical process depicted in the *Maṇimēkalai* is a central feature of medieval doxographical texts, which present different philosophical views as functioning 'together in a dialectical process' (p. 164).

While Osto and Rohlman discuss an intertextual use of dialogue that builds on the authority of earlier sources, Nicholson is claiming more of an influence in format, as doxographies – unlike the *Maṇimēkalai* – do not contain a narrative, nor do they name individual characters as representing the different views. Nonetheless, Nicholson suggests, 'there is a drama here – it is the drama of the gradual accumulation of wisdom leading to enlightenment, the same story that we find at the end of the *Maṇimēkalai*' (p. 165). An important implication of Nicholson's argument here is the crossover between philosophical and narrative literature. We have already seen, particularly when discussing the chapters of Hiltebeitel, Esposito, and Osto, how narrative texts can be vehicles for philosophical teachings. And both Rohlman and Nicholson add to this by looking at the genre of Gītā. Here, however, Nicholson is suggesting that discursive texts, which might appear to be 'technical' or 'philosophical', also seem to model their presentation of philosophy on the structures of dialogues found in narrative sources.

One key cross-cutting element throughout the chapters in Part II is the use of an old dialogical trope to legitimate a newer one. All the authors make claims about how a text can use the characters and setting of an older dialogue to deliver new teachings. Osto points out how the dialogical Buddha of the Prajñapāramitā Sūtras is more like the Buddha found in the texts of the older Pāli canon than in other more recent Mahāyāna texts. Rohlman makes a convincing case that the *Sarasvatī Purāṇa* refashions the *Kapila Gītā* into a *bhakti* revelation, and in doing so, uses the older text to legitimate the newer texts. And Nicholson shows the ways in which particular Gītās claim the *Bhāgavad Gītā* in form and at times in content but also subvert its teachings in favor of other perspectives.

Moving between Traditions

Part III of this book looks at dialogue as a way of exploring relationships between interlocutors and across religious traditions. The many common themes explored throughout this book already point to the fact that dialogue is a shared compositional feature across texts from the Hindu, Buddhist and Jain traditions. All the chapters in Part III look at how dialogues explore the interaction between participants. While Nichols and Geen both look at dialogues as a form of persuasion, where texts of a particular tradition can include dialogues that rehearse arguments in favor of their own views, Crothers examines dialogues that depict interlocutors in exchanges of distrust and deceit. Finally, Black examines dialogue as a way of exploring tolerance and accommodation of difference.

In Chapter 8, Michael Nichols looks at dialogue in the Buddhist Nikāyas, focusing on three types of exchange: the Buddha and Brahmins, the Buddha and Jains, and the Buddha and gods. As he demonstrates, 'the Buddha varies tactics depending on the unique position and identity of his interlocutor' (p. 174). In examining a number of different exchanges with Brahmins, Nichols argues that 'each dialogue is targeted toward a particular aspect of Brahminhood and employs different rhetorical techniques' (p. 177). A recurring theme is the thirty-two marks, which Nichols sees as having 'a special symbiotic, cross-legitimizing relationship between Brahmins and kings', which thus 'may be a targeted rhetoric to cast the Buddha as a new king' in his encounters with Brahmins (p. 186). Taken together, 'the overall portrayal of Brahmin–Buddha dialogue in this literature shows a mixture of tension, reorientation, and consideration, on both parts' (p. 178).

Nichols then turns his attention to dialogues between the Buddha and Jains, reflecting that 'the main thread of the Jains' dialogues involved the propriety of asceticism and its severity' (p. 187). As Nichols explains, 'the Nikāya literary dialogues with Jains tend to connect their practice of self-mortification with violence expressed towards others' (p. 180). In the three dialogues that Nichols examines between the Buddha and Nātaputta

(Mahāvīra), the text 'portrays Nātaputta defending rigorous self-mortification, i.e. violence against his own body, while verbally expressing violence against the bodies of others' (p. 181). Nichols reflects that these 'texts seem designed to give the impression of Jains as self-righteous, claimants of powers they do not actually possess, and simmering with anger and violence just below a façade of meditative calm' (p. 181). Nichols points out that these encounters occur not between the Buddha and a Jain 'but rather through a "middle man" representative of the householder sphere of life' (p. 181). As such, these '*sutta*s were less about the Jains themselves than gathering potential donors and patrons' (p. 182).

Finally, in his analysis of dialogues between the Buddha and *deva*s, Nichols reflects that a primary theme 'is the demonstration of the superior knowledge and power of the Buddha, whether the Deva(s) involved are deluded by false perceptions (Baka the Brahmā), overtly aggressive (Māra), or obsequious allies and students of the Buddha' (p. 184). As Nichols argues, the Buddha's verbal exchanges with *deva*s reflect his interactions with rival social groups, with the text mirroring 'sectarian debates by placing the words of rivals into the mouths of gods' (p. 186). In Chapter 3, Esposito also points out that gods are sometimes depicted as Mahāvīra's dialogue partners. But unlike interactions between the Buddha and gods, as seen in the Nikāyas, in the Jain sources 'the gods are usually plainly depicted as paying homage to the Jina and leaving again without further dialogues or discussions' (p. 83).

Comparing the varying characteristics of these three types of dialogues, Nichols points out that 'a different topic is at stake and thus a different rhetorical strategy is employed' (p. 186). In each case, the Buddha is depicted as superior in whichever issue is central to his interlocutor: 'Against Brahmins, the Buddha displays superior knowledge of Vedic ritual and texts, against Jains he reveals superior understanding of asceticism, and when contending with gods, he displays supernatural power beyond even their abilities' (p. 187).

Similar to Nichols, in Chapter 9 Jonathan Geen also looks at how dialogue is used as a way of exploring differences between interlocutors. But whereas Nichols' chapter focuses on how the Buddhist Nikāyas represent dialogue with rival religious groups, Geen looks at a particular type of dialogue that is found in Jain, Hindu, and Buddhist sources: conversations in which would-be renouncers attempt to convince their parents to endorse their decision to take early renunciation. Looking at two dialogues from Jain sources and two from Hindu sources (while also pointing to further examples from Buddhist sources), Geen comments on the likelihood of inter-textual borrowing. Geen suggests that a Hindu dialogue from the *Mahābhārata* shares so many features with a Jain dialogue from the *Uttarajjhayaṇasutta* that it 'appears to be a variant of the same basic dialogue' (p. 200). Comparably, a dialogue from the *Mārkaṇḍeya Purāṇa* displays a marked similarity with another dialogue from the Jain *Uttarajjhayaṇasutta*, as well as with a dialogue from Buddhist sources.

But while these similarities have interesting implications regarding shared literary features across Indian religious traditions, Geen argues that such comparable episodes are 'not entirely to be explained by inter-tradition borrowing' (p. 203). Rather, Geen suggests, the 'fact that "early" renunciation was justified in dialogues in multiple traditions speaks to the effectiveness and persuasiveness of this literary form' (p. 203). In none of the four dialogues are the young men 'invested with any special authority of their own', nor do they invoke the doctrinal authority of any particular tradition. Rather, in each case 'the persuasiveness arises out of the dialogue itself' (p. 203). In the two Jain dialogues, as well as the two Hindu dialogues, a young man is depicted as persuasively defending his desire to renounce 'all on his own, with absolute certainty and steadfast conviction' (p. 203).

Throughout his chapter, Geen brings attention to the rhetorical qualities of dialogue, maintaining that the form offers arguments of genuine persuasion that other genres do not. In comparison with third-person narrative accounts, which 'often do not explain how parental consent was obtained', dialogues 'confront the sorts of realistic objections and doubts likely to be raised by one's family' and 'how such objections were to be met' (p. 198). As Geen explains, a 'carefully constructed dialogue' can 'permit questions, objections and doubts to be repeatedly raised and answered' (p. 198). Not only might these dialogues persuade readers and listeners of these texts, but Geen speculates that such dialogue might have served as 'rehearsal-transcripts for any young man wishing to renounce and who sought the permission of his parents' (p. 199).

Geen also attempts to explain the importance of dialogue in the wider socio-historical context, in which 'the power to persuade was crucial' (p. 198) as a plurality of different religious groups competed against each other for converts. In contrast to the Vedic tradition, which had 'accrued a significant weight of ancient authority', the Jain and Buddhist traditions 'had to develop an authority of their own, based largely upon what they taught and how persuasive they were' (p. 198).

Just as Geen examines dialogues about renunciation and the effect such renunciation has on traditional relationships of trust, so too, in Chapter 10 Lisa Crothers' main focus is trust between royal interlocutors of king and advisor. Relations or exchanges of trust form the subjective basis for dialogue in religious narratives that also involve royal scenarios of rule. These intimate relations and their accompanying emotional bonds form the basis to dialogic exchanges between advisors and kings at court. As Crothers argues, such basic human relations are rarely, if ever, 'theorized' or 'explained' in these narratives – perhaps because the relational bases of dialogues are largely non-vocal. However, in these texts such bases of relationship and concourse are *shown*: for instance, in nonverbal expressions in dialogue and, paradoxically, in moments when trust is betrayed through deception. Thus, dialogic narrative encounters where trust is betrayed – or where dialogue has provided the occasion for betrayal – help us to see most clearly the intimate conditions for dialogue.

By looking at treatises of royal advice directed at success in rule, such as Kauṭilya's *Arthaśāstra*, in tandem with Buddhist *jātaka* narratives that present the Bodhisatta/Buddha exercising analogous tactics in royal relationships, Crothers focuses on the dialectical dimensions of creating trust and enacting deceptions. In her chapter, both nonverbal and verbal dimensions of enacting trust in dialogue come into view. As Crothers demonstrates, kings rely on (or question) their most trusted advisors, potential deceivers appear to be as near as one's kin, or to be in the guise of religious specialists on which individuals rely for succor, wisdom and generating religious merit. Crothers concludes by suggesting these narrative engagements with trusted deceivers point to a shared royal imaginary of trust and deception that could make or break dialogues and the royal relationships founded through them at court.

In the final chapter of this book, Chapter 11, Brian Black continues Crothers' focus on Brahmanical and Buddhist differences. He looks at three dialogues, each of which includes 'interlocutors who are defined by their differences, whether they be different castes, different religious traditions, or different genders' (p. 250). The first dialogue, from the *Bṛhadāraṇyaka Upaniṣad*, features a conversation between King Ajātaśatru and Gārgya; the second dialogue, from the *Soṇadaṇḍa Sutta* of the *Dīgha Nikāya*, features the Buddha and the Brahmin Soṇadaṇḍa; the third dialogue, from the *Mokṣasdharma* section of the *Mahābhārata*, is between the female sage Sulabhā and King Janaka. As Black comments: 'A crucial component of each dialogue is encountering and negotiating the differences between the characters' (p. 250).

But in addition to exploring the social differences between the characters, Black shows how the dialogue form plays out the contrasting philosophical views of its two interlocutors. In each dialogue, Black observes, the characters have radically different doctrinal positions, but each exchange offers a perspective that overcomes their differences. Each dialogue 'follows a certain progression, involving questions and answers, and moving from discord to harmony' (p. 252). As Black explores the flow of conversation in each dialogue, we might also think of Patton's comments about the frogs raising their voices as *Ṛg Veda* 7.103 unfolds, as well as the changing spatial relationships between the characters in the Nikāyas, as pointed out by Nichols. But Black's chapter also suggests that each dialogue has formal features of a philosophical argument. Here we might draw connections with what Nicholson says about the philosophical polemic, which was organized according to how an argument should be made.

In the third section of his chapter, Black offers an alternative reading of these dialogues, suggesting that in each case there is a degree of uncertainty or ambiguity. In making this argument, Black considers each dialogue within its larger textual context, showing that in each case the dialogue is part of an ongoing negotiation between different social groups. In exploring the inconclusive aspects of these verbal exchanges, we see an interesting distinction between these dialogues, which appear as narrative accounts of conversations, and the dialogical dimension of philosophical polemics, as discussed by Nicholson. As we have seen, a formal feature of the genre of polemic is to have each section end with a final decision. In making their points about how dialogues are resolved, both Nicholson and Black contrast the South Asian sources they examine with Plato's dialogues. While Black's exploration of the unresolved or ambiguous aspect of South Asian dialogues may at first seem to have much in common with the *aporia* found in Plato, he sees a different type of ambiguity in the South Asian context – one where 'the lack of resolution in these encounters is not presented as a philosophical conundrum, but rather as an ambivalence concerning the social hierarchy of the two characters' (p. 256). Black adds that these dialogues indicate 'an accommodative approach to social interactions, with the lack of closure allowing interlocutors to save face and opening spaces within the text to tolerate potentially subversive positions' (p. 256).

Similar to Geen, Black also addresses the degree to which literary dialogues represent 'real dialogue' outside the texts. Geen argues that it is their 'believability' or 'accuracy' that makes them persuasive. Rather than setting up a 'straw man', these dialogues engage with real arguments against renunciation, with these verbal exchanges only effective because they portray strong arguments on each side. Similarly, Black suggests that the dialogue in the text represent 'real' attempts to address difference with rival groups.

Black frames his discussion with references to the book *The Argumentative Indian*, in which Amartya Sen argues that Indian traditions have a long history of accommodation and toleration. One of Sen's central claims is that dialogue is a means through which India has maintained its toleration of diversity and, indeed, has celebrated the 'richness of variation'. By invoking Sen, Black draws a connection between the dialogues explored throughout this book and recent debates in India – and elsewhere – about secularism, pluralism, and multiculturalism. If Sen is correct about India's long tradition of accommodating diversity through dialogue, then uncovering this tradition through extended textual analysis of dialogue and debate is a vital project.

Authorities

While the three parts of this book each show thematic connections in their own right, several other broader themes weave their way through all of the chapters and suggest an intriguing texture to the dialogical mode in Indian religions. The most striking theme is that of authority, and the roles that dialogues play in mediating authority. In Vedic traditions, dialogue is the modality through which the sacrifice establishes its power, and all forms of dialogue in sacrifice are also reflected in nature, such as the reflection Patton mentions between the sacrificing Brahmins and the frogs in RV 7.103.

While the authority of the ritual is also established through sacrificial dialogue in the epics, there are also new moves which refocus authority on the role of the gods. Hiltebeitel shows the ways in which the authority of Rāma is established through the frame of an interior dialogue of Rāma with himself. The 'apostrophe', or lifting of the dialogue out of context and engaging the epic's target audience, is a way of conveying devotion and establishing the legitimacy of the god.

In the context of the Jātaka tales, Appleton argues that the Buddha's knowledge of his previous lives is best displayed through dialogue with a variety of interlocutors. His authority is enhanced by dialogue because through that genre he becomes the storyteller in his own narrative. And in the Jain tradition, Esposito also shows the ways in which Mahāvīra can display his own knowledge, and therefore establish his own authority, through dialogical engagements with his pupils. These dialogues also have the effect of creating an authoritative lineage.

So too in texts which depict conversation between traditions, dialogue can function to create a superior authority through contemplation of both traditions. Michael Nichols argues that in the Buddhist Nikāyas, the dialogues between the Buddha and Brahmins, the Buddha and Jains, and the Buddha and the gods, all show the ways in which the Buddha both considers the authority of the other tradition and then ultimately transcends it. In his study of renunciation, Geen argues that the renunciant practices of both Buddhist and Jain traditions can only be given legitimacy through dialogue, given the ancient authority of the Vedic tradition that both of the new renunciant ways of life had to overcome.

Black argues that in some dialogues, authority is not finally established, but allows for a kind of openness and lack of conclusion that is itself rhetorically powerful. The social and spiritual authority that is established through the didacticism of other dialogues is left ambiguous in these dialogues, and Black argues that this too might be intentional commentary on the lack of clarity between social classes and religious traditions.

Similarly, Osto argues that the Prajñapāramitā Sūtras depart from other texts in the Mahāyāna tradition in that they use the same technique of the dialogical Buddha, more likely to be found in the literary Buddha of the mainstream sources such as the Pāli Canon. The usage of the opening formula, 'Thus I have heard' also indicates an attempt to create an authenticating mark which reflects the oral style of the earlier mainstream tradition. This form of establishing authority through dialogue is a way of making palatable the more radical teaching of the doctrine of emptiness.

Just as the dialogue between Mahāvīra and disciple or Buddha and disciple serves to establish authority of the spiritual teacher, Rohlman argues that this is also the case in the dialogical context of the genre of the Gītā, in which a god and a devotee speaks. In the *Sarasvatī Purāṇa*, in particular, the ubiquitous dialogical form reinforces the importance of the proper lineage of knowledge. Nicholson also argues that authority remains a key element not only in the *Bhāgavad Gītā*, but in other philosophical forms that use dialogue.

In philosophical polemic, the dialogical personae are not named, and function more as generic opponents. The doxography, or compendia of philosophical views, harks back to the form of dialogue between a teacher and a pupil, they have the didactic element of graduating from the lower form to the highest truth. Thus, the final subject within the doxography becomes the most authoritative.

Frames

The framing function of dialogue also is a strong thread that runs through these texts. Specific studies of frame tales have focused on their role in the *Mahābhārata*, as well as their origins in the Vedic traditions. [9] In the Vedic ritual tradition, a narrative is frequently only implied, and thus the frame of the dialogue, if any, is frequently understood as the sacrifice itself. In the *Mahābhārata*, however, there is an explicit frame: the narrative of Vyāsa to his pupils. However, Hiltebeitel has pointed out (p. 49, note 54) that what Witzel describes as 'the dawn of a long period of story-telling in the Epic' was not necessarily explicitly or exclusively dialogical. Many frame stories, as Witzel has explained 'simply surround one story with another' within the all-encompassing Vedic ritual arena.[10]

However, the frame functions of several dialogues within the epic do become literary tropes in their own right, where complexity of layering is the goal. Hiltebeitel conceives of this framing dynamic in terms of 'braiding'.

In the long and leisurely *Mahābhārata*, such braiding extends throughout the text, but is veiled and unveiled at various points to let the reader know that even though she or he feels comfortable to have settled into its main Vaiśaṃpāyana–Janamejaya dialogue level, the braid is something never to lose track of. In contrast, the *Rāmāyaṇa* starts braiding frame elements (it would be best to call them strands rather than frames) into its main frame from the very beginning and then almost lets readers forget about them until they pop back into view.

The *Rāmāyaṇa*'s framing dialogues also become apostrophic in that they are slightly simpler and more theologically self-referential, paving the way in the Hindu tradition for the ubiquity of theological dialogue that represent the essence of Purāṇic literary style.

However, not all forms of framing complexity within dialogues have the same theological or literary goal. As Appleton argues, in some Buddhist Jātakas, the Buddha's narrative of his previous lives becomes the larger dialogical frame which encompasses all smaller ones. This self-framing of what would otherwise be a straightforward story gives a kind of self-reflective nature to texts like the *Jātakatthavaṇṇanā*, in which the Buddha muses upon his own incarnations. What is implicitly self-referential in the frame tales of the *Rāmāyaṇa* becomes explicitly so in the *Jātakatthavaṇṇanā*.

The complexity of the frame tales of the epics is also reflected in the dizzying complexity of the Jain texts like the *Vasudevahiṇḍī*. As Esposito establishes, the 'double embedding' technique of many of the Śvetāmbara texts in which all the dialogues are also placed within the dialogue of Suhamma with his pupil Jambu. As Esposito notes, 'the first and probably

---

[9] Vishwa P. Adluri, 'Frame Narratives and Forked Beginnings: Or, How to Read the Ādiparvan', *Journal Of Vaishnava Studies* 19/2 (2011): 143–210; Michael Witzel, 'On the Origin of the Literary Device of the "Frame Story" in Old Indian Literature', in H. Falk (ed.), *Hinduismus und Buddhismus: Festschrift für Ulrich Schneider* (Freiburg, 1987). pp. 380–410.

[10] Witzel, 'On the Origins of the Literary Device of the "Frame Story" in Old Indian Literature' (pp. 414; 410–11).

oldest *aṅga* is identified with Suhamma, explaining Mahāvīra's words to his pupil Jambu. Later strata of Jain canonical literature might have adopted this dialogical embedding to affix an ancient character to their texts' (p. 88). But the larger point for Esposito is that the frame's dizzying effect, beginning with this double embedding, is to reflect the incomprehensible nature of the world. We have also discovered through these chapters some unusual uses of frames. One use is the geographical frame. For Rohlman, the text's frame narrative recounts the Sarasvatī River's descent to earth and follows her course from the Himālayas, through Gujarat, to her convergence with the sea at Prabhāsa Somnāth. A wide array of tales from pan-Indic traditions is retold within this geographical framework, situating the action of each story on the banks of the Sarasvatī River in Gujarat.

Unlike the narratives used in so many of the Jain, Buddhist and Brahmanical texts, Nicholson shows the reluctance to give any kind of framing in philosophical dialogue. As he puts it, Indian philosophical commentary 'seems designed to repel the casual reader through its refusal to clearly label who each speaker is, its frequent use of technical vocabulary, and its unwillingness to explore what is at stake in human terms in the winning or losing of a debate' (p. 161). There are, then, varying intensities of framing devices, all of which tell us something important about the epistemological commitments of the texts.

Future Directions

There are many possible future directions for the study of dialogue in India following these current essays. The first and most straightforward result is the possibility of further study on a more regional level. Just as the study of South Asian religions, and South Asian Studies more broadly, is turning to the role of vernacular languages, vernacular Sanskrit in the second millennium, and so on, so too there are a wealth of vernacular forms of dialogue in those texts whose nature and functions deserve to be studied. One thinks, as a few examples among many, of the *lavani* tradition in Maharashtra, the *padya* and *pariṣat nāṭakam* traditions in Telugu, or the *paurāṇika* recitation contexts in a number of smaller Indian cities and towns.

In addition, the role of the dialogical and its relationship to theatrical performance might be another direction for students of India to take. When does a performed dialogue become a full-fledged drama, and when do particular dialogues in full-fledged dramas get lifted out to become dialogical performances in their own right? And what is the relationship between oral and written dialogical texts? On a more theoretical level, the use of the dialogical may help us reflect differently on the nature of subjectivity in early India. Judith Butler has introduced the idea of a performed self, particularly in relation to gender. The question involves gender, as do several of the chapters in this volume (Black and Rohlman in particular). However, the question of the performed self is broader even than gender identity. Butler and other theorists are interacting with a recent turn in psychological and literary theory which proposes an idea called the dialogical self.

One of the founding figures in this field is Hubert Hermans, who with T.I. Rijks and H.J. Kempen, writes that characters in a novel resist a singular description: 'Different voices, often of a markedly different character and representing a multiplicity of relatively independent worlds, interact to create a self narrative'.[11] Hermans and others are drawing

[11] H.J.M. Hermans, T.I. Rijks and H.J.G. Kempen, 'Imaginal Dialogues in the Self: Theory and Method', *Journal of Personality* 61 (1993): 208. See also H.J.M. Hermans, H.J.G. Kempen,

upon Bakhtin's notion of the polyphonic novel. Using Bakhtin's well-known essay on Dostoyevsky's poetics, dialogical theorists view the self as 'voices in dialogical relations with each other'.[12] In other words, the self is internally plural and dialogical relationships between voices lend the self-coherence. It is 'only when an idea or thought is endowed with a voice and expressed as emanating from a personal position in relation to others that dialogical relations emerge'.[13] What if we turned again to look at the nature of particular characters in epics and other classical texts in light of their dialogical subjectivity? Crothers, for example, suggests we use the lens of subjectivity when looking at narratives involving royal decision-making in both Buddhist and Brahmanical contexts.

These are just a few of the many venues in Indian religious traditions that might be explored through the lens of the dialogical. Our hope is that the pages of these essays spark in our readers many more such ideas. Our understanding of the vibrant pluralities of Indian traditions rests on such new textual, historical, literary, and ethnographic inquiries. Moreover for such inquiries to thrive, our relationships with Indian traditions themselves must remain dialogical. Our Upaniṣadic interlocutors Uddālaka Āruṇi and Citra would have wanted no less.

References

Adluri, Vishwa P., 'Frame Narratives and Forked Beginnings: Or, How to Read the Ādiparvan', *Journal of Vaishnava Studies* 19/2 (2011): 143–210.

Bakhtin, M., *Problems of Dostoevsky's Poetics* (2nd edn; trans. R.W. Rotsel) (Ann Arbor, MI: Ardis, 1973). (Original work published 1929 as *Problemy tvorchestva Dostoevskogo* [Problems of Dostoevsky's Art]).

Black, Brian, *The Character of the Self in Ancient India: Priests, Kings, and Women in the Early Upaniṣads* (Albany: State University of New York Press, 2007).

———, 'Rivals and Benefactors: Encounters between Buddhists and Brahmins in the Nikāyas', *Religions of South Asia* 3/1 (2009): 25–43.

———, 'Ambaṭṭha and Śvetaketu: Narrative Connections between the Upaniṣads and Early Buddhism', *Journal of the American Academy of Religion* 79/1 (2011): 136–61.

Bowles, Adam, *Dharma, Disorder and the Political in Ancient India: The Āpaddharmaparvan of the Mahābhārata* (Leiden: E.J. Brill, 2007).

---

and R.J.P. Van Loon, 'The Dialogical Self: Beyond Individualism and Rationalism', *American Psychologist* 47 (1992): 23–33. Also see H. Hermans and A. Hermans-Konopka, *Dialogical Self Theory: Positioning And Counter-Positioning In A Globalizing Society* (New York, 2010); H. Hermans, 'The Dialogical Self: Toward a Theory of Personal and Cultural Positioning', *Culture & Psychology* 7 (2001): 243–81; M. Bakhtin, *Problems of Dostoevsky's Poetics* (2nd edn.; R.W. Rotsel (trans.) (Ann Arbor, MI, 1973) (Original work published 1929 as *Problemy tvorchestva Dostoevskogo* [Problems of Dostoevsky's Art]).

[12] Louise Roska Hardy, 'How Social is the Self? Perspective, Interaction, and Dialogue', in Wolfgang Mack and Gerson Reuter (eds), *Social Roots of Self-Consciousness: Philosophical and Psychological Contributions* (Berlin: Akademie Verlag, 2009), p. 49.

[13] Ibid. Not surprisingly, a set of ideas is developing about the South Asian dialogical self. See Black, *The Character of the Self in Ancient India*, and Patton, 'How Do You Conduct Yourself? Gender and the Construction of a Dialogical Self in the *Mahābhārata*'. And, in relation to the *diaspora*, we might easily begin to explore with this theory of the multiple worlds that such a self must contain. See Laurie Patton and Chakravarthi Ram-Prasad, 'Hindus, Non-Hindus, and the Place for Interlogue', in John S. Hawley and Vasudha Narayanan (eds), *The Life of Hinduism* (Berkeley, 2006), pp. 98–9.

Hardy, Louise Roska, 'How Social is the Self? Perspective, Interaction, and Dialogue', in Wolfgang Mack and Gerson Reuter (eds), *Social Roots of Self-Consciousness: Philosophical and Psychological Contributions* (Berlin: Akademie Verlag, 2009), pp. 35–53.

Hegarty, James, *Religion, Narrative and Public Imagination in South Asia: Past and Place in the Sanskrit Mahābhārata* (London: Routledge, 2012).

Hermans, Hubert, 'The Dialogical Self: Toward a Theory of Personal and Cultural Positioning', *Culture & Psychology* 7 (2001): 243–81.

———, and A. Hermans-Konopka, *Dialogical Self Theory: Positioning and Counter-Positioning in a Globalizing Society* (New York: Cambridge University Press, 2010).

———, and H.J.G. Kempen, *The Dialogical Self: Meaning as Movement* (San Diego, CA: Academic Press, 1993).

_______, H.J.G. Kempen, and R.J.P. Van Loon, 'The Dialogical Self: Beyond Individualism and Rationalism', *American Psychologist* 47 (1992): 23–33.

———, T.I. Rijks, and H.J.G. Kempen, (1993). 'Imaginal Dialogues in the Self: Theory and Method', *Journal of Personality* 61 (1993): 207–36.

Hiltebeitel, Alf, *Rethinking the Mahābhārata: A Reader's Guide to the Education of the Dharma King* (Chicago: University of Chicago Press, 2001).

Minkowski, Christopher Z., 'Janamejaya's *Sattra* and Ritual Structure', *Journal of the American Oriental Society* 109/3 (1989): 401–20.

_______, 'Snakes, *sattras* and the *Mahābhārata*', in Arvind Sharma (ed.), *Essays on the Mahābhārata* (Leiden: E.J. Brill, 1991), pp. 384–400.

Olivelle, Patrick (trans. and ed.), *The Early Upaniṣads: Annotated Text and Translation* (New York: Oxford University Press, 1998).

Patton, Laurie, 'Samvada: A Literary Resource for Conflict Negotiation in Classical India', in *Evam: Forum on Indian Representations* (Delhi: Samvad India, 2003), pp. 177–90.

———, *Bringing the Gods to Mind: Mantra and Ritual in Early Indian Sacrifice* (Berkeley, CA: Univeristy of California Press, 2005).

———, 'How Do You Conduct Yourself? Gender and the Construction of a Dialogical Self in the *Mahābhārata*', in Simon Brodbeck and Brian Black (eds), *Gender and Narrative in the* Mahābhārata (London: Routledge, 2007).

_______, and Chakravarthi Ram-Prasad, 'Hindus, Non-Hindus, and the Place for Interlogue', in John S. Hawley and Vasudha Narayanan (eds), *The Life of Hinduism* (Berkeley: University of California Press, 2006), pp. 98–9.

Rāmāyaṇa, Robert P. Goldman, Sheldon Pollock, and Sally J. Sutherland (trans. and eds) Clay Sanskrit Library Series (New York: New York University Press, 2005).

Rāmāyaṇa of Vālmīki: Sanskrit Text and English Translation, Ravi Arya (ed.); M.N. Dutt (trans.) (New Delhi: Parimal Publications, 1998).

Reich, Tamar, 'The Sacrifice of Battle and the Battle of Yoga, or How to Word-Away a Discontented Wife', in Laurie L. Patton (ed.), *Notes from a Mandala: Essays in the History of Indian Religions* (Newark, NJ: University of Delaware Press, 2009), pp. 182–99.

Śabara Bhāṣya. 3 vols. Ganganatha Jha (trans.). (Baroda: Oriental Institute, 1933–36).

Śatapatha Brāhmaṇa. 5 vols (Bombay: Laxmi Venkateswar Steam Press, 1940).

Śatapatha Brāhmaṇa. Julius Eggeling (trans.). *Sacred Books of the East* (Oxford: Clarendon Press, 1882–1900).

Sukthankar, V.S. et al. (eds), *Mahābhārata: Critical Edition*, 24 vols. with *Harivaṃśa* (Poona: Bhandarkar Oriental Research Institute, 1944).

Thompson, George, 'The Brahmodya and Vedic Discourse', *Journal of the American Oriental Society* 117/1 (Jan. – Mar. 1997): 13–37.
Witzel, Michael, 'On the Origin of the Literary Device of the "Frame Story" in Old Indian Literature', in H. Falk (ed.), *Hinduismus und Buddhismus: Festschrift für Ulrich Schneider* (Freiburg: Hedwig Falk, 1987), pp. 380–410.

PART I
Dialogues Inside and Outside the Texts

Chapter 1
The Frogs Have Raised Their Voice: *Ṛg Veda* 7.103 as a Poetic Contemplation of Dialogue

Laurie Patton

First Thoughts

What does it mean to think about frogs in conversation with each other? Other chapters in this volume will address specific examples of actual dialogues in early and medieval India and contemplate their force. Are such dialogues the dramatic enforcers of doctrine? Are they ways of making us sit up and listen better to narratives? Are they modes of establishing religious authority? This chapter will begin at a slightly more microscopic level, and look at concrete imagery for dialogue in a single Vedic hymn about frogs that has puzzled, amused, and vexed Vedic interpreters both Western and Indian.

In ancient India, *Ṛg Veda* (RV) 7.103 compares the croaking of frogs to brahmins, lowing cows, and fathers and sons learning together. Later commentators, both Indian and Western, write that the hymn is designed to produce rain. The animal imagery has been the major focus of its scholarly analysis, and relatedly the vexing question of how animals, in this particular case, frogs 'mean' something in the hymn. Is the hymn (*sūkta*), and the presence of frogs, a satire? Is it another form of humour? Is it 'magico-religious?' Is it a serious invocation of natural images which are a particularly effective form of metonymic thought?

In what follows, I argue that *Ṛg Veda* 7.103 might productively be read holistically as a poetic commentary on the nature of Vedic dialogue and the development of voice. Its imagery is rich with multiple examples of conversations between characters. Even if those conversations are not enacted, references to them act as powerful constructions, which create links between the dialogical process of the sacrifice and that of the natural world. These connections could be read as a concrete, condensed, poetic means of drawing attention to the fact of dialogue in its own right.

What might I mean by a commentary on dialogue? Some comparative points might be helpful here. Many other more well-known hymns of the *Ṛg Veda* are understood by later texts and commentators to be in the actual form of dialogue, such as the conversation between Agastya and Lopāmudrā; Saramā and the Paṇis; or Indra and Agni. While I will discuss the various approaches to the dialogical hymns below, the details of their structure all involve speaking parts.

In the Agastya and Lopāmudrā hymn (RV 10.79), commentators suggest that the verses are spoken in turn between Agastya and his wife, Lopāmudrā. They are understood as a dialogue about the nature of reproduction vs. asceticism, with Lopāmudrā arguing for progeny and Agastya arguing for asceticism. In a concluding verse (the speaker of which is a matter of disagreement among commentators), the argument is 'sealed' with a statement that one can do both things – literally, 'have it both ways'.

The dialogue between Saramā and the Paṇis (RV 10.108) occurs in the midst of a narrative told extensively in later texts. The Paṇis are demons who have stolen the Aṅgiras' cows and have hidden them in caves. The gods and sages, in an attempt to get the cows back, ask the dog Saramā to pursue the cows, and she confronts the Paṇis at the cows' hiding place. The dialogue in RV 10.108 is a conversation between the dog and the demons, with the dog Saramā trying to dispel the demons and the demons trying to dissuade and then tempt Saramā with their words.

The many dialogical hymns concerning Indra involve different themes. In one (RV 10.124), Indra attempts to win Agni back from where he is hiding inside his father, an Asura, or enemy of the gods. In another (RV 10.28), Indra scolds his son, the sacrificer, for being too arrogant and hasty in his offerings. In one of the most complex hymns of the *Ṛg Veda* (10.86), Indra and his wife engage in sexual banter with the monkey Vṛṣākapi and his wife – banter which also contains discussions of appropriate offerings for Indra and his relative prowess in the sacrificial arena.

In contrast to these hymns, the commentators give no 'assigned parts' to the frog hymn of RV 7.103 as they do in the explicitly dialogical hymns. There are no clear speakers of the verses as the conversation progresses. Rather, the verses in the hymn to the frogs build upon each other to provide a progressively thicker description of dialogue itself. In the end, the similes and metaphors comparing the conversations of frogs and the conversations of brahmins are so multi-layered that dialogue becomes like a character in its own right.

The Images of the Hymn

Let us turn first then to the *sūkta* itself. Its verses begin with allusions to the coming of spring, the emergence of the frogs, and, through a series of similes about conversation and voice, ends with the brahmins celebrating the soma sacrifice and obtaining wealth.

1. After having lain for a year like brahmins keeping a vow, the frogs have raised their voice, enlivened by Parjanya, the god of rain.[1]
2. When the divine waters came upon the one that lay like a dried up leather bag in a pond, then the voice of the frogs comes together, like the lowing of cows near to their calves.[2]
3. When the rainy season has come, and it rains upon those who are longing and thirsty, one draws near to the other, like a son to a father, speaking out with a croaking sound.[3]

[1] 7.103.01a *saṃvatsarám̐ śaśayānā́*
7.103.01b *brāhmaṇā́ vratacāríṇaḥ*
7.103.01c *vā́cam parjányajinvitām*
7.103.01d *prá maṇḍū́kā avādiṣuḥ*

[2] 7.103.02a *divyā́ ā́po abhí yád enam ā́yan*
7.103.02b *dṛ́tiṃ ná śúṣkaṃ sarasī́ śáyānam*
7.103.02c *gávām áha ná māyúr vatsínīnām*
7.103.02d *maṇḍúkānāṃ vagnúr átrā sám eti*

[3] 7.103.03a *yád īm enām̐ uśató abhy ávarṣīt*
7.103.03b *tṛṣyā́vataḥ prāvṛ́ṣi ā́gatāyām*
7.103.03c *akhkhalīkṛ́tyā pitáraṃ ná putró*
7.103.03d *anyó anyám úpa vádantam eti*

4. When they have exulted in the waters that have burst forth, one of the two greets the other. When the frog leaps about, covered in rain, the dappled one mixes his voice with the green one.[4]
5. When one of them echoes the voice of the other, like the student repeats after his teacher, all the different parts are in unison, like you intone lovely voices over the waters.[5]
6. One lows like a cow; one bleats like a goat; one is dappled; one is green. They have the same name, but different shapes. As they are speaking, they fashion their voices in many ways.[6]
7. Frogs, like brahmins at the night soma sacrifice chanting around a bowl of soma, you celebrate the day of the year when the rains begin.[7]
8. Soma-pressing brahmins raised their voice, and have made their yearly prayer. Adhvaryu priests appear, hot and sweating. No one is hidden.[8]
9. They have guarded the order of the twelve month, ordained by the gods. These men do not destroy the season. When the rainy season arrives after a year, the heated bowls of milk are released.[9]
10. The one that lows like a cow and the one that bleats like a goat have enriched us. The dappled one and the green one have also. By giving us hundreds of cows, the frogs have lengthened life in a thousand soma pressings.[10]

---

[4] 7.103.04a *anyó anyám ánu gr̥bhṇāti enor*
7.103.04b *apā́m prasargé yád ámandiṣātām*
7.103.04c *maṇḍū́ko yád abhívr̥ṣṭaḥ kániṣkan*
7.103.04d *pŕ̥śniḥ sampr̥ṅkté háritena vā́cam*
[5] 7.103.05a *yád eṣām anyó anyásya vā́caṃ*
7.103.05b *śāktásyeva vádati śíkṣamāṇaḥ*
7.103.05c *sárvaṃ tád eṣāṃ samŕ̥dheva párva*
7.103.05d *yát suvā́co vádathanā́dhi apsú*
[6] 7.103.06a *gómāyur éko ajámāyur ékaḥ*
7.103.06b *pŕ̥śnir éko hárita éka eṣām*
7.103.06c *samānáṃ nāma bíbhrato vírūpāḥ*
7.103.06d *purutrā́ vā́cam pipiśur vádantaḥ*
[7] 7.103.07a *brāhmaṇā́so atirātré ná sóme*
7.103.07b *sáro ná pūrṇám abhíto vádantaḥ*
7.103.07c *saṃvatsarásya tád áhaḥ pári ṣṭha*
7.103.07d *yán maṇḍūkāḥ prāvr̥ṣī́ṇam babhū́va*
[8] 7.103.08a *brāhmaṇā́saḥ somíno vā́cam akrata*
7.103.08b *bráhma kr̥ṇvántaḥ parivatsarī́ṇam*
7.103.08c *adhvaryávo gharmíṇaḥ siṣvidānā́*
7.103.08d *āvír bhavanti gúhiyā ná ké cit*
[9] 7.103.09a *deváhitiṃ jugupur dvādaśásya*
7.103.09b *r̥túṃ náro ná prá minanti eté*
7.103.09c *saṃvatsaré prāvŕ̥ṣi ā́gatāyāṃ*
7.103.09d *taptā́ gharmā́ aśnuvate visargám*
[10] 7.103.10a *gómāyur adād ajámāyur adāt*
7.103.10b *pŕ̥śnir adād dhárito no vásūni*
7.103.10c *gávām maṇḍū́kā dádataḥ śatā́ni*
7.103.10d *sahasrasāvé prá tiranta ā́yuḥ*

Not surprisingly, given its rich imagery of water, rains, and the rainy season, the hymn has been understood by both Indian and Western commentators as a method of bringing rain. The hymn is also found in the later Veda, the *Atharva Veda* (AV), and is part of a larger sequence of AV 4.15. Later stanzas in that sequence are addressed to the frogs, and they are requested to bring rain. The earliest commentator on this hymn was Yāska, the author of the fifth-century BCE dictionary the *Nirukta.* He explains that it is a hymn addressed to Parjanya, the god of rain, mentioned in verse 2, and grouped together in typical Vedic fashion with the two preceding hymns, RV 7.102 and 7.103. The medieval commentator on the *Ṛg Veda*, Sāyaṇa, sees the *sūkta* as honouring the frogs. And he states that when recited, the frogs, like other *devas*, would be pleased and bring rain.

This usage of the hymn is something that has continued into colonial India. Jan Gonda cites Martin Haug, writing in 1871 from Varanasi, who notes that when there was drought, a group of brahmins would go to a river and recite this and the preceding hymn from the *Ṛg Veda.*[11] Many early Western Indologists, such as Martin Haug, Hermann Oldenberg, Maurice Bloomfield, and Jan Gonda see the frog hymn as parallel to other flora and fauna, from ants to plants, which help bring on the rainy season, and indeed play a double role as both harbingers and causes of its onset.

Frogs, Satire, and Similes

The religious, seasonal functions of the hymn have been the general consensus of these Indologists, although the question of satire still haunts the interpretive thread in the West. In a paper presented at the American Oriental Society in 1890, Maurice Bloomfield in particular takes Moriz Winternitz to task for continuing this popular interpretation of the hymn as satire. He argues with Winternitz's admission that, even though the satirical interpretation is obsolete, the hymn still makes a comical impression (*das alles klingt ungemein komisch*). Bloomfield emphasizes that frogs have been healing agents and most interpreters have understood their croaking sound to be auspicious bringers of rain. On the idea of satire, he notes that brahmins are respected in the Vedas on the whole, so it would seem implausible that they are also parodied at the same time. In fact, Bloomfield takes the frog-hymn so seriously, he finds the comparison flattering to brahmins:

> Their comparison with the Brāhmaṇas in vii.103 is a bit of nice diplomacy, intended as a *captatio benevolentiae* of the frogs, not as a satire upon the priests engaged in the difficult performance of the all-night sacrifice (*atirātrá*), or the still more arduous manipulation of the heated pots (*gharmá*).[12]

Echoing this standpoint, in his essay 'The So-Called Secular, Humorous and Satirical Hymns of the Ṛg Veda', Jan Gonda cautions 'western authors' who see humour where there is none, perhaps because they have no understanding of the ritual context of the ancient Indian poets. His broader purpose in the essay is to establish that every occasion, without exception, is religious in the Vedas. He takes issue with Arthur MacDonnell's classification

---

[11] Jan Gonda, 'The So-Called Secular, Humorous and Satirical Hymns of the Rigveda', *Orientalia Neerlandica, Leiden* (1948): 314.

[12] Maurice Bloomfield, 'On the Frog-Hymn, Rig Veda vii 103, Together with Some Remarks on the Composition of Vedic Hymns', *Proceedings of the American Oriental Society* 17 (1896): 178.

of wedding and funeral hymns as secular rituals in a civilization where 'the religious, [and] the magico-religious cannot be detached from the other provinces of culture, from the other domains of human thought and activity'. [13]

S.K. De also observes that early Sanskrit literature tends to be more serious than humorous. Animals – the greedy vulture, or the crafty cat – in Upaniṣadic parables or Jātaka tales are not quite vehicles of satire, but express kinship to men. De cites the frog analogy as flattering to the frogs, 'the great wizards who have the magical power of bringing rain; the simile is for flattery and not for fun, for graphic and not for satiric effect'.[14]

Wendy Doniger does not quite resurrect the idea of satire, but neither does she dismiss it altogether. If 'actual criticism of priests in general' is unlikely, she thinks it plausible there may have been a satire of 'some priests', and concludes that the comparison is a 'most elaborate and playful pun'.[15] Doniger's idea of the elaborate and playful pun speaks to another issue altogether, an issue which moves us beyond satire: the power of simile in this hymn. Gonda also writes compellingly of the case of the power of similes used in rituals:

> Now, the word often takes the form of a more or less detailed comparison, of a simile, being an expression in language of the parallelism of the magical happening. Thus a simile sometimes has a magical character: e.g. A.V. 3.24.3 (for abundance of rain) 'may they bring fatness here, like streams (bring) drift when it has rained.' As Brahmans and their texts and formulas are very powerful – they contain *brahma* – these similes in the frog-hymn may be considered as having a magical effect, as containing power. It is worth mentioning that in the 7th stanza the Brahmans perform the over-night soma-sacrifice and that in the 8th stanza they press soma: as is well known, the pressing of soma influences the coming down of the rain...[16]

Thus, a fuller understanding of the hymn would not include mockery, but elaborate likeness which creates a powerful portrait, an agent of words in the sacrifice. Frogs are serious creatures, as are brahmins, and both have power in the spring.

Ṛg Veda 7.103 as a Progressive Simile for the Development of Voice

If we take the question of simile seriously in the interpretation of RV 7.103, there are several important tasks still yet to accomplish. The first has to do with simile as 'magic'. However much Indologists like Gonda[17] assert complexity, their 'serious' refutation of the satire debate has still tended to emphasize the 'magical' or the 'magico-religious' power of making likenesses. Gonda's and others' term 'magico-religious' is a term whose use I have argued against elsewhere.[18] Putting it briefly, the primitivist connotations of the term

---

13 Gonda, 'The So-Called Secular...' : 325.

14 S.K. De, 'Wit, Humour and Satire in Ancient Literature', in *Aspects of Sanskrit Literature* (Calcutta, 1959), p. 257.

15 Wendy Doniger (trans.), *The Rig-Veda* (London, 1991), p. 233.

16 Gonda, 'The So-Called Secular...', p. 315.

17 Jan Gonda, *Remarks on Similes in Sanskrit Literature* (Leiden, 1949).

18 Laurie Patton, *Bringing the Gods to Mind: Mantra and Sacrifice in Early India* (Berkeley, 2005), pp. 38–59.

'magic' are still powerful in the world of Indology, and yet it is not at all clear that Vedic poetry or ritual was any less sophisticated than poetry or ritual in another culture or era.

In that work, I trace particular mantras and their ritual usages in two traditions of Ṛg Vedic interpretation. I look at the ritual environments in which the same poetic formula is used, and why these same verses might be applied in different ritual situations. I argue that these applications are based on perceptions of similarity between the poetic image and the ritual procedure. I further argue that the term 'metonymy' better translates the cognitive actions that are part of the sacrificial world view, where the statement of similarities based on contiguity are said to be powerful in their own right. Indeed, metonymy is a more accurate English translation of *viniyoga*, the Vedic commentarial term for the 'application' of mantra in sacrificial, domestic, and indeed all situations. Simile is not simply 'magical'; it allows for the more powerful application, or *viniyoga*, of a mantra.[19]

The category of metonymy is also an excellent way to analyse ritual agency in ancient India, as it allows us to think of verbal performance in ritual as a way of setting up possible 'associative worlds' between the uttered word and the physical surroundings within the ritual. Metonymy gives us a way of analysing ancient texts which prescribe prayers or poetic formulae within ritual; we can 'map' the words of the prayers with the reconstructed ritual situation and thus a kind of intellectual history of a ritual hermeneutic within a given situation.

Second, if similes are such powerful metonymic agents, then it would be beneficial to study them and their verbal environments more carefully. If we do so with regard to the hymn to the frogs, we see a verse by verse development of similes for the dialogical act. Every verse is a comparison of the frogs' speech to another form of speech; a likening of the frogs' conversations with another form of conversation. Verse by verse, these portraits of conversation become more deeply connected and closer to the sacrificial world.

Let us conduct the analysis to make our point. In verse 1, we see the first instance of the dialogical: the voices of the frogs are 'enlivened' by the god of rain, Parjanya (*parjányajinvitām*). Parjanya acts as a kind of impeller, like Savitṛ does of the sun in other Vedic hymns, only this time in 7.103 it is the motion of the voices and not the motion of the sun that is awakened. Here, the likeness to brahmins is also made, but only in their capacity as practitioners of a vow, not yet as practitioners of sacrifice.

In verse 2, the enlivening and impelling imagery is made even stronger. The divine waters join Parjanya in coming upon 'one who has dried up like a leather bag', possibly a lake or a pond bed. The voices of the frogs are not just enlivened, but 'come together' (*sám eti*), and are, in turn, likened to cows which come together to low over their calves. The frogs' conversation, then, is compared to the conversations of another auspicious animal and its offspring. It is well known that the cow is perhaps the most auspicious animal in the *Ṛg Veda* because the cow is itself a metaphor, or more in Vedic perspective, an actual form of wealth, harmony, light, and fertility.

In verse 3, we see not only the enlivening and the coming together of the conversational voices of the frogs, but the beginning of actual dialogue between two characters, where one frog approaches and speaks to another (*anyó anyám úpa vádantam eti*) with a croaking sound (*akhkhalīkṛ́tyā*). This speech relationship is in turn likened to a parental relationship, but not the cow and her calf of the previous verse, but the relationship between father and son (*pitáraṃ ná putró*). Through simile, the hymn has now moved the frogs' power from the natural to the animal to the human.

---

[19] Ibid., pp. 39–51.

In verse 4, the frogs are now inciting each other to speak. The cause of their coming to voice is their joyous play in the rain, and when that leaping (*kániṣkan*) happens, the frogs' voices are mingled (*sampr̥ñkté*). Although speech has been discussed earlier through many other terms, the term *vacam* is repeated here, echoing verse 1.

Verse 5 shows the development of the 'voice' with two explicit uses of the term and two similes for the process. Here, the dialogue is no longer just between two frogs, but between two frogs which are intentionally repeating after each other, and compared not just to a father and a son, but to a teacher and student (*śāktásyeva vádati śíkṣamāṇaḥ*). What is more, the voices are in harmony, even though they have different parts. This harmony is itself compared to a particular kind of voice – voices that are chanted over the waters.

Verse 6 is a further elaboration of the role of difference in harmonious dialogue, only now each frog voice has a different identity to contribute to the whole. One voice is compared to a cow, the other to a goat, and the differences in form are celebrated even as they share a name.

Verse 7 moves to the most explicit comparison yet – that frogs are not just like teacher and student, but like brahmins in their own right, who press the soma in an all-night soma sacrifice and use their voices around the soma bowl to make the sacrifice more effective (*brāhmaṇāso atirātré ná sóme sáro ná pūrṇám abhíto vádantaḥ*). This verse is indeed the lynchpin of the poem, because once this comparison has been made, the identification between frogs and sacrificing brahmins has occurred. The main focus then switches to the brahmins themselves in verse 8.

In that same verse 8, the brahmins raise their voices and emerge (*brāhmaṇā́saḥ somíno vā́cam akrata*), just as, in verse 1, the frogs did. They come out, heated and sweating (*gharmíṇaḥ siṣvidānā*), as the frogs emerge wet from their time of silence after a year. Thus the comparison is now completely reversed. While verse 1 focused on frogs being like brahmins; verse 8 focuses on brahmins being like frogs. The imagery remains that of voice in both cases; both raise their voice and become manifest in a yearly ritual.

Verse 9, in a dramatic turn, departs from the frog simile altogether, and has as its topic the brahmins who have guarded the year, and preserved the season. Like the brahmins themselves are heated, the 'heated pots' of milk offering (*taptā́ gharmā́*) are released. Moreover, such pots are like the rainy season waters that are released; they are part of the offering made in the Pravargya, or rainy season, ritual.

Finally, verse 10 brings the two elements of frog and brahmin together in the same 'diversity in harmony' imagery. The verse makes it clear that the bleating is the bleating of the brahmins, and the differences between brahmins are still frog-like in that they are speckled and green. The frogs (clearly here also the brahmins) give us hundreds of cows in the soma-pressing sacrifice (*gávām maṇḍū́kā dádataḥ śatā́ni sahasrasāvé prá tiranta ā́yuḥ*). This is the first time the subject of the sentence is explicitly frogs, and not brahmins, and the predicate of the sentence is explicitly their action in sacrifice, not the bringing of the rains. At the end of the day, the identification is complete: frogs do not just bring the rains; they also press soma in multiple-voiced chanting. And brahmins do not just press soma, they are also speckled and heated like frogs and bleat like cows and goats.

In sum, the *sūkta* grows in its dialogical portraits with every verse. Indeed, the hymn could be read as a contemplation of the growth of dialogue. As the frogs emerge, they have an enlivened but unformed voice. They are further specified in their voice as they begin to speak and call out like cows. They speak to each other in dyads like father and son. They repeat after each other in dyads, like teacher and pupil. They then emerge with individual voices, even in harmony. In those differences, they become like brahmins chanting around the lake of the soma sacrifice. Finally, the Soma-pressing brahmins' sacrificial conversation emerges, heated and sweating, from the frog conversation. They too release liquids alongside the rains. They too, now identified with frogs, give us riches through their multiple voices. The imagery throughout the hymn suggests that this multiplicity is orchestrated and collaborative, in both the natural and the sacrificial world. Thus, even in its human complexity, the sacrifice appears as inevitable as the seasons of the frogs, and vice versa.

Images for Dialogue: Beyond Historical Explanation

A final word might be in order here as we think about the genre of dialogue in early India. As mentioned above, the genre of dialogue hymns in the *Ṛg Veda* has been extensively discussed. Legends, or narratives, called *itihāsa*s, were generally used to explain a certain group of Ṛg Vedic hymns, called *saṃvāda*, which were extensively dialogical in structure. The Vedic commentators Yāska, Śaunaka, and the much later commentator, Sāyaṇa, did not give a ritual application (*viniyoga*) for these hymns, but preferred to tell a story in order to interpret them. As we shall see, in many cases, the *Bṛhaddevatā* and other authorities disagree as to whether a *sūkta* was an actual dialogue; it could also be called an *itihāsa* or an *ākhyāna* in itself.

Western scholarship, too, has had a long tradition of fascination with these dialogical hymns; early Indological work resulted in specific studies of those particular stories for which Sāyaṇa gives no ritual employment (*viniyoga*). Many of these hymns had the dialogical structure discussed above, such as the Vṛṣākapi hymn (*RV* 10.86), Saramā and the Paṇis (*RV* 10.108), the recovery of Agni (*RV* 10.51–3), Mudgala's race (*RV* 10.102), the dialogue between Pūrūravas and Urvaśī (*RV* 10.95), Lopāmudrā and Agastya (*RV* 10.179), and Indra, the Maruts, and Agastya (*RV* 10.165,170,171); the Vedic stories of Indra and Namuci, the two dogs of Yama, the marriage of Saraṇyu, as well as Trita[20] were also part of the repertoire.

Some discussion of the approaches to dialogue is important here. I have treated this issue extensively elsewhere,[21] and argued that the Indological concern throughout was with the origins of these dialogical exchanges. Western interpreters asked the question, were these dialogical hymns 'keys' to a larger, original Vedic tradition, and were the narrative interpretations of these hymns variations on an original archetypal theme? Colebrooke,[22] Rudolph von Roth,[23] Mueller, and Weber[24] took these as historical evidence of particular

---

20 Maurice Bloomfield, 'Contributions to the Interpretation of the Veda 3. 1. The story of Indra and Namuci. 2. The two dogs of Yama in a new role. 3. The marriage of Saraṇyu, Tvaṣṭar's daughter', *Journal of the American Oriental Society* 15 (1898): 143–88, and Maurice Bloomfield, 'Contributions to the Interpretation of the Veda 7. 6. Trita, the scape-goat of the gods, in relation to *AV* 6.112 and 113', *American Journal of Philology* 17 (1896): 430–37.

21 Laurie Patton, *Myth as Argument: The Bṛhaddevatā as Canonical Commentary* (Berlin, 1996), pp. 262ff.

22 Henry Thomas Colebrooke, *Essays in History, Literature and Religion of Ancient India.* (London, 1837; reprint ed., New Delhi, 1977).

23 Rudolph von Roth, *Zur Litteratur und Geschichte des Weda.* (Stuttgart, 1846).

24 Albrecht Weber, 'Episches im vedischen Ritual', *Sitzungberichte der preussischen Akademie der Wissenschaft* 38 (1891): 769–819.

religious and cultural ideas. Hermann Oldenberg[25] proposed a theory whereby the later legends comprised the prose narrative to be inserted between the verses of the original Vedic hymns. Many scholars, such as Karl Geldner and Richard Pischel,[26] and Emil Sieg,[27] followed this idea in their treatments and translations.

However, in the early twentieth century there was a reaction against this 'prose and poetry' view, particularly by Sylvain Levi, who argued that the Vedic *sūkta*s were coherent enough on their own and did not need prose narrative sections to complete the links. Johannes Hertel[28] and Von Schroeder[29] also contributed to this idea, arguing that the hymns could stand as ritual dramas on their own. Other scholars, such as A.B. Keith[30] and Jan Charpentier[31] rejected both ideas altogether.

Finally, scholarship of the mid twentieth century is marked by the study of Vedic legends with particular reference to the epic and pūraṇic material. H.L. Hariyappa's *Ṛg Vedic Legends throughout the Ages*[32] began the trend. S.A. Dange's *Legends in the* Mahābhārata,[33] Ram Gopal's 'Vedic Sources of the Sargaka Legend in the *Mahābhārata*',[34] M. Mehta's 'The Evolution of the *Suparṇa Saga* in the *Mahābhārata*',[35] and finally, Robert Goldman's 'Mortal Man and Immortal Woman: An Interpretation of Three *Ākhyāna* Hymns of the *Ṛg Veda*',[36] are some important examples. Paul Horsch, in *Die Vedische Gāthā und Śloka Literatur*, attempts to give a thorough intellectual history of the *ākhyāna* theory as a subset of the larger problem of genre in Vedic literature.[37] In an attempt to move away from the exclusively text-critical concerns, these authors are concerned with the telling of religious history through changes in themes and the treatment of characters.[38] In a masterful study, Muneo Tokunaga gives an exposition of which of the later legends might be spurious and which might be authentically connected to the dialogical hymns. My own contribution

---

25 Hermann Oldenberg, 'Das altindische *Ākhyāna*, mit besonderer Rücksichtauf das *Suparṇākhyana*', *Zeitschrift der Morgenlandischen Gesellschaft* 37 (1883): 85; Hermann Oldenberg, 'A*khyana*-Hymnen im *Rigveda*', *Zeitschrift der Morgenlandischen Gesellschaft* 39 (1885): 52–83.

26 Richard Pischel and Karl F.Geldner, *Vedische Studien* (Stuttgart, Band I, 1889; Band II, 1897; Band III, 1901).

27 Emil Sieg, *Die Sagenstoffe des* Ṛg Veda *und die indische* Itihasa-*tradition* (Stuttgart, 1902).

28 Johannes Hertel, 'Der Ursprung des Indischen Dramas und Epos', *Wiener Zeitschrift für die Kunde des Morgenlandes* 18 (1904): 59–83.

29 Leopold Von Schroeder, *Mysterium und Mimus im Rigveda* (Leipzig: 1908).

30 Arthur Berriedale Keith, 'The Birth of Pūrūravas', *Journal of the Royal Asiatic Society* (1913): 412–17.

31 Jarl, Charpentier, *Die* Suparṇasage, *Untersuchungen zur Altindischen Literatur und Sagengeschichte* (Uppsala, 1922).

32 H. L. Hariyappa, *Ṛgvedic Legends Through the Ages*, Deccan College Dissertation Series, 9 (Poona, 1953).

33 Sadavshiv Dange, *Legends in the* Mahābhārata, *With a Brief Survey of Folk-tales* (Delhi, 1969).

34 Ram Gopal, 'Vedic Sources of the Sargaka Legend in the *Mahābhārata*,' *Journal of the Ganganath Jha Research Institute* 25 (1960): 37–401.

35 M. Mehta, 'The Evolution of the *Suparṇa Saga* in the *Mahābhārata*', *Journal of the Oriental Institute, Baroda* 21/1–2 (1971): 41–65.

36 Robert Goldman, 'Mortal Man and Immortal Woman: An Interpretation of Three *Ākhyāna* Hymns of the *Ṛg Veda*', *Journal of the Oriental Institute, Baroda* 18 (1969): 273–303.

37 Paul Horsch, *Die Vedische Gāthā und* Śloka *Literatur*, (Bern, 1966), pp. 306–64.

38 See the recent special issue of *the Journal of the American Academy of Religion* 79/1 (2011) for other 'character-based' approaches to these issues of reading texts in early India.

to this debate[39] suggests that we do not look exclusively at origins (a primary focus of both sides of the debate), but rather at small changes in the legends over time as a form of intellectual history of attitudes toward poetic creation in early India.

I spend some time with this literary debate over the centuries because it gives us a good sense of the ways in which scholars have viewed dialogue in the past. For these thinkers, even in their disagreements, dialogue tends to be a structure, even a genre, which can act as a window onto the original form of Vedic poetry and ritual, but not necessarily an object of literary contemplation in its own right.

If we do take the poetic imagery about dialogue seriously as a literary trope, such as I have done in this article, we might add to this centuries-old Indological conversation (indeed a dialogue in its own right!). This approach might be analogous to the contemporary study of 'poets writing about poetry.' In such a study, we think about the ways in which poets meditate on their craft in concrete imagery.

In the same way, some less obvious Vedic hymns, such as *Ṛg Veda* 7.103, might also contribute to a larger, more expansive understanding of dialogue in early India. This contribution is not because the hymn to the frogs represents an actual dialogue, but because the imagery of dialogue is central to the *sūkta* and is deepened and developed throughout its verses, much like a character would be in a narrative. Concrete similes might be as important a key to understanding early Vedic perspectives on dialogue and voice as enacted dialogues themselves.

And relatedly, we might suggest a complementary methodology: we might read similes in the more well-known hymns, with an eye toward their literary images of speech as well as the ways in which explicit discourse about speech is developed in the *sūkta*. For example, RV 10.71, verse 7 mentions some sacrificers of speech and insight, who are 'like ponds that reach up to the mouth or shoulder, while others are deep enough to bathe in'. This image of the ponds simultaneously suggests relative degrees of depth as well as relative degrees of purity amongst sacrificers. Furthermore, the related imagery of the bath also suggests that in the proper engagement of speech, one is progressively purified. This single image achieves in a condensed manner what is elsewhere explicitly stated in the hymn: that some sacrificers succeed and others do not because of their relative knowledge of speech.

Similarly, RV 10.71.9 mentions the brahmins who use speech in a bad way, 'weaving on a weft of rags'. This imagery recalls RV 10.129, which regularly uses the imagery of weaving for the creation of the world. Thus, the single phrase reminds us that the poet is indeed attempting nothing less than to create a world, but is doing so badly, using materials that cannot actually make a cosmogonic fabric.

Another powerful simile for voice can be found in *Ṛg Veda* 2.42.1, describing the speech of the poet who also honours the bird. 'Crying repeatedly, and telling the future, may speech come to you, as a helmsman guides a boat. Be ominous of good fortune, O bird, and may no disaster come to you from anywhere.' The sage Gṛtsamada is speaking to a bird, whom he wishes to appease in order to avoid bad fortune. He compares the sending of speech to a helmsman guiding a boat – both involving considerable skill and a clear sense of direction and intention. A single image encapsulates the hoped-for efficacy of the mantra. And efficacy is what one hopes for in a hymn to dispel bad omens.

These are just some examples whereby the poetic images about voice, and of dialogue, could be powerful ways of interpreting the Veda – an additional perspective to understanding the performance of dialogue through explicitly dialogical hymns involving characters. To

[39] Patton, *Myth as Argument.*

be sure, themes of speech abound in Vedic discourse – whether they are poems in the voice of the goddess of speech, or enacted dialogical speech (in contestation as well as in riddles). But rarely has the study focused on the work of specific similes, whether they are frogs, helmsmen, or ponds.

Elsewhere in this volume, Alf Hiltebeitel writes of the effect of 'apostrophe' in the *Mahābhārata* – the sudden address to an imagined speaker – and argues that this form of address has the effect of engaging the reader. So, too, Anna Esposito writes of the change of characters in Jain dialogues as a means of gaining the attention of a different kind of audience. The similes for dialogue in the frog hymn and other parts of the Veda may well have been an earlier version of the same kind of effects: to wake the listener up and make the Vedic audience think about the nature of speech at the same time it was being spoken.

Last Thoughts

Similes for speech show themselves to be central in the hymn to the frogs. The frogs are literally 'raising their voice', verse by verse, until they become brahmins in their own right. Concrete forms of dialogue guide the imagery of the hymn, and help us move from comparison to identification between frogs and brahmins, and from the emergence of voice to a full bodied harmonious chorus. Other concrete similes for speech, and their role in the poetic construction of Ṛg Vedic hymns, await further study. The frogs and brahmins alike would delight in the exploration of such voices.

References

Bloomfield, Maurice, 'On the Frog-Hymn, Rig Veda vii 103, Together with Some Remarks on the Composition of Vedic Hymns', *Proceedings of the American Oriental Society* 17 (1896): 173–9.

———, 'Contributions to the Interpretation of the Veda 7. 6. Trita, the scape-goat of the gods, in relation to *AV* 6.112 and 113', *American Journal of Philology* 17 (1896): 430–37.

———, 'Contributions to the Interpretation of the Veda 3. 1. The story of Indra and Namuci. 2. The two dogs of Yama in a new role. 3. The marriage of Saraṇyū, Tvaṣṭar›s daughter', *Journal of the American Oriental Society* 15 (1898): 143–88.

Brown, Norman, 'Some Notes on the Rain Charms', *The New Indian Antiquary* 2 (1939): 115–19.

Charpentier, Jarl, *Die* Suparṇasage, *Untersuchungen zur Altindischen Literatur und Sagen-geschichte* (Uppsala: A.-b. Akademiska Bokhandeln i Kommission, 1922).

Colebrooke, Henry Thomas, *Essays in History, Literature and Religion of Ancient India* (London: Royal Asiatic Society, 1837; reprint ed., New Delhi: Cosmos Publications, 1977).

Dange, Sadavshiv, *Legends in the* Mahābhārata, *With a Brief Survey of Folk-tales* (Delhi: Motilal Banarsidass, 1969).

De, S.K., 'Wit, Humour and Satire in Ancient Literature', in *Aspects of Sanskrit Literature* (Calcutta: Firma Mukhopadhyay, 1959), pp. 257–89.

Doniger, Wendy (trans.), *The Rig-Veda* (London: Penguin, 1991).

Gonda, Jan, 'The So-Called Secular, Humorous and Satirical Hymns of the Rigveda', *Orientalia Neerlandica, Leiden* (1948): 312–48.

———, *Remarks on Similes in Sanskrit Literature* (Leiden: E.J. Brill, 1949).

Gopal, Ram, 'Vedic Sources of the Sargaka Legend in the *Mahābhārata*', *Journal of the Ganganath Jha Research Institute* 25 (1960): 37–401.

Goldman, Robert, 'Mortal Man and Immortal Woman: An Interpretation of Three *Ākhyāna* Hymns of the *Ṛg Veda*', *Journal of the Oriental Institute, Baroda* 18 (1969): 273–303.

Hariyappa, H.L., *Ṛgvedic Legends Through the Ages*, Deccan College Dissertation Series, 9 (Poona: S.M. Katre, 1953).

Hertel, Joannes, 'Der Ursprung des Indischen Dramas und Epos', *Wiener Zeitschrift für die Kunde des Morgenlandes* 18 (1904): 59–83.

Horsch, Paul, *Die Vedische* Gatha *und* Sloka *Literatur* (Bern: Francke Verlag, 1966), pp. 306–64.

Keith, Arthur Berriedale, 'The Birth of Pūrūravas', *Journal of the Royal Asiatic Society* (1913): 412–17.

Mehta, M., 'The Evolution of the *Suparna Saga* in the *Mahābhārata*', *Journal of the Oriental Institute, Baroda* 21/1–2 (1971): 41–65.

Oldenberg, Hermann, 'Das altindische *Akhyana*, mit besonderer Rücksichtauf das *Suparnākhyāna*', *Zeitschrift der Morgenlandischen Gesellschaft* 37 (1883): 54–86.

———, '*Akhyana*-Hymnen im *Rigveda*', *Zeitschrift der Morgenlandischen Gesellschaft* 39 (1885): 52–83.

Patton, Laurie, *Myth as Argument: The Bṛhaddevatā as Canonical Commentary* (Berlin: De Gruyter, 1996).

———, *Bringing the Gods to Mind: Mantra and Ritual in Early Indian Sacrifice* (Berkeley: University of California Press, 2005).

Pischel, Richard, and Karl F. Geldner, *Vedische Studien* (Stuttgart: W. Kohlhammer, Band I, 1889; Band II, 1897; Band III, 1901).

von Roth, Rudolph, *Zur Litteratur und Geschichte des Weda* (Stuttgart: A. Liesching and Co., 1846).

von Schroeder, Leopold, *Mysterium und Mimus im Rigveda* (Leipzig: H. Haessel Verlag, 1908).

Sieg, Emil, *Die Sagenstoffe des* Ṛg Veda *und die indische* Itihāsa-*tradition* (Stuttgart: W. Kohlhammer, 1902).

Weber, Albrecht, 'Episches im vedischen Ritual', *Sitzungberichte der preussischen Akademie der Wissenschaft*, 38 (1891): 769–819.

Chapter 2
Dialogue and Apostrophe: A Move by Vālmīki?

Alf Hiltebeitel

This chapter will explore the hypothesis that, after one looks at the similarities and differences in the ways dialogue is used in the two Sanskrit epics, it is worth exploring the possibility that Vālmīki innovates by transposing dialogue into apostrophe. By apostrophe, I content myself at the outset with a few small modifications of the first 'rhetorical' meaning given in *The New Shorter Oxford English Dictionary on Historical Principles*: 'Sudden exclamatory address; an exclamatory passage addressed to a particular person (frequently absent or dead) or thing'.[1] Considering the *Rāmāyaṇa*'s size and its vast performative and literary exfoliations, we must drop the word 'sudden', and since its principal addressee is Rāma, we should add the word 'imagined' between 'absent or dead'. I am grateful to Brian Black and Laurie Patton for appreciating that this chapter also 'gets at the vexing issue of citation practices in a broad-thinking way, and also at the larger question of what it means to 'mark' something in the literary sense of an apostrophe'.[2] But my attention to citational and grammatical meanings is almost accidental to my interest in the rhetorical meaning – which is what this essay will explore – along with the improved possibilities these two texts, especially in their Critical Editions, offer for dialogue among informed teachers, colleagues, and students. Other chapters in this volume also engage rhetorical meaning within dialogues, whether it is poetic meditations on the meanings of dialogue itself (Patton) or the rhetorical genres by which philosophical meaning is generated (Nicholson).

Behind this exploration will be the premise that, where apostrophe is used, it is used to lift dialogue 'out of context' to address the reader, that is to engage the epics' target audiences. Both dialogue in the *Mahābhārata* and apostrophe in the *Rāmāyaṇa* would have been innovative means to create new dialogical communities of those engaged in these texts. The reason to investigate this with regard to the *Rāmāyaṇa*, and to ask whether Vālmīki enhances apostrophe as a new 'move', is the fact that the *Rāmāyaṇa* is addressed first of all to its hero, Rāma.

I write from the perspective that one is justified in taking the Critical Editions of both epics to have largely successfully reconstructed the archetypal baselines from which both their smaller and larger dialogical features can and should be appreciated. The baseline texts are both works of literature. But whereas the *Mahābhārata*'s combination of heterogeneity and overarching architectural design is suggestive of composition by a committee or atelier of poets over a short period of no more than two generations, the *Rāmāyaṇa*'s greater homogeneity suggests the possibility of a single (main) poet.[3] I also consider the archetypal

---

1 Leslie Brown (ed.), *The New Shorter Oxford English Dictionary on Historical Principles* 2 vols (Oxford, 1993), pp. 1, 96. The definition is prefaced by '[L f. Gk. *apostrophē*, f. *apostrephein* turn away, f. as APO- + *strephein* to turn.].'

2 Volume editors' letter from Black, 5 March 2012.

3 For discussion, see Alf Hiltebeitel, *Rethinking the Mahābhārata: A Reader's Guide to the Education of Yudhiṣṭhira* (Chicago, 2001), pp. 20, 29 n. 20; Alf Hiltebeitel, 'Weighting Orality and

Mahābhārata a little earlier than the archetypal *Rāmāyaṇa*, and thus pose the notion of Vālmīki making a 'new move' with such a relative chronology in mind.[4] Before we can get to this new move, we must first ask how each epic treats its shorter and longer dialogical features; such an analysis will include looking at the two epics' 'subtales' and frame narratives.

Sub-stories: Shorter and Longer Dialogues

One of the ways that both epics break the main narrative flow is by the recounting of additional stories. In the *Mahābhārata*, there is a considerable body of 'ancillary stories', among which there are about sixty-seven designated 'subtales' called *upākhyānas*.[5] Stories told in the *Rāmāyaṇa* do not use this term, and are often just called *kathā*, the most conventional term for story. In both epics, all stories are dialogical in that each story-telling requires both a character who takes on the role of teller and another or others who listens.

Whereas the *Mahābhārata*'s *upākhyānas* are introduced by dialogical markers that interrupt the verse structure (typically by 'So and so said [*uvāca*]'), the *Rāṃāyaṇa*'s stories are initiated and terminated within the verses themselves. *Rāmāyaṇa* stories thus flow uninterruptedly in and out of the poem which Rāma's twin sons Kuśa and Lava address to him. Rāma is also usually the primary audience of the stories (beginning with those told by Viśvāmitra in Book 1). So we must ultimately envision him as listening to them again. And since he can also tell a story himself (as at 7.78–9 about the monthly sex-changes of Ila/Ilā before he became a royal ancestor), we must envision him listening to himself, which he would do anyway in ordinary dialogues. The net effect is to imagine Rāma involved in an interior dialogue with himself. Nothing like this goes on in the *Mahābhārata*. There, the net effect is to set up mirrors, puzzles, and echoes between subtales and the main story – and between subtales themselves[6] – and to reinforce such echoes through back-and-forth framings and multiple tellings to numerous auditors.

Writing in the Sanskrit Epics', in Petteri Koskikallio (ed.), *Epics, Khilas, and Purāṇas: Continuities and Ruptures*. Proceedings of the Third International Conference on the Sanskrit Epics and Purāṇas (Zagreb, 2002), pp. 81–111; Alf Hiltebeitel, *Dharma: Its Early History in Law, Religion, and Narrative* (New York, 2011), ch. 1; Alf Hiltebeitel, 'On Sukthankar's "S" and Some Shortsighted Assessments and Uses of the Pune Critical Edition', *Journal of Vaishnava Studies* 19/ 2 (2011): 87–126; Alf Hiltebeitel, 'The Southern Recension's "Śakuntalā" as a First Reading: a Window on the Original and the Second Reading by Kālidāsa', in Saswati Sengupta and Deepika Tandon (eds), *Revisiting Abhijñānaśākuntalam: Love, Lineage and Language in Kālidāsa's Nāṭaka* (Hyderabad, 2011), pp. 17–37; Alf Hiltebeitel, 'From *Ṛṣidharma* to *Vānaprastha*: the Southern Recension Makeover of the *Mahābhārata*'s *Umā-Maheśvara Saṃvāda*', in Adam Bowles, Simon Brodbeck, and Alf Hiltebeitel (eds), *Churning the Ocean of the Epics and Purāṇas* (in press).

[4] For my main discussion of this point, see Alf Hiltebeitel, 'Authorial Paths through the Two Sanskrit Epics, Via the *Rāmopākhyāna*', in Robert P. Goldman and Muneo Tokunaga (eds), *Epic Undertakings*, vol 2 of Petteri Koskikallio and Asko Parpola (gen. eds), *Papers of the 12th World Sanskrit Conference, Helsinki, 13–18 July 2003* (Delhi, 2009), pp. 169–214.

[5] On 'ancillary stories', see Barbara Gombach, 'Ancillary Stories in the Sanskrit *Mahābhārata*', PhD Dissertation, 2 Parts (New York: Columbia University, 2000). On *upākhyānas* and on what follows in this paragraph, see Alf Hiltebeitel, 'Not Without Subtales: Telling Laws and Truths in the Sanskrit Epics', *Journal of Indian Philosophy* 3 (2005): 467–79.

[6] See Madeleine Biardeau, *Le Mahābhārata: Un récit fondateur du brahmanisme et son interprétation* (Paris, 2002), vol. 1, pp. 412–13 on 'mirror stories' such as the Nala, Rāma, and Sāvitrī

Now, although all stories in both epics are dialogical in these varied ways, both epics use the term *saṃvāda* for units that are explicitly called 'dialogues'. This term is used frequently in the *Mahābhārata*, but is inconspicuous in the *Rāmāyaṇa*. One finds 17 references to *saṃvāda* in the *Mahābhārata*'s first five books; 5 in its war books (all but one of these in Book 6, where, 3 of the 4 cluster to describe Arjuna and Kṛṣṇa's famous dialogue in the *Bhagavad Gītā*); 47 in Book 12; 31 in Book 13; 8 in Book 14; and none thereafter in the four remaining short books of closure. The *Rāmāyaṇa* has only 9 instances. In the *Mahābhārata*, numerous dialogue chapters (*adhyāyas*) also supply colophons or 'finishing touches' that name the chapter after the *saṃvāda* within them; in the *Rāmāyaṇa* chapter (*sarga*) colophons occur rarely. Although some *saṃvādas* include the narration of illustrative stories,[7] there is next to no surface overlap in the *Mahābhārata* between *upākhyānas* and *saṃvādas*. As far as I can see, the single exception occurs in the *Mucukunda-Upākhyāna* (12.75), which is introduced with the formulaic line, 'On this they cite this old account (*atrāpyudāharantīmam itihāsaṃ purātanam*), the dialogue (*saṃvāda*) between Mucukunda and king Vaiśravaṇa [Kubera]' (12.75.3). A brief combat narrative resulting in Mucukunda's defeat by Kubera follows, after which Mucukunda recovers his kingdom (4–7, 19–20) thanks to information he got in the intervening dialogue (8–18). While Bhīṣma's postwar *dharma*-teachings to Yudhiṣṭhira shape an overarching dialogue that runs through most of Books 12 and 13, where most of the epic's *saṃvādas* occur,[8] one gets the impression that Bhīṣma lends spice to the far more frequent *saṃvādas* by occasionally interrupting them with a more colorful *upākhyāna*. Bhīṣma would seem so well informed about *dharma*-lore mostly from spending his youthful years in heaven with his mother, the celestial Gaṅgā. For he attributes many of the *saṃvādas* he cites, as well as similarly sourced 'words' (*vākyāni*; 253.1), 'sung' (*gīta*) verses (12.78.6;.93.2; 170.2; 171.4; 171.55; 251.1; 268.3; 270.13), and a speech (*vacaḥ*; 168.8), discourse (*vādam*; 194.2), and *upaniṣad* (12.94.38), to deities and heavenly sages. Bhīṣma was taught by such celestial sages as Rāma Jāmadagnya (12.117.1–2), Nārada, Vyāsa, Asita Devala, Mārkaṇḍeya, and even Vālmīki (12.200.3–5);[9] thus he could interpret *dharma* for the fractious Kurus and oversee the continuity of the Bhārata-Kuru royal line.[10]

Such formulaically highlighted *saṃvādas*, and especially those recounted by Bhīṣma in Books 12 and 13, are thus noteworthy for having a distinctive aura of sanctity. But they are

---

upākhyānas in *Mbh* Book 3; Hiltebeitel 'Not Without Subtales': 476, 487–91 on equally interactive 'puzzle pieces' like the *Kṛtaghna-Upākhyāna* (12.162–7), *Uñchavṛtti-Upākhyāna* (12.340–53), and *Nakula-Upākhyāna* (14.92–6), in each of which Yudhiṣṭhira son of Dharma encounters a figure representing his father. For further discussion, see Hiltebeitel *Dharma: Its Early History in Law, Religion, and Narrative*, ch. 9.

7 A *kathā* at *Mbh* 12.202.6; an *ākhyānam* at 12.248.11.

8 Counting slight variants, Books 12 and 13 find Bhīṣma using the full-line formula 88 of the 106 times it is used in the *Mahābhārata*. He also uses variants such as *atra te vartayiṣye 'ham itihāsaṃ purātanam*, 'On this I will tell you an old account' (*Mbh* 12.168.28; 224.6; 288.2; 291.7; 298.3; cf. 146.2; 277.2; 13.40.2).

9 Vālmīki is also mentioned among such sometimes Viṣṇu-attending Ṛṣis at 2.7.14, 3.83.102, 5.81.27, 99.11, and 13.18.7.

10 See Alf Hiltebeitel, 'Bhīṣma's Sources', in Klaus Karttunen and Petteri Koskikallio (eds), *Vidyārṇavavandanam: Essays in Honour of Asko Parpola*. Studia Orientalia 94 (2001), pp. 261–78; Hiltebeitel, *Dharma: Its Early History in Law, Religion, and Narrative*, ch. 8; and Alf Hiltebeitel, 'The *Mahābhārata* and the Stories Some People Tell about Its Tribal and Earliest Histories', in Neera Misra (ed.), *Papers from the International Seminar on the Mahābhārata: Its Historicity, Antiquity, Evolution & Impact on Civilization*, organized by Neera Misra and the Draupadi Trust. 26 April 2012 (in press).

significant as well for their technically precise mode of delivery. As Muneo Tokunaga has observed, there is a similar usage in some *dharmasūtra*s, where the *udāharanti* formula is preceded by *atha* rather than *atra.*[11] In his view,

> The particle *atha*, which matches the style of the treatise, was changed to *atra* ('as to this [point of your question]') in the dialogue of the *Mahābhārata*. Just as *atrāpi udāharanti* corroborates an instruction in the *Mahābhārata*, so *athāpy undāharanti* introduces in the Dharmasūtras a *śloka* text as an illustration or corroboration (*arthavāda*) of the injunction (*vidhi*) found in the preceding *sūtra.*[12]

Whereas *Vasiṣṭha* is the first and only *dharmasūtra* to use the quotative phrase with the source as a 'Mānavan *śloka*' (in the sense of a supposed citation of *The Laws of Manu*), the *Mahābhārata* is the first and only one of these texts to use it with the phrase *itihāsam purātanam* and thus, moreover, to use it in conjunction not only with the phrase but with the term *itihāsa*, 'so indeed it was', or 'history'.[13] However, the *Rāmāyaṇa*, *The Laws of Manu*, and the *Gautama Dharmasūtra* do not use the *athāpy/atrāpy udāharanti* formula at all.[14] It would be worth looking further into the ways that four of these 'classical *dharma* texts'[15] (*Āpastamba*, *Baudhāyana*, *Vasiṣṭha*, and the *Mahābhārata*) use it while three others (*Gautama*, *Manu*, and the *Rāmāyaṇa*) do not. We can, however, begin by noting that the first group shows a greater intertextual citational interest whereas the second group is one of texts that affect postures of standing more alone.

The first group, including the *Mahābhārata*, is one whose use of this quotative formula bears a certain resemblance to a scholarly apparatus of footnotes that would be pertinent to texts that reflect debates of a scholarly tradition on *dharma* as legal precedent, and take some delight in absorbing themselves in a world of varied and often conflicting views about it. This point may be enriched by one made by Tokunaga: that the *Mahābhārata*'s use of this formula treats the informative narrative told as exemplum as the third (middle) member of the classical Indian syllogism to provide illustration

---

11 *Āpastamba*, probably the earliest of the four surviving *dharmasūtrakāras,* begins with ten usages. Two refer to what Patrick Olivelle, *Dharmasūtras: The Law Codes of Ancient India* (Oxford, 1999), p. 30 translates as 'two verses from a Purāṇa' (*purāṇe ślokau*), one quoting Prajāpati and the other a mythological anecdote (*Ā* 1.19.13; 2.23.3–5). Others recount illustrative stories and proverbial sayings. *Baudhāyana* then generalizes the practice, using the *athāpy udāharanti* phrasing forty-nine times virtually anywhere it turns from prose to a quoted verse. *B* 2.4.26 recalls a dialogue between the two wives of the *Mahābhārata*'s Yayāti.

12 Muneo Tokunaga, 'Vedic Exegesis and Epic Poetry: A Note on *atrāpyudāharanti*', In Petteri Koskikallio (ed.) *Parallels and Comparisons*. Proceedings of the Fourth Dubrovnik International Conference on the Sanskrit Epics and Purāṇas, September 2005 (Zagreb, 2009) p. 28.

13 See my chapter 4 with the main title 'Why Itihāsa?' in Hiltebeitel, *Reading the Fifth Veda: Essays on the Mahābhārata by Alf Hiltebeitel*. Vishwa Adluri and Joydeep Bagchee (eds) (Leiden, 2011) and the further discussion in Hiltebeitel, *Dharma: Its Early History in Law, Religion, and Narrative*, ch. 7 and Alf Hiltebeitel, 'Between History and Divine Plan: The *Mahābhārata*'s Royal Patriline in Context', in Simon Brodbeck and James Hegarty (eds), *Papers from the 2010 Cardiff University Conference on Genealogy in India. Religions of South Asia* 5/1–2 (2011): 103–25.

14 *Gautama* may clear the quotative phrase out entirely from his entirely prose *dharmasūtra*.

15 I use and explain this phrase in Alf Hiltebeitel, *Dharma*, Asian Spiritualities Series (Honolulu, 2010); *Dharma: Its Early History in Law, Religion, and Narrative*. The discussion here builds on discussions there in each book's chapter 5.

or corroboration of the speaker's thesis.[16] Tokunaga shows that *Mahābhārata* usages typically occur with instruction either before or after the formula, with the instruction being about factual, moral, political, philosophical, or religious matters.[17] Along with the fact that the *Mahābhārata*'s primary self-identifying genre term is *itihāsa*, it presents its leading characters not only as 'living history' but as interested in hearing it and citing it in support of their varied views on what we may call 'precedent', and in some cases 'legal precedent', especially in several *upākhyāna*s in Book 1 and in the *Rājadharma* and *Āpaddharma* sections of Book 12.[18] This would of course help to create readerships and audiences attracted to this sense of history.[19]

The second group, including the *Rāmāyaṇa*, would then be one of texts that claim authority independent of and above such a nexus of debate. For these texts, legal precedent is to be set by the prestige of the author, in the case of 'Gautama' or 'Manu',[20] or by a virtually perfect godlike man like Rāma. Were one to want a debate, one would have to turn to him. Rather than everyone being imbued through dialogue with a sense of history, it looks like the *Rāmāyaṇa* poet is really addressing only one man with a story, or adventure, about him. If so, he does not answer. But he listens.

Now *Gautama* has no frame. *Manu* does have one that lifts its author above the *dharmasūtra* debate nexus, but as Patrick Olivelle says, it sort of 'fizzles out'.[21] In the two

---

16 In reverse, Tokunaga's point could also be taken to suggest that even the formal syllogism contains narrative and holds potential for dialogue: e.g., 'Socrates is a man; all men are mortal. …' But as Vishwa Adluri points out (personal communication), Indian systematic philosophy, and the Nyāya school above all, undercuts the Vedic and especially Upaniṣadic dialogical and initiatory philosophical current that lives on in the *Mahābhārata*. See Vishwa Adluri, *Parmenides, Plato and Mortal Philosophy: Return from Transcendence* (London, 2011), on how the dialogue form modulates philosophy in a way systematic philosophies cannot.

17 Tokunaga, 'Vedic Exegesis and Epic Poetry', pp. 24–7.

18 On 'legal precedent' in *Mahābhārata* subtales at the interface with *dharmaśāstra*, see Hiltebeitel, *Dharma: Its Early History in Law, Religion, and Narrative*, pp. 213, 360 ('Śakuntalā'); pp. 401–2, 426 (Kuntī's story about Śvetaketu), and p. 426 ('Aṇimāṇḍavya'), to which may be added 'Yayāti', and pp. 420–29, 437 on my usage of the concept 'legal precedent' with regard especially to *upākhyāna*s in Book 3.

19 Since I see the *Mahābhārata*'s generic and quotative usages going hand in hand, I do not, however, follow Tokunaga's idea that the 'moral (or dharmic) instructions' found mainly in the *Rājadharma* mark the point from which the quotative usage 'spread' to later parts of the epic (Hiltebeitel, 'Authorial Paths through the Two Sanskrit Epics', p. 27), or that usages of *itihāsa* to characterize the epic in its frames result from 'the long history of [its] textual development' as it 'gradually changed its nature under the influence of Vedic exegesis' ('Authorial Paths', p. 29). Tokunaga adopts the nineteenth-century philological programme in which gains in the study and interpretation of the *Mahābhārata* are thought to be best validated if they allow for the naming of some new layer in the text's millennia of 'redaction'. This method will obviously work better for some texts than others. Evidence mounts that it is misplaced when applied to the *Mahābhārata* and *Rāmāyaṇa*; see Vishwa Adluri and Joydeep Bagchee, *The Nay Science: A History of German Indology* (New York, 2014) and *Philology and Criticism* (London, in press); Alf Hiltebeitel, 'On Sukthankar's 'S''; Alf Hiltebeitel, 'The *Mahābhārata* and the Stories Some People Tell about It', 2 parts. *Exemplar: The Journal of South Asian Studies* 1 (Fall 2012): 1–26 and (Spring 2013); Hiltebeitel, 'The *Mahābhārata* and the Stories Some People Tell about Its Tribal and Earliest Histories'.

20 See Patrick Olivelle, 'Manu and Gautama: A Study in Śāstric Intetextuality', in *Language, Texts, and Society: Explorations in Ancient Indian Culture and Religion* (Florence, 2005), pp. 261–74. on the relation between these two texts and their shared reduction of debate to monologue.

21 Patrick Olivelle (trans.), *The Law Code of Manu* (Oxford, 2004), p. xxv.

Sanskrit epics, the frame narratives are much more complex than in *Manu*, and they certainly do not fizzle out. I have used the term 'braided' to describe the way the *Mahābhārata* intertwines dialogue levels within its larger dialogical frame structure.[22] Without using the term 'braided', I have also tried to show that something similar, with important differences, can be said about the *Rāmāyaṇa*.[23] These similarities and differences are worth re-exploring under the heading of dialogue, and in particular with reference to what I will call the largely tacit 'dialogical situations' of each epic's authorial frame.

In the long and leisurely *Mahābhārata*, such braiding extends throughout the text, but is veiled and unveiled at varied points to let the reader know that even though she or he feels comfortable to have settled into its main Vaiśaṃpāyana–Janamejaya dialogue level, the braid is something never to lose track of. In contrast, the *Rāmāyaṇa* starts braiding frame elements (it will be best to call them strands rather than frames) into its main frame from the very beginning and then almost lets readers forget about them until they pop back into view. This occurs with occasional further interventions from Nārada and Brahmā, who appear in the initial two interwoven strands. But the major flourish that ties the authorial main strand back into the main narrative occurs when Vālmīki brings Kuśa and Lava to recite the *Rāmāyaṇa* at their father Rāma's Aśvamedha sacrifice.

The *Mahābhārata*'s Braided Dialogical Frames

The *Mahābhārata* has what I have called three 'braided' frame stories, each with its own unique dialogical features. I restrict my usage to narrated framing stories such as the text presents itself.[24] One can describe the *Mahābhārata*'s three frames in various orders. The order of their disclosure in the text itself is as follows. Ugraśravas' dialogue with the Ṛṣis

[22] Alf Hiltebeitel, 'The *Nārāyaīya* and the Early Reading Communities of the *Mahābhārata*', in Patrick Olivelle (ed.), *Between the Empires: Society in India 300 BCE to 400 CE* (New York, 2006), pp. 229–33.

[23] See initially Hiltebeitel, 'Not Without Subtales': 461–64; cf. Alf Hiltebeitel, '*Mahābhārata*', in Stanley Wolpert (ed.), *Encyclopedia of India*, 4 vols (Detroit, 2006), vol. 3, pp. 82–93, and Alf Hiltebeitel, '*Rāmāyaṇa*', in Stanley Wolpert (ed.), *Encyclopedia of India*, 4 vols (Detroit, 2006), vol. 3, pp. 390–99.

[24] Uses of the term 'frame' to describe alleged late 'coatings' of the *Mahābhārata* (Reinhold Grünendahl, 'Zur Stellung des *Nārāyaṇīya* im *Mahābhārata*', in Peter Schreiner [ed.], *Nārāyaṇīya-Studien* [Wiesbaden, 1997], p. 237; see Hiltebeitel, 'On Sukthankar's "S"', p. 107) or twice-told stories that might 'frame' what occurs in the text between them (e.g., James Fitzgerald, 'The Rāma Jāmadagnya 'Thread' of the *Mahābhārata*: A New Survey of Rāma Jāmadagnya in the Pune Text', in Mary Brockington [ed.], *Stages and Transitions: Temporal and Historical Frameworks in Epic and Purāṇic Literature*. Proceedings of the Second Dubrovnik International Conference on the Epics and Purānas [Zagreb, 2002], pp. 104–7) are really no more than a continuation of the same misplaced nineteenth-century trend just mentioned in n. 19. Cf. however James L. Fitzgerald, 'The Mokṣa Anthology of the Great Bhārata: An Initial Survey of Structural Issues, Themes, and Rhetorical Strategies' (PhD dissertation, University of Chicago, 1980), pp. 281–2 with regard to the 'old accounts' and numerous authorities Bhīṣma quotes to Yudhiṣṭhira in Books 12 and 13, which 'stand[s] out .... as an overall frame' in those books. Fitzgerald limits his notion of a 'frame' here far more usefully to the 'garland of Yudhisthira's questions' and Bhīṣma's often-oblique responses, and finds this frame too uncoordinated ('The Mokṣa Anthology', p. 295), patternless ('The Mokṣa Anthology', p. 322), and 'thin and weak to be a text of any importance in its own right' ('The Mokṣa Anthology', p. 293). He does not explore its relation to the epic's encompassing frames, but is aware of the possibility: 'A few of the framing passages do express an awareness of the rest of the collection…' and 'coordination among the introductory frames' ('The Mokṣa Anthology', p. 294). See below.

of the Naimiṣa Forest (1.1),[25] and then with their leader Śaunaka (1.4), comes first with the *Mahābhārata*'s well-known 'double opening', and from this standpoint has been called the 'first dialogue level'.[26] Mention of Vyāsa's authorship is made frequently between this first and second opening as an underlying priority. And finally, the Vaiśaṃpāyana–Janamejaya dialogue is introduced third, and henceforth it becomes the main or 'second' dialogue level through which the main narrative is sustained.

The most noteworthy early mention of Vyāsa's authorship occurs at 1.2.70, where one reads that Vyāsa's *Mahābhārata* of one hundred *upaparvans* was reconfigured into eighteen major *parvans* by Ugraśravas for the Ṛṣis of the Naimiṣa Forest.[27] Presumably this would mean that Vaiśaṃpāyana told the *Mahābhārata* only from Vyāsa's hundred *upaparvan* edition, which Ugraśravas heard before coming to Naimiṣa Forest. One might take this to mean that Vaiśaṃpāyana would have stopped short of the final *upaparvans* that Ugraśravas mentions, which refer to the *Harivaṃśa*.

That solution cannot, however, explain several moments within the Vaiśaṃpāyana narration where the Ugraśravas narration breaks into it, showing that they are mixed. One such segment interjects what I have called three 'dips to the outer frame', in the third of which Vyāsa is himself the speaker quoted by Ugraśravas (Hiltebeitel, The *Nārāyanīya*). Adluri notices another fascinating case of mixture of a different kind. Just when Ugraśravas is about to tell Śaunaka the story of Āstīka up to the outcome of Janamejaya's snake sacrifice, he lets it be known that one of Śaunaka's ancestors, Ruru, once asked his father Pramati to tell him 'the entire tale of Āstīka' and that Pramati complied (*Mbh* 1.12.3, 5). Textually. Āstīka's disruption of Janamejaya's snake sacrifice coincides with the beginning of the Vaiśaṃpāyana narration. But Āstīka's intervention does not 'happen' until that narration is over. Thus in terms of the logic of the text, Pramati could not know the Āstīka story until the whole *Mahābhārata* is over and until he has heard it from (let us say) 'someone like' Ugraśravas. Adluri can thus infer that Pramati's retelling – even as 'a silent, implicit, never explicitly expressed one' (Literary Violence and Literal Salvation, 53) – is 'braided' with the Ugraśravas and Vaiśaṃpāyana frames (to which the Vyāsa frame can be added) to serve as a meta-commentary on them. As such, it would be positioned to 'witness' the whole *Mahābhārata* from the standpoint of *ahiṃsā* as the highest *dharma*, since Ruru had been introduced to that topic by a 'lizard' (really a Ṛṣi cursed to become the lizard) he had tried to kill while carrying out his own blind vendetta against snakes.[28] It may thus be that anomalies like these arise in both dialogical narrations, and are allowed to do so within the narrative 'architecture' Vyāsa devises to override them both and hold them together. But Vyāsa is never said to have authored his prior version at a dialogue level of narration.

---

25 Wherever the Naimiṣa Forest is, and I argue that it is the twinkling night sky (Hiltebeitel, *Rethinking the Mahābhārata*, pp. 95–6, 158), getting there has been a long trip for Ugraśravas. On the double opening, see now Vishwa Adluri, 'Frame Narratives and Forked Beginnings: Or, How to Read the Ādiparvan', *Journal of Vaishnava Studies* 19/2 (2011): 143–210.

26 See e.g. Grünendahl, 'Zur Stellung des *Nārāyaṇīya* im *Mahābhārata*', p. 237.

27 As noted in Simon Brodbeck, 'Analytic and Synthetic Approaches in the Light of the Poona Edition of the *Mahābhārata* and *Harivaṃśa*', *Journal of Vaiṣṇava Studies* 19/1 (2011): 231, 243 n. 32, with acknowledgment to Brian Black for bringing this to his attention.

28 See Vishwa Adluri, 'Literary Violence and Literal Salvation: Śaunaka interprets the *Mahābhārata*', *Exemplar: The Journal of South Asian Studies* 1/2 (2012): 50–54 on *Mbh* 1.8–13.2 (the Ruru story); Alf Hiltebeitel, 'Śiva's *Summa* on *Ṛṣidharma* in the *Umā-Maheśvara Saṃvāda*: The Baseline *Mahābhārata*'s Discourse on Gleaning in the Context of Contemporary Brahmanical and Buddhist Sources', unsubmitted article in progress, on *ahiṃsā* and war in both epics.

I believe it is more informative, however, to introduce these three frames in the logical order of the chronology of their transmission. First would be the 'outermost' authorial frame in which Vyāsa recites the *Mahābhārata* for the first time to his five disciples, including (and according to one passage [1.1.63] beginning with) his son Śuka. I have not been overly successful in promoting this first frame on a par with the other two, which are in their own interrelationship richly treated by Minkowski.[29] But I do view it to be indispensable to understanding their interworkings.[30] Rather than a dialogue, it is mainly a story about how Vyāsa first recited the *Mahābhārata* to his five disciples as a communication of his creation – a teaching, a 'fifth Veda'. But when we come to points where the three *Mahābhārata* frames are braided together, it will be justifiable to refer to all three as dialogical, since Vyāsa's outermost frame presumes a dialogical situation at Vyāsa's hermitage between Vyāsa and the five disciples. That situation includes dialogues between Vyāsa and Śuka in the *Mokṣadharma* section of the *Śāntiparvan*; and it refers to exchanges with all of the disciples in the Śuka story itself, and at points in the *Nārāyaṇīya* which follows 'Śuka'.[31]

Beyond such actual dialogue passages, Vyāsa's exchange with his disciples, including this outermost transmission of the *Mahābhārata* to them, is left to frame the transmission of the *Mahābhārata* through the other two frames tacitly. One might call these 'pieces' or 'outcroppings' of the outermost frame, which lies outside the two dialogical frames, the inner and outer ones. We can see at least three ways in which this outermost authorial frame superabounds both of the other two overt dialogical levels, and makes the *Mahābhārata* itself almost a pittance. Vyāsa is said to have grounded the *Mahābhārata* in his knowledge of the Veda.[32] Both dialogical narrations allege that they are presenting Vyāsa's 'thought entire'[33] which is by implication more than what they could ever narrate in the confines of the *Mahābhārata* text itself, or for that matter any text. And not least, as already mentioned, the full hundred *upaparvan Mahābhārata* mentioned by Ugraśravas includes the *Harivaṃśa*. Indeed, toward the end of that 'appendix', Janamejeya tells Vyāsa, with the sense that something is still missing, 'The *Mahābhārata* narrative has many meanings and great extent; by being agreeable to hear, it has gone by for me in a moment (*nimeṣamātram iva me sukhaśravyatayā gatam*)' (*HV* 115.11).

Second in the chronology of transmission, then, is the 'inner' generational frame in which the Pāṇḍavas' great-grandson Janamejaya performs the snake sacrifice at which (in the presence of Vyāsa and Śuka) he hears the *Mahābhārata* from Vaiśaṃpāyana, one of the four other disciples who learned it from Vyāsa. From this inner frame two other lengthy interior dialogues are pendant. First is the war account, imparted to the blind Kaurava king Dhṛtarāṣṭra by the bard (*sūta*) Saṃjaya, who is given the divine eye by Vyāsa so that he can know and relate everything that happens on the battlefield. Second is the postwar dialogue chiefly between the questioning Pāṇḍava king Yudhiṣṭhira and the by-now *dharma*-wise

---

[29] Christopher Minkowski, 'Janamejaya's *Sattra* and Ritual Structure', *Journal of the American Oriental Society* 109/3 (1989): 401–20; 'Snakes, *sattras* and the *Mahābhārata*', in Arvind Sharma (ed.), *Essays on the Mahābhārata* (Leiden, 1991).

[30] See Hiltebeitel, *Rethinking the Mahābhārata*, pp. 34, 92, 279, 300, 317; '*Mahābhārata*'.

[31] Hiltebeitel, '*Mahābhārata*', pp. 294–6.

[32] Ibid., p. 42.

[33] *Mbh* 1.1.23 for Ugraśravas; 1.55.2 for Vaiśaṃpāyana; in both cases *mataṃ kṛtsnaṃ*, See Hiltebeitel, *Rethinking the Mahābhārata*, p. 12.

patriarch Bhīṣma, who can tie together what he learned in Gaṅgāloka with the divine eye now given to him by Kṛṣṇa.[34]

Finally, third in the chronology of transmission is the 'outer' cosmological frame in which Śaunaka and the Ṛṣis of the Naimiṣa Forest hear the *Mahābhārata* from the bard Ugraśravas, who was also among those who heard it from Vaiśaṃpāyana at Janamejaya's snake sacrifice.

With the second dialogue level or inner frame narration by Vaiśampāyana to Janamejaya being central as the one to carry along the main story, with its pendant dialogues just mentioned, there are certain differences in the way the other two frames are felt as presences throughout the epic.[35] The outer Ugraśravas-Ṛṣis frame is felt by listeners/readers as an overhearing of the inner frame as retold from afar, yet also paradoxically from near enough to allow Ugraśravas to make a point or Śaunaka to ask questions that interrupt Vaiśaṃpāyana's narration. The outermost Vyāsa-and-disciples frame has something of a reverse tonality. Despite its inaccessibility as an actual text, it is felt literally and with immediacy in the course of the narration of the inner frame by the fact that Vyāsa and Śuka are themselves listening and bodily present as attendees or *sadasyas* at Janamejaya's snake sacrifice and thus at Vaiśaṃpāyana's inner-frame dialogical narration.[36]

Now there are, as mentioned, only a few places in the *Mahābhārata* where, in the course of Vaiśaṃpāyana's main inner frame dialogue with Janamejaya, there are elicitations of or 'dips' to the outer Ugraśravas–Śaunaka dialogue. The most extensive and overtly revealing occurs at 12.331 and 334–5 where the three sequential dips occur in the *Nārāyaṇīya*.[37] Unfortunately for the Poona Critical Edition, S.K. Belvalkar, the editor of the *Śāntiparvan* (the *Mahābhārata*'s twelfth book), removed these dips, basing his decision largely on Southern recension Malayālam manuscripts that had smoothed away these rather profound departures from the norm.[38] Here the listening and bodily presence of both Vyāsa and Śuka at Janamejaya's snake sacrifice is the means by which all three frames and dialogues are braided together. For Ugraśravas is positioned to report to Śaunaka three revelations by Vyāsa himself that are made off the record, as it were, from what either the first or second dialogue level could report of his original disclosure of the *Mahābhārata* to the five disciples. That is, in response to three probing questions from Śaunaka, Ugraśravas can tell about exchanges made during Janamejaya's snake sacrifice itself. These exchanges raised 'the same' questions that Śaunaka now asks of Ugraśravas. Ugraśravas can thus report what

---

[34] Contrasting these two usages of the divine eye, see Annettte Mangels, *Zur Erzähltechnik im Mahābhārata* (Hamburg, 1994); Hiltebeitel, *Rethinking the Mahābhārata*.

[35] Minkowski, 'Janamejaya's *Sattra* and Ritual Structure', p. 405, remarks that the outer frame is always felt behind the inner frame.

[36] The listening or 'overhearing' role of *sadasyas* in the *Mahābhārata* deserves further study. They are clearly off to the side somewhere, which may remind one of the stock theme in Buddhist dialogues, where interlocutors first circumambulate the Buddha and then always sit to one side. The term is inconspicuous in the *Rāmāyaṇa* (just 4 usages), with an overhearing connotation only at *Rām* 1.64.25 where *sadasyas* at Janaka's court are mentioned by him as having already heard about the many virtues of Viśvāmitra.

[37] The other elicitations of the outer frame occur at 1.1–54; 2.46.4 (a reference I owe Hudson 2006, as discussed below), 15.42–43, and 18.5 – a wraparound at the epic's end of little complexity, unlike the one at the beginning.

[38] I leave aside my demonstration of Belvalkar's error, but the matter comes up again below; see initially Hiltebeitel, 'The *Nārāyanīya* and the Early Reading Communities of the *Mahābhārata*', and now with some corrections Hiltebeitel, *Reading the Fifth Veda* ch. 7.

Vaiśaṃpāyana answered, first by quoting Vyāsa in his presence, then by speaking for Vyāsa by proxy, and finally – and most profoundly – by turning to the aged author to let him speak for himself.[39]

Dialogically speaking, however, the most intriguing and the most subtly revealing turn from the inner to the outer frame is the first one to actually interrupt the inner frame's dialogue. This occurs just after Vaiśaṃpāyana has taken three charged and informative *adhyāya*s to tell Janamejaya how Duryodhana felt demeaned at Yudhiṣṭhira's Rājasūya sacrifice handling all the tribute that was being brought to Yudhiṣṭhira; how he was laughed at when he fell into an empty pool, etc.; and how Śakuni's counsel to win it all for Duryodhana by dicing lifted the latter's spirits, whereupon they sought and got an endorsement of their plan from Dhṛtarāṣṭra. Janamejaya now asks Vaiśaṃpāyana how the 'fateful dicing match of the brethren' came about (along with a few more questions that could just lead on to the actual dicing scene), and concludes, 'I wish to hear you tell this in detail, Brahmin, for this was the root of the destruction of the world' (2.46.1–3). It is right here that 'the Bard' (*sūta*) chimes in, as it were out of the blue:

> The Bard said:
> Thus addressed by the king, Vyāsa's majestic student, who knew all the Veda, narrated it all as it happened. (2.46.4)[40]

Many have no doubt read right past his verse. But van Buitenen[41] and Hudson[42] are surely right to call attention to its importance. And although it is an exaggeration for Hudson to say that 'it is not clear at all who "the Bard" is',[43] they are right to identify the unnamed Bard as Ugraśravas. Nonetheless, two unnoticed oddities still stand out on the surface of the text. One, not at all obvious, is that Ugraśravas never breaks in like this with a single verse anywhere before or after this one instance in the entire epic. If the interruption is a significant marker of some kind, why not use the same device elsewhere? The surface obscurity of this stand-out passage does not demand the explanation that, since it only occurs this once, it must be an interpolation. The first lesson to draw, then, is that some things that occur just once in a text may do so for a reason.[44] The other oddity, more obvious, is that the Bard speaks with no input from his chief listener and dialogue partner Śaunaka. This means that it stands out as a signature statement by Ugraśravas for reasons that may be sought.

Hudson offers an interpretation based on three observations: first, since the verse comes 217 *adhyāya*s after Ugraśravas has last been mentioned, he 'is, to say the least, distant from our thoughts'; second, he is one of four 'back-to-back speakers' (in the order

39 Hiltebeitel, 'The *Nārāyanīya* and the Early Reading Communities of the *Mahābhārata*', pp. 223–49.

40 van Buitenen (trans.), *The Mahābhārata*, vol. 2., p. 115 (slightly modified).

41 Ibid., p. 815.

42 Hudson, 'Disorienting Dharma' [dissertation] pp. 195–7; *Disorienting Dharma*, pp. 168–70.

43 Hudson, *Disorienting Dharma*, p. 168.

44 See Hiltebeitel, *Dharma: Its Early History in Law, Religion, and Narrative*, p. 571 n. 9, disputing González-Reimann's stratigraphic assumptions in calling 'late' the *Mahābhārata*'s association of the onset of the Kali yuga with the fall of Duryodhana (9.59.21), one of his assumptions being that the verse's 'palpable lateness … can also be gleaned from the fact that it is put into Kṛṣṇa's mouth' (*The Mahābhārata and the Yugas: India's Great Epic and the Hindu System of World Ages* [New York, 2002], pp. 86, 101–2).

Janamejaya, Ugraśravas, Vaiśaṃpāyana, Duryodhana) who occupy different temporal niches, with Ugraśravas somewhere in the future of Vaiśaṃpāyana's narration about a Duryodhana of the past; third, 'realization that the Bard is Ugraśravas brings with it a potential moment of disorientation, which is intentional. It is as though the text is prompting us to ask ourselves: Where are we in the narrative really?'[45] The text's 'point' in 'creating this disorienting experience of time'[46] is then to signal the ways it soon 'stretches' *kāla* as 'time' in its account of the dice match.[47] But these observations are rooted in Hudson's opening point that 'it is not clear at all who "the Bard" is'. Hudson may be right that for most readers Ugraśravas is 'distant from our thoughts', and may well also be right that the text is coy in leaving it puzzling to such readers as to who he is. Indeed, in favour of this point, we may note that the Bard's single-verse utterance is a flat statement with no vocatives such as Ugraśravas uses elsewhere that would help readers to identify him in relation to Śaunaka as his outer frame dialogue partner. But once it clicks in for discerning readers that 'the Bard' cannot be anyone else but Ugraśravas, they will not be *dis*oriented about time. They will be *re*oriented about it; that is, they will be induced to recall that the *Mahābhārata* they are in dialogue with is at bottom the one Ugraśaravas imparts for the first time to a human public in the Naimiṣa Forest. Reoriented in this way, they would have no need to ask 'Where are we in the narrative really?' And if they seek the reason for Ugraśravas' statement, not disoriented themselves, they would not look ahead in the text for correspondingly disorienting ways in which time is stretched in the dice match. They would look, at least first of all, at the Bard's very loaded statement itself, which is a heads-up to his implied interlocutors, Śaunaka, the Ṛṣis of the Naimiṣa Forest, and us ideal human readers: Listen up, 'Vyāsa's majestic student, who knew all the Veda, narrated it all as it happened.' The Bard who knew Vyāsa's 'thought entire' (1.1.23) endorses Vaiśaṃpāyana who likewise knew Vyāsa's 'thought entire' (1.55.2),[48] and thereby once again – that is, for the first time in 217 *adhyāya*s – rebraids the three dialogical frames. The point of his utterance would then be sought first in what the text takes the trouble to have the Bard confirm, to an implied Śaunaka and the rest of us, that Vaiśaṃpāyana will be giving Janamejaya the real scoop he has asked for 'in detail' on what brought about 'the root of the destruction of the world'.

Thus the point Hudson attributes to the Bard's intervention looks ahead to the actual dice match rather than directly at what Vaiśaṃpāyana now recounts in six *adhyāya*s (2.46–51) that come before the invitation to the dice match is sent. She treats what she cites from those six *adhyāya*s as if Vaiśaṃpāyana were carrying on in the same vein as in the prior three (2.43–5), biding time until he will stretch its implications once the dicing begins. Such an oversight may have been encouraged by Edgerton and van Buitenen's assessments of the relationship between what both call 'versions'. Each organizes his discussion around overriding similarities and incidental differences, and each notices one red flag in particular.

Edgerton's red flag is the anomaly that Vidura goes to confer with Bhīṣma at the end of the first version with no mention of it in the second. He supposes that the first version would have 'once contained an interview between Vidura and Bhīṣma'. It is thus a matter of 'different and inconsistent accounts' that are nonetheless 'duplicate accounts of a story which (aside from that incident) is essentially the same, and this can be accounted for only on the assumption that it was composed with the use of different versions, parts of which

45 Hudson, *Disorienting Dharma*, pp. 168–9.

46 Ibid. p. 170.

47 Ibid. pp. 170–76.

48 See n. 33 above.

were incorporated side by side in this text, the ancestor of all our known MSS'.[49] Edgerton offers no opinion on the relative age of the two versions; he just says that they have been combined. But since the combination results in a loss of something from version one, it would be the less likely of the two to be the most recent.

Van Buitenen's red flag concerns Dhṛtarāṣṭra, but before getting to it he introduces a problematic terminology about the two 'versions':

> The first one, at least the one that appears chronologically first, may be called the *simplicior*; the second, being more ornate, the *ornatior*. The *simplicior* comprises chaps. 43–45, ending with Dhṛtarāṣṭra's consent to the dicing and the building of a thousand-pillared hall; the *ornatior* comprises 46–51, also ending with Dhṛtarāṣṭra's consent and the building of the hall. The *ornatior* brings more color and drama to the story, but is otherwise completely parallel. Duryodhana's resentment before Śakuni is recast as his resentment before Dhṛtarāṣṭra, with massive descriptions of the magnificence of Yudhiṣṭhira's *rājasūya* added. As in the *simplicior*, Dhṛtarāṣṭra says he will seek advice from Vidura; in both versions Duryodhana protests. The transition between both versions is Dhṛtarāṣṭra's abrupt rescinding of his permission to dice.[50]

Van Buitenen's terms 'recast' and 'added' are tip-offs that he does see the first version as earlier; so too his *simplicior–ornatior* contrast, which he almost certainly adapts from Sukthankar's well-known comparison of the *Mahābhārata*'s Northern and Southern recensions.[51] When it comes to his red flag at Dhṛtarāṣṭra's rescinding of the permission to dice, van Buitenen also deploys the idea of abruptness in the manner of a textual excavator showing a suture or seam. But Dhṛtarāṣṭra's rescinding and Vidura's talk with Bhīṣma are really just two sides of one minimalist textual strategy to make the two versions consecutive. Dhṛtarāṣṭra rescinds because, as we shall see, there will be more to his making up his mind. And in the meantime, who better than Bhīṣma to park Vidura with for an off-the-record conversation?

The very notion of 'versions' calls for more precision than Edgerton or van Buitenen give it, since the Bard's intervention with its rebraiding of the three dialogical frames comes so near the beginning of the so-called *ornatior* and implicitly 'late' version.[52] It is, of course

49 Franklin Edgerton (ed.), '*Sabhāparvan*. Introduction and Apparatus', in V.S. Sukthankar et al. (eds), *Mahābhārata: Critical Edition*, 24 vols with *Harivaṃśa* (Poona: Bhandarkar Oriental Research Institute, 1944), pp. xxxii–xxxiii.

50 J.A.B. Van Buitenen, *The Mahābhārata*, vol. 2. *Book 2 The Book of the Assembly Hall; Book 3 The Book of the Forest* (Chicago, 1975), p. 815.

51 See Sukthankar 1933, p. xxxvi: 'The Southern recension impresses us thus by its precision, schematization, and thoroughly practical outlook. Compared with it, the Northern recension is distinctly vague, unsystematic, sometimes even inconsequent, *more like a story rather naively narrated*, as we find in actual experience' (author's emphasis). Quoted out of context, the passage has misled some to think Sukthankar favors the S recension, but in context that is impossible since by 'schematizaton' and 'thoroughly practical' he means pedestrian and opportunistic.

52 Van Buitenen is misleading in two ways: 1. the terms *simplicior* and *ornatior* are precise and informative only in Sukthankar's usage in the contrast just mentioned. There is no shift here to smoother diction. 2. Sukthankar tried to maintain that 'both [recensions] spring from a common source' that 'seems to … lose itself in the mists of antiquity'. Ironically, van Buitenen would have then been right to take Sukthankar's usages as implying *simplicior* as younger and *ornatior* as later, since we now know the Southern recension to be a thoroughgoing makeover of a mainly Northern-recension baseline; see Thennilapuram Mahadevan, 'On the Southern Recension of the *Mahābhārata*, Brahman Migrations,

possible that Edgerton or van Buitenen would be correct were he to actually say the second version is later and added to the first. But how much later?

If one posits composition of the *Mahābhārata* by a committee or atelier of poets over a short period of no more than two generations, as I do, then later could mean anything from right after or consecutively to at most a few decades.[53] Yet one still finds advocates of the received view that this epic developed and grew over many centuries or even millennia. We can safely anticipate that such scholars, whom we may divide into two camps while noting that some also bridge that divide, would agree that the Bard's verse, and with it the whole second *ornatior* version, is late on the side of many centuries. On the one hand, those who have pursued the idea of a bardic oral 'core' or 'cycle' of bronze age tribal 'Kuru lays' can raise textual issues only whimsically, but they all seem to agree that their improbable precursor of the text as we have it would have been unadulterated by frame stories, not to mention dialogical frame stories, that would have been introduced along with the epic's gradual Brahmanization.[54]

On the other hand, one also meets scholars who have adopted the above-mentioned text-stratifying methods of Grünendahl, eager to substantiate his notion of 'coatings' by finding further examples of bracketing frames (as distinct from dialogical ones) and doubles.[55] For Grünendahl himself, the second dialogue level involving Ugraśravas and Śaunaka and the very idea of Vyāsa as the *Mahābhārata*'s author are among the 'thought merchandise' (*Gedankengut*) that very late redactors fanned out from the axiomatically late *Nārāyaṇīya* to coat the epic with its next-to-last layer, the last one being a final coating by Śaivites.[56]

It is plain that proponents of these two approaches, especially in combination, have long been eager to undercut any value to seeing the *Mahābhārata* that so artfully puts us in dialogue with itself as fundamentally a dialogical text! Indeed, the Bard's intervention in Book 2 probably remains apart from Grünendahl's evidence for the epic's penultimate

and Brāhmī Paleography', *Electronic Journal of Vedic Studies* 15/2 (2008): 1–143; Thennilapuram Mahadevan, 'The Three Rails of the *Mahābhārata* Textual Tradition', *Journal of Vaishnava Studies* 19/2 (2011): 23–69; Hiltebeitel, 'On Sukthankar's "S"'; Hiltebeitel, 'The Southern Recension's "Śakuntalā" as a First Reading'; Hiltebeitel, 'From *Ṛṣidharma* to *Vānaprastha*', and discussion below.

53 See the citations above in n. 3, and especially Hiltebeitel, *Rethinking the Mahābhārata*, pp. 20, 29 n. 20; Hiltebeitel, 'Weighting Orality and Writing in the Sanskrit Epics', pp. 81–111 [= Hiltebeitel, *Reading the Fifth Veda*, ch. 1], p. 88: "How late is late?' An interpolation or loose join is not evidence of the work of centuries. Within a two generation span, specific joins could be the result of a week's work and waiting, or a month's, or a decade's..' This point first came to mind in dialogue with colleagues at Dubrovnik in 2002. Cf. Hiltebeitel, 'On Sukthankar's "S"', p. 109.

54 See Hiltebeitel, 'The *Mahābhārata* and the Stories Some People Tell About It', 13–14 on E.W. Hopkins's notion of 'Kuru lays'; Frame stories in Brāhmaṇa texts in which Witzel sees 'the dawn of a long period of story telling in the Epic' are not dialogical. They 'simply surround one story with another', 'inspired by the ubiquitous ritual framework' and still older Ṛg Vedic ring composition (Michael Witzel, 'On the Origin of the Literary Device of the 'Frame Story' in Old Indian Literature', in H. Falk (ed.), *Hinduismus und Buddhismus: Festschrift für Ulrich Schneider* (Freiburg, 1987), pp. 410–11, 414.

55 See above, n. 19.

56 See Grünendahl, 'Zur Stellung des *Nārāyaṇīya* im *Mahābhārata*', pp. 237–40 for these ideas; on *Gedankengut*, see Reinhold Grünendahl, 'Zu den beiden Gandhamādana-Episoden des *Āraṇyakaparvan*', *Studien zur Indologie und Iranistik* 18 (1993): 103–18; Grünendahl, 'Zur Stellung des *Nārāyaṇīya* im *Mahābhārata*', pp. 221, 240. For critical discussion, see Hiltebeitel, 'On Sukthankar's "S"', pp. 106–7. The idea of a final Śaivite coating goes back to Adolf Holtzmann Jr; see Adluri and Bagchee, *The Nay Science*; Hiltebeitel, 'The *Mahābhārata* and the Stories Some People Tell About It', pp. 4–5.

coating only because he did not notice it while working on his *Nārāyaṇīya Studien* essays,[57] while another restraint on its being swept up into his vision of things could be Grünendahl's stricture that where versions of an event are double in the *Mahābhārata*, the later version would precede – not follow – the older one in the text.[58]

Fortunately, however, there is now an antidote to this whole method of casting about looking for late layers to the Poona Critical Edition's baseline text. As a byproduct of establishing the criteria for reconstructing the largely Northern recension baseline of that edition, Sukthankar also established the precedent, followed by all other Critical Edition editors, of working out the archetype of the Southern recension wherever it can be detected and reconstructed from uniformities in Southern recension manuscripts, and giving such interpolations the notation 'S' in that edition's Apparatus.[59] Thanks to Sukthankar, since S as a whole is actually a thoroughgoing makeover completed by or before the Kaḷabhra interregnum (ca. 300 CE) by a custodial agency that left most of N as it knew it, one can not only trace S's interpolations throughout the epic; one can also see the still later work of southern redactors writing in Malayālam, Grantha, and Telugu scripts as they tinker further with this basic S text.[60] Thus if one wants to follow Grünendahl's argumentation and apply it, as one would be bound to do, to the Sūta's verse at 2.46.4 and consider it to have come in with the *Mahābhārata*'s penultimate *Nārāyaṇīya* coating, it would help if van Buitenen's 'added' *ornatior* version had no S interpolations, while the supposedly prior *simplicior* one had them. Both have S interpolations, and they are consistent in tone and intent with others typical of S, as we shall now see.

So what then can one take home from the Bard's verse? I will answer that on two fronts: first, in terms of what Vaiśaṃpāyana tells Janamejaya in 2.46–51 that goes beyond what he has already told him in 2.43–5 that could meet the criterion set for us by the Bard of revealing the root of the destruction of the world; and second, in terms of what

57 Grünendahl is aware of 15.42–3, whose relevance to his discussion he dismisses ('Zur Stellung des *Nārāyaṇīya* im *Mahābhārata*', p. 227 and n. 162), but apparently not of 2.46.4. See Hiltebeitel, 'The *Nārāyanīya* and the Early Reading Communities of the *Mahābhārata*', p. 191.

58 See Grünendahl, 'Zu den beiden Gandhamādana', pp. 110–12; Grünendahl, 'Zur Stellung des *Nārāyaṇīya* im *Mahābhārata*', p. 224, positing a general rule that in cases of doubling newer passages are placed first. Although technically a retelling 'in detail' (a *vistareṇa* sequel) is not a double, van Buitenen goes on immediately to propose a real double where two different messengers are sent to bring Draupadī into the gambling hall; so too Edgerton (ed.), '*Sabhāparvan*. Introduction and Apparatus', pp. xxxi–xxxii, reversing the order. On Grünendahl, 'Zu den beiden Gandhamādana-Episoden des *Āraṇyakaparvan*' and 'Zur Stellung des *Nārāyaṇīya* im *Mahābhārata*', see Hiltebeitel, 'On Sukthankar's "S"', pp. 106–9, disagreeing also with points made by Christopher Austin, 'Draupadī's Fall: Snowballs, Cathedrals and Synchronous Readings of the *Mahābhārata*', *International Journal of Hindu Studies* 15/1 (2011): 111–37 in redeploying Grünendahl's *Mbh* stratigraphy to an allegedly late recurrence in Book 3 of Draupadī falling as she does at the end of Book 17. Austin notes that the Book 3 instance (3.144.1–5), in the first of two nearly back-to-back episodes in which Bhīma seeks special flowers to please Draupadī (3.140–53; 155–8), meets Grünendahl's positioning criterion in cases of doubling, and agrees with him that the whole first episode is late.

59 As Sukthankar says, 'S is the ultimate source from which all versions of the Southern recension are, directly or indirectly, derived' (1933, p. xxx).

60 Cf. Hiltebeitel, 'On Sukthankar's "S"', p. 20, and further citations at the end of n. 46 above. On the Kaḷabhra Interregnum and its impact on the earliest southern *Mbh* manuscript traditions, see Mahadevan, 'On the Southern Recension of the *Mahābhārata*'; Mahadevan, 'The Three Rails of the *Mahābhārata* Textual Tradition'; Hiltebeitel, 'From *Ṛṣidharma* to *Vānaprastha*'.

just a few little modifications by S at the most crucial moments possibly tell us about S's thoroughgoing makeover and the baseline text it drew from.

Immediately after the Bard's verse, here is how Vaiśaṃpāyana resets the stage:

> Listen to me and hear the story once more in detail (*vistareṇemāṃ kathām ... bhūyo*), best of Bharatas, if you have a mind to learn. Knowing Vidura's mind, Dhṛtarāṣṭra, son of Ambikā, spoke this word to Duryodhana when they were alone again (*vijane punaḥ*). 'Enough of this dicing, son of Gāndhārī. Vidura does not approve…' (2.46.5–7)[61]

Quickly meeting the criteria set by the Bard's verse, 'what is at the root of the destruction of the world' will arise from Dhṛtarāṣṭra's sympathetic hearing of his son's pain in a sequestered father-son dialogue. Once Dhṛtarāṣṭra has asked Duryodhana after the 'root of his grief' (*śokamūlam idaṃ katham*; 17b) even while he rules 'this great and prosperous kingdom bequeathed by father and grandfather', Duryodhana's first reply (2.46.18–35) heads right to the bottom of it, after which the rest of their impressive dialogue will all be icing on that cake. The whole two-part sequence, like so many other well-wrought segments, deserves a separate study for its artistry,[62] and this dialogue in particular for its poignant intergenerational psychology.[63] But for present purposes it must suffice to leave a few things to notes,[64] and give full attention only to how the father-son dialogue begins and what Dhṛtarāṣṭra says at the full sequence's end.

Here then are the key lines and verses in which Duryodhana begins to answer Dhṛtarāṣṭra:

---

[61] Van Buitenen (trans.), *The Mahābhārata*, vol. 2, p. 115, slightly modified. Unless similarly indicated, in what follows I reproduce van Buitenen's translation.

[62] The exemplary study of the artistry of a single *Mbh* sequence is, and will likely long remain, Simon Brodbeck, 'Ekalavya and *Mahābhārata* 1.121–28', *International Journal of Hindu Studies* 10 (2006): 1–34. See Hiltebeitel, *Rethinking the Mahābhārata*, pp. 28–9, calling for patient close readings of seemingly incongruous units and sequences 'one at a time', and (if I may update) proceeding inductively from them, along with readings of exemplary 'epic' vignettes, guided mainly by the text's architecture, and worrying about elusive formulations of the whole only such as they may arise. This approach makes a good backbone for a semester course plan on either epic.

[63] See especially Dhṛtarāṣṭra's urgings toward the beginning of their dialogue at 2.46.16: 'Commanding always this great and prosperous kingdom bequeathed by father and grandfather, you shine as the lord of the Gods shines in heaven!' – a curious statement given that Duryodhana's grandfather would likely be Bhīṣma or Vyāsa, from either of whom his hold on kingship would be even more tenuous than what he holds of it from his father. See also, near the end of their dialogue, the decisive words (50.1–28), just before Śakuni joins in, unannounced as it were, that introduce Dhṛtarāṣṭra to the idea of dicing (51.1–3). Answering Dhṛtarāṣṭra's varied appeals to paternal and maternal continuity, uxorial happiness, and cross-cousin harmony, Duryodhana says his father confuses him with his own indecisiveness and utters this resonant line, 'Discontent is the root of fortune. That is why I want to be discontented' (*asaṃtoṣaṃ śriyo mūlaṃ tasmāt taṃ kāmayāmy aham*; 18ab) – or more literally for the second *pāda*, 'That is why I want it.' Mentioning the 'root of śrī', the line could echo Janamejaya's question about 'the root of the destruction of the world', with Duryodhana holding up a mirror to the dissatisfaction of Draupadī he will soon do his major part to provoke.

[64] Van Buitenen's idea of two 'completely parallel' versions is both an over- and under-estimation; things move ahead, and as they do, some things do not fit his analysis. He is right that Duryodhana's resentment and thoughts of suicide and death are more 'dramatic' the second time they are uttered, but not because they are more elaborated. Duryodhana's first extensive account of his death wish to Śakuni (2.43.26–31) becomes, contextually, his rehearsal for this more impactful single verse to his father: 'Now that I have seen all the many and manifold gifts that the kings sent to my enemies, my suffering makes me yearn for death' (48.34). Indeed, this *ornatior* second 'version' is not only more

> Low is the man, they say, who is incapable of indignation (*amarṣam*)! A *common* fortune does not delight me (*na māṃ prīṇāti ... lakṣmīḥ sādhāraṇā*); and having seen the fortune (*śriyam*) that seemed to blaze forth at the Kaunteya's, I suffer. I have seen all the earth subject to Yudhiṣṭhira's sway, and I still stand ready here, still alive! I speak to you in pain (*duḥkhād*). ... Yudhiṣṭhira deemed me the elder and his better (*jyeṣṭho 'yam iti māṃ matvā śreṣṭhaś ceti*), and paying many compliments he charged me with the collection of the tribute. ... As I received the wealth, my hand did not hold out. ... Maya had built a lotus pond that seemed full of water but was made out of crystal with jewelled water pools – I have seen it, Bhārata. I pulled up my clothes and the Wolf-belly laughed at me as at one who is destitute of treasure and confounded by the superior wealth of the enemy. I would have killed the Wolf-belly! To be derided by a rival burns me, Bhārata. Once again, when I saw a similar pond full of lotuses, I thought it was likewise made out of crystal and I fell in the water, king. Kṛṣṇa and the Pārtha laughed at me aloud, and so did Draupadī and the women, disturbing my mind (*vyathayantī mano mama*). At the king's orders, servants gave me other clothes, because mine were wet, and that pained me more (*tac ca duḥkhataraṃ mama*). Listen as I tell you of another trick, king. When I went through what seemed to be a door but was not, I hit a crystal slab with my forehead and got hurt. The twins saw me from a distance and were amused! Mournfully they held me with their arms, and Sahadeva said to me, almost smiling, 'This is the door, go this way, prince.'[65]

Duryodhana starts with Yudhiṣṭhira recognizing him as 'elder' – as the speaker. Duryodhana probably implies Dhṛtarāṣṭra's seniority to Yudhiṣṭhira's father Pāṇḍu, but perhaps Yudhiṣṭhira spoke mockingly (both explanations could be reinforced by what follows); yet Duryodhana ends up telling how he was mocked by Draupadī, the women, and the juniors. Vaiśaṃpāyana's first un-detailed account of this episode to Janamejaya had mentioned only that Bhīma, Arjuna, and the twins 'all burst out laughing' (2.43.7), so Duryodhana's account of his own humiliation brings in Draupadī and Kṛṣṇa as additional taunters.

At this point it helps to draw in what Indian popular culture finds most memorable in this sequence, for the bombshell here is the mocking laughter of Draupadī.[66] As I learned from researching the south Indian Draupadī cult and the fourteenth-century Tamil *Villipāratam*:

> In the *Villipāratam*, it comes to be Draupadī's mockery that is repeatedly singled out (2.2.13, 215), and so it is in the [Draupadī cult's *terukkūttu*] dramas, [The play] 'The Rājasūya Sacrifice' ends on this note: 'Seeing [Duryodhana's discomfiture], Pāñcāli clapped her hands and laughed' (*kaikoṭṭi pāñcāli koṇṭu nakaitt' iṭavum*). Duryodhana

economical; its emphasis on seeing (*paśyatas*) tells us that everything Dhṛtarāṣṭra sympathetically hears he is simultaneously seeing through his son's eyes.

65 2.46.18c–20, 23, 25ab, 26–34; van Buitenen (trans.), *The Mahābhārata*, vol. 2, p. 116, italics included; slightly modified.

66 Duryodhana also tells Dhṛtarāṣṭra that laughter aggravated him again: during the conch-blowing at the Rājasūya unction, all 'the Āryan kings' fainted and keeled over while Dhṛtadyumna, the Pāṇḍavas, Sātyaki, and Kṛṣṇa laughed aloud (2.49.1, 18–19). Perhaps if Draupadī was present at the unction as queen, which I assume would be not only possible but called for, she had already had her laugh or was in a solemn mood. But it is suggestive that her brother is the first laugher mentioned, and if all five Pāṇḍavas laughed, that would include Yudhiṣṭhira. The 'Āryan kings' were differentiated from numerous barbarian ones 'turned back at the gate' during Duryodhana's elaborated account of receiving all the tribute (2.47–8).

> will frequently recall Draupadī's mockery in subsequent dramas. But it is especially in 'Dice Match and Disrobing' that he will recall her derision as provocation to humiliate her in turn.[67]

I often think of the Draupadī actor closing her hand over her mouth and tittering, as if registering just a little too late that she should not be seen laughing. What brought the situation home to me, however, was a March 2013 class in a *Mahābhārata* course I co-teach with T.P. Mahadevan. After Arjun Awasthi, a student of north Indian background, had prepared for the class by reading an assigned translation that includes only the initial 'version', he said, 'I was disappointed to find that Draupadī was not mentioned among those who make fun of Duryodhana. ... That is how I heard the story.' What gratifying grist for my mill! For I could immediately bring the class's attention to the Bard's verse and what follows it. The class had read the episode in John D. Smith's *The Mahābhārata*, which translates only 2.43–5, presumably to save space for more important things, not including 2.46–51, which Smith abridges without mentioning either the Bard's verse or anyone's laughter.[68]

Draupadī's laughter is not just Duryodhana's most aggravating humiliation taken by him as a provocation to humiliate Draupadī in turn. From the moment Duryodhana begins to answer his father's question about the 'root of his grief', he says he is pained by having had to see and handle the 'blazing fortune' (*śrī* or *lakṣmī*) that has come to Yudhiṣṭhira as tribute.[69] Draupadī, incarnation of the goddess Śrī-Lakṣmī,[70] is Duryodhana's nemesis as the personification and embodiment of that blazing fortune, which Duryodhana now speaks of not only as Yudhiṣṭhira's śrī and *lakṣmī*, but as Yudhiṣṭhira's new sacrificially acquired wealth: 'As I received the wealth, my hand did not hold out (*na me hastaḥ samabhavad vasu*

[67] Alf Hiltebeitel, *The Cult of Draupadī*, vol. 1: *Mythologies: From Gingee to Kurukṣetra* (Chicago, 1988), p. 228; additions in brackets; interior cross-references deleted. The play 'Dice Match and Disrobing', an early nineteenth-century classic in Draupadī cult stagecraft by Irāmaccantira Kavirāyar, draws ultimately from S's modifications, for it is Śakuni who hears Duryodhana's first recollection of Draupadī's laughter in this 'most astonishing and ominous vituperation' of her: '... not only did the Pāṇḍavas ridicule me (*ēḷitam paṇṇi*) but "that *paṭṭi* [low person, whore] Draupadī looked at me often, shaking in mirth [*kuluṅka nakaittāḷē*], that bitch [*kukkaṟciṟukki*: lit., 'dog-wench'] destroyed my pride [*veṭkam*], that cheat [*nīli*] abused me"' (*The Cult of Draupadi*, pp. 230–31; cf. p. 233: Duryodhana speaking again after Draupadī is staked and lost).

[68] John D. Smith, *The Mahābhārata: An Abridged Translation* (London, 2009), p. 127. Smith's summary of what I have described so far is, 'Janamejaya requests to hear the story again in greater detail and Vaiśaṃpāyana obliges.' Smith offers no opinion about the two units' relative chronology, as he does unconvincingly for the two *Udyogaparvan* scenes of 'Persuading Karṇa' (p. 339 n. 1). Thanks for this reference to T.P. Mahadevan.

[69] These thoughts have been anticipated in the first 'version' where Duryodhana tells Śakuni, 'When I saw all that blazing fortune at the Pāṇḍava's (*śriyaṃ tathāvidhāṃ dṛṣṭvā jvalantīm iva pāṇḍave*), I fell prey to resentment and I am burning' (2.43.26). See n. 64 above on 'seeing': Draupadī's part could activate an Oedipal resentment to which Duryodhana, unable to see beyond appearances, would be sensitive and the blind Dhṛtarāṣṭra complicit. Her seeing and laughing infantilizes a son whose blindfolded mother Gāndhārī chose not seeing at all, like her husband, over ever seeing her children. Cf. Hiltebeitel *Dharma: Its Early History in Law, Religion, and Narrative*, pp. 386–7; and thanks to Christopher Keats (personal communication) for spurring these connections.

[70] Draupadī is most often deemed the incarnation of Śrī (see Alf Hiltebeitel, *The Ritual of Battle: Krishna in the Mahābhārata* (Albany [1976] 1990), pp. 62 n. 7; *Dharma: Its Early History in Law, Religion, and Narrative*, p. 482), but at 18.4.10, we learn that according to Śiva she was an incarnation of Lakṣmī.

tat pratigṛhṇataḥ).'[71] Moreover, the dark earth-born Draupadī is, like 'fortune' (*śrī*) itself, a manifestations of the earth's 'prosperity' that Duryodhana covets and rivals for to make it his own.[72] Thus Draupadī's pre-eminence at the bottom of Duryodhana's humiliation, pain, and grief. Yet in back of that, and for astute readers more deeply still, the Bard's words about 'the root of the destruction of the world' are a reorientation of the words a disembodied voice spoke at Draupadī's birth. The Bard's reorientation gives such readers notice that Vaiśaṃpāyana has taken until this very moment to begin to bring to ripeness those precise heavenly words: 'Best of all women, Kṛṣṇā will lead the Kṣatra to destruction. The fair-waisted one will in time accomplish the work of the gods.'[73] In short, the Bard signals that what Vaiśaṃpāyana is about to reveal will have to do with the epic's 'divine plan' to relieve the burden of the goddess Earth.[74] The Bard can say all this because he knows, so to speak ahead of time, what Vaiśaṃpāyana will say. Even as in his own single verse he so economically rebraids all three dialogical frames for his implied audience of Śaunaka and the Naimiṣa Forest Ṛsis and his extended audience, us human beings, he knows it all himself. He and he alone is positioned to vouch that 'Vyāsa's majestic student, who knew all the Veda, narrated it all as it happened.' And where it comes to heavenly voices and the epic's divine plan, the Ṛṣis of the Naimiṣa Forest are uniquely positioned as models for such ideal readers.

Indeed, let me take this moment to remind my readers that the Naimiṣa Forest – with its etymology, *naimiṣa*: 'having to do with the moment, the blink, or the winking of the eye' – can reference the heavenly Ṛṣis as stars and allude to their Vedic Forest as one transformed now by Vedavyāsa into a forest of the literary imagination.[75]

I round off my interpretation of this sequence with the closing words of Dhṛtarāṣṭra: first, because they confirm, albeit faintly, that the Bard's intervention was an alert that Vaiśaṃpāyana was about to disclose something of the epic's divine plan. Once Dhṛtarāṣṭra gives in to Duryodhana (2.51.14–15), there are a few realignments between the two accounts. Again Dhṛtarāṣṭra orders the building of the dicing hall quickly; again he tells Vidura to go and invite the Pāṇḍavas; and again Vidura sets off reluctantly, predicting trouble. On this point, Dhṛtarāṣṭra concludes with what sounds like optimism: 'No quarrel bothers me, Steward, here, for otherwise fate would run counter to dicing. This world submits to the Placer's design. And thus does the world run, not by itself.'[76]

---

71 These words of Duryodhana's cannot be said to anticipate literally the description in three verses of Duḥśāsana's attempt to disrobe Draupadī (2.61.41–2, 48), since Duḥśāsana ends up only 'tired and ashamed' while his hands go unmentioned. Yet they do prefigure *terukkūttu* enactments of the scene, which show Duḥśāsana wringing his hands over the piles of endless saris that have passed through them; see the 'faltering Duḥśāsana's' own words to Draupadī in the play 'Dice Match and Disrobing': 'Even if my hand becomes tired, even if I lean to one side, will I leave you alone without causing your disgrace?' (Hiltebeitel, *The Cult of Draupadī*, p. 279).

72 On *śrī* as sacrificial manifestation of the radiant earth, see Biardeau, *Le Mahābhārata*, vol. 1, p. 220; vol. 2, p. 678 on *lakṣmī*; cf. Hiltebeitel, *The Ritual of Battle: Krishna in the Mahābhārata*, pp. 67–8, drawing this point from earlier studies by Biardeau.

73 *Mbh* 1.155.44–45b (the voice completes its utterance with, 'Because of her, a great fear will arise for all the Kṣatriyas').

74 See Hiltebeitel, *Rethinking the Mahābhārata*, pp. 187–8; Hiltebeitel, *Dharma: Its Early History in Law, Religion, and Narrative*, pp. 484–6, on the gratuitous character of Draupadī's birth from an earthen *vedi* or sacrificial altar as linked with the *Mbh*'s divine plan.

75 See Hiltebeitel, *Rethinking the Mahābhārata*, pp. 95–6 and passim.

76 2.51.25: *neha kṣattaḥ kalahas tapsyate māṃ/ na ced daivaṃ pratilomaṃ bhaviṣyat// dhātrā tu diṣṭasya vaśe kiledaṃ/ sarvaṃ jagac ceṣṭati na svatantram*.

As I have shown elsewhere, *Mahābhārata* characters tend to refer to the Placer (Dhātṛ), or the Placer and the Ordainer (Vidhātṛ), when for one reason or another they will not name the deity they have in mind.[77] In the case of Dhātṛ that would most typically be Brahmā, who is definitely party to the epic's divine plan, and has a higher personal agency than 'fate', which Dhṛtarāṣṭra identifies himself with more regularly and also mentions in this verse (as *diṣṭa*). Here too there is a realignment, for the prior account at 2.43–5 also ends with an evocation of the divine plan. It comes just after Dhṛtarāṣṭra has 'decided to appease Duryodhana' yet sends for Vidura because he never took a decision without consulting him:

> When the sagacious Vidura heard that the Gate of Kali was upon them and the Maw of Destruction had opened (*kalidvāram upasthitam vināśamukham utpannam*), he hastened to Dhṛtarāṣṭra. Brother approached great-spirited elder brother, and bowing with his head to his feet, he spoke this word: 'I do not welcome, my lord king, the decision you have taken. …' (2.45.50–52b)

As elsewhere in this sequence, such alignment is not one of 'duplicate accounts' that are 'completely parallel' (as Edgerton and van Buitenen respectively put it) but evidence of a larger narrative moving its finely set-up dialogically crafted pieces along.[78] Here, with the private father-son dialogue still yet to be reported, a brother-to-brother dialogue is accented, with a big difference: that in this case Vidura foresees the disaster that the divine plan has in store. The Gate of Kali that he sees opening before them bespeaks the same association that Kṛṣṇa makes, once the war is over, between the death of Duryodhana with the onset of the Kali yuga.[79] Meanwhile and nearer at hand, the Maw of Destruction is the proximate cue for Janamejaya to ask about the 'root of the destruction of the world'. Meanwhile too, though at the end of Vaiśaṃpāyana's second narrative 'in detail', Dhṛtarāṣṭra in his seeming optimism can be afforded a self-congratulatory moment. Not only can he anticipate the favourable outcome that Śakuni has promised from the dicing; with his limited insight into the link between dicing and fate he can delude himself that the Placer could leave that favourable outcome intact. Pleased finally that he could accommodate the wishes of his son, Dhṛtarāṣṭra has done his part too in contributing to what lay at 'the root of the world's destruction'.

Finally, this bringing of closure to the father-son dialogue on a note of Dhṛtarāṣṭra's contented and deluded complicity leaves two question marks over this end of the whole two-part sequence. One, which I believe we can answer, is: What is it that the Bard's verse is pointing to at the root of the destruction of the world? Is it the father-son dialogue itself, or Draupadī's laughter? The answer would have to be both, for neither occurs without the other. But that answer now poses a question that N leaves unsolvable: Did Draupadī really laugh if she is said to have done so only in Vaiśaṃpāyana's 'detailed' dialogical version but not in his straight narrative one? To be sure, the Bard's verse tells us that 'Vyāsa's majestic student, who knew all the Veda, narrated it all as it happened', but that could apply to the father-son dialogue without his vouching for Duryodhana's veracity. Vaiśaṃpāyana's detailed account raises the new possibility that Duryodhana has made up Draupadī's laughter, or exaggerated it from a smile, or that he had a 'recovered memory' of abuse that would appeal to his father in the way men talk 'in private' about a woman. Much later in

---

77 See Hiltebeitel, *Dharma: Its Early History in Law, Religion, and Narrative*, pp. 512–13, 585–9.

78 See n. 62 above.

79 At *Mbh* 9.59.21; see n. 44 above.

the epic, something similar occurs in Bhīma's first words to Duryodhana after he has felled him by breaking his thighs:

> Formerly, fool, laughing (*hasan*) at Draupadī in the hall when she was clothed in a single garment, you said 'cow, cow' to us, low-minded one; receive now the fruit of that ridicule (*tasyāvahāsya phalam*). (9.58.4)

Did Duryodhana really laugh at Draupadī when he bared his thigh to her at the dicing, or, as Vaiśaṃpāyana describes the actual scene, 'look as if he were smiling' (*smayan ivaikṣat pāñcālīm*; 2.6310c) and then also 'smiling at' (*abhyutsmayitvā*; 12a) Karṇa? By Book 9, Bhīma too seems to have a fused and selective memory. In both cases N leaves an opening that actually raises the question of what happened. No doubt one can find other exchanges in which Draupadī's laughter reverberates with Duryodhana's in an echo chamber or doubtful chain reaction.

This brings us to the second take-home from the Bard's verse. We can now say that it will have to do with little modifications by S precisely at the most crucial moments we have been noticing, and with what they can tell us about S in relation to N. The crux comes at S's handling of the two sets of verses that treat the laughter at Duryodhana's embarrassments in the hall built by Maya, and its handling of the Bard's verse itself. Since they are our current topic, I start out keeping to the verses on laughter, beginning with the first verse to mention Draupadī's joining in on the mirth (2.46.30), and work back to Vaiśaṃpāyana's initial verse on all the laughter that did not mention Draupadī (2.43.7).

As we have noted, in the reconstituted baseline text the first indication that Draupadī joined in on the mocking of Duryodhana was in Duryodhana's own words to Dhṛtarāṣṭra. Duryodhana recalls three indignities there that he endured mistaking one thing for another in the illusion-producing hall: first, he stayed dry when he expected to get wet feet; second, he got all wet when he expected to stay dry; and third, he banged his head. Amid these mishaps, verse 2.46.30 includes Draupadī's mirth over the second indignity, the one where Duryodhana gets wet. S's main alterations are not made here, but the ones it makes are still significant. Here again is van Buitenen's modified translation of that verse from the Critical Edition's baseline (N) along with a translation, using where appropriate the same phrasing, of S's modification:

> N: Kṛṣṇa and the Pārtha laughed at me aloud, and so did Draupadī and the women, disturbing my mind.

> S: Bhīma laughed at me together with Pārtha in harmony there, and so did Draupadī and the women, causing my mind to fall.[80]

So far all that stands out is that S seems to want to remove Kṛṣṇa from the laughers and to make the laughter itself a little less outward or harsh, probably because it includes Draupadī's and that of other women who might not be supposed to laugh out loud.

It turns out that S has exerted all its energy not here in Duryodhana's dialogical account itself, but in backreading information from Duryodhana's second account into

---

[80] I mention here only what Edgerton (ed.), '*Sabhāparvan*. Introduction and Apparatus', p. 229 shows to be the S archetype, not its own minor variants. In verse 2.46.30's first line S's *ahasad bhīmaḥ saha pārthena susvaraṃ* replaces N's *prāhasat kṛṣṇaḥ pārthena saha sasvanam*; and in its second line S's *pātayaṃtī* replaces *vyathayantī*.

Vaiśaṃpāyana's first narrated one. This is already significant: S takes Duryodhana's account as its model for a re-do of Vaiśaṃpāyana's. Presumably S does this because Duryodhana's is the more detailed; but we cannot rule out that S has also appreciated that Duryodhana's dialogue with his father takes us to the 'root of the destruction of the world'. The overall complexity of S's re-do can be seen from Edgerton's 'Tabular Conspectus of the sequence of stanzas 3–11 (together with all the insertions) in S'.[81] There cannot be even a shred of doubt that S's overall agenda is to remove inconsistencies from the two accounts, to 'make them square'. S does this with two foremost concerns: to make sure that the number of indignities is the same in both accounts; and to bring it about that the same people play the same roles in each of them, and that neither account is the only one to mention or omit anyone. As to the number of indignities, if Duryodhana tells of only three, so will Vaiśaṃpāyana before him, even though N's baseline text first had Vaiśaṃpāyana mention four. In brief, the rearrangement of the indignities in 2.43.3–11 can be charted as follows:

N: 1. Duryodhana stays dry; 2. gets wet; 3. stays dry 'again'; 4. bangs his head

S: 1. Duryodhana gets wet; 2. stays dry; 3. bangs his head

S achieves this result by breaking up the lines and *pāda*s that tell of the first dry indignity and redistributing most of them to its description of what had been the second, leaving only one dry indignity now second in the sequence.[82] Nor does S seem to mind that this changes the order of indignities reported by both Duryodhana in 2.46 and here by Vaiśaṃpāyana at 2.43 in N's baseline; on the contrary, in foregrounding the wet indignity by making it come first, S can have Vaiśaṃpāyana get right to the indignity that provokes (and allows S now to in effect summarize) all the main laughter. Here then is what Vaiśaṃpāyana says in N and in S about the decisive moment:

> N: When they saw him fallen in the water, the servants laughed merrily and gave him clean clothes at the king's behest. Mighty Bhīmasena saw him that way, as did Arjuna and the twins, and they all burst out laughing then.[83]

> S: When they saw him fallen in the water, the servants laughed merrily and gave him other clothes at the king's behest. Thereupon Draupadī, O king, mighty Bhīmasena, Arjuna and the twins, having seen [him], derided [him] then.[84]

---

81 Edgerton (ed.), *Sabhāparvan*. Introduction and Apparatus', p. 210.

82 The full complexity of S's changes here must be assessed from Edgerton's Tabular Conspectus ('*Sabhāparvan*. Introduction and Apparatus', p. 210) as well as from the modifications shown at 2.43.3c–4 in the Apparatus. Basically though, S relocates most of 2.43.3c–4 after 2.43.9 so that the combination describes just one dry indignity. Four of the nine S manuscripts also interpolate 420* here, which says that 'When the people saw this too, the Pāṇḍavas then laughed.' The shift thus leaves 3ab to continue into 5–7 so the wet indignity with the main laughter following it comes first. S's line adding that 'the people' saw Duryodhana could suggest a reflexive self-consciousness about S's own audiences, and be a cue to performers to draw them in.

83 *Mbh* 2.43.6–7; van Buitenen (trans.), *The Mahābhārata*, vol. 2, p 109, slightly modified.

84 S's changes are *cānyāni vāsāṃsi* [for *vāsāṃsi ca śubhāny* in 6c]; *tatraiva* (var. *tatrainaṃ*) *draupadī rājan* [for *tathāgataṃ tu taṃ dṛṣṭvā* as 7a]; and *caiva dṛṣṭvā cāpahasaṃs* [for *cobhau sarve te prāhasaṃs* in 7cd].

The verb 'deride' or 'ridicule' (*apa-√has*) is certainly stronger than 'laugh aloud' (*pra-√has*). Yet S could have transferred *apa-√has* back from Duryodhana's account where, as quoted above, he says of Bhīma's initial laughter at his first dry indignity, 'To be derided by a rival burns me' (2.46.28cd). That would be consistent with other features of S's backreading from 2.46 such as finding a general verb that can apply to Draupadī without having her laugh aloud.

Edgerton's critical edition of the *Sabhāparvan* thus enables us to bring into relief S's concern to make Vaiśaṃpāyana's account square with its own modified version of Duryodhana's plaint to Dhṛtarāṣṭra. Indeed, just on its own, Edgerton's carefully detailed 'Tabular Conspectus' on 2.43.3–11 provides renewed confirmation of Sukthankar's assessment that 'The Southern recension impresses us thus by its precision, schematization, and thoroughly practical outlook.'[85] S's removal of Kṛṣṇa from the laughers is evidence of surgical precision; schematization applies everywhere in these modifications; and the whole lot would have been thoroughly practical. For S could have foreseen one real benefit from such changes. S would henceforth provide those who read its *Mahābhārata*, and especially those who would use it for public performance and recitation, a consistent text at a pivotal juncture. Having had the good judgment to prioritize the contents of Duryodhana's dialogical 'root' account that gets to what brought about 'the destruction of the world', S could erase the apparent contradiction where Draupadī was concerned and eliminate the need to ask or answer whether she really laughed or did not.

But there are also costs to such systematization: in my opinion immense ones that outweigh the benefits. The men's laughter in outbursts loses the immediacy it has in N. S drops Duryodhana's extra surprise that Kṛṣṇa laughed with the rest of them. If, as is highly probable, this surgical strike was motivated by new south Indian theological sensitivities,[86] it erases the more interesting theological point that this deity sometimes acts like he is just one of the guys. But above all one loses the bombshell significance of Draupadī's laughter to Duryodhana that is set up by the Bard's verse. With that one misses a deferred pleasure of the text.

And now for the clincher in all this. According to Edgerton, with the exception of M1, one of two manuscripts in Malayālam out of the nine southern manuscripts collated and used for his Critical Edition of the *Sabhāparvan*, 'S omits the reference' to the Bard before the Bard's verse![87] This is an instance that bears out the necessity to consult the Critical Edition on S, and not P.P.S. Sastri's misleadingly titled *The Mahābhārata (Southern Recension) Critically Edited*, which keeps the speaker reference to the Bard as *sūta* in it (without *uvāca* following it).[88] Unlike the Poona editors, Sastri judged one large text the

---

85 Sukthankar 1933, p. xxxvi; see n. 37 above for the full contrast with N. It is renewed confirmation in that Edgerton (ed.), '*Sabhāparvan*. Introduction and Apparatus' was published eleven years after Sukthankar 1933, and one year after Sukthankar had died.

86 See Mahadevan, 'The Three Rails of the *Mahābhārata* Textual Tradition', on S's massive interpolation earlier in Book 2 of *bhakti* material drawn from the *Harivaṃśa* that would be picked up by Āḻvār Vaiṣṇavism.

87 Edgerton (ed.), '*Sabhāparvan*. Introduction and Apparatus', p. 226, abbreviating: 'S (except M1) om. the ref. – – ' The notation 'om. the ref. – – ' is used regularly, before indicating *pāda* changes, where manuscripts omit a speaker line.

88 In contrast, the Kumbhakonam edition, said to be based on Southern Recension texts yet 'includ[ing] practically all insertions of all known recensions' (Edgerton (ed.), '*Sabhāparvan*. Introduction and Apparatus', p. xxx), has a full speaker line for the Bard naming him by a typically Northern *sauti* rather than *sūta* in its *sautiruvāca* (T.R. Krishnacharya, and T.R. Vyasacharya, *Sriman*

best and worked from this principal text: a fairly early 1604 Telugu manuscript, but still chief among those that, in Edgerton's words, 'must have been extensively contaminated from the Vulgate text or his editorial principles are to me incomprehensible. For in many readings his text agrees with the Vulgate, against all our Southern MSS.'[89] Sastri's results, which Edgerton deems only 'slight' in their 'scientific interest', would have been tinged by 'Northern readings and interpolations' like those that led Edgerton to rule out three Telugu manuscripts from his Critical Apparatus.[90]

In short, Edgerton limited the southern manuscripts he would use to those from which he could reconstruct an S archetype, and of the nine that met this criterion, eight dropped the reference to the Bard. Almost as interesting, seven out of these eight go on immediately to keep the reference to Vaiśaṃpāyana as the resumed speaker of the next verse 2.46.5.[91] S thus leaves it somewhat up in the air (rather than out of the blue) who now speaks the Bard's verse. S makes only one alteration uniformly. It tones down the second *pāda* of the (former) Bard's verse to describe Vaiśaṃpāyana as 'highminded' (*mahāmatiḥ*) rather than 'majestic' (*pratāpavān*). Otherwise, only one S manuscript does something slight to improve matters unilaterally, changing its first *pāda* to read, 'When he was addressed by the king',[92] but an uncertain someone still says, 'When he was addressed by the king, Vyāsa's highminded student, who knew all the Veda, narrated it all as it happened', after which everything is left looking as much as possible as if, in removing this singular shift to the dialogue level of the Bard, S has changed nothing at all. We cannot tell whether the Bard's verse is spoken by Vaiśaṃpāyana incongruously uttering superlatives about himself before he resumes (as it were) speaking, or by a ghost in the machine. The latter reads as the better option, but only because we know about the omission behind it.

Here we face an unasked-for situation. For even if we choose to honour S for schematizing in search of consistency and for practicality in making adjustments for a southern performance milieu, dropping the Bard as speaker of 2.46.4 is an impoverishment and mediocritization of the text. It is a loss of profundity at a braided dialogical nerve point that, left alone, points to the root of the destruction of the world in a private, pivotal father-son dialogue. To put it starkly in dialogical terms, S's own custodial dialogue with its ancestral text results here in erasing one of that text's truly disorienting dialogical features about which Hudson is right:[93] that in a text where so many happenings and the whole epic itself are twice-told or more, finality is often an illusion. Many of S's interpolations can be viewed as enrichments of the *Mahābhārata* tradition, as distinct from its baseline text,

---

Mahābhāratam According to Southern Recension Based on the South Indian Texts with Footnotes and Readings. Vol. 2, *Sabhā Parva*-II. Sri Garib Das Oriental Series, No. 68. First published in Kumbhakonam (Delhi [1906–10] 1991), p. 112.

89 Edgerton (ed.), '*Sabhāparvan*. Introduction and Apparatus', p. xxx.

90 I thank T.P. Mahadevan for digging out the Sastri reference and for the information on Sastri's principal manuscript: a complete palm leaf *Sabhā Parvan* belonging to Krishnaswamy Sastrigal (email 18 April 2013). Edgerton examined three already collated southern manuscripts and decided not to use them because they were so northern in their content (Edgerton (ed.), '*Sabhāparvan*. Introduction and Apparatus', pp. xx–xxi). They do not appear to have included Sastri's principle one.

91 The Grantha manuscript G6 is the only one to 'om. the ref.' here to Vaiśaṃpāyana.

92 G1 thus reads *evamukte tu rajñā* at 2.46.4a. *Mahāmatiḥ* also occurs in Sastri, *pratāpavān* in the Kumbhkonam edition.

93 See Hudson, *Disorienting Dharma*, pp. 205–16. That is, Hudson is right about the net effect of what she calls 'narrative strategies' in this section titled 'Heaven's Riddles or the Hell Trick: The Two Conclusions of the *Mahābhārata*'. Again, her interpretation calls for further discussion.

and S is still far from being sufficiently appreciated as a marvelous scholarly tool. So even though other examples of S's mediocrity are all too easy to find,[94] it is in no one's interest to impugn S for making it a general characteristic. Nonetheless, we can be quite sure that we can hold what Sukthankar called S's 'thoroughly practical outlook' responsible for the particular loss of profundity that comes with dropping the Bard from his verse at 2.46.4. For the same kind of streamlining rationale must have lain behind the similar but more partial decision of some southern redactors to eliminate the *Nārāyaṇīya*'s three dips to the outer frame.[95] That choice too resulted in a loss of profundity at a point where an interruption from the Ugraśravas-Śaunaka outer dialogical frame led into another rebraiding of all three frames. Moreover, if Book 2's rebraiding pointed to what would lie at the root of the world's destruction, the *Nārāyaṇīya*'s rebraiding ties together interdialogical teachings that come ultimately from Vyāsa, who imparts them for the world's rectification. That loss of meaning was ignored and probably not even considered or understood by Belvalkar, and Belvalkar's erasure was tolerated by Grünendahl because it matched his view of one of the *Mahābhārata*'s late 'coatings'.

Indeed, Edgerton deserves profound thanks for recognizing that the speaker-reference *sūta uvāca* ('The Bard said',) belonged in the reconstructed archetype. He had better statistical grounds than Belvalkar to decide against including it, or to at least put the editorial wavy line denoting uncertainty – and usually incompatibility between N and S – beneath it. He may have been encouraged to leave *sūta uvāca* in, and without the wavy line, by the fact that M1 retained it.[96] I believe his decision was reinforced by three major insights that he had ahead of his time, and in which he differed from Sukthankar:

1. Regarding N as 'the ancestor of all our MSS., … this text itself was nothing "fluid"! … It is not an indefinite "literature" that we are dealing with, but a definite literary composition'[97]
2. Regarding the nine S manuscripts Edgerton edited from, 'They contain a vast number of common insertions, and an even vaster number of common readings of detail differing from those of all other MSS; many of these readings of detail in **S** (I do not say by any means all!) are probably, or in some cases quite certainly,

[94] See Sukthankar 1933, pp. xxxi–xxxvi and n. 51 above; Hiltebeitel, 'On Sukthankar's "S"', on the *Śakuntalā-Upākhyāna* preceding the *Yayāti-Upākhyāna* in N but not in S; and in press-d on S's near-total remake of the *Umā-Maheśvara Saṃvāda* with erasure of N's emphasis on *ṛṣidharma*.

[95] The driving decision to erase these three dips is reflected in the manuscripts Belvalkar calls M1, 5–7 (see Hiltebeitel, 'The *Nārāyanīya* and the Early Reading Communities of the *Mahābhārata*', pp. 233, 239; the 'M group', pp. 250–53). One might expect these manuscripts to be related to Edgerton's M2, and Edgerton's M1 to be related to Belvalkar's other manuscripts. But the only possible overlap I can see would be Edgerton's M1 with Bevalkar's M5, both coming from the Cochin State Library where their numbers, 1 and 39, leave their relation unclear (Edgerton (ed.), '*Sabhāparvan.* Introduction and Apparatus', p. x; Shripad Krishna Belvalkar (ed.), 'Śāntiparvan, with Appendix I and Critical Notes', in V.S. Sukthankar et al. (eds), *Mahābhārata: Critical Edition*, 24 vols with *Harivaṃśa* (Poona, 1966), pp. xviii–xix). The data are insufficient to conclude that the two editors worked with continuations of any of the same manuscripts.

[96] Unfortunately Edgerton does not comment on his decision, or on the slash that seems to indicate that the whole Bard's verse is absent from the Calcutta edition (Edgerton [ed.], '*Sabhāparvan.* Introduction and Apparatus', p. lxiii).

[97] Edgerton (ed.), '*Sabhāparvan.* Introduction and Apparatus', pp. xxxvi–xxxvii.

unoriginal. Therefore, the **S** MSS. constitute one "version"; they go back to a common archetype, more recent than the original.'[98]

3. On 'Sukhankar's opinion that 'in parts unaffected by the tendency of S to expand the text, it is likely to prove on the whole purer, more conservative, and more archaic than even the best Northern version', Edgerton is 'very definitely of the contrary opinion.' He found some but 'not many' cases where '**S** alone probably has preserved an original reading; but usually in such cases' N manuscripts 'are *discordant*, … they do not contain any *common* secondary reading, and hence do not tend to show derivation from a common secondary source.' Since it would take many 'common secondary readings … to establish the reality of "N" as a secondary archetype, … such a theory … is distinctly implausible.'[99]

Ironically, in rare instances where S may be 'more archaic than even the best' N manuscript, it is likely to be because S has preserved a baseline N reading better than N itself.

To close these windows into the *Mahābhārata*'s interdialogical situation, I borrow a decisively used phrase from a recent novel and film popular in India and America. Our ultimate take-home on N and S is not that N is the better text; it is 'the better story'.[100] This is not because it gets us as close as Sukthankar and his colleagues could get to an 'original'. It is because, and here Sukthankar had the feel for just the right words, 'Compared with [S], the Northern recension is distinctly vague, unsystematic, sometimes even inconsequent, *more like a story rather naively narrated*, as we find in actual experience.'[101] The Bard's verse has been good evidence, and a good reminder in taking us into a father-son dialogue that reveals what lies at the root of the destruction of the world, that having the earliest recoverable *Mahābhārata* is like having a lifeboat with a tiger in it. Draupadī, once she has endured Duryodhana's determination and Dhṛtarāṣṭra's decision to put her too at the root of the world's destruction, is both a saving boat and a tiger.[102] Thanks to Sukthankar's groundwork, the Critical Edition's identification of an S archetype allows us to appreciate both the better wilder 'primary process' story close to what the *Mahābhārata* must once have really been,[103] and what S in its genuine custodial interests sought both to preserve and tame by secondary revision.

---

98 Ibid., pp. xxxviii (author's boldface).

99 Ibid., pp. xlviii–xlix, quoting Sukthankar 1933, pp. xlvi–xlvii. I insert 'northern manuscripts' where Edgerton has 'W and E' for west and east. As he says further down the same page, 'W and E together make up Sukthankar's N.'

100 See Yann Martel, *Life of Pi* (Orlando, FL, 2001, p. 217). The reference here and the allusion below are to Yann Martel's *Life of Pi*. The phrase is equally impressive in the movie by that title.

101 See the full contrast quoted in n. 37 above.

102 Draupadī is a saving boat to the Pāṇḍavas according to Karṇa when he marvels at how she rescued them and set them ashore after the dicing (2.64.1–3). And from the dicing on, she is a tiger to one and all, and explicitly so according to Vaiśaṃpāyana where he compares a henchman of Jayadratha to a jackal approaching a tigress (3.148.17) when Jayadratha has spotted her alone in the forest and intends to abduct her.

103 On Freud's concept of primary process as 'the right metaphor' for the 'dreamwork'-like composition of both epics, see Alf Hiltebeitel 'The Primary Process of the Hindu Epics', *International Journal of Hindu Studies* 4/3 (2000): 269–88; Alf Hiltebeitel, *Uncanny Domesticities: The Goddess in the Mahābhārata and the Correspondence between Girindrashekar Bose and Sigmund Freud.* Monograph in progress (tentative title).

The Rāmāyaṇa's Interwoven Dialogical Strands

Having left the *Mahābhārata* for now with a double metaphor that fits its heroine rather well, we can quickly acknowledge that although those images would not apply to Sītā or the *Vālmīki Rāmāyaṇa*, our reading of the *Rāmāyaṇa*'s Baroda Critical Edition, despite its editorial weaknesses,[104] can still lead us to a similar assessment. It too will be the better story. Better than what? In this case, let us just say better than usually appreciated, and begin by attributing the lack of appreciation once again to the streamlining and stratifying impulses that have habituated readers to the expectation that a text's frames or framelike features would axiomatically be late.

Unlike the *Mahābhārata* with its three frame stories leisurely introduced and intermittently intertwined, and with its post-war unfolding, the *Rāmāyaṇa* has a single frame story. Moreover, it presents a single point of departure – its *Upodghāta* or 'preamble' – that leads into its whole poem by opening with a disclosure of how it came to be composed. Nonetheless, this *Rāmāyaṇa* frame can also be said to have three dialogical strands or even tiers and likewise a post-war unfolding. The *Rāmāyaṇa* frame, in only this first four-chapter (*sarga*) 'preamble', opens on to two progressive dialogical previews of the story – the first between the Ṛṣi Nārada and the Ṛṣi and poet-to-be Vālmīki; the second between Vālmīki himself, now a poet, and the god Brahmā; which ripens into the third and full unfolding, the *Vālmīki Rāmāyaṇa* itself,[105] which will include a return to the frame in the *Rāmāyaṇa*'s only post-war book, the seventh.

The first dialogue centres on Nārada's response to Vālmīki's text-opening question as to whether there is an ideal man in the world today:

> Is there a man in the world today who is truly virtuous and energetic and yet knows both *dharma* and how to act upon it? Who always speaks the truth and holds firmly to his vows? Who exemplifies proper conduct and is benevolent to all creatures? Who is learned, capable, and a pleasure to behold? Who is self-controlled, having subdued his anger? Who is both judicious and free from envy? Who, when his fury is aroused in battle, is feared even by the gods? This is what I want to hear, for my desire to know is very strong. Great Ṛṣi, you must know of such a man. (*Rām* 1.1.2–5)[106]

It sounds like a leading question, for Vālmīki certainly knows that he can expect an answer. Let us keep in mind that the second of the virtues mentioned, which Goldman translates as 'knows .... how to act on it' (*kṛtajña*), could also be translated 'grateful'. Nārada replies with a short and entirely laudatory account of Rāma's virtues and adult life, ostensibly to date (1.1.7–75). He responds as the question requires, first admitting that the 'celebrated virtues' asked for are hard to find in one person, but that upon consideration, he has the answer: Rāma. Then, having detailed Rāma's qualities, including certain godlike ones, he embarks upon Rāma's story, providing the so-called *Saṃkṣipta* ('condensed') *Rāmāyaṇa*. Hardly

---

[104] See Mahadevan, 'On the Southern Recension of the *Mahābhārata*': 99–100 n. 2 on the failure in early volumes to reckon with Malahyālam manuscripts.

[105] For discussions of the *Upodghāta* from different perspectives, see Robert Goldman (trans.), *The Rāmāyaṇa of Vālmīki*, vol. 1: *Bālakāṇḍa*. Princeton, 1984), pp. 67–73, 273–88; John Brockington, *The Sanskrit Epics*. Handbuch der Orientalistik, Zweite Abteilung, Indien, Vol. 12. J. Bronkhorst (ed.) (Leiden, 1998), pp. 2–3, 380, 395; Hiltebeitel, 'Not Without Subtales'.

[106] Goldman (trans.), *The Rāmāyaṇa of Vālmīki*, vol. 1, p. 121.

hinting at anything problematic in Rāma's life, Nārada omits Sītā's fire ordeal while going beyond it to conclude with Rāma and Sītā's return to Ayodhyā to recover his kingdom.[107] In bringing Rāma to mid-career, he speaks of his rule as already a kind of golden age ('like the Kṛta Yuga') extending into the future in which Rāma 'is performing hundreds of horse sacrifices involving vast quantities of gold', 'bringing about the establishment of royal lines of a hundred qualities, and appointing the four social classes each to its own duty in this world' – before he will go to heaven after ruling for eleven thousand years (*Rām* 1.1.76).[108] In mentioning many Aśvamedhas, Nārada leaves unmentioned the one narrated in Book 7, where the banished Sītā refuses to return to Rāma and enters the earth.[109]

I propose that Nārada's account is intentionally 'condensed' for the further iterations to unfold from it in the mind of the poet (and, of course, the listener or reader).[110] The *Rāmāyaṇa* frame thus opens onto a king who is still alive, about whom Vālmīki will be able to compose his poem to help readers, and perhaps himself, decide whether Nārada has truly answered his question. Nārada makes a later appearance to prompt Rāma to rid the world of the upstart Śūdra Śambūka (7.65), which can be taken as one of the episodes that place a question mark before the mirror that he initially holds up to Rāma's perfection.

Once Nārada leaves (1.2.2), in the *Rāmāyaṇa*'s second *sarga*, Vālmīki witnesses near his hermitage the grieving cries of a female Krauñca bird over the slaying of her mate by a 'cruel hunter'. This provokes the Ṛṣi's compassion, and Vālmīki then breaks into the utterance that creates 'verse' (*śloka*, and thus poetry) out of 'grief' (*śoka*; 1.2.12–17). For our purposes, it suffices to say that he has no dialogue either with the hunter or the surviving female crane, neither of which ever makes a follow-up appearance in the poem. The second dialogue is then with Brahmā. After Vālmīki offers brief words of homage, Brahmā reads his mind and, claiming that the inspired verse came from him (probably implying Vedic precedent for the *śloka*), urges that Vālmīki should now compose the entire adventure (*carita*) of Rāma for the world to hear, 'just as you heard it from Nārada'. With that, he gives Vālmīki the insight to see what he did not know and what is still yet to happen

---

107 Arshia Sattar, presenting 'the source' of her abridged *Rāmāyaṇa* translation as its Baroda Critical Edition (*The Rāmāyaṇa. Vālmīki. Abridged and Translated* (New Delhi, 2000), pp. viii–ix), does not explain why she would translate an interpolation from the Apparatus, but that is the case with *Rām* 107* (most often interpolated after 1.1.66ab; alternately after 69ab) on Rāma's harsh words to Sītā and her fire ordeal (*The Rāmāyaṇa. Vālmīki. Abridged and Translated*, p. 8). Sattar then misleadingly includes the passage in Nārada's account in her interpretative study of 'Vālmīki in the Story He Tells' (Arshia Sattar, 'Inside/Outside: Where is Valmiki in the Story He Tells?', in Laurie Patton and David Haberman [eds], *Notes from A Mandala: Essays in the History of Indian Religions in Honor of Wendy Doniger* [Newark, DE, 2010), p. 238). She fence-sits on matters I raised about both epics' critical editions in Hiltebeitel, *Rethinking the Mahābhārata*, incomprehensibly attributing to me the view 'that Vyāsa was the composer rather than the compiler of the *Mahābhārata*' (Sattar, 'Inside/Outside', p. 241 n. 8), and not mentioning my closing discussion of the *Rāmāyaṇa* (Hiltebeitel, *Rethinking the Mahābhārata*, pp. 285–6, 317–22) that anticipates both her own study and this one.

108 This last comes right after the *Saṃkṣipta* section, and seems to refer to the statement made twice at the end of the *Yuddhakhāṇḍa* that Rāma ruled for ten thousand years (*Rām* 6.112.82, 90). But as the conclusion of one continuous iteration, it also implies Rāma's later years that are described in Book 7, where that figure is also mentioned (7.94.12; cf. 92.16: he spent ten thousand years seeing to state affairs).

109 I do not believe one can locate Nārada's account to Vālmīki at a point in Rāma's life before Sītā's banishment or the birth of the twins, such as Sattar argues for ('Inside/Outside', pp. 238–9).

110 For different perspectives based on notions of strata and textual development, see Goldman (trans.), *The Rāmāyaṇa of Vālmīki*, vol. 1, pp. 68–9; Brockington, *The Sanskrit Epics*, p. 381.

in Rāma's life, and confirms that his poem will endure so long as rivers and mountains last on earth and that it will all be true (22–35). Brahmā thus assures Vālmīki that he will know things that Nārada omitted. Upon Brahmā's vanishing, Vālmīki now adopts the idea of composing 'the entire *Rāmāyaṇa* poem (*kāvya*) in verses such as these' (1.2.40cd). The third *sarga* then tells how Vālmīki enters this story for the first time by a sort of meditative preview (1.3.1–2), which now closes with Sītā's banishment, taking the story for the first time into Book 7 (3–28).[111] Like Nārada, Brahmā will make further appearances in the poem, being instrumental in setting in motion its divine plan (which Nārada would know of as well).[112] But most significantly, he has two dialogues with Rāma himself where he twice discloses Rāma's divinity to him after Rāma has put Sītā through her two ordeals.

Then, looking back upon the poem's completion, the fourth *sarga*, which concludes the *Upodghāta*, presumes an ongoing dialogical situation at Vālmīki's *āśrama*. Here Vālmīki names 'the whole *Rāmāyaṇa* poem (*kāvya*) the great adventure of Sītā (*sītāyāś caritaṃ mahat*) and the slaying of Paulastya [Rāvaṇa]', and teaches it to Kuśa and Lava, making the 'Munis glad at heart' (1.4.4–15). Sītā is obviously there too, but for now there is no record of any conversations involving her. Yet Vālmīki has already indicated that although Rāma's *carita* or adventure (2.30–31) was his starting point, his complete poem is about Sītā's adventure, or these two adventures that are about to unfold as one: the 'profound adventure' that Rāma prepares himself to hear at the *Upodghāta*'s end. For there, amid what I think are restrained hints at the Aśvamedha setting in which Vālmīki's poem will finally be recited by the twins to their father (21–7),[113] Rāma invites them to begin singing it before him, with the intriguing statement: 'Moreover, it is said that the profound adventure (*mahānubhāvaṃ caritam*) they tell is highly beneficial even for me. Listen to it' (1.4.26cd). We are not told whom Rāma is quoting or addressing, and we are invited to figure out how it will be of benefit to him. For this, we must wait to learn more about the scene of this recital, which will take us further beyond Sītā's banishment into the seventh book.

Just as information on the *Mahābhārata*'s frame is resumed with further revelations in the post-war Book 12 the *Rāmāyaṇa*'s frame now finally gets back to the dialogical situation at Vālmīki's hermitage in the post-war Book 7 when Vālmīki says his first words within the main story, which are also his first words to Sītā, welcoming the banished heroine to his *āśrama* with hints back to the *Upodghāta* when he tells her he knows everything by his 'concentration on *dharma* (*dharmasamādhi*)', and above all that she is 'without sin (*apāpām*)' and of 'pure character (*viśuddhabhāva*)' (7.48.9–10). Kuśa and Lava will then pick up from the *Upodghāta* directly by singing their parents' 'profound adventure' to their father in person during intervals of his horse sacrifice. Rāma orders a very large and wondrous sacrificial enclosure built for that rite beside the Gomatī River in Naimiṣa Forest, and comes there with his army after the horse is set free to wander (7.82.14; 83.2–4). With the sacrifice proceeding, Vālmīki arrives with his disciples and directs the twins to sing

---

111 Sattar, 'Inside/Outside', pp. 234–9 makes too much of Vālmīki's 'meditative trance', suggesting that he stays in it for some time and positing that it is represented in Book 7 by the divine eye by which he vouches for Sītā's purity and the twins' legitimacy before Sītā enters the earth.

112 On the *Rāmāyaṇa*'s divine plan, see Sheldon Pollock, 'Ātmānam mānuṣam manye: *Dharmākūtam* on the Divinity of Rāma', *Journal of the Oriental Institute of Baroda* 33 (1984): 505–28; Hiltebeitel, *Dharma: Its Early History in Law, Religion, and Narrative*, pp. 571–6.

113 Rāma is on a throne in an assembly (*pariṣad*). As Goldman indicates (Goldman [trans.], *The Rāmāyaṇa of Vālmīki*, vol. 1, p. 288), this could imply his court at Ayodhyā, but commentators and interpolations locate it at the Aśvamedha.

'the whole *Rāmāyaṇa* poem at the gate of Rāma's dwelling' – twenty *sargas* a day. Rāma hears the boys begin 'from the sight of Nārada (*nārada-darśanāt*; 85.11b)' – that is, from the very beginning of the *Upodghāta* on! Once the twins tell Rāma that Vālmīki is the poem's author, they agree to continue singing it at intervals in the rite (85.21). Here we learn that Vālmīki helped Sītā raise these boys, who are called *his* children, 'the children of the Muni" (*munidārakau*; 7.84.9d, 17d, and 19d). After many days, Rāma recognizes them, misses Sītā, and summons her to attest to her purity by oath in the midst of a vast assembly. But when Vālmīki brings Sītā he attests to her purity himself, tells Rāma that she herself 'will give proof of her fidelity' and that the two boys are their sons (87.15–16). Rāma accepts Vālmīki's word, and admits that Sītā has already proven her fidelity in the presence of the gods after her first ordeal by fire. Sītā nonetheless makes an oath implicitly in her only and last words: 'If I have thought with my mind of none other than Rāma, let the goddess Mādhavī [Earth] give me an opening' (88.10). When Rāma then threatens to destroy Earth unless she returns Sītā intact, Brahmā repeats what he told him after Sītā's fire ordeal, that his birth links him with Viṣṇu (7.Appendix I, No. 13, line 25).[114] Before Brahmā departs for Brahmaloka, he tells Rāma that he should listen to the rest of this 'first poem entirely established in you' (line 31) with the great Ṛṣis and the supreme Ṛṣi (presumably Vālmīki; line 40). Once Brahmā is back in Brahmaloka, the great Ṛṣis who reside there get his permission to go hear the rest of the story with Rāma about Rāma's future (lines 41–5). Rāma now tells Vālmīki about the celestial Ṛṣis' wish, and says to him, 'May you begin tomorrow morning the further recital of the future' (line 49). Rāma then takes Kuśa and Lava with him for the night to the sacrificial pavilion:

> The next morning, Rāma summoned the great Munis and said to his two sons, 'Now sing without a care.' Then when the great-souled Maharṣis had taken their seats, Kuśa and Lava recited the further part of the poem about the future. (lines 52–5)

– beginning with a recognition that Sītā had entered the earth (line 56).[115]

If we take both the *Upodghāta* and the Aśvamedha scene to be integral to the poem, Vālmīki's dramatic entry at the Aśvamedha would thus be something long prepared for, whose dialogical implications have yet to be sufficiently appreciated. Although the *Rāmāyaṇa* makes it far easier to miss, once again we see the Naimiṣa Forest as a place of intersecting cosmological planes where dialogical frames and strands are tied together. With the Brahmaloka Ṛṣis joining an audience there that includes not only Rāma but apparently Vālmīki, we can also now see that both epics' authorial frames especially have much to tell us about how each epic positions its poet-author, speakers, and audiences in a text-

---

[114] Here and in what immediately follows, *Rām* 7.App.I.13 concerns a universally attested passage discounted by the Baroda Critical Edition editor U.P. Shah for uncritical reasons: 'we feel that it is an early interpolation' and 'Without this passage of 56 lines, the continuity of narration between sargas 88 and 89 is not hampered and appears in better order' (1975, 29). Shah's feelings also led him to reject 7.App.I.9 because it tells that 'Vālmīki's poem was not unknown to the soldiers of Ayodhyā' after they stopped off at Vālmīki's *āśrama* when the twins were born, and could not have been trusted to keep their secret from Rāma (1975, 26–7).

[115] Such detail is called for to clear away Sattar's impossible and distortive idea ('Inside/Outside', pp. 233–4, 237) that the twins now stop reciting, that Rāma stops listening to the poem, and that Vālmīki recites Rāma's future to the great Ṛṣis only! It is based on selecting for translation from *Rām.* 7.App.I.13 only the lines in which Rāma tells Vālmīki to prepare for the morrow (Sattar, *The Rāmāyaṇa*, p. 678).

long braiding. But the *Rāmāyaṇa*'s frame introduces a different complexity in that it builds from the poet's dialogues with Nārada and Brahmā. Although it is more straightforwardly preliminary, shorter, and more focused, it is also more poetically traceable into the main narrative and the whole poem, and ultimately more concentrated on the poet's relations first to the hero but also ultimately to the heroine as well.

D. Talking to Sītā

Comparisons of Draupadī and Sītā have been a favorite topic in epic scholarship, Indian popular culture and media studies, and, I have found, in student papers. Taking stock of my own three efforts in this direction, they have moved from symbolism through narrative design to dialogue. I first compared Draupadī and Sītā around themes of purity and auspiciousness,[116] next in the ways they define the poets' paths through their poems[117] and lately in some words they direct to their husbands. I will return to this latter comparison, but before doing so, it will be useful to make another comparison of scenes in which both heroines are in dialogue, uniquely so in each epic, straightforwardly with other women.[118] This would be to compare Draupadī's *saṃvāda* with Satyabhāmā,[119] wife of Kṛṣṇa, with Sītā's conversation with Anasūyā, wife of the Ṛṣi Atri. Since Draupadī is not so much our concern here, it will suffice to make the formal comparison quickly before turning to what it tells us about Sītā. Each exchange takes us momentarily outside the mainly men's world of the main epic stories to offer a glimpse of the heroine handling what we might call women's shop talk. And in each case the interlocutor's interest lies in asking her about some personal or even private dimension of her marital situation. Satyabhāmā wants to know how Draupadī handles five husbands, and whether she keeps them in line with some love potion. Draupadī, even though she comes up with the most banal reply, is as feisty as ever and assures Satyabhāmā that she keeps the five Pāṇḍavas in line by nothing other than her exemplary behavior.[120] Anasūyā, on the other hand, wants a glimpse into Rāma and Sītā's first meeting, about which Sītā is rather wistful.

Anasūyā is interested in two 'stories' she has heard about Sītā: that she was born from a furrow, and that Rāma won her at a *svayaṃvara* or 'self-choice' ceremony – one in which, if the *Mahābhārata* sets the standard, the woman should have some choice in

---

[116] Alf Hiltebeitel, 'Purity and Auspiciousness in the Sanskrit Epics', in Frédérique Appfel Marglin and John Carmen (eds), *Essays on Purity and Auspiciousness, Journal of Developing Societies* 1 (1985): 41–54.

[117] Hiltebeitel, *Rethinking the Mahābhārata*; Hiltebeitel, 'Authorial Paths Through the Two Sanskrit Epics'.

[118] The description should be qualified. Draupadī dialogues with Queen Sudeṣṇā, wife of King Virāṭa, but she is in disguise and thus not speaking straightforwardly (*Mbh* 4.8.5–30; see Laurie Patton, 'How Do You Conduct Yourself? Gender and the Construction of a Dialogical Self in the *Mahābhārata*', in Simon Brodbeck and Brian Black (eds), *Gender and Narrative in the Mahābhārata* (Oxford, 2007), pp. 100, 105–7). She is also a silent party to words from Kuntī as her polyandrous married life gets initially sorted out (1.182.2–10; 184.4–6); and she and Kuntī have parting words as she leaves for exile after the dicing (2.70.4–9a). Kausalyā also has parting words for Sītā (*Rām* 2.96.21–3), and Sītā speaks with Rākṣasī women, one of whom will be mentioned below.

[119] *Mbh* 3.222–24. It is called a *saṃvāda* only in its colophons.

[120] On deeper polyphonous and performative subtleties in their exchange, see Patton, 'How Do You Conduct Yourself?'.

selecting her husband from among competing suitors who would be called upon to show some skill in arms.[121] Anasūyā is not the only one to mention Sītā's birth story. It is first recalled by Sītā's father Janaka to Rāma (1.65.14). Later Hanumān recalls it as he ponders whether the beautiful woman he has found in captivity is indeed Sītā (5.14.16). After the war while Sītā is still living in Ayodhyā with Rāma, the Ṛṣi Agastya tells Rāma that Sītā was born from a furrow after her previous life as Vedavatī (7.17.30), and Rāma recalls it to demand Sītā back from the goddess Earth just after she has re-entered her,[122] but Anasūyā is the only one to *ask* Sītā about her birth as a 'story' (*kathā*; 2.110.22; 23; 111.1). And that is also the case when she goes on to be the only person in the entire *Rāmāyaṇa* to refer to Sītā's marriage as one by *svayaṃvara*. Moreover, it is the connection between the two stories that motivates Anasūyā's inquiry. When Sītā tells Anasūyā the story of her birth, Anasūyā's question is really about her having *heard* that Sītā had a *svayaṃvara*, whereupon the two of them become the only persons to use this term for Sītā's marriage in Vālmīki's whole poem:

> Anasūyā put a question to her about a certain *story she was fond of*. 'It was at a *svayaṃvara*, they say, that glorious Rāghava obtained you, Sītā. This is at least *the story that has reached my ears*. I should *like to hear that story in full*, Maithilī, exactly as it happened, in its entirety. Would you tell it to me, please?' (*Rām* 2.110.23–24, my emphasis)

Let us appreciate the delight that Anasūyā expresses in anticipating that she will hear Sītā tell this story herself. Sītā begins by linking the two stories Anasūyā has asked about. It was her not being born from a womb that led her father, after much worry, to think of holding a *svayaṃvara* for her. The point seems to be that, even if such an abnormal birth makes it delicate to find a suitable match, lords of the land would want to vie for an earth-born bride. This would hold as much for Draupadī, who is born from an earthen altar (*vedi*), and also, like Sītā, *ayonijā*, 'not born from a womb'.[123] Sītā says Janaka had received an immense heavy bow and two quivers of divine origin, and invited the kings to win her by raising and stringing it. But the kings only looked and left, unable to lift it (in Janaka's earlier account, they actually offered a long siege [1.65.21–25]). After a long time, one day Rāma and Lakṣmaṇa came, eager to see the bow; and again Janaka brought it out. Rāma strung and drew it 'in the twinkling of an eye', and broke it (2.110.36–47). Thereupon, says Sītā,

> … my father, true to his agreement, raised up a splendid water vessel, ready to bestow me on Rāma. But ready though my father was to bestow me, Rāma would not accept me right away, for he did not know the will of his father. … So my father invited my father-in-law, … and afterwards bestowed me on the celebrated Rāma … . And that is how I was bestowed on Rāma, there at the *svayaṃvara*, and justly (*dharmeṇa*) I love my husband, the best of men. (2.110.48–52)

---

[121] For discussion, see Hiltebeitel, 'Authorial Paths through the Two Sanskrit Epics', pp. 193–6, 200 on Sītā in the *Rāmopākhyāna* (Vālmīki seems to be catching Sītā up with Draupadī); Hiltebeitel, *Dharma: Its Early History in Law, Religion, and Narrative*, pp. 359–60, 385, 488–95 on *Mahābhārata svayaṃvara*s.

[122] *Rām* 7.App.I.13, lines 13–14; see n. 115 above on this universally attested Appendix passage.

[123] See Hiltebeitel, *Dharma: Its Early History in Law, Religion, and Narrative*, ch. 10.

Sītā's story is known for a certain 'simplicity',[124] but one can also feel the narrative and emotional strains the poet leaves in it. If she had a *svayaṃvara*, it was an interrupted, disappointing, and even failed one between the suitors' departure and Rāma's arrival long after, with no rivals remaining. Nothing is left of the bride's 'self-choice'. Unlike Arjuna, who had to shoot a difficult target with arrows to win Draupadī, Rāma just broke the bow. Unlike Draupadī, who gets to garland Arjuna with a smile, it is not Sītā but her father who acted for her by lifting a vessel. Unlike Draupadī, who immediately sets off with Arjuna, Sītā had to wait until approval came from Rāma's father. Unlike the Pāṇḍavas, who fit their marriage of Draupadī to the word and law of their mother, Rāma upholds the word and law of his father. Maybe the old, chaste, ascetic Brāhmaṇī Anasūyā would have found Sītā's reassurance gladdening that, having been 'bestowed on Rāma ... according to *dharma*, I love my husband, the best of men.' To me the enthusiasm with which Sītā begins her story ends up sounding frayed, and indeed constrained by a discourse that we know will be her undoing. Sītā, Rāma, and Lakṣmaṇa are still traveling in exile together at this point, and are yet to enter the Daṇḍaka Forest where Sītā will be abducted. When she heard me make these comparisons, T. S. Rukmani commented, 'Thank you for letting us see once again that Sītā never had a chance.'[125]

This brings us to the most significant Sītā-Draupadī comparison for this essay: one in which, as described so far, each heroine directs some words to her husband.[126] More precisely, they are the first words one says to Rāma and the other to Yudhiṣṭhira after they have been violated by the males who will henceforth be their husbands' inevitable victims in war. Draupadī's words come as remonstrances to Yudhiṣṭhira early in their forest exile after her humiliation at the dicing; and Sītā's come in her first appeals to Rāma from her captivity in Laṅkā. As I hope is already apparent, the first difference between these scenes is that whereas Draupadī's words are met in a well-wrought dialogue with Yudhiṣṭhira,[127] Sītā's words to Rāma become apostrophe. If the *Upodghāta* sets up the whole *Rāmāyaṇa* as an apostrophe to Rāma, Sītā's appeal would be its apostrophe within the apostrophe – like *Hamlet*'s play within the play.[128] Since I have taken up this comparison elsewhere from different angles,[129] I will not go into Draupadī's part in it at all. But Sītā's must be summarized. Sītā makes three agonized speeches (5.23.11–20; 24.3–49; 26.3–16) while Hanumān, hiding in a tree, determines how best to speak with her without frightening her further. It is not always clear what Hanumān actually hears, since her words seem at

[124] Sheldon Pollock (trans.), *The Rāmāyaṇa of Vālmīki: An Epic of Ancient India*, vol. 2: *Ayodhyākāṇḍa* (Princeton, 1986), p. 525.

[125] This was in response to a paper of mine at the 5th Dubrovnik International Conference on the Sanskrit Epics and Purāṇas, September 2008.

[126] In Sītā's case, though not in Draupadī's, this second scene comes after the ones just described.

[127] *Mbh* 3.28–33. The *adhyāya* colophons describe it alternately as the speech (*vākya*) of Draupadī or Yudhiṣṭhira, and thus do not call it a *saṃvāda*. Early on in it, however, Draupadī uses the *atrāpy udāharantīmam itihāsaṃ purātanam* formulaic line to introduce a *saṃvāda* between Prahlāda and Vairocana (3.29.1).

[128] See David Shulman, 'Bhavabhūti on Cruelty and Compassion', in Paula Richman (ed.), *Questioning Ramayanas: A South Asian Tradition* (Berkeley, 2001), p. 63, making powerful use of this same analogy for the actual play within the play with which Bhavabhūti closes in on Rāma's despairing moods after banishing Sītā.

[129] See Hiltebeitel, *Dharma*, ch. 7 for an opening discussion; *Dharma: Its Early History in Law, Religion, and Narrative*, ch. 10 § D, with bibliography, and considering Draupadī as a materialist; *Reading the Fifth Veda*, ch. 11 § B.2, discussed from the standpoint of *bhakti*.

times to become soliloquies, particularly as she more and more addresses herself to Rāma. Between the second and third speeches a good Rākṣasī named Trijaṭā describes a dream that augurs well for Sītā, and says, 'I saw that lotus-eyed woman rise from her husband's lap to stroke the sun and moon with her hands' (25.15). But Sītā does not hear this, and it is in her third speech that her lonely soliloquy becomes apostrophe. Numbering the speeches, I supply extracts from each:

> 1. How fortunate are those who are able to see my lord – his eyes like the inner petals of a lotus – who walks with the valorous gait of a lion and is yet grateful, a speaker of what is beloved. Separated from Rāma who knows himself,[130] there is no way that I can survive any more than if I had consumed virulent poison. … Guarded by these Rākṣasīs, I will never see Rāma again. A curse on this human state! A curse on being under another's power. Although I wish to, I cannot end my life. (5.23.16–20)
>
> 2. Rāghava is renowned, wise, grateful, and compassionate. Therefore I think it must be the exhaustion of my good fortune that has made this man of good conduct uncompassionate [in not coming to rescue Sītā]. … Rāma must not know that I am alive. For if he and Lakṣmaṇa knew, it is impossible that the two of them would not scour the earth for me. Surely [Rāma] has gone – out of grief for me – from here to the world of the gods, having abandoned his body on earth. Fortunate are the gods, Gandharvas, Siddhas, and supreme Ṛṣis who can now see Rāma, my lotus-eyed lord. Or perhaps this wise royal Ṛṣi Rāma who loves *dharma* and is the Supreme Self (*paramātman*) has no use for me as his wife. There would be love for the one that is seen; there is no affection on the part of one who does not see. Ingrates destroy; Rāma will not destroy. … Or perhaps the two brothers, best of men, have laid down their weapons and are wandering in the forest as forest dwellers, subsisting on roots and fruits. Or perhaps Rāvaṇa … has slain [them] by means of some trick. … Fortunate, indeed, are those great-souled, great-fortuned Munis who are revered for their truth, their selves conquered, for whom there is neither beloved nor unbeloved. Homage to those great-souled ones who detach themselves from both! Abandoned here by my beloved Rāma whose self is known, and fallen under the power of the wicked Rāvaṇa, I shall end my life. (24.12, 37–49)
>
> 3. Oh Rāma! Oh Lakṣmaṇa! Oh Sumitra! O mother of Rāma and my own mother as well! I, this luckless woman, will perish like a ship foundering in a storm at sea. It must have been Time itself in the guise of a deer who deluded hapless me at that time when, fool that I am, I sent away my husband [and his] younger brother. … Alas, Rāma of the long arms, true to your vows! Alas, you whose face rivals the full moon! Alas, you benefactor and beloved of the living world! You do not realize that I am to be slain by Rākṣasas. My taking you for my sole divinity, my long suffering, my sleeping on the ground, and my rigorous adherence to *dharma* – this devotion to my husband has been fruitless, like the

[130] *Rām* 5.23.17: *rāmeṇa viditātmanā*, Robert Goldman and Sally Sutherland (trans.), *The Rāmāyaṇa of Vālmīki*, Vol. 5: *Sundarakāṇḍa* (Princeton, 1996), p. 180, 'celebrated'; John Brockington and Mary Brockington (trans.), *Rāma the Steadfast: An Early Form of the Rāmāyaṇa* (London: 2006), p. 207, 'sagacious'. As will be cited again with the translation 'who knows himself', *viditātman* recurs at the end of Sītā's second speech at 5.24.49. It is used frequently for Rāma, and might certainly be translated differently in different contexts. This translation here is strengthened by juxtaposition with Sītā's reference here to Rāma as *paramātman* in her second speech (5.24.40d), as discussed below.

> favors men do for ingrates. Surely this *dharma* adventure of mine has been vain and my exclusive devotion to my husband useless. For, pale and emaciated, I cannot see you; I am cut off from you without hope for our reunion. Once you have carried out your father's orders to the letter and have returned from the forest with your vow accomplished, you will, I think, make love with wide-eyed women, carefree, your purpose accomplished. But as for hapless me, Rāma, after having loved you so long, given you all my heart – to my own undoing – and practiced my vows and penances in vain, I shall abandon my accursed life. (26.8–15)

As we know from Fred Hardy,[131] later vernacular *bhakti* traditions make the woman's voice a vehicle for devotional sentiments in the mood of love in separation, and I view the *Rāmāyaṇa* as doing that already in these three speeches. The translation thus gives special weight to the tensions portrayed through the idioms of Rāma's belovedness; and of 'seeing' Rāma, wherever he may be – in heaven? through the eyes of lovers? – which Sītā cannot do except in estrangement. Sītā's words raise questions of Rāma's gratitude (as noted, one of the celebrated virtues Vālmīki asks Nārada about in the *Upodghāta*); of whether Rāma does indeed know himself, which would include his knowing his double divine and human nature, which at this point in the poem – that is, before he kills Rāvaṇa – neither Sītā nor Rāma can fully know other than by intimations, such as that when she calls him the *paramātman*!

As Sītā builds up to her final apostrophe by first calling on Rāma followed by calling on her own mother, Earth, it is what she will do again when she actually does end her life, having determined she will never call on Rāma again. Indeed, right here we find half the double metaphor that corresponds to Draupadī's. Not a saving boat, she is in her own words 'a ship foundering in a storm at sea' needing a lifeline herself from a rescuer she already questions with some penetrating accuracy. Never the tigress, we might supply the other half from the first of the forlorn similes Vālmīki has just regaled her with when she first saw Rāvaṇa coming to claim her sexually, and 'she curls up in a fetal position, trembling like a plantain tree in a gale'.[132] Yet Sītā is also resilient, and no smiles or laughter ever pass between her and her tormentor. Whatever smiles she might have left she saves for Rāma.

I have thus translated certain words in ways that sustain this *bhakti* momentum.[133] But what happens when we notice that this momentum moves more and more toward apostrophe? In a *bhakti* context, which is where I am arguing that Vālmīki's new move is made, this would mean that Sītā is giving voice to this double divine-human dimension of Rāma's portrayal. And if the *Rāmāyaṇa* itself is apostrophe to Rāma, it too is also a dialogue with God: one that draws in Rāma himself, the 'perfect man', as the poet's first conversation

---

[131] Fred Hardy, *Viraha-Bhakti: The Early History of Ka Devotion in South India* (Delhi, 1983), pp. 5–9, 331–429, 527–34.

[132] Goldman and Sutherland (trans.), *The Rāmāyaṇa of Vālmīki*, Vol. 5: *Sundarakāṇḍa*, p. 58, paraphrasing *Rām* 5.17.1–3, 'a highly figured description on the part of the poet', who continues with an 'extended series of *mālopamā*' – citing 5.13.30–35, right after which Hanumān 'was once more afflicted with uncertainty; for she seemed barely discernible like some vedic text once learned by heart but now nearly lost through lack of recitation' (13.36).

[133] See Hiltebeitel, *Dharma: Its Early History in Law, Religion, and Narrative*, ch. 10 § D; Hiltebeitel, *Reading the Fifth Veda*, ch. 11 § B.2 for specifics and some discussion. Most notably, Brockington and Brockington, *Rāma the Steadfast*, pp. 208–10 as usual inclined toward *bhakti* excisions, think Sītā originally would break off early in her second speech, and that the poem in its early state would not have included the third speech either.

partner, with any reciter or reader able to join the conversation and the beautiful but also very sad wonder of it all.

Now if we look back at what I have called the dialogical situation in Vālmīki's hermitage, we can see some reinforcement of this *bhakti* reading. Brahmā would no longer be taken, as many have done, as a god whose prominence in the *Rāmāyaṇa* exposes a pre-Viṣṇuite stage of the poem's early development. If Brahmā comes to the foreground it is because, both initially and throughout, Viṣṇu is busy being Rāma. If Brahmā has told Vālmīki that everything the poet says will be true, that would certainly include the dialogue Brahmā and the gods have with Viṣṇu in the heavens over the latter's birth as Rāma to counteract Rāvaṇa's boon (*Rām* 1.14.17–15.6). And it would also include what Brahmā himself tells Rāma twice: that he is Viṣṇu – first after Rāvaṇa's death and Sītā's fire ordeal, where, indeed, he adds that Rāma is Hṛṣīkeśa, Madhusūdana, and even Kṛṣṇa[!] (6.105.14–15), and for once that Sītā is Lakṣmī (105.25);[134] and again after Sītā has entered the earth (7 App.I.13 lines 23–26).[135] Yet as a juxtaposition of these two scenes makes as clear as can be, that alone is not where the sad but beautiful wonder of it all lies. It lies in Rāma and Sītā's humanity, through which, after she is gone, Rāma continues to hear his own and Sītā's profound adventure as the first listener.

Again, it will help to consider some traditional receptions of this text. David Shulman makes the point that where the playwright Bhavabhūti revisits Rāma's banishment of Sītā in his play *Uttararāmacarita*. The play is composed for a festival in which Śiva would be the 'first listener', much as the Kerala shadow puppet tradition makes the goddess Bhagavatī the 'primary audience' for *Rāmāyaṇa* performances, which are often presented to her without other audience present.[136] It does not require elaborate argument to say that these creations arise from the dialogical, apostrophic, structures of the seminal text. Divinity listens too. But what Shulman shows so strikingly about Bhavabhūti is that he also keeps Rāma as first listener to his own story and the play of that story 'within the play' – with Lakṣmaṇa there (as always) to 'second' his brother's being first listener when he, Lakṣmaṇa, realizes 'the whole point' of Vālmīki's 'entire poem' to be 'a long, complex, and poignant *J'accuse*'.[137]

For the *Rāmāyaṇa*'s apostrophic structure to be fully realized in performance, however, the first thing it would take would be for such a *j'accuse* to be made before a Rāma temple rather than one housing Śiva or the Goddess. And who better for us (better too for him, from what he lets us see into his thoughts) to have found his way to such a performance and tell us about it than Shulman. We are in the same sequence as Sītā's soliloquies, just a little further along, where Hanumān is about to give Sītā Rāma's signet ring as proof that he is Rāma's messenger. From what Shulman describes of Hanumān's message, one might imagine it eliciting more of a *je pardonne* from Sītā than a *j'accuse*, or, as appropriate at this hopeful point in the story, *un cri de coeur*. But since it magnifies our apostrophic structure a thousand-fold, the note of estrangement will also be identifiable. The play that Shulman and his students watched over the full month of August 2012 for twenty-nine nights is a Kuṭiyāṭṭam drama called *Aṅguliyaṅkam*, or *Drama of the Ring*, by the Kerala poet Śaktibhadra (perhaps tenth century). Hanumān imparts his message mostly in 'the

---

134 As far as I can see this is the only point where the *Rāmāyaṇa* says this of Sītā, who is usually just said to be 'like Śrī'.

135 See n. 115 and 122 above on 7 App.I.13.

136 Shulman, 'Bhavabhūti on Cruelty and Compassion', pp. 61 and 367 n. 16; Cf. Stuart Blackburn, *Inside the Drama House: Rāma Stories and Shadow Puppets in South India* (Berkeley, 1996).

137 Shulman, 'Bhavabhūti on Cruelty and Compassion', pp. 59, 80–82.

silent language of hand- and eye-gesture, *abhinaya*'.[138] Thus for most of the play, 'only a single actor is on stage, playing Hanuman as well as all other relevant roles' excepting that of Sītā, who is represented by a female performer who sits on the left side of the stage, keeps time with cymbals, and, 'through urgent speech', says 'mostly *tado tado*, "And [what happened] next?"'[139]

Once Hanumān finds Sītā,

> Most of the drama ... is taken up by a very long retrospective, in which Hanuman tells Sita, and the audience, including the god who is watching from inside the nearby temple, everything that has happened, or could ever happen, since Ravana captured her in the wilderness – and much else besides. Stories from other parts of the epic, or from its companion-text the *Mahabharata*, or from Hindu history and lore more widely... .[140]

'Every moment is intricate, action packed, resonant with' this 'whole body of pre-existing texts, and irreplaceable'.[141] Yet only 'toward the end of the twenty-ninth night' does Hanumān give Sītā the ring and promise her that Rama will soon arrive to free her.[142]

> In the course of an eight-hour tour de force, Lord Rama was made fully visible to those capable of imagining him together with the actor who manifests him in gesture. Believe me: It is no small matter to create God on stage. We then saw this god as he was, or is, after his wife was kidnapped – grief-stricken to the verge of madness: trying desperately to send her someone, anyone, a bee, a goose, as a messenger with a greeting of comfort and love; hallucinating; hopefully preparing a bed made from leaves and vines for her and for him in the vast wilderness where he is wandering; calling her again and again, in vain, to come to bed. All of the world's loneliness, which is also God's, in its immensity, variety, and depth, was called up into the final scene, an overwhelming culmination.[143]

Add the deep poignancy of Rāma's seeing all this simultaneously from his temple, just as he must listen to Sītā and others in scenes and dialogues of Vālmīki's and Bhavabhūti's staging. Whereas Bhavabhūti gives Rāma the happy ending of a reunion with Sītā, and Hanumān enacts Rāma's whole universe before her in which that fleeting reunion must occur, Vālmīki re-enters his poem only after that reunion has failed. Yet every case has the deferred gratification that Vālmīki structures into the text. Moreover, after Sītā re-enters the earth, Vālmīki leaves us with the question that hangs over from the end of the *Upodghāta*. When Rāma says there that this poem will be 'highly beneficial even for me' and that unnamed listeners should listen to it, this will have to include *first* his own listening to the fading voice of Sītā, whom not only he but nearly everyone – Anasūya, Hanumān, some Rākṣasī women, yes, even Rāvaṇa – loved to talk to. And with that, Vālmīki leaves us with

138 David Shulman, 'Creating and Destroying the Universe in Twenty-Nine Nights'. NYR Blog. http://www.nybooks/com/blogs/nyrblog/2012/nov24/creating-and-destrying-universe-twenty-nine-night/, 2 (here and below, print-out page numbers).

139 Ibid., p. 4.

140 Ibid., p. 3.

141 Ibid., p. 5.

142 Ibid., p. 3.

143 Ibid., pp. 6–7.

little to question as to how Rāma would have gone on listening: not as one who finally understood his own divinity, but 'above all' as a man.

Finally, such apostrophic reverberations are inconceivable in the *Mahābhārata*. Even if Śaunaka and the Ṛṣis of the Naimiṣa Forest may be the *Mahābhārata*'s first 'full' listeners, they and everyone else – including Kṛṣṇa in the *Bhagavad Gītā* and Vyāsa in any number of ways – are so imbricated in the winding dialogical structures of the poem that it could not be said to be addressed to anyone in particular, and certainly not to a deity. (Crothers also focuses on the role of 'listening' in the *Mahābhārata* in this volume, but focuses on the social position of the listener as advisor rather than the rhetorical effect of listening *per se*.) Yet the cases of Kṛṣṇa and Vyāsa may still be contrasted with Vālmīki's new move. As we have noted, Vyāsa is an overhearing presence to his entire creation. And Kṛṣṇa is at times quite pointedly an overhearing presence and mysterious additional listener. Twice he sits silently in the Pāṇḍavas and Draupadī's midst as they hear mysteries told about him, and each time the five and Draupadī are urged to take refuge in him and do so.[144] Vālmīki's new move would then be to bring the poet. hero, heroine, and other audiences to a new common ground by using apostrophe to lift dialogue into a textual space or Naimiṣa Forest where divine and poetic voices can overhear each other.

References

Adluri, Vishwa P., 'Frame Narratives and Forked Beginnings: Or, How to Read the Ādiparvan', *Journal of Vaishnava Studies* 19/2 (2011): 143–210.

———, *Parmenides, Plato and Mortal Philosophy: Return from Transcendence* (London: Continuum, 2011).

———, 'Literary Violence and Literal Salvation: Śaunaka interprets the *Mahābhārata*', *Exemplar: The Journal of South Asian Studies* 1/2 (2012): 45–68.

Adluri, Vishwa and Joydeep Bagchee, *Philology and Criticism* (London: Anthem Press, in press).

———, *The Nay Science: A History of German Indology* (New York: Oxford University Press, 2014).

Austin, Christopher, 'Draupadī's Fall: Snowballs, Cathedrals and Synchronous Readings of the *Mahābhārata*', *International Journal of Hindu Studies* 15/1 (2011): 111–37.

Belvalkar, Shripad Krishna (ed.), 'Śāntiparvan, with Appendix I and Critical Notes' (1954–66), in V.S. Sukthankar et al. (eds), *Mahābhārata: Critical Edition with Harivaṃśa* (24 vols, Poona: Bhandarkar Oriental Research Institute, 1933–70).

Biardeau, Madeleine, *Le Mahābhārata: Un récit fondateur du brahmanisme et son interprétation* (2 vols, Paris: Seuil, 2002).

Blackburn, Stuart, *Inside the Drama House: Rāma Stories and Shadow Puppets in South India* (Berkeley: University of California Press, 1996).

Brockington, John, *The Sanskrit Epics*. Handbuch der Orientalistik, Zweite Abteilung, Indien, Vol. 12. J. Bronkhorst (ed.) (Leiden: Brill, 1998).

[144] See *Mbh* 3.187.50–53, coming after Mārkaṇḍeya's revelations about the Ṛṣi's own emergence from the baby Kṛṣṇa's mouth during the time of the universal dissolution (3.186–7); and 12.326.120–21 in the *Nārāyaṇīya*. See Hiltebeitel, *Dharma: Its Early History in Law, Religion, and Narrative*, pp. 252–60, 591.

Brockington, John, and Mary Brockington (trans.), *Rāma the Steadfast: An Early Form of the Rāmāyaṇa* (London: Penguin, 2006).

Brodbeck, Simon, 'Ekalavya and *Mahābhārata* 1.121–28', *International Journal of Hindu Studies* 10 (2006): 1–34.

———, 'Analytic and Synthetic Approaches in the Light of the Poona Edition of the *Mahābhārata* and *Harivaṃśa*', *Journal of Vaiṣṇava Studies* 19/1 (2011): 223–50.

Brown, Leslie (ed.), *The New Shorter Oxford English Dictionary on Historical Principles* (2 vols, Oxford: Clarendon Press, 1993).

Edgerton, Franklin (ed.), '*Sabhāparvan*. Introduction and Apparatus', in V.S. Sukthankar et al. (eds), *Mahābhārata: Critical Edition*, with *Harivaṃśa* (24 vols, Poona: Bhandarkar Oriental Research Institute 1933–70).

Fitzgerald, James L., 'The Mokṣa Anthology of the Great Bhārata: An Initial Survey of Structural Issues, Themes, and Rhetorical Strategies' (PhD dissertation, University of Chicago, 1980).

———, 'The Rāma Jāmadagnya "Thread" of the *Mahābhārata*: A New Survey of Rāma Jāmadagnya in the Pune Text', in Mary Brockington (ed.), *Stages and Transitions: Temporal and Historical Frameworks in Epic and Purāṇic Literature* (Proceedings of the Second Dubrovnik International Conference on the Epics and Purānas. Zagreb: Croatian Academy of Arts and Sciences, 2002).

Goldman, Robert P. (trans.), *The Rāmāyaṇa of Vālmīki*, vol. 1: *Bālakāṇḍa* (Princeton: Princeton University Press, 1984).

Goldman, Robert P. and Sally J. Sutherland Goldman (trans.), *The Rāmāyaṇa of Vālmīki*, Vol. 5: *Sundarakāṇḍa* (Princeton: Princeton University Press, 1996).

Gombach, Barbara, 'Ancillary Stories in the Sanskrit *Mahābhārata*' (PhD Dissertation, 2 Parts, New York: Columbia University, 2000).

González-Reimann, Luis, *The Mahābhārata and the Yugas: India's Great Epic and the Hindu System of World Ages* (New York: Peter Lang, 2002).

Grünendahl, Reinhold, 'Zu den beiden Gandhamādana-Episoden des *Āraṇyakaparvan*', *Studien zur Indologie und Iranistik* 18 (1993): 103–18.

———, 'Zur Stellung des *Nārāyaṇīya* im *Mahābhārata*', in Peter Schreiner (ed.), *Nārāyaṇīya-Studien* (Wiesbaden: Harrassowitz Verlag, 1997), pp. 197–240.

Hardy, Fred, *Viraha-Bhakti: The Early History of Ka Devotion in South India* (Delhi: Oxford University Press, 1983).

Hiltebeitel, Alf, *The Ritual of Battle: Krishna in the Mahābhārata* (Albany: State University of New York Press, [1976] 1990).

———, 'Purity and Auspiciousness in the Sanskrit Epics', in Frédérique Appfel Marglin and John Carmen (eds), *Essays on Purity and Auspiciousness, Journal of Developing Societies* 1 (1985): 41–54 [= Hiltebeitel, *When the Goddess Was a Woman*, ch. 4].

———, *The Cult of Draupadī*, vol. 1: *Mythologies: From Gingee to Kurukṣetra* (Chicago: University of Chicago Press, 1988).

———, 'The Primary Process of the Hindu Epics', *International Journal of Hindu Studies* 4/3 (2000): 269–88. [= Hiltebeitel, *Reading the Fifth Veda: Essays on the Mahābhārata by Alf Hiltebeitel*, ch. 2].

———, 'Bhīṣma's Sources', in Klaus Karttunen and Petteri Koskikallio (eds), *Vidyārṇavavandanam: Essays in Honour of Asko Parpola*, *Studia Orientalia* 94 (2001), pp. 261–78 [= Hiltebeitel, *Reading the Fifth Veda: Essays on the Mahābhārata by Alf Hiltebeitel*, ch. 13].

———, *Rethinking the Mahābhārata: A Reader's Guide to the Education of Yudhiṣṭhira* (Chicago: University of Chicago Press, 2001).
———, 'Not Without Subtales: Telling Laws and Truths in the Sanskrit Epics', *Journal of Indian Philosophy* 3 (2005): 455–511. [= Hiltebeitel, *Reading the Fifth Veda: Essays on the Mahābhārata by Alf Hiltebeitel*, ch 6].
———, 'Weighting Orality and Writing in the Sanskrit Epics', in Petteri Koskikallio (ed.), *Epics, Khilas, and Purāṇas: Continuities and Ruptures*. Proceedings of the Third International Conference on the Sanskrit Epics and Purāṇas, September 2002, pp. 81–111 (Zagreb: Croatian Academy of Sciences and Arts, 2005) [= Hiltebeitel, *Reading the Fifth Veda: Essays on the Mahābhārata by Alf Hiltebeitel*, ch 1].
———, *Mahābhārata*, in Stanley Wolpert (ed.), *Encyclopedia of India* (4 vols, Detroit: Thompson Gale Corporation, 2006), Vol. 3, pp. 82–93.
———, The *Nārāyanīya* and the Early Reading Communities of the *Mahābhārata*. In Olivelle 2006, pp. 227–55) [= Hiltebeitel, *When the Goddess Was a Woman*, ch. 7].
———, *Rāmāyaṇa*, in Stanley Wolpert (ed.), *Encyclopedia of India* (4 vols, Detroit: Thompson Gale Corporation, 2006), Vol. 3, pp. 390–99.
———, 'Authorial Paths through the Two Sanskrit Epics, Via the *Rāmopākhyāna*', in Robert P. Goldman and Muneo Tokunaga (eds), *Epic Undertakings*, vol. 2 of Petteri Koskikallio and Asko Parpola (gen. eds), *Papers of the 12th World Sanskrit Conference, Helsinki, 13–18 July 2003*, pp. 169–214 (Delhi: Motilal Banarsidass, 2009) [= Hiltebeitel, *Reading the Fifth Veda: Essays on the Mahābhārata by Alf Hiltebeitel*, ch. 10].
———, *Dharma*. Asian Spiritualities Series (Honolulu: University of Hawai'i Press, 2010).
———, 'Between History and Divine Plan: The *Mahābhārata*'s Royal Patriline in Context', in Simon Brodbeck and James Hegarty (eds), Papers from the 2010 Cardiff University Conference on Genealogy in India. *Religions of South Asia* 5/1–2 (2011): 103–25.
———, *Dharma: Its Early History in Law, Religion, and Literature* (New York: Oxford University Press, 2011).
———, 'On Sukthankar's "S" and Some Shortsighted Assessments and Uses of the Pune Critical Edition', *Journal of Vaishnava Studies* 19/2 (2011): 87–126.
———, *Reading the Fifth Veda: Essays on the Mahābhārata by Alf Hiltebeitel*, Vishwa Adluri and Joydeep Bagchee, (eds) (Leiden: E.J. Brill, 2011).
———, 'The Southern Recension's "Śakuntalā" as a First Reading: a Window on the Original and the Second Reading by Kālidāsa', in Saswati Sengupta and Deepika Tandon (eds), *Revisiting Abhijñānaśākuntalam: Love, Lineage and Language in Kālidāsa's Nāṭaka* (Hyderabad: Orient Blackswan, 2011), pp. 17–37.
———, *When the Goddess Was a Woman*. Vishwa Adluri and Joydeep Bagchee (eds) (Leiden: E.J. Brill, 2011).
———, 'The *Mahābhārata* and the Stories Some People Tell about Its Tribal and Earliest Histories', in Neera Misra (ed.). Papers from the International Seminar on the *Mahābhārata*: Its Historicity, Antiquity, Evolution & Impact on Civilization, organized by Neera Misra and the Draupadi Trust (in press: 26 April 2012).
———, 'The *Mahābhārata* and the Stories Some People Tell about It', 2 parts. *Exemplar: The Journal of South Asian Studies* 1 (Fall 2012): 1–26; (Spring 2013).
———, 'From *Ṛṣidharma* to *Vānaprastha*: the Southern Recension Makeover of the *Mahābhārata*'s *Umā-Maheśvara Saṃvāda*', in Adam Bowles, Simon Brodbeck, and Alf Hiltebeitel (eds), Essays from the Epics and Purāṇas Section of the 15th World Sanskrit Conference, New Delhi, January 2012 (descriptive book title only).

———, 'Śiva's *Summa* on *Ṛṣidharma* in the *Umā-Maheśvara Saṃvāda*: The Baseline *Mahābhārata*'s Discourse on Gleaning in the Context of Contemporary Brahmanical and Buddhist Sources' (unsubmitted article in progress).
———, 'Uncanny Domesticities: The Goddess in the *Mahābhārata* and the Correspondence between Girindrashekar Bose and Sigmund Freud' (monograph in progress; tentative title).
Hudson, Emily, 'Disorienting Dharma: Ethics and the Poetics of Suffering in the *Mahābhārata*' (PhD Dissertation, Emory University, 2006).
———, *Disorienting Dharma: Ethics and the Poetics of Suffering in the Mahābhārata* (New York: Oxford University Press, 2013).
Krishnacharya, T.R. and T.R. Vyasacharya, *Sriman Mahābhāratam According to Southern Recension Based on the South Indian Texts with Footnotes and Readings*, vol. 2, *Sabhā Parva*-II. Sri Garib Das Oriental Series, No. 68. First published in Kumbhakonam (Delhi: Sri Satguru Publications, Indian Books Centre, [1906–10] 1991).
Mahadevan, Thennilapuram, 'On the Southern Recension of the *Mahābhārata*, Brahman Migrations, and Brāhmī Paleography', *Electronic Journal of Vedic Studies* 15/2 (2008): 1–143.
———, 'The Three Rails of the *Mahābhārata* Textual Tradition', *Journal of Vaishnava Studies* 19/2 (2011): 23–69.
Mangels, Annettte, *Zur Erzähltechnik im Mahābhārata* (Hamburg: Verlag Dr. Kovač, 1994).
Martel, Yann, *Life of Pi* (Orlando, FL: Harcourt, 2001).
Minkowski, Christopher Z., 'Janamejaya's *Sattra* and Ritual Structure', *Journal of the American Oriental Society* 109/3 (1989): 401–20.
———, 'Snakes, *sattras* and the *Mahābhārata*', in Arvind Sharma (ed.), *Essays on the Mahābhārata* (Leiden: E.J. Brill, 1991), pp. 384–400.
Olivelle, Patrick, *Dharmasūtras: The Law Codes of Ancient India* (Oxford: Oxford University Press, 1999).
——— (trans.), *The Law Code of Manu* (Oxford: Oxford University Press, 2004).
———, 'Manu and Gautama: A Study in Śāstric Intetextuality', in *Language, Texts, and Society: Explorations in Ancient Indian Culture and Religion* (Florence: University of Florence Press and Munshiram Manoharlal, 2005), pp. 261–74.
Patton, Laurie, 'How Do You Conduct Yourself? Gender and the Construction of a Dialogical Self in the *Mahābhārata*', in Simon Brodbeck and Brian Black (eds), *Gender and Narrative in the Mahābhārata* (Oxford: Routledge, 2007), pp. 97–109.
Pollock, Sheldon, 'Ātmānam mānuṣam manye: *Dharmākūtam* on the Divinity of Rāma', *Journal of the Oriental Institute of Baroda* 33 (1984): 505–28.
——— (trans.), *The Rāmāyaṇa of Vālmīki: An Epic of Ancient India*, vol. 2: *Ayodhyākāṇḍa* (Princeton: Princeton University Press, 1986).
Sastri, P.P.S., *The Mahābhārata (Southern Recension) Critically Edited*, vol. 3, *Sabhā Parvan* (Madras: V. Ramaswamy Sastrulu & Sons, 1932).
Sattar, Arshia, *The Rāmāyaṇa. Vālmīki. Abridged and Translated* (New Delhi: Penguin, 2000).
———, 'Inside/Outside: Where is Valmiki in the Story He Tells?', in Laurie Patton and David Haberman (eds), *Notes from A Mandala: Essays in the History of Indian Religions in Honor of Wendy Doniger* (Newark, DE: University of Delaware Press, 2010), pp. 229–43.

Shah, Umakant Premenand, *The Utttarakāṇḍa,: The Vālmīki Rāmāyaṇa*, Vol. 7, in G.H. Bhatt and U.P. Shah (eds), *The Vālmīki Rāmāyaṇa: Critical Edition* (7 vols, Baroda: University of Baroda, 1960–75).

Shulman, David. D., 'Bhavabhūti on Cruelty and Compassion', in Paula Richman (ed.) *Questioning Ramayanas: A South Asian Tradition* (Berkeley: University of California Press, 2001) pp. 49–82.

———, 'Creating and Destroying the Universe in Twenty-Nine Nights', 24 November 2012. NYR Blog. http://www.nybooks/com/blogs/nyrblog/2012/nov24/creating-and-destrying-universe-twenty-nine-night/

Smith, John D., *The Mahābhārata: An Abridged Translation* (London: Penguin, 2009).

Sukthankar, Vishnu S. (ed.), Introduction and Apparatus, '*Ādiparvan*, with Appendix I and Critical Notes', Vol. 1, with Prolegomena, i–cx, in V.S. Sukthankar et al. (eds), *Mahābhārata: Critical Edition* with *Harivaṃśa* (24 vols, Poona: Bhandarkar Oriental Research Institute, 1933–70).

Tokunaga, Muneo, 'Vedic Exegesis and Epic Poetry: A Note on *atrāpyudāharanti*', in Petteri Koskikallio (ed.), *Parallels and Comparisons*. Proceedings of the Fourth Dubrovnik International Conference on the Sanskrit Epics and Purāṇas, September 2005 (Zagreb: Croatian Academy of Sciences and Arts, 2009), pp. 21–30.

Van Buitenen, J.A.B. (trans.), *The Mahābhārata*, vol. 2. *Book 2 The Book of the Assembly Hall; Book 3 The Book of the Forest* (Chicago: University of Chicago Press, 1975).

Witzel, Michael, 'On the Origin of the Literary Device of the "Frame Story" in Old Indian Literature', in H. Falk (ed.), *Hinduismus und Buddhismus: Festschrift für Ulrich Schneider* (Freiburg: Hedwig Falk, 1987), pp. 380–410.

Chapter 3
Didactic Dialogues: Communication of Doctrine and Strategies of Narrative in Jain Literature

Anna Aurelia Esposito

In many works of Jainism, we come across a conspicuous tendency towards instruction, towards visualizing the result of right and wrong deeds and illustrating the true nature of the world. This disposition to instruct, to communicate doctrinal contents to the audience, is highly motivated by the essential role knowledge plays in Jainism: only a deep knowledge of the nature of the self and of others[1] leads to right conduct and eventually to the path of salvation. In this context the dialogical transmission of doctrinal contents is of foremost importance: the representation of doctrinal contents through a conversation between two or more people does not only make didactic communication more vivid and thus more interesting for the audience; there are far more ways to employ dialogue as a means to communicate doctrine, as Jain literature shows. Other chapters in this volume (Nicholson, Osto, Rohlman) suggest a strong link between philosophical doctrine and the dialogical genre. As I will outline below, in Jain texts dialogue can function as legitimation, as proof of the absolute and undoubtable truth of contents; it can be used as a means to embed more stories, sometimes also flashbacks, giving thus explanations for actual facts and conditions; and, in a more subtle way, dialogue can serve as a kind of illustration and recreation of the complex and incomprehensible nature of the world.

Of greatest interest in this connection is the use of dialogue in the most important corpus containing doctrinal passages, the canon of the Śvetāmbaras. Non-canonical scriptures also offer important examples regarding the use of didactic dialogues. Here, Jain narrative literature provides the most interesting approaches. For these reasons, I will limit my investigations to these two textual corpora.

Dialogue in the Canonical Scriptures of the Jains

The oldest testimonies of the Jain religion that we possess today are the canonical scriptures of the Jains, or rather, the canon of the Śvetāmbaras,[2] composed mainly in Ardhamāgadhī, a

---

[1] Compare *Dasaveyāliya* 4.64: *paḍhamaṃ nāṇaṃ tao dayā, evaṃ ciṭṭhai savvasaṃjae| annāṇī kiṃ kāhī, kiṃ vā nāhii cheya pāvagaṃ||* 'First knowledge, then compassion; thus does one remain in full control. How can an ignorant person be compassionate, when he does not know good from evil?' (trans. in Padmanabh Jaini, *The Jaina Path of Purification* (Delhi, [1979] 2001), p. 66).

[2] There are various legends concerning the division of the Jain community into two larger traditions, the Śvetāmbaras ('white-clad') and the Digambaras ('sky-clad') (Paul Dundas, *The Jains* [London and New York, 2002], pp. 46ff.). The reason for the final hardening of the boundaries between both sects was most likely the Council of Valabhī (453 or 466 CE), where exclusively Śvetāmbaras were present, attempting to codify the scriptural tradition (Dundas, *The Jains*, p. 49). The Digambaras, however, consider the canonical scriptures as lost. In the course of time, a kind of 'substitutive canon'

middle-Indic dialect. The canon is divided into several categories, beginning with the twelve *aṅga*s (with the 12th *aṅga* considered as lost), which can, according to Jaini,[3] be broadly categorized into four areas: ecclesiastical law, the examination of false views, doctrine, and finally, narratives for the edification of the laity. Subsidiary to the *aṅga*s there exist twelve *upāṅga*s, consisting of texts dealing with philosophical matters and with cosmology as well as narratives addressed to laymen and laywomen. In the remaining categories it is not possible to determine exactly which scriptures are part of the canon and which are not. The six or sometimes seven *chedasūtra*s, containing ecclesiastical law, are called by Jaini[4] 'a Jaina "book of discipline"' and compared with the Buddhist *Vinaya Piṭaka*. The *mūlasūtra*s, numbering between four and six, deal with a variety of topics pertaining to monastic law, partly in the form of narratives. The *prakīrṇa*s, ten short texts, but sometimes counting up to twenty, contain both ceremonial hymns and descriptions of the rituals to be used in preparation for a holy death. Finally, there are two *cūlikāsūtra*s, epistemological works, that include valuable summaries of the material found in other canonical texts. Since a thorough examination of all parts of the Śvetāmbara canon would go beyond the scope of this study, I would like to focus especially on the *aṅga*s and the *upāṅga*s.

Interestingly, the contents of the various parts of the canon are often embedded in dialogues: Usually, either Jina Mahāvīra's pupil Suhamma (Skt Sudharman) is telling his pupil Jambu about a former discourse given by his master,[5] or Mahāvīra himself is conversing with his pupil Goyama (Skt Gautama).[6] The narrative context is in most cases quite stereotyped: After introducing the names of the city, its king and queen, and the holy site outside the city (*ceia*, Skt *caitya*), where Mahāvīra or Suhamma stayed with their pupils, the text proceeds with the description of Mahāvīra or Suhamma respectively, the congregation approaching him to pay homage and to listen to his sermon, and finally their return home. Only after these preliminaries the conversation between master and pupil starts. To grasp fully the significance of the fact that the contents of the canon are clearly marked as the words of Jina Mahāvīra – be it directly or through the mouth of his pupil – we have to deviate shortly into Jain Universal History: The Jains consider the world as eternal

developed, which consists of a number of important texts that gained a quasi-canonical status, see Maurice Winternitz, *A History of Indian Literature*, Vol. II: *Buddhist Literature and Jaina Literature* (Calcutta: University of Calcutta, 1933), p. 474 and Dundas, *The Jains*, pp. 79–81. For an overview of the canon of the Śvetāmbaras see Jaini, *The Jaina Path of Purification*, pp. 47–77, for the 'substitutive canon' of the Digambaras see pp. 78–85. The texts of the Digambaras will not form part of this chapter.

3 *The Jaina Path of Purification*, p. 53.

4 Ibid., p. 62.

5 For example, the *Āyāraṃgasutta* (Skt *Ācārāṅgasūtra*), the 1st *aṅga*, is beginning with the formula *suyaṃ me āusaṃ! teṇaṃ bhagavayā evam akkhāyaṃ* ('O long-lived [Jambu]! I [Sudharman] have heard the following discourse from the venerable [Mahāvīra].'), while the *Sūyagaḍaṃgasutta* (Skt *Sūtrakṛtāṅgasūtra*), the 2nd *aṅga*, puts a short dialogue on the beginning: *bujjhijja tiuṭṭejjā baṃdhaṇaṃ parijāṇiyā / kim āha baṃdhaṇaṃ vīre? kiṃ vā jāṇaṃ tiuṭṭaī? //1//* ('One should know what causes the bondage of the soul, and knowing [it] one should remove it. [Jambūsvāmin asked Sudharman:] What causes the bondage [of Soul] according to Mahāvīra? and what must one know in order to remove it?' (Hermann Jacobi [trans.], *Jaina Sutras*, translated from Prakrit by Hermann Jacobi, Part II: *The Uttarādhyayana Sūtra, The Sūtrakritāṅga Sūtra* [New York, (1895) 1968], p. 235) – followed by Sudharman's answer, occupying virtually the rest of the book.

6 Three of Mahāvīra's pupils have Goyama as name of their lineage; mostly it refers to Mahāvīra's closest disciple Goyama Iṃdabhūi (Gautama Indrabhūti), see Adelheid Mette, *Die Erlösungslehre der Jaina: Legenden, Parabeln, Erzählungen: Aus dem Sanskrit und Prakrit übersetzt und herausgegeben* (Berlin, 2010), p. 314 with n. 191.

and unalterable as a whole. Two world-periods succeed each other taking turns since eternity and in eternity: A descending world-period (*avasarpiṇī*), in which the moral situation of mankind and their way of living are decreasing more and more, is followed by an ascending world-period (*utsarpiṇī*), in which the human condition becomes gradually better until finally the climax is reached again.[7] In every world-period the mostly mythological sixty-three 'great men' (*mahāpuruṣa* or *śalākāpuruṣa*) appear. Most important among them are the 24 Jinas,[8] born consecutively at a time, when the eternal wisdom, the *dharma*, has been forgotten, to spread it again among mankind. They are not regarded as discoverers, but as witnesses of the liberating truth – a significant difference from the Buddha.[9] Therefore, they are also called 'ford-makers' (*tīrthaṃkara*), that is, they who create a ford through the ocean of *saṃsāra*, revealing the path to salvation, *mokṣa*. Because they have reached the stage of omniscience (*kevala-jñāna*),[10] there can be no doubt in their words. Here, it becomes clear why the participation of Mahāvīra in the discussion is of fundamental consequence: As the last of the 24 Jinas of our descending world-period, Mahāvīra has succeeded in destroying the *karma* that is obscuring the pristine, omniscient nature of the soul. Therefore, every word of Mahāvīra has to be regarded as absolutely trustworthy, since no error is possible for somebody who has reached the stage of omniscience. Here, dialogue functions as legitimation,[11] as proof for the absolute truth of the sacred scriptures.

Conversations between Mahāvīra and his pupils, in most cases Goyama Iṃdabhūi, often take the form of instructional dialogues. The questions of the pupil alternating with the answers by the master not only structure the various subjects, but also transmit the

---

[7] Each world-period is divided into six eras. In some parts of the world, instead of the periodical change of the six eras, the same era prevails forever (for a detailed description see Helmuth von Glasenapp, *Jainism: An Indian Religion of Salvation*, trans. by Shridhar B. Shrotri, Lala Sundar Lal Jain Research Series 14 [Delhi, 1999], pp. 255–8). For further information about cosmology, cosmography and world-history of the Jains see Glasenapp, *Jainism*, pp. 241–346, and Walther Schubring, *The Doctrine of the Jainas: Described after the Old Sources* (Delhi, [1962] 2000), pp. 126–246.

[8] Furthermore, there are the twelve Cakravartin, the 'universal monarchs', destined to rule over the whole of Bharata, and the nine triads of heroes, that consist of one Vāsudeva, one Baladeva and one Prativāsudeva each that live simultaneously. The Vāsudeva and the Baladeva are half-brothers that fight together against their arch-enemy, the Prativāsudeva. The well-known heroes from the Hindu epic *Rāmāyaṇa*, Rāma, Lakṣmaṇa and Rāvaṇa, form the eigth of these triads of heroes, Kṛṣṇa, the most famous incarnation of the Hindu god Viṣṇu, appears together with his half-brother Balarāma and their enemy Jarāsandha as the ninth cathegory.

[9] See Mette, *Die Erlösungslehre der Jaina*, p. 240, as well as Padmanabh S. Jaini, 'On the Sarvajñatva (Omniscience) of Mahāvīra and the Buddha', in L. Cousins et al. (eds), *Buddhist Studies in Honour of I. B. Horner* (Dordrecht and Boston, 1974), pp. 71–90.

[10] The different kinds of knowledge are already listed in the *Nandī*- and *Anuyogadvārasūtra* that belong to the Śvetāmbara canon (see Friedrich Albrecht Weber, 'Über die heiligen Schriften der Jaina', *Indische Studien* 17 [1885]: 8ff. and 21ff.), and also in Umāsvāti's *Tattvārthādhigamasūtra* I.9 (about 2nd century CE; see Winternitz, *A History of Indian Literature*, Vol. II: *Buddhist Literature and Jaina Literature*, p. 578), a philosophical treatise that is recognized by both the Śvetāmbaras and the Digambaras. The most comprehensive form of knowledge, the *kevala-jñāna*, implies the knowledge which the soul has, once it has isolated itself from the limiting influence of *karma* (Jayandra Soni, *The Notion of Āpta in Jaina Philosophy, the 1995 Roop Lal Jain Lecture* [Toronto, 1996], p. 10). For the Jina who continues to live even after his enlightenment in the world see Soni, *The Notion of Āpta in Jaina Philosophy*, pp. 12ff.

[11] The *buddhavacana* ('word of the Buddha') in the Buddhist tradition seems to answer the same purpose, see, for example, Paul J. Griffiths, *On Being Buddha: the Classical Doctrine of Buddhahood* (Albany, 1994), p. 49.

didactical contents in a more vivid way. This kind of dialogue creates for the reader (or listener) the feeling of partaking in the conversation, to be present at Mahāvīra's sermon, and to hear the authentic words of the Jina. The sentiment to be addressed directly by the master increases the emotional identification with the contents. Dialogues of that kind are quite prevalent in the Jain canon; in most cases, the questions and answers are extremely formalized and systematized.[12] One of the most prominent canonical works containing dialogues deviating from this rigid pattern is the *Viyāhapannatti* (Skt *Vyākhyāprajñapti*, 'Proclamation of Explanations'), the 5th *aṅga*, especially the chapters I–XX.[13] It is quite difficult to describe its contents, as totally different subject-matters succeed each other, without ever being linked up in a real train of thought. Deleu remarks:

> The diversity of the topics discussed and in many cases that of the persons and the circumstances attending these discussions all but defy methodical description. That is because here we have a record, as a matter of fact the only really important canonical record, of what M[ahā]v[īra]'s teaching actually was like, not of what later systematization has made of it. Of course tradition has, in many ways, formalized this record … . The important point, however, is that … M[ahā]v[īra] here appears more as an active personality set against the background of its environmental condition and circumstances. In other words: the nucleus sayas [chapters, A.A.E.] of the Viy[āhapannatti] are, or rather contain, the only genuine dialogue text … to be found in the canon, the example imitated by would-be dialogue texts.[14]

The usual pattern in the *Viyāhapannatti* [hereafter *Viy.*] is Goyama questioning Mahāvīra on one subject after the other, mostly with a very loose concatenation of topics and ending invariably with the affirmative words *s'evaṃ bhaṃte! s'evaṃ bhaṃte!* ('So it is, lord! So it is indeed!')[15] There are, however, certain dialogues which deviate from this scheme. Thus also the disciples Roha (*Viy.* I.6, 288–308),[16] Maṇḍiyaputta (*Viy.* III.3, 133–51), Māgandiyaputta (*Viy.* XVIII.3, 56–85) and several senior monks (*Viy.* V.4, 78–82; X.5, 64–98) approach Mahāvīra as interlocutors, propounding him various problems.[17] While Roha and

[12] As Deleu remarks: 'In this connection it may be noted again that whenever we speak of "discussions", "dialogues" etc. these terms do not mean that the texts actually record real conversations. In fact the extreme formalization of the questions and answers hardly once allows of a rudimentary form of conversation…'. Jozef Deleu, *Viyāhapannatti (Bhagavaī), The Fifth Anga of the Jaina Canon: Introduction, Critical Analysis, Commentary & Indexes*, Lala Sundar Lal Jain Research Series 10 (Delhi, [1970] 1996), p. 36.

[13] Chapters I–XX may be regarded as nucleus of the *Viyāhapannatti*, to which chapter XXV is connected. Chapters XXI–XXIV and XXVI–XLI are obvious accretions, which becomes clear through their uniform contents and the uniform structure of their dialogue (or 'would-be dialogue', as Deleu calls it), Goyama invariably questioning Mahāvīra in the Guṇasilaya sanctuary near Rāyagiha (cf. Deleu, *Viyāhapannatti*, p. 19).

[14] Deleu, *Viyāhapannatti*, pp. 34ff.

[15] Contrary to this, in many canonical texts dealing with doctrinal contents we find quite uniform dialogues, Mahāvīra answering Goyama's questions, in which doctrinal domains are systematically explored. As Deleu states, there 'the would-be dialogue only serves didactical purposes' (Deleu, *Viyāhapannatti*, p. 24).

[16] The references are given as *sata*, *uddesa* and verses respectively. The numbering of the verses corresponds with the edition of the *Aṃgasuttāṇi* mentioned in the bibliography.

[17] Occasionally questions are posed in the *Viyāhapannatti* to persons other than Mahāvīra, but in such cases Mahāvīra afterwards confirms or complements the answers. This is the case in *Viy.*

Māgandiyaputta are of minor importance in the Śvetāmbara canon,[18] Maṇḍiyaputta as Mahāvīra's 6th *gaṇadhara*[19] is a more prominent figure. Interestingly enough, neither their quite formulaic characterization nor the way in which they approach their master deviates siginificantly from each other or from the main interlocutor Goyama. The same holds true for the unnamed senior monks. Thus, the order of Mahāvīra in its entirety – younger and older monks as well as prominent figures like Goyama and Maṇḍiyaputta – presents itself as a uniform entity. The uniformity is expressed particularly through the dialogues of its members with Mahāvīra.

We meet also gods approaching Mahāvīra. But contrary to the Buddhist *Nikāya*s, where gods approaching the Buddha engage in discussions resulting in a demonstration of the superior knowledge and power of the Buddha[20], the gods are usually plainly depicted as paying homage to the Jina and leaving again without further dialogues or discussions. Their presence seems to be most of all noteworthy for inspiring Goyama to pose a number of questions about the god's majesty, its karmic cause and his future. Thereupon Mahāvīra describes the former birth of the god in question, resulting in its birth as a god, answers various questions about his present power, the duration of his life-span (*sthiti*) etc., and predicts his future birth (e.g. in *Viy.* III.1, 25–53; III.2, 77–132; XVI.2, 33–40; XVIII.2, 38–55). Thus, not the displaying of the superior understanding of the Jina, but the demonstration of his omniscient knowledge of the world including the past, the present and the future seems to be the main target of his encounters with gods. This is also demonstrated by the few cases that deviate from this general pattern: In *Viy.* V.4, 83–8, for example, two gods appear and ask Mahāvīra in their mind a question, answered equally silently by the Jina. Witnessing this silent dialogue, Goyama Iṃdabhūi approaches his master – but before he can raise a question, Mahāvīra makes clear that he can read his pupil's mind like an open book. This dialogue gives Mahāvīra again the opportunity to demonstrate his ability to know everything, even the thoughts of other beings: he knows about the questions that arose in Goyama's mind, as he had before perceived the thoughts of the gods.[21]

Instructional dialogues are, however, not limited to Mahāvīra and his pupils. For example, in the *Nāyādhammakahāo* (Skt *Jñātādharmakathāḥ*, 'Examples and religious narratives'), the 6th *aṅga*, the beautiful princess and 19th *tīrthaṃkara*[22] Mallī enlightens her six suitors

II.5, 92–110, where certain Elders of Pārśva's creed instruct a group of Jain laymen. Goyama, asked by some people about his opinion, transmits the question to Mahāvīra, who approves of the tenets. Likewise in XI.12, 174–85, Mahāvīra approves of Isibhaddaputta's answers regarding divine rebirths (see also Deleu, *Viyāhapannatti*, pp. 36ff.), and in X.4, 42–63, he supports Goyama, who is not able to completely satisfy his condisciple Sāmahatthi's desire of knowledge. Only once in the *Viyāhapannatti*, in the discussion between Niyaṇṭhīputta with his condisciple Nārāyaputta (V.8, 200–207), Mahāvīra plays no role at all.

18 Roha and Māgandiyaputta are mentioned in Mehta & Chandras' *Prakrit Proper Names* only with reference to the passages above.

19 A *gaṇadhara* or 'group-leader' is the head of a group, comprising between 300 and 500 monks. Mahāvīra had eleven *gaṇadhara*s, heading nine *gaṇa*s or 'groups', see Schubring, *The Doctrine of the Jainas*, p. 44.

20 See the chapter by Nichols in the present volume.

21 In the same direction goes Mahāvīra's encounter with God Gaṅgadatta (*Viy.* XVI.5, 54–75), also deviating from the above-mentioned pattern: Mahāvīra displays his omniscient knowledge by predicting the imminent arrival of the sinless and orthodox god Gaṅgadatta, who had a dispute with a sinful heretical god and wanted to approach Mahāvīra to propound him his problem.

22 In the Digambaras' opinion, a woman cannot obtain salvation for various reasons; therefore, they reject the possibility of a female *tīrthaṃkara* and worship Mallī as male Mallinātha. For more

about the disgusting constitution of the body and the vanity of love's pleasures. As she reminds them of their former birth as prince Mahābala and his six childhood friends who renounced together the world, her suitors are ready to embrace true religion again and follow her into homelessness (*Nāyādhammakahāo* [hereafter *Nāyā.*] I.8, Vol. 1, 153b.9–154b.6). The memory of his former life also inspired minister Teyaliputta to renounce the world. His wife Poṭṭilā, who wanted to become a Jain nun, obtained his permission only on condition that she would return after her death to instruct him. She became a god and, according to her promise, led him again to the right path. Thus, remembering the thorough study of the holy scripts in his former life, Teyaliputta renounced the world and dedicated his further life to religion (*Nāyā.* I.14).

Quite interesting are dialogues culminating in the conversion of Mahāvīra's dialogue partner. Deleu mentions for the *Viyāhapannatti* seven 'well-chosen cases', that is, 'conversions of such persons as are representative of the different classes of people addressed by Mahāvīra'[23]: a monk of Pārśva's creed, a brahmin, a king, a noble lord, a noble lady, a merchant, and a dissident. In all these cases dialogue plays a crucial role; there are, however, significant differences in the individual narrations, underlined through the setting of the various dialogues. The least spectacular conversion story is that of Gaṃgeya, a monk of Pāsa's (Pārśva's) creed (*Viy.* IX.32, 77–136),[24] as it bears the most resemblance to the common dialogues between Goyama and Mahāvīra: immediately after his arrival Gaṃgeya starts to question Mahāvīra, realizing after some time that Mahāvīra is all-knowing and all-seeing.[25] As is always the case with followers of Pārśva's creed, he is admitted to the Jain order of monks by merely expressing the wish to change over from 'the fourfold dharma' to 'the dharma of five vows and confession' (*cāujjāmāo dhammāo paṃca-mahavvaïyaṃ sappaḍikkamaṇaṃ dhammaṃ uvasaṃpajjittāṇaṃ*).[26] The closeness between both faiths is underlined by the similarity of this dialogue and its setting with the conversations between Mahāvīra and his followers.

This is not the case with Mahāvīra's discourse with Khaṃdaga Kaccāyaṇa (Skt Skandaka Kātyāyana), a learned brahmin ascetic (*Viy.* II.1, 20–73). The record of his conversion abounds in details on his profession and his further spiritual career, indicating probably that it was thought of as a memorable feat.[27] Since Khaṃdaga had not been able to answer the questions presented to him by Mahāvīra's lay-disciple Piṃgalaga, he decides to approach Mahāvīra. This gives Mahāvīra the chance to demonstrate his omniscience and, finally, the superiority of Jain above brahmanical wisdom in more than one way: he informs Goyama about the imminent arrival of Khaṃdaga and the reason for his coming. Goyama

---

details about the Digambara versions of Mallinātha see Gustav Roth, Mallī-Jñāta: *Das achte Kapitel des Nāyādhammakahāo im sechsten Aṅga des Śvetāmbara Jainakanons: Herausgegeben, übersetzt und erläutert*, Monographien zur Indischen Archäologie, Kunst und Philologie, 4 (Wiesbaden, 1983), pp. 49–57.

23 Deleu, *Viyāhapannatti*, p. 40.

24 As can be understood by the canonical texts, Pāsa's system bears many similarities with that of Mahāvīra. Mahāvīra, however, developed the practical ethics beyond Pāsa's ideas, replacing 'the fourfold morality' (*cāujjāma dhamma*) by 'the dharma of five vows and confession' (*paṃca-mahavvaïya sappaḍikkamaṇa dhamma*), eliminating thus a certain vagueness in the term of his predecessor (cf. Schubring, *The Doctrine of the Jainas*, p. 30).

25 *tappabhitiṃ ca ṇaṃ se gaṃgeye aṇagāre samaṇaṃ bhagavaṃ mahāvīraṃ paccabhijāṇaï savvaṇṇuṃ savvadarisiṃ* (*Viy.* IX.32, 133).

26 See Deleu, *Viyāhapannatti*, p. 41.

27 Ibid., p. 40.

then welcomes Khaṃdaga, intimating that Mahāvīra has already foretold the circumstances of his coming. These facts are repeated again by Mahāvīra before enlightening Khaṃdaga (and the audience) on the points in question. After Mahāvīra has been able to satisfy Khaṃdaga's doubts, Khaṃdaga asks permission to join Mahāvīra's order. Compared to the conversion of Gaṃgeya, the monk of Pārśva's creed, the conversion of Khaṃdaga is much more elaborated, placing more emphasis on details of the convert and dwelling three times on the fact that he had not been able to answer Piṃgalaga's questions.[28] The dialogue as well as its setting make clear that it is obviously far more difficult – and consequently far more prestigious – to convert a learned brahmin ascetic than a monk of Pārśva's creed.

The same holds true for the conversion of King Siva of Hatthiṇāpura (Skt Hastināpura) (*Viy.* XI.9, 57–89), who after his abdication became an ascetic, representing thus at the same time Mahāvīra's royal audience and the vast comunity formed by all sorts of anchorites living on the banks of the river Ganges.[29] Having reached a limited extraordinary wisdom through his austerities, he was believed to be omniscient. Mahāvīra, however, proved the limitation of Siva's knowledge, whereupon the former king asked him permission to join his order.

Quite rapid (and quite unsteady) was the conversion of Jamāli, a young nobleman of Khattiyakuṃḍa (Skt Kṣatriyakuṇḍa, *Viy.* IX.33, 156–245): after hearing a sermon of Mahāvīra he decided immediately to renounce the world. He had to struggle hard to gain the permission of his parents, but finally they resigned. Jamāli's entering into the order was celebrated with great pomp. Jamāli studied the holy scriptures and practised many fasts; but finally he strived for independence. He left Mahāvīra's group in the company of five hundred monks that had renounced the world together with him. After some time, doubts arouse on certain points of his master's teachings. He spread his erroneous teachings, claiming even that he had reached omniscience – which was easily disproved by Goyama, unfortunately of no effect on Jamāli. Jamāli's story, very rich in lively dialogues, visualizes the tragedy of an enthusiastic youth who became, due to his stubbornness and his arrogance, the first heretic in the history of the Jain Church.

Contrary to this young nobleman, the noble woman Jayantī (*Viy.* XII.2, 41–65), already a Jain laywoman, is not rushing to join Mahāvīra's order after hearing his sermon. Only after a long conversation with Mahāvīra, discussing various topics concerning the qualities of the soul, she decides to become a nun. Jayantī's discussion with Mahāvīra does not differ substantially from dialogues between the master and his male followers. Although female speakers appear considerably less than their male counterparts, they have – at least in the tradition of the Śvetāmbaras – usually the same speaking authority as male speakers. This is reflected by the existence of a female *tīrthaṃkara*, Mallī, whose story has been mentioned above.

Exceptional is merchant Sudaṃsaṇa's dialogue with Mahāvīra (*Viy.* XI.11), as it is the only narration of this group of 'conversion stories' containing a very detailed sub-story. Questioned by the open-minded citizen of Vāṇiyaggāma (Skt Vāṇijyagrāma) about the different concepts of time, Mahāvīra illustrates one of his answers with the elaborate story of prince Mahābala, who renounced the world after witnessing a sermon of monk Dhammaghosa. After his death he gained a divine existence in the heaven Baṃbhaloga (Skt

---

[28] First this fact is told in the course of the story, then it is repeated by Goyama and finally by Mahāvīra, linked to the question if this account is true – which is answered by Khaṃdaga in the affirmative.

[29] Ibid.

Brahmaloka); then he was born again as the same merchant Sudaṃsaṇa in Vāṇiyaggāma. In hearing this account, Sudaṃsaṇa gained knowledge of his previous lives and decided to join Mahāvīra's order.

In each of these seven cases, the dialogue is not simply a means to document the conversion of the dialogue partner in question. Through its special setting, its close resemblance to conversations of the master and his disciples, or its conspicuous elaboration, the dialogue conveys subtle differences between the individual converts and highlights the Jina's superiority over them.

Quite interesting are in this connection dialogues that contain refutations of dissidents,[30] in some cases even leading on to the opponent's conversion. In the *Viyāhapannatti* we witness, besides the quite stereotyped refutation of some anonymous opponents' views,[31] the doubts of eleven dissidents (probably Ājīvikas)[32] regarding the fundamental entities (*atthikāya*, Skt *astikāya*). Kālodāi, one of the group, enters into a dispute with Mahāvīra and is rather rapidly[33] converted (*Viy.* VII.10, 212–33) – again a clear sign of the superiority of Mahāvīra's doctrine and his charismatic personality. In the *Nāyādhammakahāo*, Thāvaccāputta, a pupil of the 22nd *tīrthaṃkara* Ariṭṭhanemi, has to spend comparatively more energy to convince Suya, a follower of the Sāṃkhya school. In this dialogue, Thāvaccāputta is not outwitted by the ambiguity of Suya's three questions, defining the ambiguous words thoroughly and thus enlightening his opponent (*Nāyā.* I.5, Vol. 1, 112b.13–114a.3).[34] One of the most impressive and elaborated examples in Jain canonical literature is the vivid discussion between the materialistic King Paesi and the princely renouncer Kesi.[35] 'The Story of Paesi', *Paesikahāṇayaṃ* (Skt *Pradeśikathānaka*), forms the kernel of the *Rāyapaseṇiya*

---

30 *annaütthiya*, Skt *anyayūthika* or rather **anyatūrthika* (Pischel, *A Grammar of the Prākrit Languages*, §58), also *paraütthiya.*

31 The *annaütthiya*s of anonymous dissidents are generally treated in the following way: Goyama informs Mahāvīra about a particular view of the dissidents and asks his opinion on it. Mahāvīra declares this view as heretical and proclaims another view in this concern. For a thorough description and references in the *Viyāhapannatti* see Deleu, *Viyāhapannatti*, p. 39.

32 Ibid., p. 38.

33 After a concise description of the five *atthikāya*s Mahāvīra answers two questions put forward by Kālodāi. Kālodāi, enlightened, asks to hear the true religion and subsequently joins the spiritual order of Mahāvīra.

34 As Bollée remarks (Willem B. Bollée, *The Story of Paesi (Paesi-kahāṇayaṃ): Soul and Body in Ancient India. A Dialogue on Materialism. Text, Translation, Notes and Glossary*. Beiträge zur Kenntnis südasiatischer Sprachen und Literaturen 8 [Wiesbaden, 2002], p.1), this dialogue in the *Nāyādhammakahāo* is dependent on the nearly identical dispute between the brahmin Somila and Mahāvīra in *Viy.* XVIII.10, 204–24. Suya (in *Viy.* Somila) first asks in Thāvaccāputta's (in *Viy.* Mahāvīra's) well-being. As the words used can be understood also in another way, Thāvaccāputta (Mahāvīra) feels constrained to accurately define the terms. The same applies for the next question, namely whether *sarisavayā, māsa* and *kulatthā* may be eaten (again the quite ambiguous words are carefully defined in the answer). Finally Suya (Somila) wants to know whether Thāvaccāputta (Mahāvīra) is one or two, imperishable, immutable and stationary or whether he has different forms in past, present and future. Thāvaccāputta (Mahāvīra) declares himself to be all of these. After his explanations Suya (Somila) is convinced. While in the *Nāyādhammakahāo* Suya, the follower of the Sāṃkhya school, joins with his disciples Thāvaccāputta's order, in the *Viyāhapannatti* the brahmin Somila becomes a layman.

35 The discussion of Paesi and Kesi has in Buddhist literature a parallel in the dialogue between King Pāyāsi and *kumāra* Kassapa in *Dīghanikāya* II.316ff. See Ernst Leumann, *Das Aupapātika Sūtra, erstes Upāṅga der Jaina. I. Theil: Einleitung, Text und Glossar*, Abhandlungen für die Kunde des Morgenlandes, VIII.2 (Leipzig, 1883), pp. 470–90, and Bollée, *The Story of Paesi*, pp. 1–9.

(Skt *Rājapraśnī*?),[36] the second *upāṅga* of the Śvetāmbara canon, and is embedded in a dialogue between Mahāvīra and his pupil Goyama. The *Rāyapaseṇiya* starts with the description of the setting of the story and the persons involved: the city Āmalakappā, the holy site Aṃbasālavaṇa outside the city, King Seya and Queen Dhāriṇī. Then the scene shifts to the god Sūriyābha (Skt Sūryābha) in his heavenly abode. Thanks to his unrestricted vision, he realizes that Mahāvīra stays at the holy site Aṃbasālavaṇa near the city Āmalakappā. With great pomp he visits the holy site and pays homage to the Jina. Asked by his pupil Goyama,[37] Mahāvīra describes the magnificence of Sūriyābha and narrates, how he got all this glory – and here the *Paesikahāṇayaṃ* starts: In his last birth, god Sūriyābha had been born as Paesi (Skt Pradeśin), ruler of Seyaviyā (Skt Setavyā) and a wicked materialist. One day he meets the princely renouncer Kesi (Skt Keśin).[38] A lively (and not always polite) dialogue about the existence of a soul independent of the body developes, in which the king's thesis or objection and the renouncer's antithesis or refutation succeed one another.[39] Finally Kesi is able to dispel Paesi's doubts, and the king is ready to hear the doctrine. The former materialist Paesi turns into a pious layman and no longer pays attention to his affairs, his subjects or even his harem. Feeling neglected, his queen Sūriyakantā puts an end to his life. He is reborn in the Sohammakappa as god Sūriyābha and will attain in his following birth final emancipation, as Jina Mahāvīra lets Goyama know in the frame dialogue.

The *Rāyapaseṇiya* is by far not the only example of a dialogue that forms a frame story for a number of secondary stories – or even other dialogues. One example out of many in the canonical literature is the *Vivāgasuyaṃ* (Skt *Vipākaśrutam*, 'the text of the ripening [of actions]'), the 11th *aṅga*. Its different chapters proceed invariably according to the following pattern: Iṃdabhūi sees some extraordinary things happen and questions his master Mahāvīra about it. Mahāvīra explains the actual incident and tells Iṃdabhūi all about the former and future births of the persons involved. This dialogue is only possible with a *kevalin*[40] like Mahāvīra as narrator – nobody else's account about past and future events could be regarded as absolutely reliable, and, above all, as credible for the audience.[41]

---

36 Already Weber ('Über die heiligen Schriften der Jaina', *Indische Studien* 16 [1883]:. 382–4) and Leumann (*Das Aupapātika Sūtra*, 1883, p. 2, and 1885, p. 536) had various suggestions concerning the origins, namely the sanskritized forms of 'Rāyapaseṇiya / Rāyapaseṇaïyya' and 'Paesi'; for a summary and further suggestions see Bollée, *The Story of Paesi*, pp. 9ff., as well as Piotr Balcerowicz, 'Monks, Monarchs, and Materialists,,' *Journal of Indian Philosophy* 33 (2005): 571ff. For a German translation of the *Rāyapaseṇiya* see Leumann (*Das Aupapātika Sūtra*, 1885, pp. 503–27), and for an English translation with valuable annotations, see Bollée, *The Story of Paesi*, pp. 15–221.

37 Here we leave the frame narration; for the rest of the *Rāyapaseṇiya*, except for some lines at the end, the narrator is Mahāvīra. In his narration a further dialogue, that of Paesi and Kesi, is embedded.

38 Kesi is called a follower of Pāsa, the 23rd *tīrthaṃkara*. In Bollée's opinion (*The Story of Paesi*, p. 273), Passa / Pāsa is 'wrongly sanskritized as Pārśva'. He proposes a new etymology and suggests '*(U)pāśva(sena)*'. For a discussion of this suggestion and some futher notes see Balcerowicz, 'Monks, Monarchs, and Materialists: 577–9.

39 Paesi's arguments can be summarized in the following way: If a soul independent from the body would exist, his grandparents would have warned him from their infernal or heavenly abode, respectively. Furthermore, in experiments with the bodies of criminals he had found no evidence of a soul. And if a soul different from the body would exist, all beings should have the same abilities, independent from their age, size etc.

40 A *kevalin* is somebody who possesses *kevala-jñāna*, omniscience.

41 The same pattern occurs more often in the Jaina canon: In the 8th *upāṅga*, called *Nirayāvalī* or *Kappiyāo* (Skt *Kalpikāḥ*), ten queens of the deceased King Seṇia ask Mahāvīra about the future of their sons who are fighting on the battlefield. Mahāvīra informs them of the death of their sons. Questioned

Furthermore, in the *Vivāgasuyaṃ* Mahāvīra's words are embedded in another dialogue – the dialogue between Mahāvīra's pupil Suhamma (Skt Sudharman) and his pupil Jambu, who questions his master about the contents of the 11th *aṅga* preached by Jina Mahāvīra. This 'double dialogue' as frame story we also encounter partly[42] in the aforementioned *Nāyādhammakahāo*, where, on the demand of Jambu, Suhamma narrates the stories told by Mahāvīra to his monks, in order to show them the consequences of wrong and right behaviour – in this and in the next lives. Actually, several parts of the Śvetāmbara canon are embedded in this 'double dialogue'[43] – a quite astonishing fact that raises the question of why Mahāvīra's conversations with his pupils had to be framed by Suhamma's dialogue with Jambu. One explanation for this phenomenon may lie in the fact that in Jain canonical literature the unnamed speaker of the *Āyāraṃgasutta* (Skt *Ācārāṅgasūtra*, 'the book of conduct'), the first and most probably oldest *aṅga*, is identified with Suhamma, explaining Mahāvīra's words to his pupil Jambu. Later strata of Jain canonical literature might have adopted this dialogical embedding to affix an ancient character to their texts. This form of dialogical embedding is not only continued in the narrative literature of the Jains, but even developed to perfection, adding through artfully intertwined dialogues an important didactic dimension, as we will see in the following.

Didactic Dialogues in Jain Narrative Literature[44]

In the canonical scriptures of the Jains, dialogue is used strategically to legitimate and to embed the doctrinal contents; this is continued in Jain narrative literature, carrying certain features to extremes. Quite interesting in this respect is the oldest preserved text of Jain narrative literature, the *Vasudevahiṇḍī* ('Vasudeva's wanderings', ca. 5th century CE) of the Jain monk Saṅghadāsa, written in an old style of Jaina-Māhārāṣṭrī.[45] The *Vasudevahiṇḍī* links the contents of the nowadays lost *Bṛhatkathā* of Guṇāḍhya, the source of many Indian narrative and dramatic texts, in an unique way with the Jain Universal History described above. Contrary to the other works[46] of the *Bṛhatkathā*-tradition, however, the intention to transmit didactical contents through entertaining stories, is much more evident in the

by Iṃdabhūi, he reveals in which hell the single princes are dwelling at present and what will be their future destiny. In the 10th and 11th *upāṅga*, the *Pupphiāo* and the *Pupphacūliyāo* (Skt *Puṣpikāḥ* and *Puṣpacūlikāḥ*), Mahāvīra is narrating to his pupil the past history of various gods and godesses, who have arrived to pay him homage.

42 Here only in some chapters (*Nāyā*. I.1, I.6, I.10, I.11, I.13 and I.16) the 'original' dialogue – Mahāvīra replying to Goyama Iṃdabhūi's question – is retained.

43 As, for example, the *upāṅgas* 8–12.

44 I will limit myself here on Jain narrative literature of the classical period, including works on the *mahāpuruṣas*.

45 The author, Saṅghadāsa, claims in his foreword that the adventures of Vasudeva that he is going to tell have been transmitted from teacher to teacher (*guruparaṃparāgayaṃ vasudevacariyaṃ*) (*Vasudevahiṇḍī* [*Vh.*] 1.16), back to Mahāvīra's pupil Sudharman, who told the story to his disciple Jambu (*Vh.* 2.2 f.). As we can assume that this transmission has taken place orally, it might account for the distinctive dialogical structure of the *Vasudevahiṇḍī*.

46 Apart from the *Vasudevahiṇḍī* we have the following surviving versions of the *Bṛhatkathā*: Three works written in Sanskrit, Buddhasvāmin's *Bṛhatkathāślokasaṃgraha* (8th or 9th century CE), Kṣemendra's *Bṛhatkathāmañjarī* (dated 1037 CE) and Somadeva's *Kathāsaritsāgara* (composed between 1063 and 1081 CE); furthermore, one work written in Old Tamil, Koṅku Vēḷir's *Peruṅkatai* (10th century CE).

Vasudevahiṇḍī.[47] The main story of the *Bṛhatkathā* serves thereby as a kind of framework, that is not only overgrown with an abundance of secondary stories, but also wrapped in several narrative layers of pure Jain origin. The means to connect the various stories with each other is in most cases the dialogue. As it is not only the oldest work of its kind, but also a prime example of different usages of the didactic dialogue, I will focus in the following primarily on the *Vasudevahiṇḍī*.

Most conspicuous is in the *Vasudevahiṇḍī*, as in some other works of Jain narrative literature, the continuation of the 'double dialogue' as frame story, in which Suhamma and Mahāvīra are the narrators.[48] Contrary to the parallel situations in the Jain canon, their dialogue partners shift in Jain narrative literature from the sphere of spirituality to a more worldly realm: Suhamma is not conversing any more with his pupil Jambu, but with King Koṇia, and telling him about a former conversation of Jina Mahāvīra with Koṇia's father, King Seṇia of Rāyagiha (Skt Rājagṛha).[49] In this way the respective works follow apparently the canonical tradition, legitimizing their contents as words of the Jina and thus as absolutely true. By replacing the ascetic dialogue partner with a royal one, however, the shifting of emphasis becomes implicitly clear: The contents are of a more secular kind, pure doctrinal passages are rare and integrated into fascinating stories, more suitable for the new target audience consisting of laymen and laywomen instead of monks and nuns.[50]

The *Vasudevahiṇḍī*, however, does not content itself with a mere two narrative layers as frame story. Dialogues between various characters lead us deeper and deeper into the different narrative layers and leave ample space for parables, similes and instructive stories. Instead of narrating a story in a chronological way as, for example, Hemacandra (CE 1089–1172) does in his *Triṣaṣṭiśalākāpuruṣacarita* (The lives of sixty-three illustrious persons) and the proceeding *Sthavirāvalīcarita* (The lives of the line of the [Jain] Elders), the *Vasudevahiṇḍī* often uses not one, but several frames, thus presenting the narrative as a series of embedded conversations from different times and places. This accumulation of narrative layers through dialogues is well known from the epic and narrative literature of the Hindus, but it is surpassed by Jain narrative literature, particularly in the *Vasudevahiṇḍī*. I would like to illustrate this peculiarity by a quite striking example: the story of the former births of Usabha (Skt Ṛṣabha), the first *tīrthaṃkara* of this world-period. It is enwrapped in several narrative layers:[51] The first narrative layer consists in King Koṇia's dialogue with

47 For a more detailed comparison of the *Vasudevahiṇḍī* and the *Bṛhatkathā* / *Bṛhatkathā*-tradition in this respect see Anna Aurelia Esposito, 'How to Combine the *Bṛhatkathā* with Jain Universal History – Reflections on Saṅghadāsa's *Vasudevahiṇḍī*', in Jayandra Soni (ed.), *Jaina Studies: Proceedings of the DOT 2010 Panel in Marburg, Germany* (New Delhi, 2012), pp. 201–12.

48 In Jinasena's *Ādipurāṇa* (9th century, written in Sanskrit), Gautama takes the place of his fellow pupil Suhamma, equally in Puṣpadanta's *Mahāpurāṇa Tisaṭṭhimahāpurisaguṇālaṃkāra* (completed in 965 CE, written in Apabhraṃśa).

49 Seṇia (Skt Śreṇika) is identical with King Bimbisāra of Buddhist sources, his son Koṇia (also Kūṇia, Skt Kūṇika) with Ajātasattu.

50 The fact that in the *Vasudevahiṇḍī* Mahāvīra's dialogue partner is of royal descent does not necessarily suggest that this text was meant for courtly audiences – or rather, not for courtly audiences only. The text as a whole clearly shows an urban setting, attaching great weight to 'middle-class' professional groups like merchants. I would suggest as target group of the *Vasudevahiṇḍī* a literate urban audience, comprising besides educated citizens also the aristocracy.

51 For an overview see Figure 3.1 on p. 95. For a study of the different versions of the story of Jina Usabha and their position in the respective works see Anna Aurelia Esposito, 'Life Before Life Before Life – an Exceptional Perspective on Jina Usabha's Biography', *International Journal of*

the Jain monk Suhamma. During their conversation, Suhamma tells Koṇia about an earlier meeting between Jina Mahāvīra and King Seṇia, Koṇia's father (second narrative layer). During that meeting Mahāvīra told Seṇia the story of King Vasudeva's grandsons (third narrative layer). In the course of this narration, Vasudeva recounts his own adventures to his grandsons (fourth narrative layer). Here starts the actual main story of the *Vasudevahiṇḍī*, borrowed from the *Bṛhatkathā*-tradition. It is interspersed with numerous secondary stories, leaving room not only for various narrations about the *śalākāpuruṣa*s, the sixty-three 'great men' of Jain Universal History, but also for the transmission of religious contents. The means to insert all these stories is exclusively the dialogue. As in the case of the former lives of Jina Usabha, an old, (seemingly) low-caste woman[52] is offering Vasudeva her granddaughter in marriage. Vasudeva refuses, pointing to their difference in social status. The old woman responds with a long story about the origins of her family, containing Usabha's birth, life and renunciation, and his first begging for alms (fifth narrative layer). In this strain of the narrative, passers-by ask Sijjaṃsa (Śreyāṃsa), Usabha's first donor, how he knew what alms were to be given. Sijjaṃsa then has occasion to relate his and Usabha's former births: Their birth as twins in the Uttarakurus (sixth narrative layer) and the female twin's memory of their former life as the god Laliyaṃga and his wife Sayaṃpabhā, as she tells her brother (seventh narrative layer). The God Laliyaṃga in turn narrates Sayaṃpabhā his former birth as King Mahābala (eighth narrative layer), during which his friend Sayaṃbuddha told him a series of moral stories (ninth narrative layer). King Mahābala renounces the world and dies after submitting himself to extreme austerity (eighth narrative layer), as God Laliyaṃga narrates his wife. Now we are back in the seventh narrative layer and witness the continuation of God Laliyaṃga's and Goddess Sayaṃpabhā's lives. After their death they are reborn as Prince Vaïrajaṃgha and Princess Sirimaī. In her youth Sirimaī remembers her former birth as Goddess Sayaṃpabhā and her existence as a despised girl with no name (or without a *proper* name), Niṇṇāmiyā (Nirnāmikā), as she tells her nurse (eighth narrative layer). Vaïrajaṃgha and Sirimaī marry and their life continues happily until they are poisoned by their own son, as the female twin in the Uttarakurus remembers in the sixth narrative layer. Now the story continues chronologically. The twins are reborn as gods in Sohamma-heaven, then as the physician Kesava and his friend Abhayaghosa, again as gods in Accua-heaven, as Prince Vaïranābha and his friend Sujasa. After their birth as gods in Savvaṭṭhasiddha-heaven they were, as Sijjaṃsa recalls, reborn in this very life as Usabha and as his great-grandson and first donor Sijjaṃsa. Here we are back in the 'narrative present', the fifth narrative layer. The story – and the fifth narrative layer – closes with Usabha preaching the *dharma*, and in the fourth narrative layer King Vasudeva's adventures continue, interspersed with many similar conversations, containing dialogues that include still more narrations.

The presentation of a story through different narrators involved in separate dialogues and accumulating more and more narrative layers is at a certain point quite difficult to grasp. What is the use of telling a story in such a confusing way? Would it not be much easier for the audience to narrate everything in a chronological way, like Hemacandra, Jinasena and other authors do in their works about Jain Universal History? But exactly this apparent chaos acts as a visualization of the baffling diversity of bygone lives and the relativity of

Jaina Studies (forthcoming). As the text is written in Jaina-Māhārāṣṭrī, I shall give the names in the original language.

[52] As she admits at the end of her story, she and her family were only disguised as low-castes.

any relationship between people whatsoever.[53] To present such stories in a dialogical form, jumping to and fro between different narrators and listeners, between different times and places, adds to the dizzying sensation. Quite important for this creation of confusion is that on no occasion is the audience reminded of the main frame or of any sub-frame, like, for example, in the *Mahābhārata*, where the dialogical frames and strands are 'braided'.[54] The reader is deliberately abandoned in the wilderness of dialogues; he has to lose track of the main story with all its sub-tales to experience the sensation to be completely lost – lost not only in this thicket of stories, but also in the complex and incomprehensible nature of the world, recreated by these inscrutable narrations.

Who are the narrators of such puzzling stories? The rememberance of former lives is not easy to gain; it presupposes in general an individual that is firmly grounded in the true faith – that is, of course, Jainism. So it is no surprise that in many dialogues of this type monks or nuns are involved. In Haribhadra's *Samarāiccakahā* (The tale of Samarāditya, 8th century CE), for example, it is a common pattern that a monk is asked for the reason why he had renounced the world. The monk then tells the story of his life (or sometimes lives), inspiring the enquirer to follow him on the path to salvation, either as a layman or as an ascetic. This motif is not so frequent in the *Vasudevahiṇḍī*. Here monks – especially those who have obtained omniscience – are involved in general in more complex dialogical situations, referring not only to former and sometimes also future lives of the people in question, but also to various narrations about the sixty-three 'great men' of Jain Universal History. The reason for inserting long stories into the main narrative can be quite insignificant: Vasudeva once met two monks, who came from the Tīrtha of Jina Santi. Asked to tell about this Jina, they give a long account, running over 38 pages (*Vh.* 310.5–348.9) and including, besides the previous births of the Jinas Santi, Kunthu and Ara, also the story of Tiviṭṭhu, Ayala and Āsaggīva, the first *vāsudeva*, *baladeva* and *prativāsudeva* of this world-period. Also Mahāvīra's pupil Suhamma, asked by King Koṇia, why his pupil Jambu had renounced the world, answers with a long story that contains, strictly speaking, the rest of the *Vasudevahiṇḍī*. Suhamma refers to an earlier meeting between Koṇia's father, Seṇia, and Jina Mahāvīra. Their dialogue started with the story of King Pasannacanda and his younger brother Vakkalacīri, the Jain Śunaḥśepa, to focus on a god named Vijjumāli, who had come to celebrate Pasannacanda reaching the state of omniscience. Mahāvīra explained to Seṇia the former births of god Vijjumāli and predicted that he will attain in his next birth the final emancipation. He will be born as the son of merchant Usabhadatta in Rāyagiha. The person in question is, of course, Jambu, the starting point for this dialogue between Koṇia and Suhamma. Suhamma also relates Seṇia's next question to Koṇia – is it possible to gain the fruit of one's own deeds in this and also in the next life – and Mahāvīra's answer takes up the rest of the *Vasudevahiṇḍī*, more than 350 pages. Hemacandra, by the way,

---

53 Phyllis Granoff ('Life as Ritual Process: Remembrance of Past Births in Jain Religious Narratives', in Phyllis Granoff and Koichi Shinohara [eds], *Other Selves: Autobiography and Biography in Cross-Cultural Perspective* [Oakville, 1994], pp. 17ff.) even suggests 'that in their [the narratives, A.A.E.] radical deconstruction of our notions of a stable hierarchical social order they usher in an important step in a larger process of change that the person who is hearing the story is undergoing'. For an example of a quite dizzying rebirth story, containing the artfully intertwined former lives of seven protagonists, see Anna Aurelia Esposito, 'Wer war wer? Eine komplexe Wiedergeburtsgeschichte aus der *Vasudevahiṇḍī* des Saṅghadāsa', in Eli Franco and Monika Zin (eds), *From Turfan to Ajanta: Festschrift for Dieter Schlingloff on the Occasion of his Eightieth Birthday* (Lumbini, 2010), pp. 321–34.

54 See Hiltebeitel's chapter in the present volume.

disentangles in his *Sthavirāvalīcarita* this complex dialogical situation by recounting the story of Pasannacanda, Vakkalacīri, God Vijjumāli and Jambu in a chronological way. As mentioned above, it is characteristic for the *Vasudevahiṇḍī* to use dialogue in the form of flashbacks as a stylistic and didactic device.

The dialogues that have the most obviously didactic purposes are sermons, parables and instructive tales. While sermons are in general given only by religious specialists, monks and nuns,[55] parables and instructive tales are also told by advanced laymen and, less frequently, laywomen.[56] We encounter in Jain narrative literature also gods who enter in a dialogue with humans to instruct them,[57] or who pay advanced monks a visit to be enlightened by them.[58] As Jain narrative literature is located predominantly in the bourgeois milieu, the main participants in didactic dialogues are traders, merchants and aristocrats, but the listeners can originate from all sections of society.[59] Even animals get the opportunity to make progress on the path to salvation due to instructions by monks and laymen.[60] Quite interesting are in this connection two dialogues of the *Vasudevahiṇḍī* that are interspersed by various parables and instructive tales. The narrators are in both cases not monks, but laymen who are on the brink of renouncing the world, ranking thus almost among religious specialists: Sayaṃbuddha, minister of King Mahābala (one of the former incarnations of Jina Usabha), wants to win his king over to a religious life. He has to reason against his

---

55 In the *Vasudevahiṇḍī,* for example, monk Sivagutta delivers a sermon about the consequences of *karma* (*Vh.* 219.14–23), monk Pīiṃkara speaks about the bondage of the soul and the path to salvation (*Vh.* 259.11–18), and monk Saṃjayanta discusses the dangers of wrath (*Vh.* 262.13–264.2). The nun Hirimaī admonishes her daughter, Queen Rāmakaṇhā, that she should not neglect the true religion (*Vh.* 254.13–23). Having understood the worthlessness of shallow joys, the queen renounces the world. Vasudeva, the hero of the *Vasudevahiṇḍī*, represents an exception: Requested by some hermits, who took him for a divine being, to give a religious sermon, he explained to them the vows of an ascetic (*mahāvrata*s, 'the big vows'), and their origin (*Vh.* 266.14–267.4).

56 An interesting example of a laywoman instructing a monk is Nāilā, (former) wife of Bhavadeva. The happily married Bhavadeva had been forced by his elder brother, who was a monk, to join his order. After his brother's death he wanted to return to his former wife. Nāilā, however, reproached him for his weak-mindedness and convinced him to remain in the order by telling an instructive story. After his death, Bhavadeva became a god; he later incarnated as Jambu, son of merchant Usabhadatta (*Vh.* 20.19–23.6).

57 Often these gods were in a former life very close to the people they instruct. The kings Mahābala (*Vh.* 169.6–12), Acala (*Vh.* 174.27–175.20), and Siridāma (*Vh.* 261.11–27), for example, were advised by gods who had been their former grandfather, mother and brother respectively. Princess Sumati renounced the world after hearing the sermon of a goddess who had been her former sister (*Vh.* 328.5–19).

58 Some gods approach the monks with specific questions, like the god from Sohamma heaven, who wanted to know from an omniscient monk how he could proceed on the path to salvation in the next life (*Vh.* 87.10–16), or god Sakka, who asked Jina Usabha about the different kinds of donations (*Vh.* 183.11–184.3). Other gods arrive to show an advanced monk their reverence and get enlightened by his sermon, like god Lohiyakkha (*Vh.* 274.30–275.8; 278.31–279.12).

59 In such a setting courtesans cannot be absent: Sāmidatta, a pious layman, explains to courtesan Aṇaṅgaseṇā and her chaste daughter Kāmapaḍāgā the prescriptions for laypeople (*aṇuvrata*s, 'the little vows'), illustrating them with various instructive tales (*Vh.* 294.12–297.18).

60 Merchant Cārudatta, for example, instructed a goat before it was slaughtered, whereupon it was reborn as a god (*Vh.* 149.15–23; 151.16–18). Equally, the minister of King Jiyasattu advised the buffalo Bhaddaga, who acquired after his death a birth as a god (*Vh.* 273.21–274.10). Monk Sīhacanda instructed the elephant Asaṇivega, who had been in a former life his father (*Vh.* 256.15–23). After a couple of alternating births as god and prince he obtained the final emancipation.

co-minister Saṃbhiṇṇasoya, who advocates the enjoyment of life. Finally he is able to convince King Mahābala, who thus sets foot on the way to salvation (*Vh.* 166.12–170.31). Jambu, the son of merchant Usabhadatta, plays an even more distinctive role than Sayaṃbuddha. In the frame story of the *Vasudevahiṇḍī* he has to argue against the prince-cum-burglar Pabhava, who challenges his resolve to renounce the world. He refutes each argument of Pabhava, illustrating his view with a parable or instructive story.[61] Finally Pabhava, convinced of the worthlessness of mundane joys, decides to renounce the world together with Jambu (*Vh.* 7.19–15.27). Jambu's accomplished argumentation, however, makes the reader feel to witness the sermon of an experienced monk, not of a mere layman. The reason might be twofold: First, Jambu's firm resolve to renounce the world the next morning gives him already the aura of a monk. Second, Jambu is well known from the canonical scriptures as pupil of Mahāvīra's disciple Suhamma and as such ranks among the most prominent elders of the Jain religion. No other words than those of a great saint can be expected from him.

Didactic dialogues have not only the ability to instruct the opponent and to remove the errors and doubts that keep him from following the right path – beyond that, they can possess a downright healing power. Rāhuga, for example, was mute by birth. One day he met the Jain monk Sacca. Sacca, who had acquired supernatural knowledge (*avadhī-jñāna*), apprehended the true reason behind Rāhuga's muteness: In one of his former lives Rāhuga had been a greedy merchant. After two births as animals, he had been born as the son of his former son. In catching sight of his parents' familiar faces, he remembered his bygone lives. As it seemed impossible for him to address his former son and daughter-in-law as father and mother, he decided to remain mute for the rest of his life. Having this knowledge of Rāhuga's state of mind, monk Sacca informed Rāhuga of the true nature of things. Rāhuga, enlightened, was instantly healed from his muteness (*Vh.* 86.21–88.16).[62]

A special place is occupied by philosophical discussions, which are rather rare in Jain narrative literature. Interestingly enough, in most discussions the opponent is either a follower of the materialistic doctrine (*nāstikavādin*) or at least uses arguments that follow along the same lines as those of the materialists – probably to intensify the difference between both opponents. As we have seen above, the canonical scriptures contain in the *Paesikahāṇayaṃ* a quite impressive example of a materialist's encounter with a Jain monk. Haribhadra follows in the 3rd *bhava*[63] of his *Samarāiccakahā* [*Sama.*] quite closely the authoritative canonical text. Here minister Bambhadatta's son Sihi wants to renounce the world at the feet of monk Vijayasiṃha. One of his father's followers, the *nāstika* Piṅgakesa, tries to dissuade him and enters into a discussion with the Jain monk.[64] Vijayasiṃha

[61] Amongst other things, Pabhava argues that Jambu has the duty to enjoy at least for a short time the wealth gained with difficulty by his forefathers. Furthermore, he is responsible for the wellbeing of his wives and the oblations for his deceased parents. Jambu, in turn, shows Pabhava vividly the danger of wealth, the relativity of all human bonds and the irrelevance of oblations for the dead, using six parables and instructive stories.

[62] A similar story is told in the 6th *bhava* of Haribhadra's *Samarāiccakahā* (Hermann Jacobi [ed.], *Samarāicca Kahā. A Jaina Prākṛta Work. Volume I: Text and Introduction*, Bibliotheca Indica, 169 [Calcutta, 1926], 475.5–477.13).

[63] The main plot of the *Samarāiccakahā* is divided into the description of nine births (*bhava*) of the hero and the antagonist, in which they were connected with each other.

[64] Piṅgakesa's arguments show strong parallels to Paesi's in the *Paesikahāṇayaṃ*: Also he argues, if a soul independent from the body would exist, his evil grandfather and his pious father would have warned him from their infernal or heavenly abode, respectively. Furthermore, in experiments with

refutes Piṅgakesa's arguments one by one and in the end reduces him to silence. By this discussion both Bambhadatta and Piṅgakesa are awakened and adopt the law of laymen (*Sama.* 164.18–175.6).

An outstanding example is Vasudeva in his role as philosopher. Contrary to Sayaṃbuddha and Jambu mentioned above, he would not dream of renouncing the world, at least for the years to come. He is in the middle of exciting adventures, gaining one wife after another and showing his abilities in various fields. It is small wonder that he, as the son of a king, is accomplished in the arts[65] and an authority in weaponry; but the role of a philosopher, of an authority in the sacred scriptures – that's rather fitting for an ascetic than for a warrior. Twice he is able in the *Vasudevahiṇḍī* to show in this way his keen intelligence and, above all, his firmness in Jain doctrine. His first opponent is Puṇṇāsa, instructor of King Abhaggaseṇa's sons and a convinced materialist. He challenges Vasudeva in the presence of the king, contradicting Vasudeva's statement that the soul (*āyā*, Skt *ātmā*)[66] is the authority behind any action. After Puṇṇāsa's explanation of the materialistic world view and the consequent impossibility of the existence of a soul independent from the body, Vasudeva refutes his opponent's view with various arguments, culminating in the conclusion that a soul distinct from the elements does exist (*Vh.* 202.13–203.8).[67] In the following, neither is Puṇṇāsa's reaction reported nor is he mentioned again. He simply vanishes from our narrative.

Vasudeva's second philosophical discussion is still more astonishing. Again he shows himself as superior in penetrating philosophical subjects, but this time his opponent is an ascetic – a representative of the religious specialists. Vasudeva comes across him in a grove near the city Kañcaṇapura, where he is in deep meditation. Vasudeva pays his respects, and the mendicant invites him to sit down. Questioned by Vasudeva, the ascetic states that he had been reflecting on the relationship between *pagaï* (Skt *prakṛti*, matter) and *purisa* (Skt *puruṣa*, soul). Now a vivid discussion with alternating arguments evolves,[68] in which Vasudeva is able to contradict and correct the ascetic's reflections. 'Pleased by this and other statements,' as King Vasudeva narrates later to his grandsons, 'the ascetic invited me to accompany him to his dwelling-place' (*Vh.* 360.20–361.21). Although this episode is treated in the *Vasudevahiṇḍī* as a rather trivial incident, it is in reality quite extraordinary: Here a mere layman is confronting an ascetic, a representative of the religious specialists, contradicting and correcting him in a discussion with pure philosophical contents! Here

---

the bodies of criminals he had found no evidence of a soul. Additionally he presents a short summary of the materialists' world view: As the body consists exclusively of the five material elements (and thus produces also the consciousness), there is no soul independent from the body.

65 In his 'autobiography' Vasudeva relates that he was taken to a teacher to learn the arts when he was eight years old. He was able to satisfy his teacher due to his 'distinguished intelligence and understanding' (*visiṭṭha-mehā-mati-guṇeṇa*, *Vh.* 118.25).

66 For the form *āyā*, attested by Pischel only for Ardhamāgadhī, see Anna Aurelia Esposito, "The Prakrit of the *Vasudevahiṇḍī* – an Addendum to Pischel's Grammar', *Studien zur Indologie und Iranistik* 28 (2011 [2012]), p. 31. As Adelheid Mette (*Die Erlösungslehre der Jaina: Legenden, Parabeln, Erzählungen: Aus dem Sanskrit und Prakrit übersetzt und herausgegeben* [Berlin, 2010], p. 233, n. 65) remarks, older sources use for 'soul' often *āyā* instead of *jīva*.

67 For a more detailed account see Anna Aurelia Esposito, 'Vasudeva the Philosopher – Soul and Body in Saṅghadāsa's *Vasudevahiṇḍī*', in Peter Flügel and Olle Qvarnström (eds), *Jaina Scriptures and Philosophy* (London: Routledge, forthcoming). It is quite striking that this passage shows no affinity at all with the *Paesikahāṇayaṃ*, that in all probability has been known by the author.

68 Contrary to the aforementioned dispute with the materialist Puṇṇāsa, where two monolithic blocks of arguments were opposing each other!

Figure 3.1
The narrative embedding of Jina Usabha's former lives in the *Vasudevahiṇḍī* (ca. 5th cent. CE)

1st layer:	King Koṇia's conversation with *gaṇadhara* Suhamma
2nd layer:	King Seṇia's meeting with Jina Mahāvīra, narrated by *gaṇadhara* Suhamma
3rd layer:	The story of King Vasudeva's grandsons, narrated by Jina Mahāvīra
4th layer:	Vasudeva's adventures, narrated by himself
5th layer:	The story of Jina Usabha, narrated to King Vasudeva by an old woman
6th layer:	The previous birth of Jina Usabha as a male twin, narrated by Sijjaṃsa, Jina Usabha's first donor
7th layer:	The previous birth of the male twin as god Laliyaṃga, narrated by the female twin
8th layer:	The previous birth of god Laliyaṃga as King Mahābala, narrated by himself
9th layer:	Different moral stories, narrated to King Mahābala by his friend Sayaṃbuddha
8th layer:	The previous birth as King Mahābala, continued
7th layer:	The previous birth as god Laliyaṃga (and goddess Sayaṃpabhā), continued
	The previous birth as Prince Vaïrajaṃgha (and Princess Sirimaī)
8th layer:	Princess Sirimaī narrates her former birth as Niṇṇāmiyā
7th layer:	The previous birth as Prince Vaïrajaṃgha and Princess Sirimaī, continued
6th layer:	The previous birth as twins, continued
	The birth as gods in Sohamma-heaven
	The birth as physician Kesava (and his friend Abhayaghosa, son of a Seṭh)
	The birth as gods in Accua-heaven
	The birth as Prince Vaïranābha (and his friend Sujasa, his charioteer)
	The birth as gods in Savvaṭṭhasiddha-heaven
5th layer:	The story of Jina Usabha, narrated to King Vasudeva by an old woman, continued
4th layer:	Vasudeva's adventures, narrated by himself, continued

doctrine is communicated by the king, not by the monk. This may appear surprising at a first glance; there are, however, strong parallels to another textual corpus of ancient India: the Upaniṣads. As Black states, 'the literary trope of the *kṣatriya* who teaches the brahmin is one of a number of narrative features in the early Upaniṣads that makes these stories directly appealing to a *kṣatriya* audience'.[69] In the *Vasudevahiṇḍī* it is the king as representative not only of the nobility, but of educated Jain laymen in general, who challenges successfully the religious specialist and makes the didactic contents all the more appealing for the bourgeois target audience of Jain narrative literature.

Conclusion

Dialogue proves already in the canonical scriptures to be pivotal in several regards: Dialogues between Jina Mahāvīra and his pupils not only frame and structure the various topics, they also transmit the doctrinal contents more vividly and therefore in a more appealing way for the audience. Above all, remarks of an omniscient being like Jina Mahāvīra act as legitimation, as proof for the absolute truth of the subjects transmitted. Jain narrative literature not only continues, but also expands upon these features established in the canonical literature: Some works imitate the canonical texts by using the same narrative framing. At the same time, they underline, by replacing the ascetic dialogue partner with a royal one, the new target audience, consisting of laypeople instead of monks and nuns. To reach this new audience, the authors locate most stories in a bourgeois millieu, which can even result in the dialogical victory of a layman over a monk. In addition, the authors try to conceal doctrinal contents behind entertaining stories and to insert as much of them as possible into the main narrative. Thus, as Appleton and Hiltebeitel also show in this volume, narrative framing has multiple purposes. The best means to integrate all these various tales in a plausible way is the dialogue. Dialogues between various characters, mostly in the form of flashbacks, lead us deeper and deeper into the different narrative layers, creating a dizzying sensation and thus visualizing the bewildering diversity of bygone lives and the relativity of any relationship between people whatsoever. Here dialogue is not only used as a stylistic, but also as a didactic device, as a means to illustrate and recreate the complex and incomprehensible nature of the world.

References

Balcerowicz, Piotr, 'Monks, Monarchs, and Materialists', *Journal of Indian Philosophy* 33 (2005): 571–82.

Black, Brian, *The Character of the Self in Ancient India: Priests, Kings, and Women in the Early Upaniṣads*, SUNY Series in Hindu Studies (Albany: State University of New York Press, 2007).

Bollée, Willem B., *The Story of Paesi (Paesi-kahāṇayaṃ): Soul and Body in Ancient India. A Dialogue on Materialism. Text, Translation, Notes and Glossary*. Beiträge zur Kenntnis südasiatischer Sprachen und Literaturen 8 (Wiesbaden: Harrassowitz, 2002). [Reprint: Bombay, 2005].

[69] Brian Black, *The Character of the Self in Ancient India: Priests, Kings, and Women in the Early Upaniṣads* (Albany, New York, 2007), p. 129.

Dasaveyāliya (Sirisejjaṃbhavatherabhadaṃtaviraiyaṃ Dasaveyāliyasuttaṃ, Aṇegatherabhadaṃtaviraiyāiṃ Uttarajjhayaṇāiṃ Āvassayasuttaṃ), Puṇyavijaya Muni and Amṛtalāla Mohanalāla Bhojaka (eds), *ca*, Jaina-Āgama-Granthamālā 15 (Bambaī: Śrī Mahāvīra Jaina Vidyālaya, 1977).

Deleu, Jozef, *Viyāhapannatti (Bhagavaī), The Fifth Anga of the Jaina Canon: Introduction, Critical Analysis, Commentary & Indexes*, Lala Sundar Lal Jain Research Series 10 (Delhi: Motilal Banarsidass, [1970] 1996).

Dundas, Paul, *The Jains* (London and New York: Routledge, 2002).

Esposito, Anna Aurelia, 'Wer war wer? Eine komplexe Wiedergeburtsgeschichte aus der *Vasudevahiṇḍī* des Saṅghadāsa', in Eli Franco and Monika Zin (eds), *From Turfan to Ajanta: Festschrift for Dieter Schlingloff on the Occasion of his Eightieth Birthday* (Lumbini: Lumbini International Research Institute, 2010), pp. 321–34.

———, 'The Prakrit of the *Vasudevahiṇḍī* – an Addendum to Pischel's *Grammar*', *Studien zur Indologie und Iranistik* 28 (2011 [2012]): 29–50.

———, 'How to Combine the *Bṛhatkathā* with Jain Universal History – Reflections on Saṅghadāsa's *Vasudevahiṇḍī*', in Jayandra Soni (ed.), *Jaina Studies: Proceedings of the DOT 2010 Panel in Marburg, Germany* (New Delhi: Aditya Prakashan, 2012), pp. 201–12.

———, 'Vasudeva the Philosopher – Soul and Body in Saṅghadāsa's *Vasudevahiṇḍī*', in Peter Flügel and Olle Qvarnström (eds), *Jaina Scriptures and Philosophy* (London: Routledge, forthcoming).

——— 'Life Before Life Before Life – an Exceptional Perspective on Jina Usabha's Biography', *International Journal of Jaina Studies* (forthcoming).

Glasenapp, Helmuth von, *Jainism: An Indian Religion of Salvation*, trans. Shridhar B. Shrotri, Lala Sundar Lal Jain Research Series 14 (Delhi: Motilal Banarsidass, 1999). [German original: *Der Jainismus. Eine indische Erlösungsreligion. Nach den Quellen dargestellt*. Berlin: Alf Häger Verlag, 1925].

Granoff, Phyllis, 'Life as Ritual Process: Remembrance of Past Births in Jain Religious Narratives', in Phyllis Granoff and Koichi Shinohara (eds), *Other Selves: Autobiography and Biography in Cross-Cultural Perspective* (Oakville: Mosaic Press, 1994), pp. 16–34.

Griffiths, Paul J., *On Being Buddha: the Classical Doctrine of Buddhahood* (Albany: State University of New York Press, 1994).

Haribhadra, *Samarāiccakahā*, in Hermann Jacobi (ed.). *Samarāicca Kahā. A Jaina Prākṛta Work. Volume I: Text and Introduction*, Bibliotheca Indica 169 (Calcutta: Asiatic Society of Bengal, 1926).

Jacobi, Hermann (trans.), *Jaina Sutras, Translated from Prakrit by Hermann Jacobi, Part II: The Uttarādhyayana Sūtra, The Sūtrakritāṅga Sūtra* (New York: Dover Publications, [1895] 1968).

Jaini, Padmanabh S., 'On the *Sarvajñatva* (Omniscience) of Mahāvīra and the Buddha', in L. Cousins et al. (eds), *Buddhist Studies in Honour of I. B. Horner* (Dordrecht and Boston: Reidel, 1974), pp. 71–90.

———, *The Jaina Path of Purification* (Delhi: Motilal Banarsidass, [1979] 2001).

Leumann, Ernst. *Das Aupapātika Sūtra, erstes Upāṅga der Jaina. I. Theil: Einleitung, Text und Glossar*, Abhandlungen für die Kunde des Morgenlandes VIII.2 (Leipzig: Deutsche Morgenländische Gesellschaft, 1883. Reprint, Nendeln, Liechtenstein: Kraus Reprint Ltd, 1966).

———, 'Beziehungen der Jaina-Literatur zu anderen Literaturkreisen Indiens', *Actes du VIe congrès international des Orientalistes* III/2 (1885): 469–564 [= *Kleine Schriften* 29–124].

———, *Kleine Schriften. Herausgegeben von Nalini Balbir*, Glasenapp-Stiftung 37 (Stuttgart: Franz Steiner Verlag, 1998).

Mehta, Mohan Lal, and K. Rishabh Chandra, *Prakrit Proper Names* (2 vols, Ahmedabad: L.D. Institute of Indology, 1970–72).

Mette, Adelheid, *Die Erlösungslehre der Jaina: Legenden, Parabeln, Erzählungen: Aus dem Sanskrit und Prakrit übersetzt und herausgegeben* (Berlin: Verlag der Weltreligionen, 2010).

Nāyādhammakahāo, in Candrasāgarasūri (ed.), Śrījñātādharmakathāṅga Śrī Anandacandragranthābdhau Grantharatnam 16, 18 (2 vols, Mumbāi: Śrīsiddhacakra-Sāhityapracāraka-Samiti, 1951–52).

Paesikahāṇayaṃ, see Bollée.

Pischel, Richard, *A Grammar of the Prākrit Languages*, trans. from German by Subhadra Jhā (Delhi: Motilal Banarsidass, 1999). [German original: *Grammatik der Prakrit-Sprachen*. Strassburg: Karl Trübner, 1900].

Roth, Gustav, *Mallī-Jñāta: Das achte Kapitel des Nāyādhammakahāo im sechsten Aṅga des Śvetāmbara Jainakanons: Herausgegeben, übersetzt und erläutert*, Monographien zur Indischen Archäologie, Kunst und Philologie 4 (Wiesbaden: Franz Steiner Verlag, 1983).

Saṅghadāsa, *Vasudevahiṇḍī*, in Caturvijaya Muni and Puṇyavijaya Muni (eds), *Pūjyaśrīsaṅghadāsagaṇivācakavinirmitā Vasudevahiṇḍī* (Gandhinagar: Gujarat Sahitya Akadami, [1930–31] 1989).

Schubring, Walther, *The Doctrine of the Jainas: Described after the Old Sources*, translated from the revised German edition by Wolfgang Beurlen, with the three indices enlarged and added by Willem Bollée and Jayandra Soni (Delhi: Motilal Banarsidass, [1962] 2000). [German original: *Die Lehre der Jainas. Nach den alten Quellen dargestellt*. Berlin: Walter de Gruyter (Grundriß der indo-arischen Philologie und Altertumskunde III.7), 1935].

Soni, Jayandra, *The Notion of* Āpta *in Jaina Philosophy*, the 1995 Roop Lal Jain Lecture (Toronto: University of Toronto, 1996). [Reprint in: Joseph T. O'Connell (ed.), *Jain Doctrine and Practice: Academic Perspectives*, South Asian Studies Papers 13 (Toronto: University of Toronto, Centre for South Asian Studies, 2000), pp. 50–68].

Viyāhapannatti (= *Bhagavatī*), in Nathamala, Muni (ed.), *Bhagavaī (Viāhapaṇṇattī): Aṃgasuttāṇi, Vol. 2: Original Text Critically Edited* (Lāḍanūṃ: Jaina Viśva Bhāratī, 1974).

Weber, Friedrich Albrecht, 'Über die heiligen Schriften der Jaina', *Indische Studien* 16 (1883): 211–479; 17 (1885): 1–90. (Reprint 1973, Hildesheim: Georg Olms Verlag. Translated into English by Herbert Weir Smyth as *Weber's Sacred Literature of the Jains* [Bombay: Education Society's Steam Press, 1893]. Citations refer to original German edition.)

Winternitz, Maurice [= Moriz], *A History of Indian Literature, Vol. II: Buddhist Literature and Jaina Literature* (Calcutta: University of Calcutta, 1933). [German original: *Geschichte der indischen Litteratur. Band 2: Die buddhistische Litteratur und die heiligen Texte der Jainas*. Leipzig: C.F. Amelangs Verlag, 1920].

Chapter 4
The Buddha as Storyteller: The Dialogical Setting of *Jātaka* Stories

Naomi Appleton

Introduction

Jātaka stories, or stories relating to episodes in the past births of the Buddha, are ubiquitous in Buddhist texts and societies. Although there are many texts which contain *jātaka* stories, the largest and most well-known collection is that preserved by the Theravāda school and entitled *Jātakatthavaṇṇanā* or *Jātakaṭṭhakathā* (henceforth JA).[1] This collection of around 550 stories is partly canonical, for the verses are considered to be *buddhavacana* ('word of the Buddha'), and form part of the *Khuddaka Nikāya* of the Pāli scriptures. The prose, which in most cases contains the bulk of the narrative, is officially commentarial, and in its final form cannot be dated to before the fifth century CE. However, an early prose commentary must always have accompanied the verses since they are incomplete alone, and there is evidence to suggest that the text has held a quasi-scriptural position since early times.[2] The verses and prose fit together according to a set structure. First we find the story of the present, which sets the scene and explains the reasons for the Buddha telling the story of the past. For example, a community of monks might be discussing Devadatta's recent attempt to kill the Buddha, and the latter comments that this is not the first time he has done so, and tells a story of the past. This story of the past is considered to be the *jātaka* proper since it is here that the events of a previous birth (*jāta*) of the Buddha are related. Somewhere within or shortly after the story of the past are the verses, which may record a moral, some dialogue, or part of the narrative. At the end of the story the consequences of hearing it, such as the listeners attaining a specified stage of the path, are related, and finally the Buddha explains the 'connection' between the stories by identifying himself as one of the characters of the past; sometimes he also identifies other characters of the present (often members of his audience) with those in the past.[3] Unsurprisingly, the focus of most scholarship on this text has been the stories of the past, many of which have parallels in other story collections, both Buddhist and non-Buddhist. However, the framing of the

---

[1] V. Fausbøll (ed.), *The Jātaka Together With Its Commentary being Tales of the Anterior Births of Gotama Buddha* (6 vols, London, 1877–96). E.B. Cowell (ed. – several translators), *The Jātaka or Stories of the Buddha's Former Births* (6 vols, Cambridge, 1895–1907). N.A. Jayawickrama (trans.), *The Story of Gotama Buddha (Jātaka-nidāna)* (Oxford, 1990).

[2] The genre (if not the text) forms one of the nine *aṅgas*, or 'limbs' of scriptures, and had its own tradition of *bhāṇakas*, or oral reciters who preserved the texts. This and other evidence for the antiquity of the genre is explored in Chapter 3 of Naomi Appleton, *Jātaka Stories in Theravāda Buddhism: Narrating the Bodhisatta Path* (Farnham, 2010). I refer to the stories of the JA by the numbering found in Fausboll's edition and Cowell's translation.

[3] For further explanation of the history and structure of the text see Oskar von Hinüber, *Entstehung und Aufbau der Jātaka-Sammlung* (Stuttgart, 1998).

stories in the teaching career of the Buddha is also worthy of attention, and is the focus of this chapter. Other chapters in this volume (Hiltebeitel, Esposito) discuss the complex question of framing, and argue similarly that the frame of the dialogue determines how it might be understood by the reader or hearer.

As far as we are aware, no other Buddhist school had a collection of *jātaka*s on anything like the scale of the JA. Indeed the tendency was not to gather the stories into a single collection at all; rather they form integral parts of other texts. Birth stories are frequently narrated in biographical texts (such as the *Mahāvastu*) and works of *vinaya* (especially the copious *Mūlasarvāstivāda vinaya*), and collections of narrative that include birth stories of the Buddha alongside those of other figures are common. There are also literary *jātaka* compositions, the most famous example being Āryaśūra's *Jātakamālā*, an elegant Sanskrit work from around the fourth century CE that retells thirty-four stories from an unknown source. In this text there is no story of the present; indeed the stories are not narrated by the Buddha at all, but are rather outlined by the author relying upon traditional accounts. The same holds true for most other retellings of *jātaka* stories, right up to the present, where stories are frequently found in children's books or modern media with no suggestion that they were originally narrated by the Buddha himself. The JA would therefore appear to be unique in that it exclusively contains *jātaka* stories and places these in a dialogical frame involving the Buddha and a variety of interlocutors.[4]

Given the set structure of the JA, and especially the emphasis in this text on providing a 'story of the present' that identifies the narrator (the Buddha) and his audience, we might ask what difference this makes to the text. Does it matter whether or not a story of the Buddha's past birth was narrated by him? Why does the JA include him as narrator and many other characters of the present as his interlocutors and audience if the focus is really the stories of the past? Who constitutes the audience for *jātaka* stories and what is their role? In sum, why are *jātaka* stories placed in a dialogical setting in the JA? This chapter is an attempt to answer such questions. Focusing on the JA, I will first investigate the role of the Buddha as narrator, rememberer, and revealer. Next, I will examine the audience for the stories within the narrative frame, and ask what their role is in requesting and receiving the stories, and what they tell us about the perceived purpose of the stories. Finally, I will examine the relationship between the Buddha and his audience, and the characters in the stories of the past. I will suggest that the dialogical narrative frame of the JA, though deemed dispensible in other texts, adds extra layers of meaning and power to the stories.

The Narrator

Author and Authority

Let us begin with the first question: Does it matter whether or not a story of the Buddha's past birth was narrated by him? There are two sides to this question: what the Buddha's identification as narrator says about the Buddha, and what it says about the stories. We may begin with the latter.

[4] The dialogical setting is not of course unique in Buddhist scripture, where many if not most texts are framed by biographical narrative and/or include indications of when, where and to whom the teaching was given.

It has been widely commented that the JA contains a lot of stories that have no discernable Buddhist content. Animal fables and stories of men whose wit and worldly wisdom get them out of sticky situations abound, sometimes at the expense of Buddhist ideals. For example, there is more than one story in which the Bodhisatta (Buddha-to-be) is a hero who kills his adversary, going against the central Buddhist precept of refraining from killing and providing a dubious example of the behaviour required by someone on the path to buddhahood. One such example is the story of the cat (JA 128) who pretends to be an ascetic and gradually eats his way through a group of mice-devotees, of which the Bodhisatta is the leader. Realizing eventually that something is amiss, the Bodhisatta catches the cat (or jackal, as he is in the prose) as he is about to pounce, bites his throat and puts an end to his life, after which 'the company of mice returned and ate the jackal with a crunch crunch crunch. Or rather, I have heard, the first that came got meat, but those that were behind got none.'[5] This rather gruesome tale is also found in several non-Buddhist sources, which might explain the multiple identities of the villain, who is a cat in the title and verse but a jackal in the prose.[6]

The cat story is not the only story that has parallels in other texts, nor is it the only story that fits awkwardly into a Buddhist context. One way in which the JA functions is as a repository of narrative. Many stories were collected together into the text, and established as authentically Buddhist by being placed in the teaching career of the Buddha. The text contains everything from a Buddhist version of the *Rāmāyaṇa* (JA 461) to a version of the well-known Aesopic fable 'The Ass in the Lion's Skin' (JA 189). By collecting popular stories into the text, the JA indicated that the Buddha was the source of all these narratives and the worldly wisdom contained within them. The Buddha tells you how to deal with sham ascetics, how to escape murderous courtesans, how to avoid the dangers of sea travel, how to win kingdoms, and how to deal with difficult wives. He is also a skillful raconteur: he knows which story to tell for which purpose, is witty and has a keen sense of humour. With such a broad source of narratives, the collection contains a story for almost every conceivable purpose, truly demonstrating the all-emcompassing wisdom of the Buddha.

There is a danger inherent in this: that the close association between the Buddha and worldly matters taints him and makes him appear less perfect. However, the Buddha's narration of the stories, and the Bodhisatta's participation in them, keep a careful balance between identification and distance through an alternation of first and third person narration. Both the stories of the present and of the past are actually narrated in the third person, the former by an anonymous narrator, and the latter by the Buddha. The only use of the first person is during the identification of the births, when the Buddha declares that 'I was such-and-such a character at that time.' Sarah Shaw assesses the effect of this narrative style as follows:

> The threads of the Buddha, described in the third person, the 'he' of the Bodhisatta and the 'I' at the end of each tale are woven in and out of each other like a plait, evoking a succession of lives. These three elements suggest neither the 'eternalist' view, an abiding

---

[5] *Mūsikagaṇo nivattitvā sigālaṃ murumurā ti khāditvā agamāsi. Paṭhamam āgatā va kir'assa maṃsaṃ labhiṃsu, pacchā āgatā na labhiṃsu.* Fausbøll, *The Jātaka*, vol. 1, p. 461.

[6] It seems likely that the identity of the villain was changed between the time of the composition of the verses (which must have been influenced by other Indian versions of the story) and the fixing of the prose. A jackal may have been deemed a more appropriate identification because of his similar characterizations in other *jātaka* stories.

> self, nor the 'annihilationist' view that the self ceases at death.... A moving point, like a kind of 'middle way', arises from the process itself, in the constant movement between the first person acknowledgement of the Buddha and his third-person character, the bodhisatta.[7]

As Shaw argues, the weaving together of first- and third-person narration in the JA allows the Buddha to identify himself with the story whilst simultaneously stepping back from it.

That the mix of first- and third-person narration in the JA allows the Buddha to balance his worldly and Buddhist authority is demonstrated further through comparison with other *jātaka* texts. For example, the *Cariyāpiṭaka* (henceforth CP), a late scriptural text of the Theravāda, contains 35 stories narrated entirely in the first person. These stories, predominantly retold from the JA, claim to demonstrate the qualities acquired by the Bodhisatta during his quest for awakening. The stories are concisely narrated by the Buddha in the first person and are focused upon specifically Buddhist qualities, the perfections (*pāramī*s or *pāramitā*s) required for buddhahood. Presumably because of this close identification between the stories and the Buddha (and buddhahood) there appears to be an attempt in the CP to distance the Bodhisatta from the morally problematic or insignificant actions that are found in the JA, and whole portions of narrative are therefore omitted. For example, the *Khaṇḍahāla-jātaka* (JA 542) is found as the six-verse *Candakumāracariyaṃ* (CP 1.7) in the chapter on *dāna* (generosity). In the JA this story relates how a king, wishing to go to heaven and under the influence of an evil brahmin (the Buddha's cousin Devadatta in a previous birth), plans a large sacrifice which includes his wives and children, most notably his son Prince Canda (the Bodhisatta). Prince Canda tries to get himself (and implicitly the other sacrificial victims) freed but is eventually rescued only thanks to his wife's declaration of truth and the intervention of the god Sakka. In the CP this whole dramatic narrative is omitted and the story relates simply that after being freed from the sacrifice Canda gave great gifts. Strikingly, Canda has been made the hero of this tale, in contrast to the passive or even impotent role he plays in the JA, and the focus is therefore shifted to the virtues that qualify him for eventual buddhahood. Even more striking evidence of the CP's preoccupation with the Bodhisatta's qualities is found in the *Kapirājacariyaṃ* (CP III. 7), which is told in the section demonstrating *sacca* (truth) and relates the failed attempt of a crocodile to kill a monkey (the Bodhisatta). In the parallel stories of the JA (57. *Vānarinda-jātaka*; 208. *Suṃsumāra-jātaka*; 342. *Vānara-jātaka*) the monkey tells a lie to the crocodile in order to outwit him. In the CP we find the line: 'No lie was spoken to him, I acted according to my word'.[8] This looks like a deliberate attempt to rewrite the stories already popular in the JA in order to give them a cleaner ethic, one that can be more closely associated with the Buddha and Bodhisatta. In contrast, the distance provided by the primarily third-person narration in the JA allows the Bodhisatta to have a wider variety of roles and act out much more human situations.

Āryaśūra's *Jātakamālā* (henceforth JM) is located at the other end of the spectrum, for it presents birth stories narrated by an author wholly unconnected with the events. Thirty of the thirty-four stories in this text have parallel versions in the JA, and in some cases whole verses or phrases are identical, whilst other stories show significant variation from their Pāli

[7] Sarah Shaw, 'And that was I: How the Buddha Himself Creates a Path between Biography and Autobiography', in Linda Covill et al. (eds), *Lives Lived, Lives Imagined: Biography in the Buddhist Traditions* (Boston, 2010), pp. 36–7.

[8] *Na tassa alikaṃ bhaṇitaṃ yathā vācaṃ akās'haṃ*; N.A. Jayawickrama (ed.), *Buddhavaṃsa and Cariyāpiṭaka* (London, 1974), p. 30, verse 310.

counterparts. Whatever source Āryaśūra had at his disposal, his aim – as he tells us in his prologue – is to 'celebrate the wonders performed by the Holy One in previous incarnations' which are 'like conspicuous signs pointing the way to perfection' and by thus doing he hopes that 'these edifying tales give greater enjoyment than ever before'.[9] The enjoyment is indeed great: the Sanskrit is elegant and the stories are told concisely but not without colour or sophistication. As a literary composition, the text certainly exalts the Buddha by glorifying his past actions, yet it also seems very far removed from him. The absence of the Buddha from the narrative raises issues of authenticity, for the text is clearly authored many centuries after the time of the Buddha, by a named individual. This individual is only qualified to tell the story because he relies upon traditional accounts; that he is aware of this requirement is clear from the phrase 'according to tradition' (*tadyathānuśrūyate*) which begins each story. With the absence of the Buddha, even the Bodhisatt(v)a seems distant, narrated in the third person by someone hundreds of years after the character attained his final *nirvāṇa*. Quite simply, this text makes no claim to be scriptural or to preserve the words of the Buddha himself. It is thus far removed from both Buddha and Bodhisatta, in contrast to the JA's careful balance of connection and distance.

Visionary and Revealer

The JA, therefore, manages to avoid letting the Buddha's identification as the narrator of its stories compromise his perfection, yet still allows his narration to give authority and authenticity to a rather diverse collection. Indeed, rather than compromising his spiritual authority, the stories actually bolster it, for as well as identifying the Buddha as the source of all popular narrative, the JA demonstrates his ability to *know* the stories. In other words, he is shown to be a visionary who can see his own past lives and those of other people, and who can use these past lives in his teaching career. Whereas the CP and JM glorify the actions of the Buddha in his past lives, the JA also glorifies the Buddha's ability to remember these past lives.

Several formulaic phrases found in the JA demonstrate the importance that is placed upon the Buddha's unrivalled vision. When the Buddha is entreated to tell a story of the past it is because his interlocutor acknowledges that he cannot see it himself. For example, in the very first story of the JA the Buddha responds to a situation by mentioning events of the past, and the great lay supporter Anāthapiṇḍika, says to him that these past events are 'concealed from us and known only to you'.[10] He continues with a request that the Buddha 'make it clear to us, as if making the full moon rise in the sky'.[11] Assenting to Anāthapiṇḍika's request the Buddha tells the story of the past, 'making clear that which was concealed from them by rebirth'.[12] Similarly, in the introduction to the second story, the community of monks tell the Buddha that whilst they understand the present faint-heartedness of the monk under discussion, they do not know about his past acts of perseverence, for these are 'known only to you, the all-knowing one'.[13] Again, the Buddha assents to their request

---

[9] Peter Khoroche (trans.), *Once the Buddha Was a Monkey: Ārya Śūra's Jātakamālā* (Chicago and London, 1989), p. 3.

[10] *amhākaṃ paṭicchanno tumhākam eva pākaṭo* (Fausbøll, *The Jātaka*, vol. 1, pp. 97–8).

[11] ākāse puṇṇacandaṃ uṭṭhāpento viya imaṃ kāraṇaṃ pākaṭaṃ karotu (Fausbøll, *The Jātaka*, vol. 1, p. 98).

[12] *bhavantarena paṭicchannakāraṇaṃ pākaṭaṃ akāsi* (Fausbøll, *The Jātaka*, vol. 1, p. 98).

[13] *tumhākaṃ sabbaññūtaññāṇasseva pākaṭo* (Fausbøll, *The Jātaka*, vol. 1, p. 107).

that he tell them the story of the past, thereby once more 'making clear that which was concealed from them by rebirth'.[14] This phrase recurs in each story until number thirteen, when the commentator states:

> From now on we will not mention the entreaty of the monks or that which is obscured by rebirth, but will say only 'he spoke of the past.' But when this is said, all that has been said above – the entreaty, the simile of setting the moon free from the clouds, and making clear what was concealed by rebirth – are understood and should be said.[15]

These formulae then disappear from our text, but should – we are told – remain in our minds.

The term that I have here translated as 'rebirth' (*bhavantara*) literally means between (*antara*) becomings or existences (*bhava*) and is understood to refer to the experience of moving from one birth to the next. During this process certain memories are lost, thus the actions and experiences of one life are not remembered in the next. According to early Buddhism these memories can be revisited by practising the *jhāna* meditations. As an adept at these meditations, the Buddha is said to be able to see his own previous births as well as the workings of *kamma* on other beings as they fall away and take up new births; indeed these abilities form the first two of the three superknowledges that characterize the attainments of the Buddha during the night of his awakening. The ability to see past births is not limited to the Buddha, however, or indeed to Buddhist practitioners, though Buddhaghosa remarks that non-Buddhists can only remember as far back as forty eons, since their understanding is so weak.[16] The ability to tell these stories is not, therefore, proof of buddhahood, nor even of awakening, but it is proof of having reached an advanced spiritual state. This acts as another counterbalance to the worldly contents of the stories themselves. Thus by placing its stories in the mouth of the Buddha, the JA not only lends authority to a vast and diverse body of tales, it also demonstrates the spiritual achievements of the narrator and the great experience he has had of the world over many lives.

The Audience

The Buddha is not simply an assumed author or a disembodied narrator in the JA; rather, his narration is located in specific times and places, which are almost always specified in the story of the present, along with the subject of the story. In addition, most stories specify the people who make up the audience for the stories, and sometimes their reason for requesting the story from the Buddha. So whom was the Buddha believed to tell these stories to?[17] The audience are most clearly divided along gender lines as well as according

---

[14] *bhavantarena paṭicchannakāraṇaṃ pākaṭam akāsi* (Fausbøll, *The Jātaka*, vol. 1, p. 107).

[15] *Itoparaṃ pana bhikkhūnaṃ yācanaṃ bhavantarapaṭicchannatañ ca avatvā "atītaṃ āharī"ti ettakameva vakkhāma, ettake vutte pi āyācanaṃ valāhakagabbhato candanīharaṇūpamā ca bhavanta rapaṭicchannakāraṇabhāvo cā 'ti sabbam etaṃ heṭṭhāvuttanayen' eva yojetvā veditabbaṃ.* (Fausbøll, *The Jātaka*, vol. 1, pp. 153–4).

[16] *Visuddhimagga* XIII 16; Bhikkhu Ñāṇamoli (trans.), *The Path of Purification (Visuddhimagga) by Bhadantācariya Buddhaghosa* (5th edn, Kandy, 1991), p. 407. The Buddha can see millions of aeons, and the varying types of followers varying degrees in between.

[17] I am not of course suggesting that the JA preserves an accurate record of the telling of *jātaka* stories by the Buddha during his teaching career. The absence of an equivalent text in other Buddhist schools, and the many-layered compositional history of the JA, suggest it was a compilation of stories

to the lay–monastic distinction, and so my focus here will be the fourfold community of monks, nuns, laymen, and laywomen.[18]

Out of around 480 stories that give explicit identifications of the Buddha's audience, eighty percent are told to a monastic audience.[19] More than two thirds of these are addressed to the *bhikkhu*s as a unit, with the remainder directed at individual monks, often those unnamed monks who are tempted to return to the lay life and need a story to dissuade them. The 20 per cent of stories addressed to a non-monastic audience include stories told to various laypeople, including kings, merchants, brahmins, and even a *brahmā* god called Baka.[20] Only six stories are told to the lay community as a whole,[21] in comparison with around 275 told to the monastic *saṅgha*. There is clearly a heavy bias towards a monastic audience within the narrative frame. This monastic bias might reflect the process of transmission of the stories, for these were preserved by monks. The claim that these stories were originally heard by monks and have been transmitted within the monastic community may have bolstered the perceived authority of monks to tell the stories.

Despite the heavy monastic presence within the narrative, it has often been assumed that *jātaka* stories are primarily teachings for the laity, that they are a form of popular Buddhism, and that they entertain more than they elucidate.[22] The fact that the internal audience is predominantly monastic might shed doubt on this assumption, though having different audiences within and outside of the narrative is perfectly possible. The main reason for believing the stories to have a lay audience is the content, which, as we noted above, is often rather worldly. However, these worldly stories are often specifically aimed at illustrating or solving *monastic* problems, particularly the difficulty of leaving behind (and resisting the temptation of returning to) one's wife. The story of a man whose wife repeatedly cheats on him until he eventually outwits her might seem very worldly, but its effect on a monk who misses his wife is very much in accordance with monastic ideals. In addition, whilst many stories do play a part in sermons to the laity, they are also still used in both educational and ritual contexts within the monastery. The idea that *jātaka* stories are simple moral fables for the laity is thus a significant misunderstanding of the audience both within and outside of the narrative.

---

made several hundred years after the death of the Buddha. Some of the settings may be accurate records, but most are formulaic and were probably regulated by a similar injunction to that in the *Mūlasarvāstivāda-vinaya* explored by Schopen (Gregory Schopen, 'If You Can't Remember, How to Make It Up: Some Monastic Rules for Redacting Canonical Texts', in Petra Kieffer-Pülz and Jens-Uwe Hartmann (eds), *Bauddhavidyāsudhākaraḥ: Studies in Honour of Heinz Bechert on the Occasion of His 65th Birthday* (Swisttal-Odendorf, 1997), pp. 571–82). It is thus important to remember that the stories of the present are as much part of the narrative as the *jātaka* stories themselves.

[18] In some cases specific characters or backgrounds are given, for example see note below. Whilst these specific identifications are interesting, the broader picture is best illuminated, in my view, through concentrating on the gender and monastic division. The reasons for this will, I trust, become clear as we proceed.

[19] In the vast majority of the remaining stories, the implied audience is the community of monks, but this is not made totally clear.

[20] According to my statistics, 23 stories are told to kings, 12 to the wealthy layman Anāthapiṇḍika, four to members of the Buddha's family, five to brahmins, and one each to an Ājīvika and Baka Brahmā.

[21] JA 421, 490, 494, 506, 511 and 543.

[22] As one example amongst many, J.G. Jones states as fact that 'the Jātaka was mainly concerned with the preoccupations of layfolk and had its currency mainly within the lay community'. John G. Jones, *Tales and Teachings of the Buddha: The Jātaka Stories in Relation to the Pāli Canon* (2nd edn, Christchurch, New Zealand, 2001), p. 72.

As well as the monastic bias, it is clear that women were not considered to have heard many of the stories of the JA. There is no explicit mention of a nun being told a *jātaka* story, though it is possible that nuns were considered to be included in the massed monastic audience. Some of the stories involve characters identified with nuns, for example Rāhula's mother, Mahāpajāpatī Gotamī, and Uppalavaṇṇā, suggesting perhaps that they were believed to be present in the audience. Many more stories concern the dangers of interaction with women, and one assumes that these stories were aimed solely at a male audience.

In its absence of dialogue between the Buddha and nuns the JA is in keeping with the oldest Theravāda scriptures. Von Hinüber has recently pointed out that 'the Buddha is never mentioned as talking to any individual nun in the four Nikāyas of the Suttapiṭaka'.[23] Indeed, these scriptures do not show any nuns being directly ordained by the Buddha, whilst individual nuns are only rarely mentioned at all, and only Ānanda and two other monks are said to have talked directly to nuns. On the basis of this evidence von Hinüber concludes that there was no order of nuns during the time of the Buddha, but that this was founded shortly after his death. Von Hinüber suggests that there were two rival factions after the Buddha's death, one loyal to Mahākassapa and the other to Ānanda. The latter, on the basis of social pressures such as the need 'not to be disadvantaged against any other religious movements such as Jainism',[24] won the battle for the founding of the nuns' order.

Von Hinüber's observations make absorbing reading, but I find myself unconvinced by his argument, for three reasons.[25] Firstly, as he points out, there is *some* evidence from the earliest texts that nuns existed at the time of the Buddha, for he is shown talking about them and ordering a monk to go and preach to them.[26] Secondly, there is evidence from the *Vinaya* as well as from material in the *Khuddaka-nikāya* that nuns were considered to have conversed with the Buddha. For example, ten of the nuns in the *Therīgāthā* claim to have met the Buddha in person, and Bhaddā the former Jain claims that he ordained her directly in the same manner in which he ordained the earliest monks.[27] Some of the nuns named as members of the earliest community are said to have lived at the same time as the Buddha, and furthermore Mahāpajāpatī Gotamī, who is credited with founding and leading the order of nuns, is traditionally said to have predeceased the Buddha; the *Vinaya* records that the Buddha himself went to preach to her on her deathbed.[28] These texts are admittedly likely to be later than the *suttanta*s that form von Hinüber's evidence, but not by so much that the history of the nuns' order could have been totally rewritten to obscure the fact that the Buddha never founded an order of nuns. Finally, and in my view most

[23] Oskar von Hinüber, 'The Foundation of the Bhikkhunīsamgha: A Contribution to the Earliest History of Buddhism', *Annual Report of the International Research Institute for Advanced Buddhology at Soka University* 11 (2008): 21.

[24] Von Hinüber, 'The Foundation of the Bhikkhunīsamgha': 25.

[25] Since writing this I have come across a more detailed critique of von Hinüber's hypothesis to which I refer interested readers: Ven. Anālayo, 'Theories on the Foundation of the Nuns' Order – A Critical Evaluation', *Journal of the Centre for Buddhist Studies, Sri Lanka*, 6 (2008): 105–142.

[26] The evidence is presented in von Hinüber, 'The Foundation of the Bhikkhunīsamgha': 22–4.

[27] See the verses of Jentī, Bhaddā, Vāsiṭṭhī, Sujātā, Anopamā, Cālā, Upacālā, Sīsūpacālā, Sundarī, and Subhā Jīvakambavanikā. Bhaddā the former Jain declares (verse 109): 'Having bent the knee, having paid homage to him, I stood with cupped hands face to face with him. "Come, Bhaddā," he said to me; that was my ordination.' Norman's translation in Mrs C.A.F. Rhys-Davids and K.R. Norman (trans.) *Poems of Early Buddhist Nuns (Therīgāthā)* (Oxford, 1989).

[28] For all the sources which depict Mahāpajāpatī Gotamī's interactions with the Buddha see G.P. Malalasekera, *Dictionary of Pāli Proper Names* (Oxford, 1997).

convincingly, one has to ask how the early Buddhist community would have been able to sanction female renunciants if the Buddha himself had not, especially if we accept von Hinüber's scenario of competing factions in the argument. Given the presence of nuns in the Jain community, with which the early Buddhist community competed, the question of female ordination must have been raised with the Buddha, and either he sanctioned it (reluctantly or otherwise) or he did not. If the latter, then it is hard to imagine how it could have been sanctioned after his death.

A preferable explanation for the lack of dialogue between the Buddha and his nuns is perhaps that the monks' and nuns' communities lived rather independently, and may even have preserved different records of their own interactions with the Buddha and experiences of the Buddhist path. The *Therīgāthā* and *Therī-apadāna* appear to be examples of texts preserved by the nuns' community as counterparts to male-authored texts.[29] The four main *nikāya*s present a predominantly androcentric world, but this does not mean that there were no nuns, for as an undergraduate lecturer of mine used to say, absence of evidence is not evidence of absence. The androcentrism of these texts may simply reflect the fact that they were preserved by monks, and that these monks marginalized the nuns' community. The lack of nuns in the audience for the Buddha's *jātaka* stories suggests that the JA was also most likely preserved and used by monks.

Whereas nuns are never mentioned explicitly as listening to *jātaka* stories in the JA, there are a few that are said to have been told to laywomen. The Buddha tells one story (JA 512) to the laywoman Visākhā and her friends, who visit the Buddha during a drinking festival. Since Visākhā's five hundred friends have been joyfully participating in this festival, they dance, quarrel, and make improper gestures in the Buddha's presence. After having first sobered them up with a terrifying display of magical powers, at Visākhā's request the Buddha tells a story about the origins of drink. An un-named laywoman forms the audience for another story (JA 223) which the Buddha tells to reassure her that her husband will one day appreciate her kind nature. In a similar vein are two stories (JA 320, 333) that are told to the wife of a landowner, after the latter shows his ingratitude and lack of affection. In addition, laywomen are explicitly said to be included in the lay community on at least one occasion when they are listening to a *jātaka* story. Their presence in the narrative frame of the JA is therefore minimal, but they are at least represented.

Once again it is instructive to compare the audience within the narrative with that outside it. With the nuns' lineage only recently reintroduced in Theravāda countries after a long absence, we have little evidence to suggest whether or not *jātaka* stories formed a part of a nun's education. With laywomen we are on firmer ground, for the majority of the active lay community in Theravāda countries is female. Laywomen request and receive sermons, participate in rituals and festivals, and are generous donors to the monastery and temple. It is curious, therefore, that whilst the audience for *jātaka* stories within the JA is made up predominantly of monks, the audience for sermons (of which *jātaka* stories are often a part) is predominantly laywomen: the opposite to monks in all respects. There are no reliable sources to suggest which stories are most popular in sermons, but one assumes that the plethora of stories recommending that men be suspicious of women are glossed

[29] On the female authorship of the *Therīgāthā* see Kathryn R. Blackstone, *Women in the Footsteps of the Buddha: Struggle for Liberation in the Therīgāthā* (Richmond, 1998). On the *Therī-apadāna* see Sally Mellick, 'A Critical Edition, with Translation, of Selected Portions of the *Pāli Apadāna*' (Oxford University D.Phil. Thesis, 1993), and Jonathan S. Walters, 'A Voice from the Silence: The Buddha's Mother's Story', *History of Religions* 33/4 (1994): 358–79.

over in favour of those narratives advocating generosity and good conduct, which are equally numerous.

Studies into how *jātaka* stories are and have been used in Buddhist societies are sadly lacking, so it is difficult to compare the uses within the narrative with those outside it.[30] However, these internal examples of how the stories were believed to have been used by the Buddha do provide a possible model for later uses. In addition the audience are a model audience, requesting the Buddha's help in understanding their experiences, and responding appropriately. Explanations about when, where, and to whom particular stories were told also preserve something of the original Buddhist community. Time after time we see poorly behaved monks dragged reluctantly to receive a telling-off from the Buddha. We learn about the character traits of key followers of the Buddha: the elder monk Sāriputta, we are told, was very stubborn; the king of Kosala respected the advice of the Buddha; many monks found a celibate life difficult.[31] In this way the JA is not just about the Buddha, but also all those people who had the great fortune of meeting him and hearing his stories. Many of these people became the last links with the Buddha after his passing, and were responsible for the continuation of his teachings, given to a variety of people to comment on or transform a variety of their situations.

Once again comparison with the other texts is instructive. With no audience within the JM to receive the stories and respond to them, we see no example of how to use the stories. Perhaps as a consequence of this omission, a redactor has added colophons to each story that suggest suitable purposes for it. For example, the first story is that of the starving tigress, who is saved from the temptation of eating her own newborn cubs by the Bodhisatta's generous gift of his own body as food. The colophon explains that this story inspires faith and demonstrates the importance of listening attentively to the *dhamma*, as it was brought to us with great difficulty. It should be used in sermons on compassion, as it demonstrates that great compassion has a reward.[32] In the case of the CP we have no evidence as to its use, though the purpose is clear: to glorify the Buddha and his path to buddhahood through an illustration of the perfections he acquired. Whether this is a narrative for monks, nuns, laypeople, or unbelievers is not clear, and neither is the appropriate audience response: should we worship the Buddha or aspire to be like him? Both the JM and CP may be more organized and elegant than the JA, and they are certainly more concise, but their lack of dialogical framing renders them less effective as teachings, because we have no model audience. In addition, they do not preserve any of the anecdotal tradition of the

---

[30] Some evidence on the various uses of *jātaka* stories is found scattered through ethnographic works. I draw together this material and supplement it with my own observations in Chapter 7 of Appleton, *Jātaka Stories in Theravāda Buddhism*.

[31] JA 69 tells of how Sāriputta gave up meal-cakes after being jokingly accused of overindulgence. His refusal to ever eat them again was much talked of by his fellow monks, prompting the Buddha to tell of similarly determined behaviour in the past, when Sāriputta was a snake who refused on pain of death to suck back his poison from a bite. JA 77 and 314, amongst others, show King Pasenadi approaching the Buddha for advice. Jones counts 24 stories that are told to a monk who is having difficulties resisting the charms of women (usually his former wife). Jones, *Tales and Teachings of the Buddha*, p. 73.

[32] J.S. Speyer (trans.), *The Jātakamālā: Garland of Birth-Stories of Ārya-śūra* (London, 1895), p. 8. In the prologue to his edition Kern notes that the language of these epilogues is somewhat different to the stories but that he cannot be sure that they are interpolations, since they seem to represent a very old tradition. Hendrik Kern (ed.) *The Jātaka-māla, Stories of Buddha's Former Incarnations, Otherwise Entitled Bodhisattva-avadāna-mālā, by Ārya-çūra* (Cambridge MA, 1943 [first published 1891]), p. x.

Buddha's great storytelling occasions. These texts are solely about the Bodhisatta's great acts of the past.

Textual Community

We have now examined the role of the Buddha as narrator and of the audience for his stories, as it is presented within the narrative frame of the JA. We have seen that the dialogical setting allows the Buddha to be viewed as the source of all wisdom (worldly and Buddhist) and a man with a solution to every problem. His ability to recount his own past and that of other people establishes him as a great spiritual leader, with supernormal vision into the way the universe operates. The audience within the story are preserved as representatives of all Buddhists, requesting and receiving these nuggets of insight from the All-Knowing One. They model the learning process, trusting the Buddha's understanding of *kamma* and of human nature, and applying his wisdom to their own lives and paths. The predominantly monastic audience establishes the authority of the monastic redactors who have compiled and preserved the text, and thereby reinforces the authenticity of the text itself. These many benefits are brought about by the simple narrative frame of the stories of the JA.

When this frame is lost, as in the case of the JM and CP, there is a tendency to view *jātaka*s solely as stories illustrating the actions and path of the Buddha, both in order to glorify the person of the Bodhisatta and to instruct those wishing to emulate him. This is clearly the purpose of both the JM and the CP, but it is not an interpretation that can be read back into the JA. In fact, the oldest birth stories we have – those embedded in *sutta* texts of the *nikāya*s – demonstrate that this was far from the earliest use of the stories. Instead these stories demonstrate the inferiority of the Bodhisatta in comparison to the Buddha. The actions of the Bodhisatta are good, but solely in a non-Buddhist context: he is a skilled craftsman (*Pacetana sutta*, AN 3, 15), organizes a great bloodless sacrifice (*Kūṭadanta sutta*, DN 5), amasses great wealth (*Mahāsudassana sutta*, DN 17) and gives it away to various worthy recipients (*Velāma sutta*, AN 9, 20), or renounces and teaches the way to the heavenly realms (*Mahāgovinda sutta*, DN 19; *Makhādeva sutta*, MN 83). In each story the Buddha makes an explicit comparison between the skills and activities of the Bodhisatta and his own superior achievements, so – he points out – teaching the way to heaven is inferior to teaching the eightfold path to *nibbāna*, and being skilled in dealing with the flaws of wood is not as good as being skilled with regard to the flaws of body, speech and mind. Far from glorifying the Bodhisatta's long path to eventual buddhahood, these early *jātaka* stories highlight the inferiority and mundane skills of the Bodhisatta. This is not done in order to demonstrate the failings of the Bodhisatta, however, but rather to highlight the limited opportunities for spiritual progress that are found in a world without Buddhism. Thus, in these texts the Buddha tells *jātaka* stories in order to make the audience appreciate his great achievements and the benefit he has brought to the world.

This early ideology of *jātaka* stories – that they demonstrate the superiority of the Buddha and the great contribution he has made to humankind by founding the Buddhist community and teaching the *dhamma* – is preserved to a certain extent in the JA, where the Buddha's presence seems at least equally important to that of the Bodhisatta. That the JA is in some sense *about* the Buddha rather than Bodhisatta is suggested by the *Nidāna-kathā*, a long biographical preface to the JA that traces the Buddha's long career from his initial resolve at the foot of Dīpaṅkara Buddha, right through to the donation of the Jeta Grove to the Buddhist monastic community by Anāthapiṇḍika. The Jeta Grove is the setting in which the Buddha is said to have related many of his birth stories, including the first one, which is – one suspects not coincidentally – related to Anāthapiṇḍika. The *Nidāna-kathā* thus acts as a preface to the stories of the present, rather than the stories of the past, and provides an explanation for how the Buddha has become able to tell these many stories. The setting of *jātaka* narrations in a biography of the Buddha is also found in the *Mahāvastu*, a Lokkotaravādin text that traces a similar biography to the *Nidāna-kathā*. In this text, *jātaka* stories are primarily told to illustrate certain events in the Buddha's final life, for example there is a cluster of stories surrounding the courting of the Buddha's wife, who, we discover, has been his wife many times in the past. Whether or not the Buddha had to win his bride in the past too would seem to fit better into a discussion of the Buddha than of the Bodhisatta or his path.

As I have discussed elsewhere, the JA is a very important text in the history of the *jātaka* genre, since its many layers of composition reflect both the old association of stories with glorifying the Buddha's achievements, and evolving ideas about the *bodhisatta* path and the extent to which it should be emulated by Buddhist practitioners.[33] By the end of the compositional history of the JA the *jātaka* genre was understood as being about the Bodhisatta and his path, and so subsequent texts saw the frame narrative that depicts the Buddha, as omniscient narrator, as dispensible. However, the stories of the present in the JA clearly demonstrate the importance of the Buddha in an understanding of his birth stories, as well as the centrality of his audience, who request and listen to his narrations.

It is not only in the stories of the present that other characters play a role: on many occasions characters in the past are identified with specific members of the early Buddhist community. In many of the stories of the past the Bodhisatta is not even the central character, but is rather a passer-by or witness, later recalling the actions of other people.[34] For example in the *Lakkhaṇa-jātaka* (JA 11) the Buddha tells of how the senior monk Sāriputta was born as a stag who judiciously led a herd of deer to safety, whilst his brother – a previous birth of the schismatic monk and quintessential villain Devadatta – led his herd to ruin. The Bodhisatta was their father, but played a minimal role in the story. The JA is therefore not a text simply about the Bodhisatta's actions, but is about the experiences of the founder of the Buddhist community, and his interactions with other members of that community both in the past and during his final life.

For the JA, the dialogue between the Buddha and his audience is not an incidental frame that can be ignored at will. As Esposito also states in the case of Jain literature, the embedded nature of dialogue matters. It gives the text its very meaning, granting authenticity to the stories and their redactors, glorifying the narrator, and creating a sense of community both past and present. Modern audiences are part of this community, modelling their actions

---

33 See in particular Chapters 3–5 of Appleton, *Jātaka Stories in Theravāda Buddhism*. Briefly speaking, I argue that the framing of the stories by the JA and the addition of the *Nidāna-kathā* transformed *jātaka*s from stories about events witnessed by the Buddha to stories about the *bodhisatta* path. The individual stories predate this focus upon the Bodhisatta and his path, which explains why so many of them sit uneasily with the tradition's definition of *jātaka*s as stories about the gradual acquisition of the qualities required for buddhahood (stated in the introductory verses of the JA and assumed by texts such as the *Cariyāpiṭaka*).

34 The identification of one character – even a silent and totally uninvolved witness – with the Bodhisatta, despite the Buddha's ability to also see the past births of other people as well as himself, is a requirement of the JA and the *jātaka* genre more widely, but should not be seen as indicating the *jātaka*s are always *about* the Bodhisatta.

on audience members or on the Buddha himself, or perhaps identifying themselves with characters in the past. They too are in a dialogue with the Buddha and his early followers.

Abbreviations

AN	Aṅguttara Nikāya
CP	Cariyāpiṭaka
DN	Dīgha Nikāya
JA	Jātakatthavaṇṇanā
JM	Jātakamālā
MN	Majjhima Nikāya

References

Anālayo, Ven., 'Theories on the Foundation of the Nuns' Order – A Critical Evaluation', *Journal of the Centre for Buddhist Studies, Sri Lanka* 6 (2008): 105–42.

Appleton, Naomi, *Jātaka Stories in Theravāda Buddhism: Narrating the Bodhisatta Path* (Farnham: Ashgate, 2010).

Blackstone, Kathryn R., *Women in the Footsteps of the Buddha: Struggle for Liberation in the Therīgāthā* (Richmond: Curzon, 1998).

Cowell, E.B. (ed. – several translators), *The Jātaka or Stories of the Buddha's Former Births* (6 vols, Cambridge: Cambridge University Press, 1895–1907).

Fausbøll, V. (ed.), *The Jataka Together With Its Commentary being Tales of the Anterior Births of Gotama Buddha* (6 vols, London: Trübner and Co., 1877–96).

von Hinüber, Oskar, *Entstehung und Aufbau der Jātaka-Sammlung* (Stuttgart: Franz Steiner Verlag, 1998).

———, 'The Foundation of the Bhikkhunīsamgha: A Contribution to the Earliest History of Buddhism', *Annual Report of the International Research Institute for Advanced Buddhology at Soka University* 11 (2008): 3–29.

Jayawickrama, N.A. (ed.), *Buddhavaṃsa and Cariyāpiṭaka* (London: Pali Text Society, 1974).

——— (trans.), *The Story of Gotama Buddha (Jātaka-nidāna)* (Oxford: Pali Text Society, 1990).

Jones, John G., *Tales and Teachings of the Buddha: The Jātaka Stories in Relation to the Pāli Canon* (2nd edn, Christchurch, New Zealand: Cybereditions, 2001).

Kern, Hendrik (ed.), *The Jātaka-māla, Stories of Buddha's Former Incarnations, Otherwise Entitled Bodhisattva-avadāna-mālā, by Ārya-çūra* (Cambridge MA: Harvard University Press, 1943, first published 1891).

Khoroche, Peter (trans.), *Once the Buddha Was a Monkey: Ārya Śūra's Jātakamālā* (Chicago and London: University of Chicago Press, 1989).

Malalasekera, G.P., *Dictionary of Pāli Proper Names* (Oxford: Pali Text Society, 1997).

Mellick, Sally, 'A Critical Edition, with Translation, of Selected Portions of the Pāli Apadāna' (Oxford University D.Phil. Thesis, 1993).

Ñāṇamoli, Bhikkhu (trans.), *The Path of Purification (Visuddhimagga) by Bhadantācariya Buddhaghosa* (5th edn, Kandy: Buddhist Publication Society, 1991).

Rhys-Davids, C.A.F. and K.R. Norman (trans.), *Poems of Early Buddhist Nuns (Therīgāthā)* (Oxford: Pali Text Society, 1989).

Schopen, Gregory, 'If You Can't Remember, How to Make It Up: Some Monastic Rules for Redacting Canonical Texts', in Petra Kieffer-Pülz and Jens-Uwe Hartmann (eds), *Bauddhavidyāsudhākaraḥ: Studies in Honour of Heinz Bechert on the Occasion of His 65th Birthday* (Swisttal-Odendorf: Indica et Tibetica Verlag, 1997), pp. 571–82.

Shaw, Sarah, 'And that was I: How the Buddha Himself Creates a Path between Biography and Autobiography', in Linda Covill et al. (eds), *Lives Lived, Lives Imagined: Biography in the Buddhist Traditions* (Boston: Wisdom Publications, 2010), pp. 15–47.

Speyer, J.S. (trans.), *The Jātakamālā: Garland of Birth-Stories of Ārya-śūra* (London: Henry Frowde, 1895).

Walters, Jonathan S., 'A Voice from the Silence: The Buddha's Mother's Story', *History of Religions* 33/4 (1994): 358–79.

PART II
Texts in Dialogue

Chapter 5
Orality, Authority, and Conservatism in the Prajñāpāramitā Sūtras

Douglas Osto

Introduction

No other corpus of Mahāyāna texts has captured the modern scholarly imagination more than the collection of Prajñāpāramitā Sūtras (Perfection of Wisdom scriptures) has in the last half century. Among these the *Aṣṭasahaśrikā-prajñāpāramitā* (*Aṣṭa*) has garnered the most attention since the late Edward Conze proclaimed it to be the oldest Perfection of Wisdom text, leading some to speculate that it is the oldest Mahāyāna sūtra.[1] Although the *Aṣṭa* can no longer claim special status as the oldest Mahāyāna scripture,[2] its antiquity is confirmed by its inclusion among the oldest Chinese translations of Mahāyāna sūtras and a recently discovered Gāndhārī manuscript fragment.[3] No doubt some of the scholarly focus on the Prajñāpāramitā texts is due to Edward Conze's pioneering translation work. This in turn must be due in part to the survival of many of these sūtras within the extant Nepalese and Pāla manuscript collections. While the popularity of the *Heart Sūtra* and *Diamond Sūtra* in the Tibetan and East Asian Buddhist traditions have made them common objects of scholarly inquiry,[4] the

[1] See Edward Conze, *Prajñāpāramitā Literature* (Tokyo, 1978). Several scholars accept Conze's assertion of the *Aṣṭasāhasrikā*'s antiquity and draw conclusions about early Mahāyāna based on this. See especially Lewis Lancaster, 'The Oldest Mahāyāna Sūtra: Its Significance for the Study of Buddhist Development', *The Eastern Buddhist* 8 (1975): 30–41; Andrew Rawlinson, 'The Position of the *Aṣṭasāhasrikā Prajñāpāramitā* in the Development of Early Mahāyāna', in Lewis Lancaster and Luis O. Gómez (eds.), *Prajñāpāramitā and Related Systems: Studies in honor of Edward Conze* (Berkeley, 1977); and Stephen A. Kent, 'A Sectarian Interpretation of the Rise of Mahayana', *Religion* 12 (1982): 311–32.

[2] Other sūtras such as the *Pratyutpanna-buddha-saṃmukhāvasthita-samādhi-sūtra* and the *Ugraparipṛcchā* may be just as old, if not older than the *Aṣṭa*. See Paul Harrison (trans.), *The Samādhi of the Direct Encounter with the Buddhas of the Present: An Annotated English Translation of the Tibetan Version of the* Pratyutpanna-Buddha-Saṃmukhāvasthita-Samādhi-Sūtra (Tokyo, 1990); and Jan Nattier (trans.), *A Few Good Men: The Bodhisattva Path According to the Inquiry of Ugra* (Ugraparipṛccha) (Honolulu, 2003).

[3] For the various dates of the *Aṣṭa*'s translations into Chinese, see Lancaster, 'The Oldest Mahāyāna Sūtra'. At the conference for the International Association of Buddhist Studies held at Emory University in Atlanta, Harry Falk presented a paper, 'Another Collection of Kharosthi manuscripts from Gandhara' (27 June 2008), in which he referred to a manuscript fragment of the *Aṣṭa* in the Gāndhārī language dated to possibly as early as the first century CE.

[4] For three important studies on the *Heart Sūtra*, see Donald S. Lopez, Jr., *The* Heart Sūtra *Explained: Indian and Tibetan Commentaries* (New York, 1988); Donald S. Lopez, Jr., *Elaborations on Emptiness: Uses of the* Heart Sūtra (Princeton, 1996); and Jan Nattier, 'The Heart Sūtra: A Chinese Apocryphal Text?', *Journal of the International Association of Buddhist Studies* 15/2 (1992): 71–102. For a study and translation of the Sanskrit manuscript of the *Diamond Sūtra* from Gilgit, see Gregory Schopen, 'The manuscript of the Vajracchedikā found at Gilgit', in Luis Gómez

Indian commentarial tradition demonstrates the continued attention that Perfection of Wisdom Sūtras received within the Indian Buddhist intellectual tradition.[5]

Much of the work done on the *Aṣṭa* and other Prajñāpāramitā texts has focused on philosophical aspects, or attempted to reconstruct the 'early Mahāyāna' from them. However, few studies have investigated these texts as literature, and examined how they employ certain literary devices in order to promote their specific brand of Buddhism. One exception to this trend has been the recent monograph by Alan Cole, *Text as Father: Paternal Seductions in Early Mahāyāna Buddhist Literature*.[6] In this provocative and highly original work, Cole interrogates four Mahāyāna sūtras (the *Lotus Sūtra*, the *Diamond Sūtra*, the *Tathāgatagarbha Sūtra* and the *Vimalakīrtinirdeśa*) in order to expose their various rhetorical strategies. Following Cole's approach, I will in the following pages investigate several Prajñāpāramitā Sūtras as literature existing within the larger textual system of Indian Buddhism. Specifically, I investigate the following themes found in the Prajñāpāramitā Sūtras: the conceit of orality, the construction of textual authority, the employment of certain mainstream Buddhist characters, the concept of radical negation, and religious conservatism.[7]

In his chapter on the *Diamond Sūtra*, Cole makes two insightful observations about the text: the *sūtra*'s illusion of orality and its strong conservatism despite its radical program of philosophically negating the substantial nature of all phenomena.[8] These same two themes I will address in relation to several other Prajñāpāramitā texts. A primary conclusion of the current investigation is that as a whole the Prajñāpāramitā corpus also demonstrates the characteristics that Cole has witnessed in the *Diamond Sūtra*. Moreover, because these traits span numerous texts within the corpus throughout several centuries, their appearance cannot be analysed solely in terms of a relative chronology vis-à-vis other Mahāyāna *sūtra*s, but must be considered as one particular cluster of ideological postures in relation to a spectrum of religious orientations existing (both synchronically and diachronically) within Indian Buddhism.

Sources

I will limit my study to these Prajñāpāramitā texts: *The Perfection of Wisdom in 8,000 Lines* (*Aṣṭasahaśrikā-prajñāpāramitā*),[9] *The Perfection of Wisdom in 25,000 Lines*

---

and Jonathan Silk (eds.), *Studies in the Literature of the Great Vehicle: Three Mahāyāna Buddhist Texts* (Ann Arbor, 1989), pp. 89–139.

5 Some of the most important and influential commentaries are Maitreya's *Abhisamayālaṃkāra*, Haribhadra's *Abhisamayālaṃkārāloka*, Nāgabodhi's *Mahāprajñāpāramitāśāstra*.

6 Alan Cole, *Text as Father: Paternal Seductions in Early Mahāyāna Buddhist Literature* (Berkeley, 2005).

7 Other chapters in this volume, particularly those of Esposito, Nicholson, and Rohlman, elucidate the complex relationship between literary and philosophical genres in Jain and Hindu traditions as well as Buddhist ones.

8 Cole, *Text as Father*, pp. 174ff.

9 For an English translation, see Edward Conze (trans.), *The Perfection of Wisdom in Eight Thousand Lines & Its Verse Summary* (San Francisco, 1973 [1958]). For a Sanskrit edition, see P.L. Vaidya (ed.), *Aṣṭasāhasrikā Prajñāpāramitā* (Darbhanga, 1960). The *Aṣṭa* was first translated into Chinese by Lokakṣema as the *Dàoxíng bōrě jīng* 道行般若經 (T. 224) in 179 CE. See Charles Muller

(*Pañcaviṃśatisāhasrikā-prajñāpāramitā*),[10] *The Perfection of Wisdom in 2,500 Lines* (*Sārdhadvisāhasrikā-prajñāpāramitā*),[11] *The Perfection of Wisdom in 700 Lines* (*Saptaśatikā-prajñāpāramitā*),[12] and *The Heart Sūtra* (*Prajñāpāramitā-hṛdaya*).[13] Edward Conze divides the development of the Prajñāpāramitā corpus into four phases: (1) the elaboration of a basic text (ca. 100 BCE – 100 CE), which constitutes the original impulse; (2) the expansion of that text (ca. 100 CE – 300 CE); (3) the restatement of the doctrine in short texts and versified summaries (ca. 300 CE – 500 CE); (4) the period of Tantric influence and the absorption into magic (600 CE – 1200 CE).[14] Conze identifies the *Aṣṭa* and its verse summary (the *Ratnaguṇa-saṃcaya-gāthā*) as representing the earliest strata.[15] *The Pañcaviṃśatisāhasrikā* (*Pañcaviṃśati*) falls approximately within phase 2 (expansion phase); while the *Sārdhadvisāhasrikā*, *Saptaśatikā*, *Diamond* and *Heart Sūtra*s fall roughly into phase 3 (restatement of doctrine in short texts).[16] I must emphasize at this point that I am not strongly committed to definitive dates for these texts. As is well known, the dating of Mahāyāna *sūtra*s is notoriously difficult and relies largely on the dates of Chinese translations. Here I merely use Conze's scheme as a rough approximation to demonstrate the strong likelihood that the Perfection of Wisdom texts evolved over several centuries.[17] In what follows I will not attempt to develop a more definitive relative or absolute chronology of these texts. Rather, I hope to demonstrate the continuity of certain themes such as the conceit of orality, the construction of authority, the appearance of mainstream Buddhist literary figures, the rhetoric of radical negation, and an underlying conservatism within these texts.

(chief editor), *The Digital Dictionary of Buddhism* (http://www.buddhism-dict.net/ddb/; accessed 16 July 2010).

[10] For an English translation, see Edward Conze (trans. and ed.), *The Large Sutra on Perfect Wisdom with Divisions of the Abhismayālaṅkāra* (Berkeley, 1975). For the Sanskrit text, see Nalinaksha Dutt (ed.), *The* Pañcaviṃśatisāhasrikā Prajñāpāramitā *edited with critical notes and introduction* (London, 1934). The *Pañcaviṃśati* was first translated into Chinese by Dharmarakṣa as the *Guāngzàn bōrě bōluómì jīng* 光讚般若波羅蜜經 (T. 222.8.147a–216b) in 286 CE (Muller, *Digital Dictionary of Buddhism*).

[11] For an English translation, see Edward Conze (trans.), *Perfect Wisdom: The Short Prajñāpāramitā Texts* (London, 1973), pp. 1–78. For the Sanskrit text, see P.L. Vaidya (ed.), *Mahāyānasūtrasaṃgrahaḥ*, Part I (Darbhanga, 1961), pp. 1–74. This *sūtra* was translated by Upaśūnya as the *Shèngtiānwáng bōrě bōluómì jīng* 勝天王般若波羅蜜經 (T. 231) in 565 CE (Muller, *Digital Dictionary of Buddhism*).

[12] For an English translation, see Conze, *Perfect Wisdom*, pp. 79–107. For the Sanskrit text, see Vaidya (ed.), *Mahāyānasūtrasaṃgrahaḥ*, Part I, pp. 340–51. The Chinese translation translated by Mandra is known as the *Wénshūshīlì suǒshuō móhēbōrě bōluómì jīng* 文殊師利所說摩訶般若波羅蜜經 (T. 232.8.726a–732c) (Muller, *Digital Dictionary of Buddhism*).

[13] For an English translation, see Conze, *Perfect Wisdom*, pp. 140–43. For the Sanskrit text, see Vaidya (ed.), *Mahāyānasūtrasaṃgrahaḥ*, Part I, pp. 97–8. The *Heart Sūtra* was translated seven times into Chinese; the most popular translations were by Kumārajīva and Xuanzang (Muller, *Digital Dictionary of Buddhism*).

[14] Conze, *Prajñāpāramitā Literature*, p. 1.

[15] Ibid.

[16] See Conze, *Perfect Wisdom*, pp. i–iii.

[17] The Chinese translations of the *Aṣṭa* clearly demonstrate this development over time. See Lancaster, 'The Oldest Mahāyāna Sūtra'.

The Conceit of Orality

The oral nature of the early Vedic and Buddhist textual traditions is universally recognized. The original medium of composition of the earliest Mahāyāna sūtras is unknown, but in recent decades some scholars have speculated that they were originally written compositions. Beginning in the 1990s, a debate began within Buddhist studies over the oral versus written composition of Mahāyāna sūtras. Sparked by the emergence of 'Orality Studies', and the recognition that the earliest use of writing for Buddhist texts seemed roughly to correspond to the time when the Mahāyāna began, some scholars imagined a possible connection between the new technology of writing and the emergence of the Mahāyāna. Richard Gombrich first put forth the idea that the Mahāyāna began as a written tradition.[18] Discussing the several Mahāyāna sūtras known to proclaim the merit acquired through writing them down and enshrining them for worship, Gombrich states: 'My feeling is that these texts preserve a sense of wonder at this marvelous invention [writing] which permits an individual's opinions or experiences to survive whether or not anyone agrees or cares.'[19] More recently, Alan Cole has also argued for the written nature of the early Mahāyāna in his *Text as Father*.[20] One point raised by Cole is the fact that Mahāyāna sūtras often refer to themselves as texts that should be copied and transmitted to others. Moreover, the word 'book' commonly appears and the act of writing is specifically mentioned.[21] Cole admits that these elements might have been added later to an oral tradition; however, he sees another type of evidence as militating against this idea: there is change in the style of presenting the voice of the Buddha often on a level of narrative sophistication not found in non-Mahāyāna sources.

While it is true that Mahāyāna sources often mention the merit of copying sūtras, they also frequently praise the memorizing, reciting, and hearing of *sūtras*.[22] Moreover, written texts from Gandhāra radiocarbon dated to as early as the second century CE demonstrate the early use of writing by non-Mahāyāna Indian Buddhists as well.[23] No doubt there existed in the ancient Indian Buddhist world a complex relationship between oral and written texts. We know that early Chinese translators such as Dharmarakṣa (third century CE) worked from written Indic texts.[24] It also seems likely that some sūtras were transmitted orally from

---

18 Richard Gombrich, 'How the Mahāyāna Began', in Tadeusz Skorupski (ed.), *The Buddhist Forum, Vol. I: Seminar Papers 1987–88* (London, 1990).

19 Ibid. (brackets mine). For the now famous article on this 'cult of the book' in the Mahāyāna, see Gregory Schopen, 'The Phrase "*sa pṛthivīpradeśaś caityabhūto bhavet*" in the *Vajracchedikā*: Notes on the Cult of the Book in Mahāyāna', *Indo-Iranian Journal* 17 (1975): 147–81. For a recent critique of this article, see David Drewes, 'Revisiting the phrase "*sa pṛthivīpradeśaś caityabhūto bhavet*" and the Mahāyāna Cult of the Book', *Indo-Iranian Journal* 50 (2007): 101–43. In this writer's opinion, while many of Drewes' criticisms are accurate, the fact that many Mahāyāna sūtras mention the merit gained through the copying and worshipping of the written text remains an important insight of Schopen's study.

20 Cole, *Text as Father*, pp. 14–17.

21 Cole does not give a Sanskrit term; however, *pustaka* is often used in the surviving Sanskrit sources such as the *Lotus Sūtra*.

22 David Drewes, 'Early Indian Mahāyāna Buddhism I', *Religion Compass* 3 (2009): 6 (accessed electronically, Doi 10.1111/j.1749–8171.2009.00195.x).

23 Ibid.

24 See Daniel Boucher, *Bodhisattvas of the Forest and the Formation of the Mahāyāna: A Study and Translation of the* Rāṣṭrapālaparipṛcchā-sūtra (Honolulu, 2008), p. 93.

an Indic language into written Chinese. However, this transmission from Indic oral text to written Chinese text does not mean that an Indic written archetype did not exist. The mixing of media between oral and written was most likely complex and interwoven. However, the oral/aural component of this complex relationship has been lost to us. All we possess now are the linguistic remains of a written tradition. Furthermore, there is no definitive way of demonstrating from the written records that any Mahāyāna sūtra, or part of a sūtra, existed in a prior state as a strictly oral text.

In sum, while parts of the earliest strata of the Perfection of Wisdom literature may have existed in strictly oral form, we find evidence that sometime in the early centuries of the Common Era these texts appear in writing. The creation and/or appearance of Buddhist sūtras in writing generated a particular problem of authority in the Indian context. It is widely agreed that the earliest Buddhist sūtras were memorized and passed down orally for generations prior to the use of writing for religious purposes. The oral nature of these texts is reflected in the standardised opening phrase found at the beginning of every *sūtra*: 'Thus have I heard, at one time the Lord dwelled…' (*evaṃ mayā śrutam ekasmin samaye bhagavān… viharati sma*). Traditionally, these words were believed to be recited at the first Buddhist council following the final *nirvāṇa* of the Buddha, by Ānanda, faithful monk-servant and cousin of the Buddha, who not only was present at practically all of the Buddha's sermons, but also possessed an eidetic memory and could recall verbatim every teaching occasion of the Buddha. In this way, the phrase 'Thus have I heard' became the authenticating mark of a text as sūtra, endowing it with all the authority of the 'Buddha's words' (*buddhavacana*).

With the advent of written Mahāyāna *sūtra*s a dilemma was generated: does authority now reside in the written text or in the testimony of a faithfully transmitted oral tradition? Donald Lopez phrases the problem thus:

> The question of the identity of the rapporteur, then, is the question of where authority should lie: in what is written, or in the testimony as to what has been heard. If there is to be resolution, it would seem to come in the moment that is so difficult to imagine, when a monk puts stylus to palm leaf and penned the words, *evaṃ mayā śrutam ekasmin samaye…*[25]

Like their mainstream Buddhist counterparts, all Mahāyāna *sūtra*s begin with the 'Thus have I heard' opening phrase. While some Mahāyāna *sūtra*s such as the *Avataṃsaka* and *Gaṇḍavyūha*[26] seem happy to apply this required stamp of authentication to their beginnings and then quickly transition to highly ornate visually overloaded descriptions of the cosmically baroque, other *sūtra*s such as the Perfection of Wisdom texts demonstrate a style reminiscent of their oral ancestors. About the *Diamond Sūtra*, Cole makes the follow comments:

---

[25] See Donald S. Lopez, Jr., 'Authority and Orality in the Mahāyāna', *Numen* 42/1 (1995): 42.

[26] For an English translation of the *Avataṃsaka*, see Thomas Cleary (trans.), *The Flower Ornament Scripture: A Translation of the Avatamsaka Sutra* (Boston, 1993). For a study of visual metaphor in the Mahāyāna, see David McMahan, *Empty Vision: Metaphor and Visionary Imagery in Mahāyāna Buddhism* (New York, 2002). For a recent study of the *Gaṇḍavyūha*, see Douglas Osto, *Power, Wealth and Women in Indian Mahāyāna Buddhism: The Gaṇḍavyūha-sūtra* (London and New York, 2008).

> Though the first line of the text announces in traditional form, 'Thus I heard,' the narrator disappears until the closing lines. Hence the narrative, while obviously a composition, is attempting to present its content as a historical, oral moment, unaffected by the medium that it inhabits. Slipping from awareness of a constructed narrative into the impression of unadulterated orality presumably brings the reader more intimately into the discussion and obviates addressing both problematic sides of the narrative composition: the authorial work in bringing the Real into narrative-textual form and then the reader's hazardous work of interpreting that discourse... The studied effacement of the narrator gives the illusion that spoken words were transmitted perfectly into narrative and then into written words, with no subsequent shift in form, content, or meaning.[27]

Here we witness in the *Diamond Sūtra* an attempt to capture the 'oral moment' of the traditional *sūtra* genre, and thereby efface or conceal its written nature. This move is a basic strategy of the Perfection of Wisdom *sūtra*s, and it is achieved primarily through the use of dialogue. Through their seeming reproduction of historical, oral discourse, these texts demonstrate a basic anxiety about their own authority. Thus the position of the Prajñāpāramitā Sūtras is both highly traditional and innovative. In their literary mode, they are traditional in that one of the means of establishing the authority of the *sūtra*s is by simulating the 'unadulterated orality' of dialogues faithfully memorized by the monastic tradition. On the other hand, in their doctrine the Perfection of Wisdom's teaching of radical negation by means of the doctrine of 'emptiness' (*śūnyatā*) is philosophically innovative.

Now let us examine in more detail how the Prajñāpāramitā texts attempt to establish their religious authority.

Authority

The beginning of the *Perfection of Wisdom in 8,000 Lines* (*Aṣṭasāhasrikā Prajñāpāramita*, or *Aṣṭa*) reveals a number of characteristic features of the Perfection of Wisdom corpus. It reads:

> Thus have I heard at one time the Lord dwelled at Rājagṛha on Gṛdhakūṭa Mountain together with a great assembly of monks, with 1250 monks, all of whom were arhats whose cankers were destroyed, who were without defilements, controlled, with minds completely liberated, who were completely freed through wisdom, who possessed perfect knowledge, who were well-bred steeds, who were great serpents, whose work was done, who had done what needed to be done, who had put down their burden, whose aim had been obtained, whose bondage to existence had been destroyed, whose minds were liberated through perfect knowledge, who had obtained the supreme perfection of control over all their thoughts, except for one person – namely the Venerable Ānanda.
>
> At that time, the Lord addressed the Venerable Elder, Subhūti, 'Subhūti, reveal[28] to the bodhisattvas, the great beings, the perfection of wisdom such as how bodhisattvas, the great beings, ought to go forth to the perfection of wisdom'.

---

27 Cole, *Text as Father*, pp. 173–4.

28 In the expression *pratibhātu te subhūte*... (literally, 'Let it be [made] clear by you, Subhūti...'), *te* seems most likely to be a Buddhist hybrid form of the second person, instrumental case. See Franklin Edgerton, *Buddhist Hybrid Sanskrit Grammar and Dictionary, Volume I* (New Haven, 1953), §20.22.

> Then the thought occurred to the Venerable Śāriputra, 'Will the Venerable Elder Subhūti expound the perfection of wisdom to the bodhisattvas, the great beings, by himself through his own application and his own power from the force of inspired wisdom, or through the might of the Buddha?'
>
> The Venerable Subhūti, through the might of the Buddha, perceived with his mind these thoughts of the Venerable Śāriputra and said to him, 'Venerable Śāriputra, whatever the disciples of the Lord say, teach, explain, utter, illuminate, declare; all this is to be known as the heroic work of the Tathāgata. What is the reason for this? Whatever dharma is taught by the Tathāgata, they practice that preaching of the dharma, and realize and preserve its essence; having realized and preserved its essence, they say, teach, explain, utter, illuminate, and declare only just that; all of this is compatible with the essence of dharma.'[29]

In this introductory passage (*nidāna*) to the *sūtra* we find a number of features distinctive of the Perfection of Wisdom literature. The first point of interest is the rather brief and modest (for Mahāyāna *sūtra*s) introduction of who was present before the Buddha, here referred to by his common titles as 'Lord' (*bhagavān*), and Tathāgata ('Thus Gone One'). Noteworthy in the Sanskrit version is the fact that no *bodhisattva*s are mentioned as specifically present, nor are any particular bodhisattvas named. I will return to this point below.

The next distinctive feature of this passage is the presentation of the characters that are present before the Buddha. These are the 1250 monk disciples of the Buddha described as *arhat*s ('worthies') who have attained (with the exception of one) a number of spiritual accomplishments, each of which is actually a different way of saying that they

---

Graeme MacQueen, 'Inspired Speech in Early Mahāyāna Buddhism II', *Religion* 12 (1982): 49, translates *pratibhātu te subhūte...* as 'May something be clear to you, Subhūti...' This completely misses the sense that the Buddha is commanding (politely with the third person, imperative form of the verb) Subhūti to expound the Perfection of Wisdom to the bodhisattvas. Edward Conze's 'Make it clear now, Subhūti...' captures the correct sense here. See Conze, *The Perfection of Wisdom in Eight Thousand Lines*, p. 83.

[29] *evaṃ mayā śrutam / ekasmin samaye bhagavān rājagṛhe viharati sma gṛdhakūṭe parvate mahatā bhikṣusaṃghena sārdham ardhatrayodaśabhirbhikṣuśataiḥ, sarvairarhadbhiḥ kṣīṇāsravair niḥkleśair vaśībhūtaiḥ suvimuktacittaiḥ suvimuktaprajñair ājñair ājāneyair mahānāgaiḥ kṛtakṛtyaiḥ kṛtakaraṇīyair apahṛtabhārair anuprāptasvakārthaiḥ parikṣīṇabhavasaṃyojanaiḥ samyagājñāsuvimuktacittaiḥ sarvacetovaśiparamapāramiprāptair ekaṃ pudgalaṃ sthāpayitvā yaduta āyuṣmantam ānandam //*

tatra khalu bhagavānāyuṣmantaṃ subhūtiṃ sthaviram āmantrayate sma – pratibhātu te subhūte bodhisattvānāṃ mahāsattvānāṃ prajñāpāramitām ārabhya yathā bodhisattvā mahāsattvāḥ prajñāpāramitā niryāyur iti //

atha khalv āyuṣmataḥ śāriputrasyaitadabhavat – kim ayamāyuṣmān subhūtiḥ sthavira ātmīyena svakena prajñāpratibhānabalādhānena svakena prajñāpratibhānabalādhiṣṭhānena bodhisattvānāṃ mahāsattvānāṃ prajñāpāramitām upadekṣyati utāho buddhānubhāveneti?

atha khalvāyuṣmān subhūtirbuddhānubhāvena āyuṣmataḥ śāriputrasya imam evarūpaṃ cetasaiva cetaḥparivitarkamājñāya āyuṣmantaṃ śāriputram etad avocat – yatkiṃcidāyuṣman śāriputra bhagavataḥ śrāvakā bhāṣante deśayanti upadiśanti udīrayanti prakāśayanti saṃprakāśayanti, sa sarvastathāgatasya puruṣakāro veditavyaḥ / tatkasya hetoḥ? yo hi tathāgatena dharmo deśitaḥ, tatra dharmadeśanāyāṃ śikṣamāṇās te tāṃ dharmatāṃ sākṣātkurvanti dhārayanti, tāṃ dharmatāṃ sākṣātkṛtya dhārayitvā yadyadeva bhāṣante, yad yad eva deśayanti, yad yad eva upadiśanti, yad yad evodīrayanti, yad yad eva prakāśayanti, yad yad eva saṃprakāśayanti, sarvaṃ tad dharmatayā aviruddham. See P.L. Vaidya (ed.), *Aṣṭasāhasrikā Prajñāpāramita* (Darbhanga, 1960), pp. 1–3. My translation.

have achieved the ultimate goal of mainstream Buddhism: *nirvāṇa*. The one exception is Ānanda, who had not attained the goal due to his emotional attachment to the Buddha. The other two monks mentioned by name are Śāriputra and Subhūti, two important figures in mainstream Buddhist *sūtras*. I will return to the use of these types of literary figures in the Prajñāpāramitā literature below. For now, I only wish to emphasize that these disciples are positively portrayed as having attained a worthy goal, and the ones mentioned by name (Ānanda, Śāriputra, and Subhūti) would have been familiar to any Buddhist audience in ancient India.

One of the most significant aspects of this passage is Subhūti's statement that 'whatever the disciples of the Lord say, teach, explain, utter, illuminate, declare; all this is to be known as the heroic work of the Tathāgata'. Graeme MacQueen has written how this passage from the *Aṣṭa* borrows the ideas from mainstream Buddhism concerning the 'Buddha's words' (*buddhavacana*), and 'inspired speech' (*pratibhāna*), but interprets them in a new manner.[30] Whereas the concept of inspiration (*pratibhāna*), or inspired speech is found in mainstream sources such as the Pāli Canon to authorize the words of others (often disciples of the Buddha) as extended *buddhavacana*, in the *Aṣṭa pratibhāna* becomes the basis for the new revelation of the sūtra. MacQueen speculates that the Dharma preachers (*dharmabhāṇaka*) mentioned in the Mahāyāna *sūtras* may have employed this new idea in order to generate new sūtras, thus leading him to conclude that:

> Mahāyāna has brought about a truly radical shift in the relationship between *buddhavacana* and *pratibhāna*: no longer is *buddhavacana* the truth that once came to the community, to the formulation of which the *pratibhāṇa* of people other than the Buddha contributed a small part (as extended *buddhavacana*) but beyond which such *pratibhāna* no longer had any authority; rather *buddhavacana* is that which comes to the community *now* and comes not otherwise than through *pratibhāna*.[31]

Thus MacQueen sees Subhūti's statement as demonstrating a strategy to legitimize what follows as *buddhavacana*; and that this passage is one example of a method whereby the Mahāyāna established the authority of its new *sūtras*.

In order to appreciate better the nature of this legitimating strategy, we can contrast this approach with another found in the Mahāyāna *Gaṇḍavyūha-sūtra*. The *Gaṇḍavyūha* begins:

> Thus have I heard at one time the Lord was dwelling at Śrāvastī in Jeta Grove, the pleasure park of Anāthapiṇḍada, within the Great Array pavilion accompanied by five thousand bodhisattvas with the bodhisattvas Samantabhadra and Mañjuśrī foremost among them – namely the bodhisattva, the great being Jñānottarajñānin, Sattvottarajñānin, Asaṅgottarajñānin, Kusumottarajñānin....[32]

---

[30] Graeme MacQueen, 'Inspired Speech in Early Mahāyāna Buddhism I', *Religion* 11 (1981): 303–19; and MacQueen, 'Inspired Speech in Early Mahāyāna Buddhism II'.

[31] MacQueen, 'Inspired Speech in Early Mahāyāna Buddhism II'.: 60. Emphasis his.

[32] *evaṁ mayā śrutam| ekasmin samaye bhagavān śrāvastyāṁ viharati sma jetavane'nāthapiṇḍadasyārāme mahāvyūhe kūṭāgāre sārdhaṁ pañcamātrairbodhisattvasahasraḥi samantabhadramañjuśrībodhisattvapūrvaṁgamaiḥ| yaduta jñānottarajñāninā ca bodhisattvena mahāsattvena| sattvottarajñāninā ca| asaṅgottarajñāninā ca| kusumottarajñāninā ca* | (P.L. Vaidya [ed.], *Gaṇḍavyūhasūtra* [Darbhanga, 1960], p. 1). My translation. A list of 153 *bodhisattvas* follows grouped in sets of ten according to the final compound members in their names (*-jñānin*, *-dhvaja*, *-tejas*, etc.). There are 153 rather than 150, because the fifth group (*-netra*) contains 12 members, and the eighth group (*-ketu*) has 11 members.

In this way the Lord dwelled together with five thousand of the foremost bodhisattvas all of whom had embarked upon the vow to follow the course of the bodhisattva Samantabhadra, whose range was unobstructed due to their pervasion of all buddha fields, who had entered an infinitude of proclamations due to their unceasing approach toward the perfect awakening of all the tathāgatas, whose splendour was endless due to having obtained the light of gnosis of an ocean of principles of all the teachings of the buddhas, whose elucidation of good qualities would not end after endless eons due to the purity of their special knowledge, whose purity and range of supreme knowledge was unchecked all the way to the realm of space due to their seeing the Form Body as the basis for the world, who were free from darkness through the knowledge of the realm of beings as without beings or souls, whose gnosis was equal to the sky through their pervading nets of light-rays throughout the entire Dharma Realm.[33]

Also present were five hundred disciples with great psychic powers of whom all had perfectly awakened to the essence of the principle of reality, who had arrived at the direct perception of the limit of the real, who had penetrated into the nature of phenomena, who had escaped from the ocean of becoming, whose range was the sky of the Tathāgata; who had turned back the fetters, evil dispositions and evil latent tendencies; whose residence was an unobstructed firm basis; whose abode was sky-like peace; who had uprooted doubt, uncertainty and scepticism with regard to the Buddha; who had penetrated the path of resolution to attain the ocean of gnosis of the Buddha.[34]

The text proceeds to describe how the *bodhisattva*s, disciples, and others in attendance wondered about the previous bodhisattva practices of the Buddha. Thereupon,

reading the thoughts of the bodhisattvas, the Lord entered a trance called 'The Lion's Yawn' that was an array illuminating the world.... And immediately upon this occurrence, the Lord's Great Array pavilion became infinite in size. The pavilion became an array with a ground-surface of unsurpassed diamonds, with a surface that appeared to be a royal net of all jewels, covered with many gem flowers, evenly dispersed with great jewels, adorned with pillars of lapis lazuli, with royal ornaments evenly distributed, with jewels illuminating the world and a multitude of pairs of all gems.[35]

---

[33] *evaṁpramukhaiḥ pañcamātrairbodhisattvasahasraiḥ sarvaiḥ samantabhadrabodhisattvacaryāpraṇidhānābhiniryātairasaṅgagocaraiḥ sarvabuddhakṣetraspharaṇatayā| anantakāyādhiṣṭhānaiḥ sarvatathāgatopasaṁkramaṇatayā| anāvaraṇacakṣurmaṇḍalaviśuddhaiḥ sarvabuddhavikurvitadarśanatayā| vijñaptiṣvapramāṇagataiḥ sarvatathāgatābhisaṁbodhimukhopasaṁkramaṇāpratiprasrabdhatayā| anantālokaiḥ sarvabuddhadharmasamudranayajñānāvabhāsapratilabdhatayā| anantakalpākṣīṇaguṇanirdeśaiḥ pratisaṁvidviśuddhyā| ākāśadhātuparamajñānagocaraviśuddhyanigṛhītair yathāśayajagadrūpakāyasaṁdarśanatayā| vitimirair niḥsattvanirjīvasattvadhātuparijñayā| gaganasamaprajñaiḥ sarvadharmadhāturaśmijālaspharaṇatayā|* (Vaidya, *Gaṇḍavyūhasūtra*, p. 3). My translation.

[34] *pañcabhiśca śrāvakamaharddhikaśataiḥ sarvaiḥ satyanayasvabhāvābhisaṁbuddhair bhūtakoṭipratyakṣagatair dharmaprakṛtyavatīrṇair bhavasamudroccalitais tathāgatagaganagocaraiḥ saṁyojanānuśayavāsanāvinivartitair asaṅgālayanilayairgaganaśāntavihāribhir buddhakāṅkṣāvimativicikitsāsamucchinnaiḥ buddhajñānasamudrādhimuktipathāvatīrṇaiḥ||* (Vaidya, *Gaṇḍavyūhasūtra*, p. 3). My translation.

[35] *atha khalu bhagavāṁsteṣāṁ bodhisattvānāṁ cetasaiva cetaḥparivitarkamājñāya. siṁhavijṛmbhitaṁ nāma samādhiṁ samāpadyate sma jagadvirocanavyūham| samanantarasamāpannasya ca bhagavato mahāvyūhaḥ kūṭāgāro 'nantamadhyavipulaḥ saṁsthito 'bhūt|*

The *Gaṇḍavyūha* continues to describe a similar transformation of Jeta Grove and how countless other 'buddha fields' (*buddhakṣetra*) are made manifest and are likewise arrayed with jewels.

In these passages we see a number of features that sharply contrast with the beginning of the *Aṣṭa*. Foremost is the foregrounding of the *bodhisattva*s. Not only are there said to be 5,000 present, but 155 are mentioned by name. Moreover, their spiritual abilities and powers are described before those of the disciples. Next, is the *Gaṇḍavyūha*'s rather baroque visionary description of how the Buddha's trance (*samādhi*) transformed his pavilion, Jeta Grove and countless other buddha lands. However, more significant for our current discussion is the polemical turn that occurs following the description of this visionary experience.

The omniscient narrator of the *Gaṇḍavyūha* states that the great disciples present before the Buddha did not perceive this transformation. The narrator then informs his target audience of the many reasons why this was the case. The first and foremost reason given is that the disciples lacked the 'corresponding roots of merit'.[36] In other words, they had not developed enough good karma and subsequently established themselves on the Mahāyāna path. About this contrast between the *bodhisattva*s and disciples (*śrāvaka*) in this passage, David McMahan states, 'The fact that the *bodhisattva*s are depicted as seeing the vision, while the *śrāvaka*s remain oblivious, is at once an assertion of the value of seeing over hearing and the Mahāyāna over the "Hīnayāna".'[37] Based on this and other examples, McMahan develops the idea that the Mahāyāna employed these types of visionary accounts as a legitimating strategy and that the emergence of Mahāyāna corresponded to a shift from auditory means of knowing to more visually based means of knowing. Moreover, he speculates that this transformation may have been the result of the shift from an oral mainstream tradition to a written Mahāyāna tradition.[38] However, as we have seen, the *Aṣṭa* quite clearly right from the start claims legitimacy through 'inspired speech', not through visionary experience.

The insights of MacQueen and McMahan demonstrate that there are multiple means of establishing legitimacy and authority in Mahāyāna sūtras. While more visionary texts such as the *Gaṇḍavyūha* and others *sūtra*s from the *Avataṃsaka* collection may place more emphasis on the seeing of visions, the *Aṣṭa* and other *sūtra*s from the Perfection of Wisdom corpus stress the discourses and dialogues as inspired speech. Moreover, the Prajñāpāramitā texts employ characters from the mainstream Indian Buddhist tradition in a much more positive light than many other Mahāyāna sūtras, a point to which I shall now turn.

Characters

One of the most distinctive features of the Perfection of Wisdom literature is the presence of important roles given to certain characters drawn from 'mainstream'[39] Indian Buddhism.

---

aparājitavajradharaṇītalavyūhaḥ sarvamaṇiratnarājajālasaṁsthitabhūmitalamanekaratnapuṣpābhikīrṇo mahāmaṇiratnasuvikīrṇo vaiḍūryastambhopaśobhito jagadvirocanamaṇirājasuvibhaktālaṁkāraḥ sarvaratnayamakasaṁghāto. (Vaidya, *Gaṇḍavyūhasūtra*, pp. 4–5). My translation.

36 *kuśalamūlāsabhāgatayā* (Vaidya, *Gaṇḍavyūhasūtra*, p. 13).

37 David McMahan, 'Orality, Writing, and Authority in South Asian Buddhism: Visionary Literature and the Struggle for Legitimacy in the Mahāyāna', *History of Religions* 37/3 (1998): 269.

38 This idea is fully articulated in David McMahan, *Empty Vision: Metaphor and Visionary Imagery in Mahāyāna Buddhism* (New York, 2002).

39 The term 'mainstream' has now entered common scholarly usage for Indian Buddhist schools that are non-Mahāyāna (and often represent pre-Mahāyāna Buddhist ideas).

Recently Brian Black and Jonathan Geen suggest that when one South Asian religious tradition borrows characters from another, 'the characters may be popular or may strongly present authority, leading one tradition to adopt another's characters with a sort of me-too attitude'.[40] Often this is clearly the case when Mahāyāna *sūtra*s introduce mainstream Buddhist figures into their narratives. As a new religious movement in India, the Mahāyāna must have struggled to legitimate itself to the wider Buddhist community. By employing characters from the mainstream tradition, the Prajñāpāramitā Sūtras attempt to borrow the authority of these characters, use their traditional personas as a means of critiquing the views of earlier schools, and present its new philosophical message as if it were part of the original teachings of the Buddha. In this section, I briefly discuss the most significant mainstream characters occurring in the Perfection of Wisdom texts and detail how their roles differ from their use in mainstream sources such as the Theravādin Pāli Canon.

The most important character found in mainstream Indian Buddhist sources is, of course, the 'historical' Buddha, Siddhārtha Gautama (Pāli: Siddhattha Gotama), also known as Śākyamuni Buddha. Although the Buddha has always been considered by Buddhists to be more than merely human, non-Mahāyāna sources such as the Pāli Canon often present a rather human side to the Buddha. For instance, in mainstream sources, we find the Buddha at times getting annoyed with his monks,[41] making jokes[42] and suffering back pain.[43] But most importantly, in mainstream *sūtra*s the Buddha teaches the *dharma* through his many discourses. While this might seem obvious, it is important to note the significant changes that occur concerning the Buddha in many Mahāyāna *sūtra*s. As we have seen from the *Gaṇḍavyūha*, the Mahāyāna Buddha sometimes does not speak at all but instead enters a trance (*samādhi*) that leads to some magical display, which has some beneficial effect upon his audience. On some occasions instead of teaching, the Buddha performs other miracles such as causing light-rays to shoot forth from his forehead illuminating far-distant Buddha lands.[44] Although these more 'theistic' and miraculous aspects of the Buddha are also present in the Perfection of Wisdom texts, they are less significant and less common.[45] As MacQueen points out, the Prajñāpāramitā Sūtras tend to emphasise the perfection of wisdom (*prajñāpāramitā*) as the ultimate source of enlightenment and the 'mother' of all Buddhas.[46] In relation to this idea, we find that the Buddha of these *sūtra*s teaches the perfection of wisdom in discourses and enters into dialogues and lively debates with his disciples and *bodhisattva*s. This type of dialogical Buddha is more in line with the literary Buddha of mainstream sources such as the Pāli Canon.

---

40 See Brian Black and Jonathan Geen, 'The Character of 'Character' in Early South Asian Religious Narratives: An Introductory Essay', *Journal of the American Academy of Religion* 79/1 (2011): 16.

41 See John Powers, *A Bull of a Man: Images of Masculinity, Sex and the Body in Indian Buddhism* (Cambridge: 2009), p. 152, wherein Powers recounts an incident from *Vinaya Piṭaka* I.351–2, of the Buddha entering solitary retreat after becoming disgusted with his arguing monks.

42 See for example, Shayne Clark, 'Locating Humour in Indian Buddhist Monastic Law Codes: A Comparative Approach', *Journal of Indian Philosophy* 37 (2009): 311–30.

43 See for example, *Aṅguttara-Nikāya* V.122ff.

44 See for example, P.L. Vaidy, (ed.), *Saddharmapuṇḍarīka* (Darbhanga, 1960), pp. 2–3.

45 For a discussion of 'theistic and non-theistic' aspects of the Buddha in Mahāyāna sources with special reference to the *Aṣṭa*, see MacQueen, 'Inspired Speech in Early Mahāyāna Buddhism II'.

46 Ibid.

Another commonly occurring figure in the Perfection of Wisdom Sūtras is Śāriputra. In the Pāli sources, Śāriputra (Pāli: Sāriputta) is described as the foremost disciple (*aggasāvaka*) of the Buddha.[47] He is said to be first among those that possess great wisdom,[48] second only to the Buddha himself. About this Malalasekara points out, 'Several instances are given of Sāriputta instructing the monks and preaching to them of his own accord on various topics–apart from the preaching of the well-known suttas [such as the *Dasuttara* and *Saṅgīti Sutta*s] assigned to him.'[49] Significant for his role in the Perfection of Wisdom Sūtras is Sāriputta's special proficiency in the Abhidhamma (Sanskrit: Abhidharma),[50] which presents a philosophical elaboration of the Buddha's discourses based on the theory of fundamental 'factors' (Pāli: *dhamma*; Sanskrit: *dharma*)[51] that make up experience.

The single most distinctive feature of Śāriputra in the Prajñāpāramitā texts is that he does not maintain the same exalted status that we find attributed to him in such mainstream sources as the Pāli Canon. This demotion may have to do with his association with the Abhidharma. The philosophical thrust of the entire Perfection of Wisdom corpus may be summarized as the doctrine of 'emptiness' (*śūnyatā*). This is the notion that all *dharma*s (factors, elements, phenomena) lack inherent existence, essence or 'own-being' (*svabhāva*). This position is both an extension of the Buddhist notion of no-self (*anātman*, Pāli: *anatta*) and an attack on the Abhidharma doctrine (maintained by the most influential and widespread Buddhist school in India, the Sarvāstivāda), that *dharma*s possess *svabhāva*. From the point of view of Sarvāstivādin Abhidharma, the existence of such things as individual selves, souls, tables, chairs, trees and medium-size dry goods are only conventionally real; whereas *dharma*s possess ultimate existence or 'own-being'. The Perfection of Wisdom Sūtras attack this notion, claiming that even *dharma*s are only conventionally real; ultimately all things lack an essence and are therefore 'empty'. I will discuss these philosophical issues in more detail below. However, I hope it is now clear why Śāriputra, as the master of the Abhidharma, becomes demoted in Perfection of Wisdom discourse – he embodies the very view these *sūtra*s so rigorously attack. Thus, his views are often shown to be in need of 'correction' by the Buddha or the disciple Subhūti, to whom I shall now turn.

The disciple Subhūti is an important figure in the Prajñāpāramitā texts. He is the main interlocutor in the *Aṣṭasahaśrikā*, the *Pañcaviṃśati*, and the *Diamond Sūtra*s. Unlike Śāriputra, Subhūti plays a much less significant role in the Pāli Canon than he does in the Perfection of Wisdom Sūtras. In the Pāli sources, it is said that after his ordination he dwelled in the forest and attained sainthood (arhatship) through his 'meditation on loving-kindness' (*mettājhāna*).[52] In the *Aṅguttara Nikāya*, the Buddha declares Subhūti to be the foremost among those that 'dwell in peace', and of those 'worthy of gifts'.[53] Also in the

---

47 See G.P. Malalasekera, *Dictionary of Pāli Proper Names, Volume II* (New Delhi, 1995), p. 1108.

48 *etadaggaṃ bhikkhave mama sāvakānaṃ bhikkhūnaṃ mahāpaññānaṃ yadidaṃ sāriputto* (*Aṅguttara-Nikāya* I.14.1.2, Pāli Text Society edition, 1885–1900, p. 23). Reference sourced from Malalasekera, *Dictionary of Pāli Proper Names, Volume II*, p. 1109.

49 Ibid. My brackets.

50 Ibid., p. 1116.

51 *dharmas*/*dhammas* are also often translated as 'elements' or 'phenomena'.

52 Malalasekera, *Dictionary of Pāli Proper Names, Volume II*, p. 1235.

53 *etadaggaṃ bhikkhave mama sāvakānaṃ bhikkhūnaṃ araṇavihārīnaṃ yadidaṃ subhūti / etadaggaṃ bhikkhave mama sāvakānaṃ bhikkhūnaṃ dakkhiṇeyyānaṃ yadidaṃ subhūti*... (*Aṅguttara-*

Udāna (VI.7), the Buddha praises Subhūti for his skill in meditation.[54] Why Subhūti was promoted to such an exalted status in the Perfection of Wisdom corpus is unclear. Perhaps the composers and Indian target audience considered his special skills of forest-dwelling and meditation particularly useful in penetrating into the profound reality of the perfection of wisdom. However, such a suggestion at this stage is merely conjecture.

Also present to a lesser degree in Prajñāpāramitā Sūtras are other mainstream disciples such as Ānanda, Mahākāśyapa, Mahāmaudgalyāyana, Pūrṇa, and Mahākātyāyana.[55] Either little is said regarding these characters, or what is stated appears to reinforce their traditional personas. For example, Ānanda, as the cousin and faithful servant of the Buddha, was thought to be present at practically every occasion of the Buddha's discourses. Although known in mainstream sources for his unshakable loyalty and unfailing memory, Ānanda was considered unable to attain enlightenment during the Buddha's lifetime due to his emotional attachment to the Lord. As seen from the translated passage of the *Aṣṭa* above, this view of Ānanda remained unchanged in the *Perfection of Wisdom* texts.

Significantly, the Prajñāpāramitā corpus generally possesses a positive attitude toward the Buddha's disciples. While Subhūti seems to take pride of place in several important Perfection of Wisdom texts, Śāriputra often plays an important role; and even if his insight may at times be wanting, he nevertheless is portrayed respectfully.[56] And as we have seen in the opening passage of the *Aṣṭa* translated above, other disciples are mentioned as present and are referred to in salutary terms. However, the Prajñāpāramitā texts seem at times to go beyond mere respect for the Buddha's disciples and imply that some of these at least may have been 'crypto-bodhisattvas'.

Following the opening scene (translated and discussed above) of the *Perfection of Wisdom in 8,000 lines* (*Aṣṭa*), Subhūti, Śāriputra, and the Buddha enter into discussion concerning the perfection of wisdom. Subhūti is the main interlocutor throughout the entire text and often engages in dialogue with Śāriputra, clarifying or correcting the views of the latter with the Buddha's approval. Here Subhūti explains, in the dialogical style common to the text, how a bodhisattva ought to train in the perfection of wisdom:

> Śāriputra: How then must a bodhisattva course if he is to course in perfect wisdom?
>
> *Subhūti*: He should not course in the skandhas [aggregates], nor in a sign, nor in the idea that the 'skandhas are signs', nor in the production of the skandhas, in their stopping or destruction, nor in the idea that 'the skandhas are empty,' or 'I course,' or 'I am a bodhisattva'… . The Bodhisattva then has the concentrated insight 'Not grasping at any dharma' by name, vast, noble, unlimited and steady, not shared by any of the Disciples or Pratyekabuddhas… .

Nikāya I.14.2.4–5, Pāli Text Society edition, 1885–1900, p. 24). See also, Malalasekera, *Dictionary of Pāli Proper Names, Volume II*, p. 1235.

54 Malalasekera, *Dictionary of Pāli Proper Names, Volume II*, p. 1235.

55 See for example, the introduction to the *Perfection of Wisdom in 700 Lines* (Conze, *Perfect Wisdom*, p. 79).

56 This is not always the case in Mahāyāna *sūtra*s. See for example, the *Vimilakīrtinirdeśa* wherein Śāriputra is made the object of ridicule and transformed into a goddess. For an English translation, see Robert Thurman, *The Holy Teaching of Vimalakīrti: A Mahāyāna Scripture* (University Park, 1976), pp. 56–63. For the Sanskrit text, see Study Group on Buddhist Sanskrit Literature, Tokyo, The Institute for Comprehensive Studies of Buddhism, Taisho University (eds.), *Vimalakīrtinirdeśa, A Sanskrit Edition Based upon the Manuscript Newly Found at the Potala Palace* (Tokyo, 2006), chapter 6.

> Śāriputra: Can one show forth that concentration?
>
> *Subhūti*: No, Śāriputra. Because that son of good family neither knows nor perceives it.
>
> Śāriputra: You say that he neither knows nor perceives it?
>
> *Subhūti*: I do, for that concentration does not exist.
>
> *The Lord*: Well said, Subhūti. And thus should a Bodhisattva train therein, because then he trains in perfect wisdom.
>
> Śāriputra: When he thus trains, he trains in perfect wisdom?
>
> *The Lord*: When he thus trains, he trains in perfect wisdom.
>
> Śāriputra: When he thus trains, which dharmas does he train in?
>
> *The Lord*: He does not train in any dharma at all. Because the dharmas do not exist in a way as foolish untaught, common people are accustomed to suppose.[57]

Here we find Subhūti explaining the profundities of the perfection of wisdom to Śāriputra, known in the mainstream sources as the foremost disciple in wisdom. Interesting is the fact that Subhūti, a disciple in mainstream sources, details how a bodhisattva should train. I would suggest that implicit in this dialogue and in many others of the vast Perfection of Wisdom corpus in which Subhūti is the main interlocutor is that Subhūti himself is a *bodhisattva*. How else would he have the necessary insight to understand the profound and paradoxical philosophy of emptiness (*śūnyatā*) as it is found in these texts? This conception that certain disciples of the Buddha were actually crypto-*bodhisattva*s fits in well with the *Prajñāpāramitā* idea mentioned above that a true *bodhisattva* does not maintain the idea that 'I am a *bodhisattva*'. Though these *bodhisattva*-disciples are actually *bodhisattva*s in the guise of disciples, as true *bodhisattva*s, they would never admit to being *bodhisattva*s, because the false conception of '*bodhisattva*' as a truly existent *dharma* with 'own-being' never occurs in their minds.

This incorporation of disciples into the Mahāyāna as secret *bodhisattva*s in the Perfection of Wisdom texts is made more explicit in sūtras such as the *Gaṇḍavyūha*. For example, following the elaborate visionary experiences of the *bodhisattva*s in the introduction of the *sūtra* (discussed above), which were not seen by the great disciples, the Bodhisattva Mañjuśrī departs to the south of India to teach the Mahāyāna. Then Śāriputra, 'by the authority of the Buddha',[58] sees the *bodhisattva* leaving the Jeta Grove, and thinks that he

---

[57] Conze, *Perfection of Wisdom in Eight Thousand Lines*, pp. 86–7. Brackets mine. Here and in the follow passages from Conze's translations, I have modified his translations by adding the proper diacritics to the disciples' names to maintain consistency with the rest of this chapter. NB: Conze often abbreviates his translations by omitting repetitions. For the Sanskrit text, see Vaidya, *Aṣṭasāhasrikā Prajñāpāramita*, pp. 6–7.

[58] *buddhānubhāvena* (Vaidya, *Gaṇḍavyūhasūtra*, p. 36.21). Here we find the term 'authority' (*anubhāva*) instead of 'power' (*adhiṣṭhāna*), but the general idea is the same: Śāriputra is able to see Mañjuśrī leaving because of the Buddha.

should go with him. Śāriputra approaches the Buddha with sixty monks[59] and asks the Lord's consent to follow Mañjuśrī. Permission granted, the venerable monk goes to the *bodhisattva* and describes Mañjuśrī's spiritual qualities to his fellow monks. These words inspire the monks and produce Mahāyānist attributes in them such as faith in the *bodhisattvas*, great compassion (*mahākaruṇā*), great vows and faith in omniscience (*sarvajñatāprasāda*).[60] Mañjuśrī teaches them a discourse, which causes the monks to enter into a trance (*samādhi*) called 'Domain of the Unobstructed Eye Seeing All Buddhas',[61] which firmly establishes them in 'the course of conduct of the Bodhisattva Samantabhadra'.[62] In other words, the disciples are converted to the Mahāyāna, and thereby become *bodhisattvas*. Thus it seems that for both the *Aṣṭa* and the *Gaṇḍavyūha* it was necessary to incorporate at least some of the Buddha's disciples into the Mahāyāna fold. While the *Aṣṭa* does this more through the implication that Subhūti was secretly a *bodhisattva*, the *Gaṇḍavyūha* includes a passage, which explicitly narrates the conversion of Śāriputra and sixty of his monastic brothers to the Mahāyāna.

Why would the *Aṣṭa* and other Perfection of Wisdom texts take such great pains to employ traditional oral means of legitimation and traditional mainstream Buddhist characters? Perhaps one possibility might have been to cushion the blow of their radical philosophical innovation—namely the doctrine of 'emptiness'. To this concept I shall now turn.

Radical Negation

The *Perfection of Wisdom in 25,000 Lines* (*Pañcaviṃśatisāhasrikā-prajñāpāramitā*, or *Pañcaviṃśati*) is one of the older Perfection of Wisdom Sūtras, and a massive text consisting largely of dialogues between and among the Buddha, Subhūti and Śāriputra. Within its pages (repeated over and over again) is found the Mahāyāna notion of emptiness represented through the 'radical negation' typical of the Prajñāpāramitā corpus. To convey this radical negation of conventional thought and language, the Prajñāpāramita texts employ paradoxical language. Since the *Pañcaviṃśati* is much too long for a detailed discussion here, I will merely cite one short passage from literally hundreds of pages following a similar style:

> Śāriputra: For what reason, Subhūti, do you say that 'Although we speak of a 'self', yet absolutely the self is something uncreated'?
>
> *Subhūti*: Absolutely a self does not exist; how then could its real creation take place? And that is true also of the synonyms of 'self', like being, soul, etc.; and also of form, etc., and all dharmas.

---

59 The narrator mentions ten by name: Sāgarabuddhi, Mahāsudatta, Puṇyaprabha, Mahāvatsa, Vibhudatta, Viśuddhacārin, Devaśrī, Indramati, Brahmottama, Praśāntamati (Vaidya, *Gaṇḍavyūhasūtra*, p. 36.27–9).

60 Vaidya, *Gaṇḍavyūhasūtra*, p. 37.13–19.

61 *sarvabuddhavidarśanāsaṅgacakṣurviṣayaṃ* (Vaidya, *Gaṇḍavyūhasūtra*, p. 38.15).

62 *samantabhadrabodhisattvacaryāpratiṣṭhitā* (Vaidya, *Gaṇḍavyūhasūtra*, p. 38.29). This expression is a synonym for the *bodhisattvacaryā*, or *bodhisattvamārga* in the *Gaṇḍavyūha* and indicates that Samantabhadra functions in the text as a personification of the highest spiritual realisation.

> Śāriputra: For what reason has the Ven. Subhūti said that 'all dharmas have no own-being'?
>
> *Subhūti*: Because an own-being acting in causal connection does not exist.
>
> Śāriputra: Of what is there no own-being acting in causal connection?
>
> *Subhūti*: Of form, etc. By this method all dharmas are without own-being. Moreover, Śāriputra, all dharmas are impermanent, but not because something has disappeared.[63]

Here we witness the philosophy characteristic of the Perfection of Wisdom Sūtras and much of the Mahāyāna: the position that all factors of existence (*dharma*s) lack inherent existence, an essence, or 'own-being' (*svabhāva*). As mentioned above this position is a hallmark of Prajñāpāramitā thought and may be seen as a further development of the mainstream Buddhist notion of no-self. As philosophically innovative as this idea may be, note that it is here presented in a traditional oral style in the form of a dialogue between characters familiar to a mainstream audience—the disciples Śāriputra and Subhūti.

The *Perfection of Wisdom in 2,500 Lines* (*Sārdhadvisāhasrikā-prajñāpāramitā*, or *Sārdha*), also known as the *Questions of Suvikrāntavikrāmin*, begins with the Bodhisattva Suvikrāntavikrāmin asking the Buddha questions. Although this *sūtra* starts with a *bodhisattva* (a non-mainstream character) asking questions, substantial portions of what follows include dialogues among and between mainstream characters such as the Buddha, Śāriputra (here called Śāradvatīputra), Ānanda and Subhūti. Particularly striking from the fourth chapter is a passage that continues for several pages wherein the Buddha and Śāriputra engage in a philosophical tit-for-tat dialogue on the emptiness of the perfection of wisdom itself:

> Śāradvatīputra: This perfection of wisdom is hard to see!
>
> *The Lord*: Because it does not admit of being seen by anyone.
>
> Śāradvatīputra: Hard to understand, O Lord, is the perfection of wisdom!
>
> *The Lord*: Because in it no fully real dharma is apprehended which it has fully known.
>
> Śāradvatīputra: Indefinable, O Lord, is the perfection of wisdom!
>
> *The Lord:* Because it has not been set up by the definition of any dharma.
>
> Śāradvatīputra: Without own-being is this perfection of wisdom.
>
> *The Lord*: Because of the absence of own-being in form, etc....[64]

---

[63] Conze, *The Large Sutra on Perfect Wisdom*, p. 191. For the Sanskrit text, see Dutt, *The Pañcaviṃśarisāhasrikā Prajñāpāramitā*, pp. 251–2.

[64] Conze, *Perfect Wisdom*, p. 30. For the Sanskrit text, see Vaidya, *Mahāyānasūtrasaṃgrahaḥ*, Part I, p. 28.

Here again, we see the characteristic philosophy of emptiness presented in the dialogical style between mainstream characters. In this case, however, the very perfection of wisdom, which is said to be the source of enlightenment of all Buddhas, is claimed to also lack independent existence or 'self-nature'. In this way, we witness how no concept, no matter how sacred, was considered immune to the philosophical critique of radical negation.

In the *Perfection of Wisdom in 700 Lines (Saptaśatikā-prajñāpāramitā*, or *Saptaśatikā*) the primary characters are the Buddha, the Bodhisattva Mañjuśrī, Śāradvatīputra (Śāriputra) and Mahākāśyapa. Mañjuśrī as the embodiment of wisdom is an important Mahāyāna *bodhisattva* appearing in numerous *sūtra*s. In the *Saptaśatikā*, he engages in lively discourse with the Buddha and Śāriputra on various topics important to the religio-philosophical position of the Perfection of Wisdom collection. For example:

> Śāradvatīputra: If, Mañjuśrī, you see in such a way those who use the vehicle of the Disciples, how then do you see those who use that of the fully enlightened Buddhas?
>
> *Mañjuśrī*: I do not review a dharma called 'bodhisattva', nor a dharma 'set out towards enlightenment', or a dharma called 'he fully knows'. It is in this fashion that I see those who use the vehicle of the fully enlightened Buddhas.
>
> Śāradvatīputra: How then, Mañjuśrī, do you see the Tathāgata?
>
> *Mañjuśrī*: Leave the great Nāga out of it, Rev. Śāradvatīputra! Do not busy yourself about the great Nāga!
>
> Śāradvatīputra: 'Buddha', Mañjuśrī, of what is that a synonym?
>
> *Mañjuśrī*: Of what then is the term 'self' a synonym?
>
> Śāradvatīputra: It is a synonym of non-production.
>
> *Mañjuśrī*: So it is, Rev. Śāradvatīputra. The word 'self' denotes the same thing which the word 'Buddha' denotes.... For 'self' and 'Buddha' are synonymous. Just as the self does absolutely not exist, and cannot be apprehended, so also the Buddha.[65]

Here again we find a good example of the extent the Perfection of Wisdom texts emphasize their doctrine of the ultimate emptiness of all concepts. Even such hallowed ideas as 'Buddha' are no more real than the false conception of a 'self'.

The most famous of all Perfection of Wisdom texts, the *Heart Sūtra* survives in a longer and shorter version (both little more than a page long in translation).[66] In the longer version, the Buddha enters a trance (*samādhi*), and then Śāriputra asks the Bodhisattva Avalokiteśvara (the Mahāyāna personification of compassion) a question about how one is to train in the perfection of wisdom. The shorter version lacks the typical introduction (*nidāna*) giving the occasion of the *sūtra*, and begins abruptly with Avalokiteśvara

---

[65] Conze, *Perfect Wisdom*, p. 87. For the Sanskrit text, see Vaidya, *Mahāyānasūtrasaṃgrahaḥ*, Part I, pp. 346–7.

[66] Conze, *Perfect Wisdom*, pp. 140–43. For Sanskrit versions, see Vaidya, *Mahāyānasūtrasaṃgrahaḥ*, Part I, pp. 97–8.

'coursing' (*caramāṇa*) in the profound perfection of wisdom. The bulk of the *sūtra* is the *bodhisattva*'s response to the disciple beginning with his famous statement that the five aggregates of the putative person are empty (*śūnya*) of essence (*svabhāva*) and that 'form (*rūpa*) is emptiness (*śūnyatā*) and that very emptiness is form'.[67] The *bodhisattva* then gives his discourse addressed to Śāriputra. Once again, emptiness is the theme of the *sūtra* and paradoxical language is employed claiming such things as that in emptiness there is 'no arising of suffering, no extinction, no path, no gnosis,' and so on.

Thus we see in the *Sārdha, Saptaśatikā* and *Heart Sūtra*s the continuation of themes from the longer and supposedly older texts (*Aṣṭa* and *Pañcaviṃśati*). Although important Mahāyāna *bodhisattva*s such as Mañjuśrī and Avalokiteśvara now appear in central roles, the disciples are still present and continue to engage in dialogue with the Buddha and *bodhisattva*s. Moreover, until the *Heart Sūtra*, the Buddha continues to give discourses in a traditional manner, rather than entering a trance or performing miracles as a primary method of teaching. However, the main philosophical message of emptiness and the corresponding radical negation of all concepts (including the 'perfection of wisdom', the 'Buddha', and the 'path') through the use of paradoxical language is maintained throughout the corpus.

Conservatism

Several elements of the Prajñāpāramitā texts mentioned thus far seem to imply a level of religious conservatism despite their radical doctrinal message. One possible example of this conservatism may be found in the absence of *bodhisattva*s mentioned in the beginning of the *Aṣṭa*. This absence of *bodhisattva*s may well be an attempt to align the *Aṣṭa* more closely to the traditional sūtras, which make no mention of bodhisattvas. One might be tempted to infer that this absence is due to the fact that the *Aṣṭa* is one of the earliest Mahayāna *sūtra*s. However, as Jan Nattier has pointed out, in the two earliest Chinese translation of the *Aṣṭa* (late second century CE, and mid-third century CE), *bodhisattva*s are mentioned in the introduction.[68] Only in one of the translations by Xuanzang several centuries later do we find a Chinese version similar to the surviving Sanskrit version.[69] I would like to suggest that if this absence of *bodhisattva*s is indicative of conservatism, the evidence found in the Chinese translations suggest that this conservatism endured throughout the centuries in India, becoming more entrenched over time. Also, as mentioned above, the Perfection of Wisdom texts seem to imply that some of the Buddha's disciples were actually crypto-*bodhisattva*s. This implication rather than assertion of *bodhisattva* status may also be a sign of their conservative nature. Less conservative Mahāyāna sūtras disregard the disciples, or as in the case of the *Gaṇḍavyūha*, detail the conversion of certain disciples to the Mahāyāna, thereby asserting their status as *bodhisattva*s outright.

As mentioned above, MacQueen sees Subhūti's statement in the beginning of the *Aṣṭa* concerning inspired speech (*pratibhāna*) as constituting the words of the Buddha (*buddhavacana*) as a means by which the *sūtra* legitimates its own religious authority. This

---

67 *pañca skandhāṃstāṃś ca svabhāvaśūnyān samanupaśyati sma | rūpaṃ śūnyatā, śūnyataiva rūpam* (Vaidya, *Mahāyānasūtrasaṃgrahaḥ*, Part I, p. 98).

68 Jan Nattier, 'Avalokiteśvara in Early Chinese Buddhist Translations: Preliminary Survey', in William Magee and Yi-hsun Huang (eds.), *Bodhisattva Avalokiteśvara (Guanyin) and Modern Society: Proceedings of the Fifth Chung-Hwa International Conference on Buddhism* (Taipei, 2007), p. 196.

69 Ibid.

strategy is significant in that it employs speech acts and preserves the dialogical style of the oral discourses found in the earlier mainstream traditions, thereby suggesting a stylistic conservatism of the Prajñāpāramitā Sūtras. In this regard, MacQueen's concluding statement in his study of inspired speech in early Mahāyāna is worth quoting: 'of all the attempts made in early Mahāyāna to open the tradition to the recognition of new revelation without changing the essentials of the religion, that of the Perfection of Wisdom school is surely one of the most impressive'.[70] As mentioned above, this stylistic conservatism may have been employed to soften the blow of the radical nature of the texts' philosophical message.

As a whole, the Prajñāpāramitā Sūtras' use of sermons and dialogues, representing a literary style that is closer to mainstream Indian Buddhism in its recreation of oral discourse, is a more conservative solution to the problem of legitimacy than the more radical approach employing visionary accounts such as those found in the *Gaṇḍavyūha-sūtra*. This type of stylistic distinction would allow us to begin to plot Mahāyāna *sūtra*s based on a continuum of conservative to more radical responses to issues of authority and legitimation. Note that such distinctions are not necessarily diachronic developments within the Indian Buddhist tradition, but may represent synchronic choices within different Buddhist communities existing in the Indian subcontinent.

Conclusion

The Prajñāpāramitā Sūtras consist of a vast body of literature, which developed over many centuries within the Indian subcontinent. Although these texts vary in size from a single page to many hundreds of pages in length, and must have been composed by diverse authors often separated from each other by centuries, they demonstrate a remarkable consistency in their philosophical message. The central religio-philosophical thrust of the entire corpus is the *bodhisattva*'s quest to attain the perfection of wisdom by realizing that all *dharma*s lack inherent existence, or are empty (*śūnya*) of an essence (*svabhāva*). As philosophically radical as this message may have been, its form of presentation was in many ways quite conservative. A wide-ranging strategy of legitimation employed by these *sūtra*s is the use of dialogue in order to preserve the appearance that they capture 'oral moments' of historical discourses as found in mainstream Indian Buddhist *sūtra*s. Related to this strategy is the depiction of the Buddha as giving sermons and engaging in discussions and debates with his disciples, rather than teaching through magical displays of cosmic visions as found in some less conservative Mahāyāna *sūtra*s such as the *Gaṇḍavyūha* and *Lotus Sūtra*s. Moreover, we find important figures from the mainstream tradition such as Śāriputra and Subhūti discussing and debating with the Buddha and *bodhisattva*s on the finer points of the Mahāyāna perfection of wisdom.[71] I suggest that employing these traditional characters as the mouth-pieces for the Prajñāpāramitā cushions the impact of its otherwise radical philosophy and further demonstrates the conservatism of these Mahāyāna sūtras.

Finally, given that the message of the Perfection of Wisdom developed, expanded, contracted and was rephrased numerous times for over a millennium, using the same dialogical style with the same familiar characters, such stylistic conservatism combined with philosophical innovation should be viewed as one particular ideological posture in relation

---

[70] MacQueen, 'Inspired Speech in Early Mahāyāna Buddhism II': p. 62.

[71] In their pieces in this volume, Black, Crothers, and Nichols also address the use of these traditional Buddhist figures to establish authority.

to a spectrum of religious orientations existing (both synchronically and diachronically) within Indian Buddhism.

References

Black, Brian and Jonathan Geen, 'The Character of "Character" in Early South Asian Religious Narratives: An Introductory Essay,' *Journal of the American Academy of Religion* 79/1 (2011): 6–32.

Boucher, Daniel, *Bodhisattvas of the Forest and the Formation of the Mahāyāna: A Study and Translation of the* Rāṣṭrapālaparipṛcchā-sūtra (Honolulu: University of Hawaii Press, 2008).

Clark, Shayne, 'Locating Humour in Indian Buddhist Monastic Law Codes: A Comparative Approach,' *Journal of Indian Philosophy* 37 (2009): 311–30.

Cleary, Thomas (trans.), *The Flower Ornament Scripture: A Translation of the Avatamsaka Sutra* (Boston: Shambala, 1993).

Cole, Alan, *Text as Father: Paternal Seductions in Early Mahāyāna Buddhist Literature* (Berkeley: University of California Press, 2005).

Conze, Edward (trans.), *The Perfection of Wisdom in Eight Thousand Lines & Its Verse Summary* (San Francisco: Four Seasons Foundation, 1973 [1958]).

——— (trans.), *Perfect Wisdom: The Short Prajñāpāramitā Texts* (London: Luzac & Company Limited, 1973).

——— (trans. and ed.), *The Large Sutra on Perfect Wisdom with Divisions of the Abhismayālaṅkāra* (Berkeley: University of California Press, 1975).

———, *Prajñāpāramitā Literature* (Tokyo: Reiyukai, 1978).

Drewes, David, 'Revisiting the phrase "*sa pṛthivīpradeśaś caityabhūto bhavet*" and the Mahāyāna Cult of the Book', *Indo-Iranian Journal* 50 (2007): 101–43.

———, 'Early Indian Mahāyāna Buddhism I', *Religion Compass* 3 (2009): 1– 11 (accessed electronically, Doi 10.1111/j.1749–8171.2009.00195.x).

Dutt, Nalinaksha (ed.), *The* Pañcaviṃśatisāhasrikā Prajñāpāramitā *edited with critical notes and introduction* (London: Luzac & Co., 1934).

Edgerton, Franklin, *Buddhist Hybrid Sanskrit Grammar and Dictionary, Volume I* (New Haven: Yale University Press, 1953).

Falk, Harry, 'Another Collection of Kharosthi manuscripts from Gandhara' (Oral presentation, International Association of Buddhist Studies Conference, Atlanta, 27 June 2008).

Gombrich, Richard, 'How the Mahāyāna Began', in Tadeusz Skorupski (ed.), *The Buddhist Forum, Vol. I: Seminar Papers 1987–88* (London: School of Oriental and African Studies, 1990).

Harrison, Paul (trans.), *The Samādhi of the Direct Encounter with the Buddhas of the Present: An Annotated English Translation of the Tibetan Version of the* Pratyutpanna-Buddha-Saṃmukhāvasthita-Samādhi-Sūtra (Tokyo: The International Institute of Buddhist Studies, 1990).

Kent, Stephen A., 'A Sectarian Interpretation of the Rise of Mahayana', *Religion* 12 (1982): 311–32.

Lancaster, Lewis, 'The Oldest Mahāyāna Sūtra: Its Significance for the Study of Buddhist Development', *The Eastern Buddhist* 8 (1975): 30–41.

Lopez Jr., Donald S., *The* Heart Sūtra *Explained: Indian and Tibetan Commentaries* (New York: State University of New York Press, 1988).
———, 'Authority and Orality in the Mahāyāna', *Numen* 42/1 (1995): 21–47.
———, *Elaborations on Emptiness: Uses of the* Heart Sūtra (Princeton: Princeton University Press, 1996).
MacQueen, Graeme, 'Inspired Speech in Early Mahāyāna Buddhism I', *Religion* 11 (1981): 303–19.
———, 'Inspired Speech in Early Mahāyāna Buddhism II', *Religion* 12 (1982): 49–63.
Malalasekera, G.P., *Dictionary of Pāli Proper Names, Volume II* (New Delhi: Asian Educational Services, 1995).
McMahan, David, 'Orality, Writing, and Authority in South Asian Buddhism: Visionary Literature and the Struggle for Legitimacy in the Mahāyāna,' *History of Religions* 37/3 (1998): 249–74.
———, *Empty Vision: Metaphor and Visionary Imagery in Mahāyāna Buddhism* (New York: Routledge, 2002).
Muller, Charles (chief ed.), *The Digital Dictionary of Buddhism* (http://www.buddhism-dict.net/ddb/; accessed 16 July 2010).
Nattier, Jan, 'The Heart Sūtra: A Chinese Apocryphal Text?', *Journal of the International Association of Buddhist Studies* 15/2 (1992): 71–102.
——— (trans.), *A Few Good Men: The Bodhisattva Path According to the Inquiry of Ugra* (Ugraparipṛccha) (Honolulu: University of Hawaii Press, 2003).
———, 'Avalokiteśvara in Early Chinese Buddhist Translations: Preliminary Survey', in William Magee and Yi-hsun Huang (eds.), *Bodhisattva Avalokiteśvara (Guanyin) and Modern Society: Proceedings of the Fifth Chung-Hwa International Conference on Buddhism* (Taipei, 2007).
Osto, Douglas, *Power, Wealth and Women in Indian Mahāyāna Buddhism: The Gaṇḍavyūha-sūtra* (London and New York: Routledge, 2008).
Powers, John, *A Bull of a Man: Images of Masculinity, Sex and the Body in Indian Buddhism* (Cambridge: Cambridge University Press, 2009).
Rawlinson, Andrew 'The Position of the *Aṣṭasāhasrikā Prajñāpāramitā* in the Development of Early Mahāyāna', in Lewis Lancaster and Luis O. Gómez (eds.), *Prajñāpāramitā and Related Systems: Studies in honor of Edward Conze* (Berkeley: Berkeley Buddhist Studies, 1977).
Schopen, Gregory, 'The Phrase "*sa pṛthivīpradeśaś caityabhūto bhavet*" in the *Vajracchedikā*: Notes on the Cult of the Book in Mahāyāna', *Indo-Iranian Journal* 17 (1975): 147–81.
———, 'The manuscript of the Vajracchedikā found at Gilgit', in Luis Gómez and Jonathan Silk (eds.), *Studies in the Literature of the Great Vehicle: Three Mahāyāna Buddhist Texts* (Ann Arbor: University of Michigan, 1989), pp. 89–139.
Study Group on Buddhist Sanskrit Literature, Tokyo, The Institute for Comprehensive Studies of Buddhism, Taisho University (eds.), *Vimalakīrtinirdeśa, A Sanskrit Edition Based upon the Manuscript Newly Found at the Potala Palace* (Tokyo, 2006).
Thurman, Robert, *The Holy Teaching of Vimalakīrti: A Mahāyāna Scripture* (University Park, PA: Pennsylvania State University Press, 1976).
Vaidya, P. L. (ed.), *Aṣṭasāhasrikā Prajñāpāramita* (Darbhanga: Mithila Institute, 1960).
———, *Aṣṭasāhasrikā Prajñāpāramita* (Darbhanga: Mithila Institute, 1960).
———, *Gaṇḍavyūhasūtra* (Darbhanga: Mithila Institute, 1960).
———, *Saddharmapuṇḍarīka* (Darbhanga: Mithila Institute, 1960).
———, *Mahāyānasūtrasaṃgrahaḥ*, Part I (Darbhanga: Mithila Institute, 1961).

Chapter 6
The Dialogue of Tradition: Purāṇa, Gītā, and Theological Heritage

Elizabeth M. Rohlman

While this volume focuses explicitly on dialogue, *sammukham*, as speech act – that is, as a literary discourse between two characters – textual studies in Indology often approach dialogue from an entirely different angle. I refer to the wealth of scholarship addressing the metaphorical dialogue through which texts engage with and respond to each other. That Indic texts engage in this type of discourse, often across differences of history and locale, is well documented. This literary device was perhaps most poetically described by the late A.K. Ramanujan in his seminal essay, 'Where Mirrors are Windows'.[1] Ramanujan described the ways in which Indic texts engage with their literary forbearers as 'intertextual reflexivity', though subsequent scholars have more often referred to this literary practice simply as textual, or inter-textual, dialogue. This chapter aims to consider the ways in which literary dialogue within a text facilitates this more metaphorical dialogue between texts. It will do so by asking how discourse between characters – *sammukham* as speech act – facilitates dialogue between texts. Taking as a starting point the literary form of Gītā, or 'song', it will consider the ways in which divine speech is employed to create conversations between members of the larger genre of Purāṇa.

Taking as an example the *Sarasvatī Purāṇa*, a medieval Sanskrit text from the mytho-historical Purāṇa genre, this chapter engages a text with an explicitly and narrowly defined regional provenance. Originally composed between the twelfth and fifteenth centuries and later rewritten into a second recension, the narrative of the *Sarasvatī Purāṇa* locates itself in the western Indian region of Gujarat through specific geographical and historical motifs. The process of regionalization is achieved through an extended celebration of the sacred and elusive River Sarasvatī and her place in the sacred landscape of Gujarat. The text's frame narrative recounts the Sarasvatī River's descent to earth and follows her course from the Himālayas through Gujarat to her convergence with the sea at Prabhāsa Somnāth. A wide array of tales from pan-Indic traditions are retold within this geographical framework, situating the action of each story on the banks of the Sarasvatī River in Gujarat. The result is a narrative marriage of regional vision and pan-Indic, trans-regional literary lineage.

The frame narrative of the *Sarasvatī Purāṇa* retells the story of the Sarasvatī River's descent to earth that is found in the Prabhāsa Khaṇḍa of the *Skanda Purāṇa*.[2] As a fire named Vadava threatens to consume the heavenly abode of the gods, he is convinced by the gods that the proper starting place for his destruction is the ocean, who is first among all

---

[1] A.K. Ramanujan, 'Where Mirrors are Windows: Towards an Anthology of Reflections', in Vinay Dharwadker (ed.), *The Collected Essays of A.K. Ramanujan* (Delhi, 1999).

[2] The text of this narrative of Sarasvatī's descent is found in *The Skanda Purāṇa: Prabhāsa Khaṇḍa*, trans. D.V. Tagare, Ancient Indian Tradition and Mythology: Purāṇas in Translation Series number 67 (Delhi, 2003).

deities. He consents to descend to earth and pursue the ocean on the singular condition that he is carried on his journey by a virgin girl. At the request of her father Brahmā, Sarasvatī descends to earth and travels through Gujarat to her confluence with the sea at Prabhāsa Somnāth, where she deposits the fire in the ocean, thus extinguishing it and nullifying its threat to the heavens. Amendments to the story as it is found in the *Skanda Purāṇa* mark the *Sarasvatī Purāṇa* as the regional text that it is. The space and time between Sarasvatī's descent to earth and her arrival at the ocean are filled with narratives of her travels through the medieval kingdom of Gujarat. The course of the Sarasvatī here does not match the course of the 'lost' river recounted in other Indic texts or reconstructed from archaeological evidence. Instead, the text reflects local tradition in linking three minor rivers of Gujarat and claiming them to be the lost Sarasvatī. The only geography this text shares with pan-Indic literary traditions are the source and the mouth of the river – though the tradition of the Sarasvatī River ending at Somnāth is not unwaveringly universal, either.

While all extant versions of the *Sarasvatī Purāṇa* include the same frame-narrative, two distinct recensions defined by opposing theologies survive. One is unapologetically Śaiva, promoting worship of the god Śiva, and the other is Vaiṣṇava, promoting worship of the god Viṣṇu. The differing theologies are represented by sub-narratives recounted in the dialogic style of the Purāṇas, which itself is illustrative of the metaphorical dialogue that takes place between texts and traditions. The text was originally composed as a Śaiva Purāṇa, reflecting the dynastic identity and sectarian affiliations of early medieval Gujarat. It was later reworked to reflect the changing sectarian and theological identities in the area of its composition and circulation. The Vaiṣṇava theology of the later recension reflects the changing religious landscape of Gujarat after the fifteenth and sixteenth centuries witnessed the overwhelming influence of the *bhakti* poet Narasiṅgh Mehta and the theologian Vallabhācārya. The exact workings of this process is fodder for another discussion. For the purposes of this discussion, I will focus on the Vaiṣṇava recension of the text, the shorter and later of the two versions, and on the ways in which this version of the *Sarasvatī Purāṇa* draws on other textual and theological traditions to create intertextual discourse.[3]

The central theological argument of the Vaiṣṇava recension relates the story of Kapila, an incarnation of Viṣṇu. The story of Kapila is retold from the celebrated *Bhāgavata Purāṇa*, and is, in fact, the only narrative in either recension of the text in which another text is cited explicitly. In addition to relating the story of Kapila's conception and birth, the *Sarasvatī Purāṇa* refashions the famed *Kapila Gītā*, which, in the *Bhāgavata Purāṇa*, serves as a treatise on Sāṃkhya Vaiṣṇava devotionalism and some rudimentary aspects of the Saṃkhya *darśana*.[4] The *Sarasvatī Purāṇa*, by contrast, refashions this *gītā* into a *bhakti* revelation more compatible with the Vaiṣṇava traditions of late medieval Gujarat. By directly citing, and then refashioning, the *Kapila Gītā*, the *Sarasvatī Purāṇa* uses the dialogue of its characters

---

[3] All citations in this chapter are taken from the *Sarasvatī Purāṇa* contained in the L.D. Institute of Indology Ahmadabad, Printed Book number K1843, entitled *Sarasvatī Māhātmya*. This version contains the twenty-seven *adhyāya* Vaiṣṇava recension and is printed on seventy-two folia with twelve lines per side. This edition was prepared by Harajīvan Kevalarām Śarmā for the Bombay City Press in Samvat 1943 (circa AD 1888). While it is a printed book, it is not a critically edited version and is printed in the unbound folia style of a traditional Sanskrit text. For this reason, I have treated it as a manuscript throughout my research.

[4] Throughout this discussion I use the title *Kapila Gītā* to refer explicitly and exclusively to the *Kapila Gītā* of the *Bhāgavata Purāṇa*, though at least three other texts with the title *Kapila Gītā* exist. See Knut Jacobsen, *Kapila: Founder of Sāṃkhya and Avatāra of Viṣṇu* (New Delhi, 2008), p. 2 and *passim*.

to create a theological dialogue between the pan-Indic Vaiṣṇava traditions associated with the *Bhāgavata Purāṇa* and the more regionally defined Vaiṣṇava traditions of Gujarat.

The use of the Gītā form, that is, a direct didactic exchange between a god and a devotee, makes this text a particularly fruitful stage for reflecting on the art of dialogue. Because the *Kapila Gītā* of the *Sarasvatī Purāṇa* is a refashioning of a prior narrative and *gītā* from the *Bhāgavata Purāṇa*, the dialogue here works on two levels: as a discourse between god and devotee and as a discourse between regional and pan-Indic textual and theological traditions. While the appeal to the beloved *Bhāgavata Purāṇa* is clearly an assertion of textual authority, it is also an act of engaging another text in direct theological and narrative dialogue. As such, the dialogue between the god and his devotee becomes inter-textual dialogue, which, in turn, becomes theological dialogue. Thus, dialogue here serves as both theological polemic and inter-textual narrative discourse. It is through this process of inter-textual dialogue that the *Sarasvatī Purāṇa* articulates a uniquely regional religious vision while simultaneously claiming a larger and longer theological heritage.

Purāṇa

More than any other genre of Indic literature, the nature and scope of the Purāṇic literature continues to puzzle Indologists. This is in part because there is not an easy (if imperfect) correlate in Western literature for the Purāṇas, or 'old stories', in the way that *kāvya* relates to poetry or *darśana* to philosophy. The closest approximations of the genre in Western terminology are mythology, or, in the broadest possible view, narrative, though these, too, fail to evoke the entirety of this vast and diverse body of literature. The consternation surrounding the Purāṇas also results from the fact that the Purāṇic tradition itself plays so fast and loose with its own boundaries that a definition based on the overwhelming wealth of extant Purāṇic literature seems an impossibility. This leaves scholars in a continuing conundrum that requires nearly every statement made about the Purāṇas to begin by defining what, in that specific instance, is meant by Purāṇa and thus to rehearse a litany of well-known arguments and definitions.

What, in this discussion, is meant by Purāṇa? Overall, I take the term to indicate a much broader and inclusive category than is meant in some traditional Indological scholarship. I begin, of course, with the definitions provided by the Indic tradition. Tradition enumerates eighteen great (*maha*) and eighteen lesser (*upa*) Purāṇas, all of which are identified with the *pañcalakṣaṇa*, five 'marks' or topics that all *purāṇas* are supposed to address. These five topics cover the essentials of cosmic, divine, and human history and, while the Purāṇas are consistently defined by the five marks, extant Purāṇas seldom, if ever, actually cover all five of the topics. Often, the *pañcalakṣaṇa* is only a cursory element of a Purāṇa. In its place, however, can be almost any topic imaginable, from aesthetics to the art of warfare. While generations of scholars have puzzled over the disjuncture between Purāṇas as they survive and as the traditions have defined them, the most fruitful approach thus far has been suggested by both Velcheru Narayana Rao and Greg Bailey. They argue that the *pañcalakṣaṇa* should be viewed as an artefact of cultural literacy, suggesting that this definition of a Purāṇa would have been known by readers and listeners of the texts and would have coloured their reception of the texts regardless of the actual content therein.[5] It has also been argued by

---

[5] See Velcheru Narayana Rao, 'Purāṇā as Brahminic Ideology', in Wendy Doniger (ed.), *Purāṇa Perennis: Reciprocity and Transformation in Hindu and Jaina Texts* (Albany, 1993); and

Greg Bailey that Purāṇas might be better defined by their didactic function. Each Purāṇa seems designed to promote a specific theological vision.[6] Historically, the theologies of the Purāṇas were increasingly colored by the influence of *bhakti* devotional movements. Perhaps the only formal quality that is universal to all Purāṇic literature is the manner in which these theological teachings are presented, as a dialogue between a guru and his student. Dialogue, therefore, is an essential means of furthering the didactic function of the Purāṇas.

The extent, as well as the content, of the genre poses a vexing problem. The tradition is inconsistent as to which texts belong to the traditional list of thirty-six *purāṇas*, and the reality is that, when Purāṇas that are unique to specific regional and sectarian communities are counted, the tally far exceeds thirty-six. The text that occupies our discussion, the *Sarasvatī Purāṇa*, is one of the later, regional texts unaccounted for in the classical lists of thirty-six Purāṇas. The manuscript record indicates that the text was composed and circulated within the region that is now the modern state of Gujarat. In addition to texts that bear the name *purāṇa*, Ludo Rocher has argued that other types of texts, namely Māhātmyas and Stotras, do not differ in essence from Purāṇas and should be treated as members of the larger Purāṇic genre.[7] Once again, the *Sarasvatī Purāṇa* itself is illustrative of the difficulty in distinguishing between the various types of texts included in the Purāṇic genre. Among the manuscript record, the text at various times refers to itself as the *Sarasvatī Māhātmya*, the *Sarasvatī Purāṇa*, and the *Sarasvatī Mahapurāṇa*.[8] When all such variants across the entirety of Purāṇic literature are added up, the sheer volume of extant Purāṇic texts is overwhelming.

The essential didactic format that unites this literature – the question and answer format of the Purāṇas – evokes a tradition of learning centered around the guru–student relationship that is prominent throughout Indic traditions and that stretches back at least to the Upaniṣads. As Brian Black argues, dialogue ties learning and knowledge to particular individuals and social contexts, with an emphasis on intersubjectivity.[9] The Upaniṣadic model of philosophical inquiry is one where knowledge is arrived at through discussion – usually between a guru and his students – and is therefore a process that requires at least two actors.[10] At the time of the Upaniṣads, this represented an important change, as the means of acquiring knowledge and insight shifted from learning and performing the ritual texts of the Vedas to intellectual inquiry.[11] The dialogic format of this shift made the lineage of gurus more important than one's paternal lineage, and, as noted above, anchored specific thought to specific individuals.[12] In essence, the guru was established as the embodiment of

---

Greg Bailey, *Gaṇeśapurāṇa Part I: Upāsanākhaṇḍa*, Tübingen Purāṇa Research Publications number 4 (Wiesbaden, 1995).

6 Bailey, *Gaṇeśapurāṇa*, pp. 13–14.

7 Ludo Rocher, *The Purāṇas*. A History of Indian Literature vol. 2, fasc. 3 (Wiesbaden, 1986), p. 71.

8 For a detailed account of the manuscript record of the *Sarasvatī Purāṇa*, see Elizabeth M. Rohlman, 'Manuscripts of the *Sarasvatī Purāṇa* in the Archives of Western India', *Journal of the Oriental Institute* 59/1–2 (2010): 151–62.

9 Brian Black, *The Character of the Self in Ancient India: Priests, Kings, and Women in the Early Upaniṣads* (Albany, 2007), p. 22.

10 Ibid., p. 22.

11 Ibid., pp. 37–8.

12 Ibid., p. 30.

knowledge. While the knowledge he embodied was generated out of the didactic practice of discourse, the end result was identified with him as an individual.

By the time of the Purāṇas, especially that of the later, regional Purāṇas, this revolutionary turn of the Upaniṣads was established as the status quo. Purāṇas are universally narrated in a question and answer format, in which the apt student asks a question and the guru, generally a noted sage, answers by relating a story. In the case of the *Sarasvatī Purāṇa*, the discourse occurs between the noted sage *Mārkaṇḍeya* and his eager and inquisitive pupil, Sumati. Wendy Doniger notes that knowledge in the Purāṇas is always transmitted *param-parā*, from one to another, giving the knowledge itself a lineage.[13] In Doniger's discussion of the *Bhāgavata Purāṇa* she observes that the *Bhāgavata*, like all Purāṇas, identifies more with the *Mahābhārata* than with either the Vedas or the Upaṇiṣads.[14] It is common, in fact, for the gurus and sages who narrate the Purāṇas to allude to other texts, especially the *Mahābhārata*, in answering their students' questions. Knowledge in this context is no longer tied exclusively to the human lineage of gurus so central to the Upaniṣads. It is just as likely to originate in the textual lineage, as Purāṇic gurus cite a wide array of texts from the ever-expanding Sanskrit literary canon as the sources of their knowledge. This reflects the fact that, throughout Purāṇic discourse, dialogue represents not only the means by which knowledge is acquired but also the source of its authority.

The dialogic format of the Purāṇas is thus a formal necessity. Within the winding and complex narratives of the Purāṇas, the students' persistent questions may give the impression of a mere mechanical device through which new topics and stories are introduced. But the punctuation of narrative with periodic *param-parā* discourse (and the didactic functions this indicates) is in fact essential to the ability of any text to effectively function as a Purāṇa.[15] The fact that the didactic format of the Upaniṣadic sages is preserved in this manner indicates the universality and apparent necessity of the dialogue form throughout the Purāṇas. This form is one of the very few traits that is found across the wide spectrum of Purāṇic literature. The preservation of the dialogic form also illustrates that narrative, as well as knowledge, requires discourse in these texts. The essential role of the guru as narrator enables the narrative to move forward and, as in the Upaniṣads, continues to tie knowledge to specific figures. The guru, then, continues to be the embodiment of knowledge. This is particularly significant in the case of a Gītā, when the guru involved is also a god.

Gītā

Gītā, or 'song', refers to the heightened elocution of teachings revealed by an incarnated deity. The most famous *gītā*, of course, is the *Bhagavad Gītā* of the *Mahābhārata*. Like Māhātmyas and Stotras, Gītās are embedded within epic and Purāṇic literature but often circulate as independent texts. As opposed to most other Purāṇic literature, including Māhātmyas and Stotras, Gītās minimize mythic narratives and employ hymns and promises only occasionally. C. Mackenzie Brown identifies the common structure of Gītās as covering

---

13 Wendy Doniger, 'Echoes of the *Mahābhārata*: Why is a Parrot the Narrator of the *Bhāgavata Purāṇa* and the *Devībhāgavata Purāṇa*?', in Wendy Doniger (ed.), *Purāṇa Perennis: Reciprocity and Transformation in Hindu and Jaina Texts* (Albany, 1993), p. 30.

14 Ibid., p. 32.

15 For more on the dialogic and didactic functions that define Purāṇas, see Bailey, *Gaṇeśapurāṇa*.

a set range of topics, including the nature of the deity in both his cosmic and mundane forms, the nature and genesis of the world, the nature of the individual soul, the role of the supreme deity in the creation and destruction of the world, the paths or disciplines leading to liberation, and the idealized life of a devotee.[16] Certainly, these topics are common in Māhātmyas and, indeed, most Purāṇic literature. Brown argues that the essential distinction of Gītā literature is one of perspective: whereas Purāṇas and Māhātmyas are told from the perspective of the devotee, the Gītā is related from the perspective of the deity. This difference in perspective also impacts the literary form of the genre. The emphasis in Māhātmyas is on the use of narrative to praise and eulogize deities, places and persons.[17] The divine perspective of the Gītā allows for more direct teaching of theological and philosophical truths, and the dialogical and didactic structure of the text is more explicit. As in all Purāṇic literature, Gītās are related in the form of a dialogue between a guru and student. In this case, however, the guru is an incarnation of god, and the speech is therefore direct and divine revelation. Based on the model of the *Bhagavad Gītā*, knowledge is conveyed through both the deity's speech and also through the direct revelation of the deity's cosmic form.

Throughout Purāṇic literature, Gītās that model themselves on the *Bhagavad Gītā* are quite common. Brown has referred to such texts as 'imitation' Gītās.[18] Texts that explicitly mimic the *Bhagavad Gītā* include the Śaiva-oriented Sūta and Guru Gītās of the *Skanda Purāṇa* and various Sakta Gītās, most notably the Devī Gītās of the *Devī Bhāgavata Purāṇa* and the *Kūrma Purāṇa*. In fact, the Devī Gītā of the *Devī Bhāgavata Purāṇa* often quotes Kṛṣṇa's teachings from the *Bhagavad Gītā* directly.[19] The *Kapila Gītā* of the *Bhāgavata Purāṇa* itself can be read as an imitation of the *Bhagavad Gītā* of the *Mahābhārata*. The Bhagavad Gītā certainly prefigures much of the *Kapila Gītā*'s content, from Kṛṣṇa's claim that he was Kapila among the *siddhas* to the Sāṃkhya ontology that structures much of the text.[20] The *Kapila Gītā* of the *Sarasvatī Purāṇa* is, in turn, an imitation of the *Bhāgavata Purāṇa*'s *Kapila Gītā*.

The *Sarasvatī Purāṇa* introduces its *Kapila Gītā* by narrating the story of the birth of Kapila, an incarnation of Viṣṇu. The student of the text, Sumati, asks his guru, Mārkaṇḍeya, how it was that Kapila was born at the Bindu Lake near Patan, the intellectual and political capital of medieval Gujarat. Mārkaṇḍeya's response to this inquiry is the only place in either recension of the text where another text is cited directly. Mārkaṇḍeya claims that this same question was once asked of the sage Maitreya by his student Vidura in the *purāṇa* beloved by Viṣṇu and that he, Mārkaṇḍeya, will retell that story.[21] In this instance, the *purāṇa* 'beloved by Viṣṇu' is the *Bhāgavata Purāṇa*, and the text here is referencing the story of Viṣṇu's Kapila incarnation told in chapters 22–3 of the text's third *skanda*. In fact, nearly all of the story of Kapila's birth is quoted directly from the *Bhāgavata Purāṇa*.[22] It is related, however, in a much briefer form. Though it quotes the *Bhāgavata Purāṇa* directly,

---

16 C. Mackenzie Brown, *The Triumph of the Goddess: The Canonical Models and the Theological Visions of the Devī-Bhāgavata Purāṇa* (Albany, 1990), p. 181.

17 Brown, *The Triumph of the Goddess*, pp. 180–1; C. Mackenzie Brown, *The Devī Gītā: The Song of the Goddess, A Translation, Annotation, and Commentary* (Albany, 1998), p. 9.

18 Ibid., pp. 8–9.

19 Ibid., p. 2.

20 Jacobsen, *Kapila: Founder of Sāṃkhya and Avatāra of Viṣnu*, pp. 57–8.

21 *Sarasvatī Purāṇa* 19:3–4AB. *Mārkaṇḍeya uvāca, asmin nartha purā pṛṣṭo Maitreyo bidureṇa ca, tṛtīye ca ṣubheskaṇdhe purāṇe viṣṇuvallabhe. Ahaṃ tadanusāreṇa pravakṣyāmi tavāgrataḥ.*

22 As compared with *The Bhāgatavata Purāṇā* Volume I, ed. H.G. Shastri (Ahmadabad, 1996).

many verses are omitted, resulting in sometimes jarring narrative leaps. This may reflect an assumption on the part of the *Sarasvatī Purāṇa* that its audience would already know the story of Kapila's birth. The text may be assuming that its audience, or at least the Purāṇic *sūtas* who would ideally preserve and perform the text, would know the full and exact text of the *Bhāgavata Purāṇa*, and would thus be able to fill in the missing verses. Alternatively, it may reflect the fact that the lineage and authority of the *Bhāgavata Purāṇa* – that is, the cultural ideal of the text – is more essential to the *Sarasvatī Purāṇa's* polemics than its line-by-line content.

The story of Kapila's birth begins with the sage Kardama, who worships Viṣṇu in the hopes of procuring a wife and children. Viṣṇu appears, already aware of Kardama's desires, and offers him a well-made marriage to Devahūti, the daughter of Brahmā. Viṣṇu promises that, due to Kardama's practices of great *tapas*, the strength of his seed will be increased nine-fold, thus foreshadowing the simultaneous birth of Kardama and Devahūti's nine daughters. Kardama is also promised that when he forsakes the householder's life, Viṣṇu himself will take birth through Devahūti. This promise is conveniently forgotten, and the story of Kardama and Devahūti's marriage, their hundred years of travel in Kardama's celestial palace, and the birth of their nine daughters unfolds.

After the birth of their daughters, Kardama wishes to leave the householder's life and retreat to the forest. Devahūti tearfully pleads with Kardama to stay. She reminds him that they have nine daughters to marry off, and that she herself will need companionship and protection when he is gone. At this point, Kardama recalls Viṣṇu's forgotten promise. He promises Devahūti that Viṣṇu himself will soon enter her womb. His birth will bestow fame upon his father, and his life teachings will provide his mother with knowledge of the true nature of reality and cut the ties of attachment that bind her to the corporeal world.

Kapila's birth is immediate and spectacular, as he is said to be born of Kardama and Devahūti as fire is born in wood. All of the expected auspicious and miraculous occurrences surround his birth, and these signs attract the god Brahmā accompanied by nine great sages to Kardama's *āśrama*. After they have worshipped the newly born Kapila properly, the nine daughters are given in marriage to these nine sages, wrapping up Kardama's obligations to Devahūti nicely. Kardama leaves for the forest and, with Devahūti in her son's care, the stage is set for the *Kapila Gītā*, in which the god incarnate will bestow upon his mother the knowledge required for liberation.[23]

It is at this point that the *Sarasvatī Purāṇa*'s telling of these events departs from the *Bhāgavata Purāṇa*. Whereas the *Kapila Gītā* of the *Bhāgavata Purāṇa* is associated alternately with the Sāṃkhya *darśana* and the Sāṃkhya Vaiṣṇava devotional movement, the *gītā* of the *Sarasvatī Purāṇa* relates a path of *bhakti* devotionalism that is more reflective of the theological traditions of fifteenth- and sixteenth-century Gujarat. By relating the story of Kapila's birth from the much better known, and better respected, *Bhāgavata Purāṇa*, the *Sarasvatī Purāṇa* has situated itself within a particular textual lineage. Compounding the authority that this lineage carries with it is the fact that its theology is presented in the form of a *gītā*. It is, quite literally, god speaking these teachings. Within the long-standing tradition of anchoring knowledge to specific individuals through dialogue, the discourse of the divine presents the most powerful and persuasive knowledge of all.

---

[23] While this issue is beyond the scope of this discussion, it is interesting to note the family and gender dynamics of Kapila instructing his mother. This trope of god instructing a female relative is also found in the Gurugītā (of the Santakumārasaṃhitā of the Uttarakhaṇḍa of the *Skanda Purāṇa*), in which Śiva administers teachings to Pārvatī.

Theological Heritage

In refashioning the *Kapila Gītā*, the *Sarasvatī Purāṇa* is altering a regional text to reflect the changing sectarian affiliations of its region. Aspiring to greater authority by appealing to pan-Indic teachings, it simultaneously emphasizes the regional aspects of the text to promote their importance within the region of Gujarat and, quite possibly, abroad.[24] As it does this, the *Sarasvatī Purāṇa* is conversing with, and therefore altering, at least two textual traditions. It is conversing with the regional textual tradition of the *Sarasvatī Purāṇa* as a once Śaiva text and with the trans-regionally popular *Bhāgavata Purāṇa* and its particular vision of Vaiṣṇava theology. By choosing the form of Gītā, the text is using an uniquely direct dialogic form to redefine the theology of this particular regional textual tradition.

If the dialogic format links knowledge to particular individuals, the *Kapila Gītā* of the *Bhāgavata Purāṇa* is an excellent example of how the embodiment of knowledge in a particular guru is maintained across a variety of texts and adaptations. Kapila, as an *avatāra* of Viṣṇu, serves as guru while his mother, Devahūti, plays the role of student. The knowledge that Kapila conveys *param-parā*, from one to another, establishes him as the father of an entire philosophical school and establishes the site of his teachings as a significant devotional and ritual location. The *Kapila Gītā* of the *Bhāgavata Purāṇa* is also known as the *Sāṃkhya Śāstra* and is celebrated as recounting the origins of the Sāṃkhya *darśana*. From this perspective, Kapila instructs Devahūti in the intricacies of the Sāṃkhya *darśana*, including teachings in cosmogony, the doctrines of *prakṛti* and *puruṣa*, the workings of *saṃsāra*, and the sufferings of the various modes of existence. These cosmological teachings are paired with instructions in both *bhakti* and *aṣṭānga yogas*. This, then, is the source of Kapila's association with both the Sāṃkhya *darśana* and the location of Siddhapur, near the medieval Gujarati capital of Patan.

While this interpretation of the Gītā associates Kapila with the Sāṃkhya *darśana*, it has been argued that the contents of this *gītā* are not, in fact, related to the *darśana*, but convey a particular strain of Vaiṣṇava *bhakti* known as Sāṃkhya Vaiṣṇavism.[25] Knut Jacobsen notes the existence of two distinct Sāṃkhyas – the philosophical school of the Sāṃkhya *darśana* and Vaiṣṇava Sāṃkhya, a form of *bhakti* emphasizing the path of knowledge (*jñāna*) over those of action (*karma*) or devotion (*bhakti*).[26] Jacobsen bases this assessment on the fact that Kapila teaches these two distinct traditions to two different pupils at various points in the *Bhāgavata Purāṇa*. The fact that Kapila seems to occupy two different positions in lists of Viṣṇu's incarnations offered in the text indicates that there may have once been two distinct Kapilas associated with these two Sāṃkhyas. In the *Bhāgavata Purāṇa*, he is listed as either the fifth or third of twenty-two *avatāras*. This seems to underscore the fact that there were, at one point, two Kapilas: one the founder of the Sāṃkhya *darśana*, and the other the teacher of Sāṃkhya Vaiṣṇavism.[27]

---

24 On the possibility of a readership for the *Sarasvatī Purāṇa* outside of Gujarat, see Elizabeth M. Rohlman, 'Sectarian Polemics and Textual Travels: Reconstructing the History of the *Sarasvatī Purāṇa* in Light of Two Newly Discovered Manuscripts', *Journal of the Oriental Institute*, forthcoming. On the ways in which the *Sarasvatī Purāṇa* engages in textual discourse with both regional and pan-Indic sources, see Elizabeth Rohlman, 'Geographical Imagination and Literary Boundaries in the *Sarasvatī Purāṇa*', *International Journal of Hindu Studies* 15/2 (2011): 139–63.

25 Jacobsen, *Kapila: Founder of Sāṃkhya and Avatāra of Viṣṇu*, pp. 3, 59.

26 Ibid., p. 57.

27 Ibid., pp. 59–60.

Of course, inconsistencies of this sort are common throughout the Purāṇas and, just as variant manuscript versions of a single *purāṇa* tend not to affect the cultural identity of that *purāṇa*, such philosophical variants do not necessarily impact the cultural identity of a literary figure. In contemporary tradition, the two Kapilas and their two Sāṃkhyas are generally treated as one and the same. While the sage (or sages) Kapila is associated with both Sāṃkhyas, the *gītā* of the *Bhāgavata Purāṇa* most directly links Kapila to Vaiṣṇava Sāṃkhya through his teachings to his mother, Devahūti. The narrative also links Kapila to the *tīrtha* of Siddhapur in a manner that is consistent with the prominence of regional geography in the *Sarasvatī Purāṇa*'s narrative design. Because Kapila's teachings lead his mother to *mokṣa* here, Siddhapur is to this day identified as the location where *śrāddha* rituals to one's female ancestors should be performed. Thus, it is a feminine alternative to such pilgrimage destinations as Gaya and Vārāṇasī. There are, of course, some similarities between the Sāṃkhya *darśana* and the Sāṃkhya Vaiṣṇavism taught in the *Kapila Gītā*, namely the emphasis on creation composed of the male and female elements *puruṣa* and *prakṛti*. Thus, the devotional Sāṃkhya teachings convey some of the fundamentals of the Sāṃkhya *darśana's* cosmogony. The differences between the Sāṃkhya *darśana* and Vaiṣṇava Sāṃkhya, in fact, might be qualified as differences of style more than ontological substance. The *darśana* relates the workings of the world from an ontological perspective, while Vaiṣṇava Sāṃkhya relates the workings of the world from an emotive, *bhakti*-driven perspective. Sāṃkhya is seen throughout the epics and Purāṇas, and thus often comes in close contact with *bhakti* teachings. Indeed, aspects of Sāṃkhya thought are found in the Bhagavad Gītā, the idealized *gītā* to which all others aspire, through Kṛṣṇa's teachings on the three *guṇas*, or qualities of existence.[28] But regardless of the consistencies or inconsistencies between the philosophical and devotional teachings, later tradition treats the two Kapilas – the founder of the Sāṃkhya *darśana* and the proponent of Sāṃkhya Vaiṣṇava *bhakti* – as a single figure. He is the guru who embodies the knowledge of both aspects of Sāṃkhya. And from the Purāṇic accounts of this figure, we get the association of Kapila with Siddhapur. This makes Kapila, even as he is presented in a text of pan-Indic appeal, a distinctly regional figure. He is, then, a regional guru and deity who embodies the knowledge of both a philosophical and a theological lineage.

While it relies heavily on the *Bhāgavata Purāṇa* and its associated intellectual heritage, the *Sarasvatī Purāṇa* also presents its own, unique version of the *Kapila Gītā*. The *adhyāya* in which the *Kapila Gītā* appears is divided into two sections, the *gītā* proper and an accompanying Māhātmya that extols the merits of the location of Kapila's teachings and Devahūti's liberation. Reflecting the multiple Kapila traditions noted by Jacobsen, only brief mention is made of the Sāṃkhya *darśana*, despite Kapila's strong association with this school of thought. Devahūti interrupts Kapila only once in these teachings, to offer extended praises of Kapila as the supreme deity and to equate him with the divine essence, Brahman. The accompanying Māhātmya emphasizes the fruits born to those who go on pilgrimage to the Bindu Lake, near Siddhapur, where these teachings were revealed, and the merits of those who are devoted to Viṣṇu in the form of Kapila.

The theological teachings of the *Sarasvatī Purāṇa*'s *gītā*, that is, the *gītā* proper, are divided roughly into three sections. Much of these teachings draw substantially on the organization of the *Kapila Gītā* of the *Bhāgavata Purāṇa* or the *Bhagavad Gītā* of the

---

[28] Angelika Malinar has discussed the use of Sāṃkhya to provide a philosophical framework for Kṛṣṇa-*bhakti* in the *Bhagavad Gītā* extensively. See Angelika Malinar, *The Bhagavadgītā: Doctrines and Contexts* (Cambridge, 2007).

Mahābhārata. Kapila instructs his mother in the efficacy of Vaiṣṇava *bhakti*, emphasizing that only the lowest of humans are unable to truly know the lord and are therefore trapped in *saṃsāra*, teaching the proper practices of four-fold *bhakti* and the importance of practicing in the company of good people. Kapila teaches that from good company, the four instruments (*sādhanas*) of *bhakti* arise. These instruments are listed as the sense of distinction between what is permanent and impermanent; detachment from the enjoyments of both the human world and the world beyond; the cultivation of the qualities of appeasement of one's senses, separation from worldly desires, cessation of attachment, tolerance of pleasure and suffering, contemplation, and faith; and the desire for *mokṣa*.[29] The second section of Kapila's teachings presents the principles of *jñāna yoga*, drawing strongly on the Upaniṣadic teachings in citing the *mahāvākya*, '*tattvamasi*', and offering commentary on its meaning by explaining what the self is, or rather, is not. Following this are teachings of *karma yoga*. This again is related to Upaniṣadic ideals by asserting knowledge of Brahman as the ultimate goal of *karma yoga* and citing common Upaniṣadic metaphors, such as the non-distinction of thread and cloth, for the non-distinction of the self and the world.[30] The third and final section of teachings begins with an extended discussion of the meanings of words, beginning with the concepts of indicative (*lakṣaṇā*) and denotative (*śakti*) and becoming increasingly detailed from there. This discussion of meaning is employed as a metaphor for the relationship between the individual soul and the ultimate soul, which supports the closing argument for the unity of the paths of *jñāna* and *bhakti yoga* and their superiority over the path of *karma yoga*.

The Vaiṣṇava recension of the *Sarasvatī Purāṇa* reflects a Gujarat in transition from an epoch of Śaiva kings and a courtly culture dominated by Jain intellectuals to a new reality of Muslim rule and populist Vaiṣṇava *bhakti* movements. Given that the likely composition window of this recension begins with the late fifteenth or early sixteenth century, the text reflects a time of marked and dramatic change in the religious composition of this western Indian region.[31] In fact, the Vaiṣṇava recension of the text, which is itself a reworked version of the earlier Śaiva recension, was most likely the direct result of this period of change. Gujarat of the fifteenth and sixteenth centuries was dominated by the introduction of a new *bhakti* devotional theology focusing on the god Viṣṇu and especially on his incarnation as Kṛṣṇa. This departure from the Śaiva sentiments that dominated the courts of early medieval Gujarat was largely shaped by two figures: the *bhakti* poet Narasiṅgh Mehta (circa AD 1414–1480) and the theologian Vallabhācārya (AD 1479–1531). The great poet-saint Narasiṅgh Mehta, who holds the lauded position of 'first poet' of the Gujarati language, spread Kṛṣṇaite *bhakti* throughout Gujarat with his enormously popular songs. Vallabhācārya founded the Vaiṣṇava tradition of the Puṣṭimārg, or the path of grace, and represented an enormous theological influence in sixteenth-century Gujarat. The Puṣṭimārg sect emphasized pure non-dualism, the superiority of *bhakti* devotionalism, and the role of the grace of the lord in the religious experiences of devotees. The *Kapila Gītā* of the *Sarasvatī Purāṇa* is a product of these cultural and theological changes and brings them

[29] *Sarasvatī Purāṇa* 20:7–15. The *Sarasvatī Purāṇa* associates the desire for *mokṣa* with an affinity for listening to Vedānta, which provides an interesting and elusive aside in the context of the prominent Sāṃkhya orientation of the text.

[30] *Sarasvatī Purāṇa* 20:16–29.

[31] On the role of regional *purāṇas* as a response to the shifting political realities and religious landscape of late medieval Gujarat, see: Samira Sheikh, *Forging a Region: Sultans, Traders, and Pilgrims in Gujarat, 1200–1500* (New Delhi, 2010), Chapter 4.

into conversation with pan-Indic narrative and theology. Francois Mallison has argued that pre-Vallabhā literature demonstrates the influence of sophisticated Vaiṣṇava literature, including the *Harivaṃśa*, the *Viṣṇu Purāṇa*, and the *Bhāgavata Purāṇa*, on Gujarati writers by the late fifteenth century.[32] The historical reality that the *Bhāgavata Purāṇa* was known in Gujarat at this time bears witness to the theological and sectarian movements that were shaping Gujarat as the Vaiṣṇava recension of the *Sarasvatī Purāṇa* was being composed.

In quoting directly from the *Bhāgavata Purāṇa*, the *Sarasvatī Purāṇa* is therefore making a powerful assertion with respect to its own theological heritage. As in the narrative of Kapila's birth, large portions of the teachings from the *Bhāgavata Purāṇa*'s *Kapila Gītā* are omitted. This may reflect an assumption that the *Sarasvatī Purāṇa*'s audience would have strong knowledge of the original text. It is equally, if not more, likely that the extensive omissions reflect the much greater stylistic and literal brevity of the *Sarasvatī Purāṇa* as compared with the *Bhāgavata Purāṇa*. The Vaiṣṇava recension of the *Sarasvatī Purāṇa*, in particular, is marked by stylistic brevity and economy of language; this quality is notable even in comparison to the earlier Śaiva recension of the text.[33] The *Sarasvatī Purāṇa* does, however, follow the basic structure of the original *Kapila Gītā* just as it follows the narrative of Kapila's birth. While the text ends its reliance on direct quotation from the *Bhāgavata Purāṇa* at the beginning of Kapila's teachings, it continues to follow the text in spirit. That is, the *Sarasvatī Purāṇa* continues to convey a similar range of topics and continues to convey these topics in the literary mode of Gītā. The similarities here are rooted, in part, in the standard list of topics shared by all Gītās discussed above: the genesis, nature, and destruction of the world; the nature of the deity, the human soul, and the paths of liberation; and, most notably, the philosophical and theological foundations of the devotee's idealized life. Note, again, that these topics are similar to those addressed in the *pañcalakṣaṇa*, the five marks that define idealized Purāṇas. The distinction between the two is in the point of view and method of delivery of the teachings: a narrative related from the perspective of a devotee versus theological teachings offered from the perspective of the deity through direct, divine speech. The revelatory status of the direct speech of the deity is common to both versions of the *Kapila Gītā* and is, indeed, their most significant shared characteristic.

While the *Sarasvatī Purāṇa* draws on the textual lineage of the *Bhāgavata Purāṇa*, the *Kapila Gītā* is not reproduced exactly in the *Sarasvatī Purāṇa*. Rather, the adaptation of the text is a reflection of a specific historical and cultural reality, emphasizing those teachings that were most compatible with the Vaiṣṇava traditions indigenous to late medieval Gujarat. The songs of Narasiṅgh Mehta and the Puṣṭimārg theology of Vallabhācārya dominated the *bhakti* devotional traditions of medieval Gujarat, and continue to do so today. These traditions assert a theology that places devotion and the grace of the lord before the intellectual attainments emphasized in the Sāṃkhya Vaiṣṇavism of the *Bhāgavata Purāṇa*'s Kapila Gītā – that is, they hold the path of *bhakti*, devotion, in higher esteem than the path of *jñāna*, knowledge. Here, the text's editorial choices are key. Primarily, the teachings that dwell on issues of cosmogony and ontology, and therefore that bear the strongest resemblance to the Sāṃkhya *darśana*, are omitted, in keeping with the emotive *bhakti* orientation of the *Sarasvatī Purāṇa*. Far more emphasis, as well, is placed on the geographical location of these events, reflecting the continued ties of this text to the medieval kingdoms of Gujarat

[32] Francois Maillison, 'Early Kṛṣṇa Bhakti in Gujarat', in *Studies in South Asian Devotional Literature*, ed. Alan W. Entwistle and Francois Mallison (Paris, 1994), pp. 53–7.

[33] For more on the narrative style of the *Sarasvatī Purāṇa* in a comparative sense, see Rohlman, 'Geographical Imagination and Literary Boundaries in the *Sarasvatī Purāṇa*'.

and the idealized sacred landscape they inhabited. The text may aspire to transcend its regional identity, but it is retelling a pan-Indic narrative and relating its associated theology in a way that emphasizes its regional ties.

The marriage of the regional and trans-regional tradition is also reflected in the text's editorial choices and the subtle changes to Kapila's *bhakti* instruction they represent. The *Sarasvatī Purāṇa* is most faithful to the original *Kapila Gītā* in its narrative of Kapila's birth, a story that is consistent with a theological emphasis on the grace of Viṣṇu and the fruits of abject devotion. This emphasis on devotion and grace is seen, for example, in Viṣṇu's original greetings to Kardama, in which he reveals that he already knows the contents of Kardama's mind and the specific boon he will request.[34] Viṣṇu promptly arrives at Kardama's *āśrama* fully aware of Kardama's desires, indicating both that devotion to Viṣṇu bears valuable fruit and that the lord has an intimate emotional connection with his devotees. The narrative underscores the fact that any devotee with faith and devotion to Viṣṇu will attain similar rewards, just as it underscores the notion that few humans are truly incapable of benefitting from Viṣṇu's grace. The *Sarasvatī Purāṇa* is least faithful to the original *Kapila Gītā* and strays the most from its text in the theological content of Kapila's revelation to Devahūti. Here, the *Sarasvatī Purāṇa* softens the teachings of the *Bhāgavata Purāṇa*'s *Kapila Gītā* on the superiority of the path of knowledge, or *jñāna yoga*. The Sāṃkhya Vaiṣṇava argument for the superiority of the *jñāna yoga* over the *bhakti yoga*, or path of devotion, is omitted from this adaptation of the text. In its place, the *Sarasvatī Purāṇa* argues for the compatibility of the paths of knowledge and devotion, and ultimately asserts that they are, in fact, the same path. In keeping with the teachings of Puṣṭimārg, the path of grace, and with the emotive poetry of Narasiṅgh Mehta, the grace of the lord and the superior *bhakti* devotional path ultimately prevail. In softening the *Kapila Gītā*'s claims about the superiority of the path of knowledge, the text is more consistently reflective of its cultural-historical context.

In keeping with the original geographical vision of the Śaiva *Sarasvatī Purāṇa*, the Vaiṣṇava recension of this same text places far more emphasis on the location of the Kapila *avatāra*'s birth at Siddhapur than does the *Bhāgavata Purāṇa*. This places the Vaiṣṇava tradition of this new *Kapila Gītā* very near Patan, the intellectual and political capital of early modern Gujarat, thus bringing the lauded, pan-Indic *Bhāgavata Purāṇa* into a specifically regional articulation of Vaiṣṇavism. The fact that there is far more emphasis on the location of the events at Siddhapur and the fruits for pilgrims of visiting this location indicates the dual purposes of the text. One aspiration of the text is to exalt the regional identity of the *Kapila Gītā*, that is, to claim it as a thoroughly Gujarati tradition. Another is to tie the *gītā* and the entire *Sarasvatī Purāṇa* to the immensely authoritative *Bhāgavata Purāṇa*, and to thus place it on par with pan-Indic theological and devotional traditions. The text aspires to both promote and transcend its regional origins. By drawing on the Kapila Gītā, it is claiming the authority of Kapila, Viṣṇu, the *Bhāgavata Purāṇa*, and the Sāṃkhya *darśana*. As the guru, Kapila embodies the knowledge he teaches and gives it the power of divine speech. The *Sarasvatī Purāṇa* and its *gītā* draw on the authority of the Kapila *avatāra* as well as the heritage of the most beloved and influential of Vaiṣṇava Purāṇas, the *Bhāgavata Purāṇa*.

The Vaiṣṇava *Sarasvatī Purāṇa* is a text in transition, and this transition is effected through dialogue. Here, dialogue as the relating of teachings from guru to student is used to erase one theological identity and replace it with another. It is, in essence, used to redefine

---

[34] *Sarasvatī Purāṇa* 20:10–11.

the lineage of knowledge embodied in the text. By introducing the form of Gītā, the guru who embodies the text's knowledge is changed. If the guru embodies particular knowledge, and if lineage of intellectual tradition is significant, there is perhaps no more effective means of establishing a new theological heritage. As if to underscore this, the guru who establishes this theological heritage is Viṣṇu incarnate. His teachings are, therefore, not mere philosophical instruction but divine revelation.

In a grander sense, the discourse between Kapila and Devahūti facilitates a metaphorical dialogue between texts. Dialogue serves to create the lineage of the knowledge contained in the text. This knowledge has a lineage defined by location and culture, as established by the frame narrative; by parentage, through the narrative of Kardama; by textual association, through the citation of the *Bhāgavata Purāṇa*; by divine association, through Kapila's role as Viṣṇu incarnate; and by the lineage of gurus, through Kapila's role as the guru relating knowledge directly to his pupil, Devahūti. In this instance, dialogue is entirely in service of establishing a lineage of knowledge as a theological heritage. Not only is the knowledge revealed by Kapila dispersed *param-parā*, from one to another, but it is also dispersed from text to text. Kapila's story, and Sumati's questions about it, provide an opportunity to cite the beloved *Bhāgavata Purāṇa*. Because this opportunity is used to change the theological vision and sectarian affiliation of the *Sarasvatī Purāṇa*, the discourse between texts is also a discourse between traditions. Through its frame narrative, the text clearly situates itself in a specific location and regional culture. Through its adaptation of the *Kapila Gītā*, it situates itself with equal clarity in a specific and trans-regional theological and intellectual lineage. The revelatory speech of god and the direct citation of another text work in tandem to establish an overwhelming authority for this newly adapted text. Concurrently, the preservation of the *Sarasvatī Purāṇa* frame narrative and the Māhātmya that accompanies the new *Kapila Gītā* serve to both retain and exalt the regional provenance of the text.

That Mārkaṇḍeya cites the *Bhāgavata Purāṇa* directly makes this use of dialogue between texts explicit. But this process of intertextual dialogue occurs throughout the Purāṇas in more subtle ways. Purāṇic literature represents a remarkably malleable genre in which narrative and textual progress takes place through dialogue. This may take shape through the varying perspectives of Māhātmyas, Stotras, or Gītās, but the end result is the same. Dialogue inevitably serves as a means of adapting a plastic and pliable text. It is through this textual elasticity that texts that are defined by specifically articulated and limiting situations of space and time claim grander statements of authority, lineage, and heritage.

References

Sanskrit Texts

Bhāgavata Purāṇa. Volume I. (ed.) H.G. Shastri. Ahmadabad: B.J. Institute of Learning and Research, 1996.

Sarasvatī Māhātmya (also known as *Sarasvatī Purāṇa*). Edited by Harajīvan Kevalarām Śarmā. Bombay: Bombay City Press, Samvat 1943 (circa AD 1888). Printed book number K1843, L.D. Institute of Indology, Ahmadabad, Gujarat.

Secondary Sources

Bailey, Greg, *Gaṇeśapurāṇa Part I: Upāsanākhaṇḍa*. Tübingen Purāṇa Research Publications 4. (Wiesbaden: Harrassowitz Verlag, 1995).

Black, Brian, *The Character of the Self in Ancient India: Priests Kings, and Women in the Early Upaniṣads* (Albany: State University of New York Press, 2007).

Brown, C. Mackenzie, *The Triumph of the Goddess: The Canonical Models and the Theological Visions of the Devī-Bhagavata Purāṇa* (Albany: State University of New York Press, 1990).

———, *The Devī Gītā: The Song of the Goddess: A Translation, Annotation, and Commentary* (Albany: State University of New York Press, 1998). [Reprint New Dehli: Sri Satguru Publications, 1999].

Doniger, Wendy, 'Echoes of the *Mahābhārata*: Why is a Parrot the Narrator of the *Bhāgavata Purāṇa* and the *Devībhāgavata Purāṇa*?', in Wendy Doniger (ed.), *Purāṇa Perennis: Reciprocity and Transformation in Hindu and Jaina Texts*, (Albany: State University of New York Press, 1993).

Jacobsen, Knut, *Kapila: Founder of Sāṃkhya and Avatāra of Viṣnu, with a Translation of Kapilāsurisaṃvāda* (New Delhi: Munshiram Manoharlal, 2008).

Maillison, Francois, 'Early Kṛṣṇa *Bhakti* in Gujarat', in Alan W. Entwistle and Francois Mallison (eds), *Studies in South Asian Devotional Literature* (Paris: École Française d'Extrême-Orient, 1994).

Malinar, Angelika, *The Bhagavadgītā: Doctrines and Contexts* (Cambridge: Cambridge University Press, 2007).

Narayana Rao, Velcheru, 'Purāṇa as Brahminic Ideology', in Wendy Doniger (ed.), *Purāṇa Perennis: Reciprocity and Transformation in Hindu and Jaina Texts* (Albany: State University of New York Press, 1993).

Ramanujan, A.K., 'Where Mirrors are Windows: Towards an Anthology of Reflections', in Vinay Dharwadker (ed.), *The Collected Essays of A.K. Ramanujan* (Delhi: Oxford University Press, 1999).

Rocher, Ludo, *The Purāṇas*. A History of Indian Literature 2, fasc. 3 (Wiesbaden: Otto Harrassowitz, 1986).

Rohlman, Elizabeth M., 'Manuscripts of the *Sarasvatī Purāṇa* in the Archives of Western India', *Journal of the Oriental Institute*, 59/1–2 (2010): 151–62.

———, 'Geographical Imagination and Literary Boundaries in the *Sarasvatī Purāṇa*', *International Journal of Hindu Studies* 15/2 (2011): 139–63.

———, 'Sectarian Polemics and Textual Travels: Reconstructing the History of the *Sarasvatī Purāṇa* in Light of Two Newly Discovered Manuscripts', forthcoming in *Journal of the Oriental Institute.*

Sheikh, Samira, *Forging a Region: Sultans, Traders, and Pilgrims in Gujarat, 1200–1500* (New Delhi: Oxford University Press, 2010).

Tagare, D.V. (trans.), *The Skanda Purāṇa: Prabhāsa Khaṇda* Ancient Indian Tradition and Mythology: Purāṇas in Translation Series 67 (Delhi: Motilal Banarsidass, 2003).

Chapter 7
Dialogue and Genre in Indian Philosophy: Gītā, Polemic, and Doxography

Andrew J. Nicholson

Whether or not we accept that 'philosophy' is a universal human phenomenon, it is clear that the modes in which it is expressed – the genres of texts that are labelled as philosophical – vary from culture to culture. This textual aspect of philosophy is frequently overlooked or ignored by philosophers, who often deem such concerns as outside the scope of philosophy itself. But if it is granted that there is an important relation between form and content, that the form in which philosophers adopt to express their ideas has some bearing on the ideas they express, then this is a significant oversight. One of the central goals of a university education in philosophy is acquainting a student with a certain kind of 'philosophical' text, usually of a quite particular sort. In time, reading such texts becomes second nature, to the extent philosophers become blind to questions of textuality, forgetting that this particular moment in the history of philosophy is marked by particular kinds of texts – for instance, the journal article and the monograph – that have their own institutional histories. Had philosophical conventions developed differently, Donald Davidson might have presented his ideas in dialogue form, or Quine might have written rhymed couplets.[1]

One of the challenges when confronting philosophical works from a foreign culture is the often vastly different assumptions about texts and textuality in those cultures. It is not only a language barrier that holds us back, but also the unwritten conventions of how ideas are to be expressed. This issue of philosophical form, I believe, is one of the biggest obstacles to having Asian philosophy recognized as philosophy per se – the texts of philosophers in India and China just do not look like the sorts of texts that students of philosophy, whether 'continental' or 'Anglo-American', are trained to read. But this burden is not borne by Asian philosophers alone. Take the following example:

> The goddess said:
>
> One ought to say and to conceive that being is, for it is possible to be;
>
> And nothing is not possible [to be]: I bid you consider these things.
>
> For from this first road of inquiry I restrain you,

---

[1] One of the most disorienting aspects of Indian philosophy is that many philosophers did write in verse, although not rhymed. Buddhist philosophers such as Nāgārjuna and Hindus such as Śaṅkara at times employed the anuṣṭubh poetic meter as the vehicle for their philosophies (verses of four quarters, each quarter containing eight syllables). See David J. Kalupahana (ed. and trans.), *Mulamadhyamakakarika of Nagarjuna: The Philosophy of the Middle Way* (Delhi, 2006), and Sengaku Mayeda (ed. and trans.), *A Thousand Teachings: The Upadesasahasri of Sankara* (Albany, 1992).

> But then from this one (the road), on which mortals, knowing nothing,
>
> Wander two-headed, for helplessness in their
>
> Breasts guides their wandering thought, and they are carried,
>
> Deaf and blind equally, bewildered, undiscerning tribes,
>
> For whom to be and not to be are thought the same
>
> And not the same, and the path of all is back-turning.[2]

This dogmatic-sounding pronouncement comes not from the Hindu goddess of speech (Vāc) or of learning (Sarasvatī), but from the Greek goddess of night.[3] Is Parmenides' poem *On Nature*, the work that this citation comes from, a work of philosophy? Clearly the speaker seems to be concerned with what in later times was labelled ontology, the inquiry into being. But there is little in the way of explicit philosophical argumentation here. Instead, as in Hindu texts such as the *Bhagavad Gītā*, this text takes the form of a supernatural being addressing mortals and exhorting them to think in a certain way. It appears to lack what the British philosopher Antony Flew identified as the essence of philosophy, namely, explicit philosophical argument. He made this claim in the beginning of his introductory work in philosophy, as part of a justification of his exclusion of non-Western philosophy: 'philosophy as the word is understood here, is concerned first, last, and all the time with argument. It is, incidentally, because most of what is labeled *Eastern Philosophy* is not so concerned – rather than any reason of western parochialism – that this book draws no materials from any source east of Suez.'[4] Yet whether or not Antony Flew would have considered the *Bhagavad Gītā* and Parmenides' *On Nature* to be philosophy, both texts certainly interested philosophers in later times, philosophers who understood them as containing reasoned argument.[5] There is no doubt that much of what classical Greeks and Indians said and wrote now sounds strange to us. But that strangeness is no reason to ignore these writings. On the contrary, their foreignness presents an opportunity for engagement with another way of thinking, a type of cross-cultural fusion of horizons that is not available in picking up a recently published journal or a book from a university press. Like the other essays in this volume by Osto, Rohlman, and Eposito, in this chapter I hope

---

2 Parmenides, *On Nature*, fragment six, translated in Vishwa Adluri, *Parmenides, Plato, and Mortal Philosophy: Return from Transcendence* (New York, 2011), p. 140.

3 See John Palmer, *Parmenides and Presocratic Philosophy* (Oxford, 2009), pp. 59–61.

4 Antony Flew, *Introduction to Western Philosophy: Ideas and Argument from Plato to Popper* (London, 1971). Other philosophers, such as Heidegger and Husserl, have also understood philosophy as a project specific to Western civilization. See also Wilhelm Halbfass, *India and Europe: An Essay in Understanding* (Albany, 1988).

5 Besides attracting the attention of Śaṅkara, Rāmānuja, Tilak and Gandhi in India, the *Bhagavad Gītā* has also been the inspiration for thinkers in Europe and America since the nineteenth century. For instance, Hegel reviewed Wilhelm von Humboldt's lectures on the *Bhagavad Gītā*; see Herbert Herring (trans. and ed.), *On the Episode of the Mahabharata Known by the Name Bhagavad-Gita* (Delhi, 1995). Bimal Matilal's *Ethics and Epics: The Collected Essays of Bimal Krishna Matilal, volume 2* (New York, 2002) is a remarkable example of a contemporary analytic philosopher taking the *Bhagavad Gītā* and *Mahābhārata* seriously as a source of ethical reflection.

to shed some light on reasoned argument and its relationship to other genres, particularly narrative, in India.

Dialogue is the form of writing that stands with Socrates near the beginning of the Western canon, yet it is rare in the modern academy. Amidst the increasing professionalization of the field of philosophy, the dialogue form has only been attempted occasionally and with some risk by nineteenth- and twentieth-century philosophers.[6] But dialogue, or more precisely, dialectic, is one entrée into the textual world of ancient South Asia, as it was perhaps even more central to the activity of philosophy there than it was in classical Greece. According to Aristotle, dialectic involves two parties, a questioner and respondent. Aristotle distinguished dialectic from logical demonstration insofar as dialectic concerns issues of probability rather than certainty.[7] While demonstration begins from first principles and ends with a conclusion that is certain, he maintains that dialectic starts from common opinions and shows what can be deduced from these. The questioner tries to lead the respondent to state the most unacceptable consequences of the original thesis, in order to illustrate the thesis's unlikelihood. The respondent gives examples that support the thesis he is trying to prove, while the questioner attempts to find counter-examples to illustrate the unsoundness of the argument.[8] In this regard, Aristotelian dialectic is reminiscent of the five-step syllogism of the Nyāya school of philosophy.[9] The Nyāya school saw as its central mission the systematization of arguments concerning issues such as the existence of God and the nature of cognition. This school developed the so-called 'Indian syllogism', which has five rather than three steps. One well-known formulation is as follows:

> There is fire on the hill.
>
> Because there is smoke.
>
> As in a kitchen.
>
> This is such a case.
>
> Therefore it is so.

Students of Western logic will find things both familiar and strange in this sequence of statements. It may seem at first glance that the entire five-step sequence can easily and more efficiently be translated into a Western-style deductive proof:

---

[6] One of the rare recent studies that remarks upon the decline of the dialogue as a philosophical genre is Timothy Smiley (ed.), *Philosophical Dialogues: Plato, Hume, Wittgenstein*, Proceedings of the British Academy 85 (Oxford, 1995), p. ix.

[7] For a brief summary of Aristotle's understanding and a lucid discussion of dialectic in Indian and Tibetan philosophical traditions, see Georges B.J. Dreyfus, *The Sound of Two Hands Clapping: The Education of a Tibetan Buddhist Monk* (Berkeley, 2003).

[8] In the example of the smoke and fire, the questioner would try to offer counter-examples that show some places in which the presence of smoke is not accompanied by the presence of fire. In Indian logic, this invariable concomitance of two things is known as 'pervasion' (*vyāpti*). For more on *vyāpti*, see Bimal K. Matilal, *The Character of Logic in India* (Albany, 1998).

[9] On the attempts of European scholars to find the source of the 'Indian syllogism' in Greece, see Jonardon Ganeri, 'The Hindu Syllogism: Nineteenth-Century Perceptions of Indian Logical Thought', *Philosophy East and West* 46/1 (1996): 5–6.

1. All places with smoke are places with fire.
2. The hill is a place with smoke.
3. Therefore, the hill is a place with fire.

This attempt at translation is missing certain parts of its Indian counterpart that may seem, at first glance, completely inessential for the task of proving the conclusion at hand, 'the hill is a place with fire'. The most notable is the third step in the Indian syllogism, the example (*udāharaṇa*). It is the Indian logicians' insistence on this step as indispensable that sets apart Indian logic from logic in the West. For, while Western logic from Aristotle to the present day has been exclusively concerned with the validity of arguments, Indian logicians have also been concerned with their soundness (in other words, whether the conclusion is actually true). It is such real-world concerns as finding examples to substantiate the truth of an argument that marks Indian logic as not being a *formal* logic.[10] Or, to adopt Aristotelian terminology, what the 'Indian logicians' are doing is not strictly speaking logic at all, but rather dialectic.

While we may concede that the third part of the Indian syllogism at least provides some new information that may be relevant to the argument, the fourth and fifth steps ('this is such a case' and 'therefore it is so') seem wholly redundant, merely pointing the listener back again to steps one and two. But these final steps further indicate the use of this five-step procedure developed by the Naiyāyikas in India, not as a formal proof but as an outline of debating procedure. Formal debaters, whether in ancient India or in the modern West, follow a similar model: first, proposing a thesis to be proven ('resolved: there is fire on the hill'), second, providing an argument for why the thesis should be accepted, and third, providing examples ('as in a kitchen') and arguing against counterexamples that possess only superficial relevance to the question at hand. By this time, the audience of the debate may well have forgotten what precisely was stated in the original thesis! For that reason, the fourth step explicitly connects the examples to the original thesis, and finally, the fifth restates the original thesis.

In the remainder of this chapter, I will focus on three dialogical genres of text in India that, while familiar to anyone with a first-hand acquaintance of philosophical writing in Sanskrit, have not been as widely discussed as the 'Indian syllogism' mentioned above. The first genre, the 'Gītā' or 'song', is famous because of its well-known exemplar, the *Bhagavad Gītā*. Less well known is that there are dozens of other Gītās, most of them resembling the *Bhagavad Gītā* in depicting a dialogue between a mortal human being and a god. The second genre, what I here call 'polemic', is the genre of philosophical writing familiar among philosophical commentators in India. Commentators on the *Brahma Sūtra*s and the *Mīmāṃsā Sūtra*s divided these texts up into sections (*adhikaraṇas*) each concerned to explore one disputed topic (*viṣaya*). Similar to some European texts, each of the sections contains a type of stylized dialogue between a questioner (*pūrvapakṣin*) and a respondent (*uttarapakṣin*), eventually culminating in an established conclusion (*siddhānta*). The third genre I discuss is doxography.[11] Made famous in the late medieval period with Mādhava's fourteenth-century *Sarvadarśanasaṃgraha* (Compendium of all philosophical systems), such late Advaita Vedānta doxographies have at their root a kind of dialectical structure,

[10] For more on formal versus informal logics, see Matilal, *Character of Logic*, pp. 1–18.

[11] For a more in-depth discussion of doxography in India, consult Andrew J. Nicholson, *Unifying Hinduism: Philosophy and Identity in Indian Intellectual History* (New York, 2010), pp. 144–84. My remarks in this chapter are adapted from the discussion there.

more in the Hegelian than the Aristotelian sense. Furthermore, I claim that this genre developed out of earlier narrative forms such as the sixth-century CE Tamil Buddhist poem *Maṇimēkalai*, whose chapters 27–9 comprise the earliest doxography in India. They depict a series of dialogues between the courtesan Maṇimēkalai and a number of different teachers, each presenting their own distinctive philosophical view (*darśana*). In outlining each of these three dialogical genres of text, I hope to show how the form of each relates to its content. These three genres of text may appear exotic or strange next to their modern Western counterparts. In my conclusion I will return to the question of whether these texts, and the work of Parmenides cited earlier, can be called 'philosophy' *sensu stricto*.

Gītās

The *Bhagavad Gītā*, like Parmenides' *On Nature* mentioned above, might seem at first glance to be a religious rather than philosophical text. One of the two dialogue partners in this work, the warrior Arjuna, faces a crisis: he must choose whether to fight the cousins who have usurped his kingdom, or to lay down his arms and respect the ancient laws prohibiting the killing of kinsmen. The second character is the charioteer Kṛṣṇa, who over the course of this dialogue reveals his divinity to Arjuna. He is actually the highest god among all the gods, and his method of persuasion includes an awe-inspiring theophany that leaves Arjuna begging Kṛṣṇa to revert back to his human disguise. Although interspersed with such extra-philosophical passages, this text has also held the fascination of philosophers of the medieval and modern eras, who have found in its themes of duty and freedom much that is relevant beyond the battlefield of Kuru where the dialogue takes place.[12]

However, scholars of philosophy and religion have been somewhat late in acknowledging the importance of the many other texts labeled 'Gītās' in India, not to mention the commentaries on these texts.[13] Much of this is due to a lingering historicist bias. According to influential twentieth-century scholars such as Franklin Edgerton and R.C. Zaehner, the Gītās postdating the *Bhagavad Gītā*, starting with the *Anugītā* in the *Mahābhārata* itself, are pale imitations with none of the poetic beauty or philosophical rigor of the original. Since this has been the assessment of indologists, these texts have generally been left untranslated, and are generally unknown to modern audiences in modern India and in the West.[14]

The assessment that these Gītās are mere recapitulations of the original is encouraged by the texts themselves. The *Anugītā*, for instance, appears near the end of the epic poem *Mahābhārata*, after the carnage of battle has ended. At that point, Arjuna tells lord Kṛṣṇa somewhat surprisingly that he was not paying attention before, and has forgotten what Kṛṣṇa told him in the *Bhagavad Gītā* – would he repeat it one more time? Kṛṣṇa replies that he cannot: he was *yogayukta*, deep in meditative concentration during the *Bhagavad Gītā*, and is no longer in that state. He agrees, however, to provide another teaching whose essence is identical to the essence taught in the *Bhagavad Gītā*. Kṛṣṇa then goes

---

12 See note 5.

13 For instance, the *Īśvara Gītā*, an eighth-century work portraying Śiva as the ultimate god, has been largely neglected by modern scholars, yet it was the subject of at least four Sanskrit commentaries in the medieval period.

14 On the neglect of the *Anugītā*, see Arvind Sharma, 'The Role of the Anugītā in the Understanding of the Bhagavadgītā', *Religious Studies* 14 (1978): 262–3.

on to give a teaching that differs drastically from the *Bhagavad Gītā*. In the *Anugītā*, the path of action (*karmayoga*) is mentioned only briefly and devotion (*bhakti)* hardly at all. Instead, the *Anugītā* regards knowledge (*jñāna*) and renunciation (*saṃnyāsa*) as most appropriate for liberation. One reason for this difference in teaching, as Herman Tieken has pointed out, is the different purpose that the *Anugītā* serves in the narrative context of the *Mahābhārata*.[15] The *Bhagavad Gītā*, coming immediately before the great battle, serves the purpose of exhorting Arjuna to fight. By the time of the *Anugītā*, the Pāṇḍavas have achieved their Pyrrhic victory and the epic is drawing to a close. Kṛṣṇa's teachings there serve to encourage Arjuna and his brothers to renounce their lives on earth and draw the epic to a close. The *Anugītā*, far from being a watered-down repetition of the *Bhagavad Gītā*, claims the authority of Kṛṣṇa's teaching in order to displace it, to portray a world in which renunciation, not dispassionate action, is the best way of life.

There are over one hundred texts called 'Gītās', which at least implicitly make reference to the *Bhagavad Gītā* and derive some of their own authority from the lustre of its reputation in premodern India. Many of these texts share the same tendency as the *Anugītā*. They claim the authority associated with the *Bhagavad Gītā* while simultaneously subverting parts of the *Bhagavad Gītā*'s message. In the *Īśvara Gītā*, an influential section of the *Kūrma Purāṇa*, this is done by Śiva literally upstaging Viṣṇu. After the sages ask to hear from Viṣṇu the origin of the universe and the nature of the self, Śiva swoops down to answer their questions as Viṣṇu bows and acknowledges him as the greatest of gods. In some verses, Śiva repeats Kṛṣṇa's teachings from the *Bhagavad Gītā* word-for-word.[16] But by immediately juxtaposing these passages with verses that do not appear in the *Bhagavad Gītā*, Kṛṣṇa's words are put in the service of a teaching that sees the eight-limbed yoga of Patañjali and the meditative visualizations of the Pāśupata sect as superseding the path of devotion.

As C. Mackenzie Brown has observed, in the *Purāṇa*s the line between a Gītā and a Māhātmya ('glorification' text) is a thin one.[17] Generally speaking, the perspective of a Māhātmya is that of the devotee, who listens to the deeds of the divinity and extols his or her majesty. In the Gītā, the perspective is primarily that of the divinity, who instructs the devotee. Part of the neglect of these Gītās in the modern period is due to their heavily theistic trappings. This also explains the recent popularity of the *Aṣṭāvakra Gītā*, one *gītā* that consists of a dialogue between two human beings, instead of a human and a god. Swami Chinmayananda, a twentieth-century Advaita Vedāntin, even asserts that 'in communicating to the seekers the unsurpassing beauty and indefinable perfections of the Absolute, the Upaniṣads stammer, the Brahma-sūtras exhaust themselves, and the *Bhagavad Gītā* hesitates with an excusable shyness … . We must admire the *Aṣṭāvakra Gītā* for the brilliant success it has achieved in communicating the nature and glory of the Supreme Reality.'[18]

---

[15] Herman Tieken, 'Kill and be Killed: The *Bhagavadgītā* and *Anugītā* in the *Mahābhārata*', *Journal of Hindu Studies* 2/2 (2009): 210–12.

[16] There are 40 verses in the *Īśvara Gītā* that have one or more quarters identical to a passage from the *Bhagavad Gītā*. At four places, the *Īśvara Gītā* repeats verses from the *Bhagavad Gītā* in their entirety: *Īśvara Gītā* 2.34 (identical with *Bhagavad Gītā* 12.30), *Īśvara Gītā* 8.10 (*Bhagavad Gītā* 13.27), and *Īśvara Gītā* 8.11 (*Bhagavad Gītā* 13.28). For more on the relationship of the *Īśvara Gītā* to the *Bhagavad Gītā*, see Andrew J. Nicholson (ed. and trans.), *Lord Śiva's Song: The Īśvara Gītā* (Albany, 2014).

[17] C. Mackenzie Brown, *The Triumph of the Goddess* (Albany, 1990).

[18] Swami Chinmayananda (trans.), *Ashtavakra Geeta* (Madras, 1972).

But it is a mistake to think that the theistic orientation of these texts leads them to extol *bhakti* as the highest path. As in the *Anugītā*, many of these texts are not primarily concerned with the path of *bhakti*. Often the lavish praise of the deity in earlier chapters is primarily in order to establish the deity's epistemic authority. The teaching given by the deity in the Purāṇic Gītās generally consists of some combination of Vedānta and theistic Sāṃkhya. The Vedānta of these texts is sometimes but not always Advaita (Non-dual) Vedānta. In texts where the Advaita message of *nirguṇa Brahman* is presented, that message remains in tension with other passages where the *saguṇa* form of the deity is portrayed as the highest reality.[19] Another feature of many of these texts is instructions on yoga that go far beyond the *Bhagavad Gītā*'s. Many Gītās are heavily influenced by Patañjali's *Yoga Sūtra*s; later Gītās often integrate tantric yoga and insist that the eight-limbed yoga he taught is incomplete without tantra.[20]

Even the *Kapila Gītā*, a dialogue that would seem to be between two human beings, Sāṃkhya sage Kapila and his mother Devahūti, relies heavily on the epistemic authority of a god. In this *gītā*, a part of the *Bhāgavata Purāṇa*, Kapila is an incarnation of Lord Kṛṣṇa, who compassionately enters Devahūti's womb in order to provide her a son. This text's primary concern is not to subvert of the message of the *Bhagavad Gītā*, but rather to subvert the message of *atheistic* schools of Sāṃkhya. In Kapila's theistic Sāṃkhya, he himself is the god who provides the necessary impetus to set in motion the Sāṃkhya principles of *prakṛti* and *puruṣa*.

Since Charles Wilkins' first translation of the *Bhagavad Gītā* into English in 1785, many Westerners and Indians alike have taken it to be the greatest expression of the Hindu mind, and even the pinnacle of Sanskrit literature.[21] This modern obsession with the *Bhagavad Gītā* has led some scholars to underestimate the influence of other texts, such as the widely disseminated *Bhāgavata Purāṇa*, a text that was arguably more important in medieval Hinduism than the *Bhagavad Gītā*. We should avoid the temptation to overemphasize the relation each of these Purāṇic Gītās have to the *Bhagavad Gītā*, and in so doing to miss the heavily inter-textual nature of the various sub-genres of Purāṇic Gītās among themselves.[22] The Śaiva and Śākta Gītās, for instance, borrow motifs and teachings from one another that appear nowhere in the *Bhagavad Gītā*. The Purāṇic Gītās are interesting both from a historical and a philosophical standpoint. They often go far beyond the message of the *Bhagavad Gītā*, developing philosophical ideas further and in greater depth than the author of the *Bhagavad Gītā* was able or willing to do. Concepts like *śakti* (power), *avidyā*

---

[19] For instance, the *Sūrya Gītā* teaches Viṣiṣṭādvaita; other texts have a Bhedābheda message.

[20] One clear example of a *gītā* that teaches tantric yoga is the *Devī Gītā*. See C. Brown, *The Triumph of the Goddess*, pp. 1–31.

[21] H.D. Thoreau wrote, 'in the morning I bathe my intellect in the stupendous and cosmogonal philosophy of the Bhagavat Geeta … in comparison with which our modern world and its literature seem puny and trivial' (*A Week on the Concord and Merrimack Rivers* [New York, 1989], p. 559). Thoreau, however, also criticizes the *Bhagavad Gītā*'s conservatism and casteism in other parts of *A Week on the Concord and Merrimack Rivers*. According to the philologist and statesman Wilhelm von Humboldt, the *Bhagavad Gītā* was 'the most beautiful, perhaps the only true philosophical song existing in any known tongue' (quoted in Jawaharlal Nehru, *The Discovery of India* [Delhi, 1981], pp. 108–9). He was likely unfamiliar with the existence of the other Gītās in Sanskrit.

[22] On the intertextuality of the Gītās, also see Elizabeth Rohlman's contribution to this volume. On the general theme of intertextuality in the South Asian literatures, see A.K. Ramanujan, 'Where Mirrors are Windows: Towards an Anthology of Reflections', in Vinay Dharwadker (ed.), *The Collected Essays of A.K. Ramanujan* (New Delhi, 1999), pp. 6–33.

(ignorance), and the distinction between *nirguṇa Brahman* and *saguṇa Brahman*, barely touched upon in the *Bhagavad Gītā*, are developed in sometimes bewildering, sometimes illuminating ways. For the bewildering parts, we also have the systematic reflections of the philosophical commentators, who are ready to serve as our guides through the jungle of Gītās yet to be translated or appreciated by modern scholars.

Polemic

It is peculiar that although the commentaries written by the Vedānta philosophers Śaṅkara and Rāmānuja are among the most widely read and cited in the modern era, until recently little time has been spent reflecting on the form employed in the writing of these texts, and in particular their debt to the methods of analysis designed by the Mīmāṃsā school of Vedic exegesis that preceded them.[23] The format I designate here as 'polemic' is another dialectical model favoured by philosophers in India. These philosophical commentators usually divided their works into 'sections' (*adhikaraṇas*), each section corresponding to one 'topic' (*viṣaya*) under discussion. The five-fold breakdown of each section is said by the Mīmāṃsakas to reflect the natural interaction between a teacher and pupil:

topic (*viṣaya*)
doubt (*viśaya* or *saṃdeha*)
prima facie view (*pūrvapakṣa*)
response (*uttara* or *uttarapakṣa*)
final decision (*nirṇaya*)[24]

First comes the introduction of a topic (*viṣaya*) of discussion, for instance, 'the imperishability of the self'. Next comes some doubt (*viśaya*), which creates the need for a discussion and final decision about the topic; if a topic is wholly without controversy, there is no reason to take it up in the first place. So, a doubt about the self might arise: 'Is the self perishable or imperishable?' First comes the prima facie view (*pūrvapakṣa*), which will eventually be opposed in steps four and five. A student or opponent puts forward the view that the self is perishable, and introduces an argument or series of arguments attempting to establish this position. After this comes the response to the prima facie view, refuting

23 Francis Clooney's analysis of Śaṅkara's commentarial strategies in the *Brahma Sūtra Bhāṣya* (in *Theology After Vedānta: An Experiment in Comparative Theology* [Albany, 1993], pp. 45–58) was one of the first to note Vedānta's formal reliance on Mīmāṃsā commentaries. For details of the Sanskrit conventions associated with commentary, see Gary Tubb and Emery Boose, *Scholastic Sanskrit: A Manual for Students* (New York, 2007), pp. 239–52.

24 While all agree that the *adhikaraṇa* is divided into five parts, the specific terminology of this five-fold division of the *adhikaraṇa* varies according to different Pūrva Mīmāṃsā and Advaita commentators. One late medieval Mīmāṃsā commentator from Varanasi, Śambhu Bhaṭṭa, cites the mnemonic verse '*viṣayo viśayaś caiva pūrvapakṣas tathottaraḥ / prayojanaṃ ca pañcāṅgaṃ śāstre 'dhikaraṇaṃ viduḥ*' (N.S. Ananta Krishna Sastri, *The Bhāṭṭa Dīpikā of Khaṇḍadeva with Prabhāvalī, the Comentary of Śambhu Bhaṭṭa* [New Delhi, 1987], vol. 1, p. 9). Another variation is '*viṣayo viśayaś caiva pūrvapakṣas tathottaram / nirṇayaś ceti pañcāṅgaṃ śāstre 'dhikaraṇaṃ smṛtam*' (Shree Narayan Mishra, personal communication). The most common understanding of the Vedānta *adhikaraṇa* includes 1. topic (*viṣaya*), 2. doubt (*saṃdeha*), 3. prima facie view (*pūrvapakṣa*), 4. response (*uttarapakṣa*), and 5. established view (*siddhānta*) (see Clooney, *Theology After Vedānta*, p. 47).

each of the arguments advanced by the opponent and offering independent arguments for the proponent's view, that the self is imperishable. Last is the final decision (*nirṇaya*), that the self is permanent. After this decision is made, the next topic is taken up, ideally a topic that follows naturally from the previous argument. After a statement of relevance (*saṃgati*) is made to show how the next topic follows naturally from the previous, the new section begins, with its different but related topic.[25]

This format for organizing philosophical texts in India is widely used by many schools yet was first fully elaborated by the Pūrva Mīmāṃsā system. Like the 'Indian syllogism', it is also a kind of formalized structure based on Indian theoreticians' ideas of what a conversation between a teacher and pupil does or should look like.[26] It is also an immediately recognizable genre of text. Indeed, it is sometimes portrayed as the Sanskrit equivalent of the Socratic dialogue, or even the only genre of philosophical text in India. Both of these portrayals are false, to be sure. There are substantial differences between the polemical form of the five-fold 'section' (*adhikaraṇa*) and the Socratic dialogue, beginning with thc identification of the characters in the Socratic dialogue.[27] Unlike the Socratic dialogue, the opponent (*pūrvapakṣin*) is rarely named, and often the argument he advances is not explicitly identified as belonging to any particular school. The identities of the philosophical schools in question would have been evident to those living at the time of the text's author. But today many of the arguments we find in these texts are quite obscure. Even when we can put a name to an argument advanced as a prima facie view, the greater details of the opponents' views have often lost with the decline of their sects' popularity centuries ago.[28]

Another difference between the Socratic dialogue and the format of the *adhikaraṇa* is the formal requirement that each section end with a 'final determination' (*nirṇaya* in Mīmāṃsā) or 'established conclusion' (*siddhānta* in Vedānta). One of the remarkable features of the Socratic dialogue is that often there is no clearly established conclusion; the end of the dialogue is marked by the destruction of the interlocutor's thesis, yet Socrates advances no alternative that might take its place. Instead, all that the reader is left with is the agreement between Socrates and his interlocutor that they must continue to pursue the truth, since they have not yet reached a satisfactory conclusion. This tendency in some of Socrates' dialogues lent itself to a particular interpretation by the Academic sceptics in

---

25 For an example of the *saṃgati*, see Clooney, *Theology After Vedānta*, pp. 59–63.

26 On the prescriptive (as opposed to descriptive) tendencies of Indian *śāstra*, see Sheldon Pollock, 'The Theory of Practice and the Practice of Theory in Indian Intellectual History', *Journal of the American Oriental Society* 105/3 (1985): 499–519. Also relevant here is the Naiyāyikas' enumeration of three types of debate: 1. Constructive debate (*vāda*), in which the goal is to ascertain the truth; 2. Confrontational debate (*jalpa*) in which the goal is to have one's own point of view declared the superior (*jalpa*), which may involve various types of rhetorical tricks; and 3. Destructive debate (*vitaṇḍā*), in which the only goal is to disprove the other party's thesis, without advancing any thesis of one's own. The first of these types is considered the type pursued between a teacher and pupil. The second of these is the type engaged in between philosophical rivals.

27 My use of the term 'polemic' is not meant in any pejorative sense, but is rather simply an attempt to find an English term less unwieldy than '5-fold *adhikaraṇa* format'. The *adhikaraṇa* is a polemic in the sense of 'a controversial argument' since according to its theory the topic is controverted in parts two and three of the *adhikaraṇa*.

28 For instance, the Ājīvika school was once a thriving sect with distinctive philosophical views, but now only available to us through the writings of their opponents. On one attempt to reconstruct the views of the Ājīvikas, see Johannes Bronkhorst, *Greater Magadha: Studies in the Culture of Early India* (Leiden, 2007), pp. 38–51.

Greece: the purpose of dialectic is purely negative, and that the ultimate goal of philosophy is the suspension of all dogmatic views.[29] But the Greek sceptics' goal of disproving all theses without offering any alternative thesis of their own is actually a violation of the rules of debate, as agreed upon by most Indian dialecticians. [30] The Nyāya school terms this 'destructive argument' (*vitaṇḍā*), the lowest of the three types of dialectics.[31]

Contrasting the standard polemical form of the Indian commentators, the five-fold *adhikaraṇa*, with the more familiar form of Socratic dialogue helps to emphasize just how broad the category of 'the dialogical' is, and the many different functions that dialogical genres can perform. On the one hand, the five-fold form of commentarial polemic is a systematic method of argumentation for establishing one's own conclusions and overturning those of one's opponents, who are always inevitably vanquished in order for the final decision (*nirṇaya*) to appear. It is a kind of machine for debate, and unapologetically dogmatic.

By contrast, Plato created a new philosophical genre in Greek, the 'aporetic dialogue with pseudo-historical setting', for almost opposite purposes.[32] As argued by Ruby Blondell, this new form of text has two functions, to avoid dogmatism and to draw its audience in as emotional participants in the debate.[33] There is constant ambiguity in these works as to whether any set of opinions voiced by Socrates in a given dialogue are those belonging to the historical Socrates, to Plato (using Socrates as a kind of ventriloquist's dummy for his own views), or, most likely, some combination of the two. In some dialogues, Plato uses narrative framing techniques to further distance himself as author from the views being expressed. So, in the *Phaedo*, for instance, Phaedo gives his own recollection of a conversation in prison between Socrates and two other men shortly before Socrates' execution.[34] These dialogues are dramatic in a way that the Indian five-fold polemic is not, in the Aristotelian sense of drama as a mimetic art depicting 'people doing things'.[35] Not only does Phaedo relate the words exchanged between Socrates and his interlocutors. He also describes Socrates calmly drinking the hemlock potion, and the bravery with which he faces death as the coldness spreads throughout his entire body.[36] The pathos of this dialogue's conclusion has parallels to some of the episodes of the Indian epics, but no parallel in a work of Indian

---

29 On the Academic sceptics, see Katja Vogt, 'Ancient Skepticism', *Stanford Encyclopedia of Philosophy* (16 December 2010).

30 The most notable exception to this in India was the school of Prāsaṅgika Madhyamaka Buddhism, which saw itself as only refuting the viewpoints of others without offering any alternative. For a comparison of this school to the Greek sceptics, see Jay Garfield, *Empty Words: Buddhist Philosophy and Cross-Cultural Interpretation* (New York, 2003), pp. 3ff.

31 See Richard King, *Indian Philosophy: An Introduction to Hindu and Buddhist Thought* (Edinburgh, 1999), p. 130 and p. 141.

32 See Charles H. Kahn, *Plato and the Socratic Dialogue* (New York, 1996), pp. 95–100. Kahn's thesis is that Plato invents this new genre of philosophical writing for heuristic purposes. Dialogues such as the *Laches*, the *Charmides* and the *Euthyphro* were designed to prepare Athenians for the doctrines that were to come later in the *Symposium*, the *Phaedo* and the *Republic*.

33 See Ruby Blondell, *The Play of Character in Plato's Dialogues* (New York, 2002), p. 39.

34 On 'framing' devices in Plato's writings, see ibid., pp. 47–8 and pp. 78–9. An obvious point of comparison is the copious use of frames in the Indian epic, although I have never seen an in-depth comparison. On frame structures in the Sanskrit epics, see, for instance, C.Z. Minkowski, 'Janamejaya's Satta and Ritual Structure', *Journal of the American Oriental Society* 109/3 (1989): 401–20.

35 See Blondell, *The Play of Character in Plato's Dialogues*, p. 30.

36 Plato, *The Collected Dialogues of Plato*, ed. Edith Hamilton and Huntington Cairns (Princeton, 1996), pp. 97–8.

philosophical commentary.[37] This emotional power and accessibility is one of the reasons the Socratic dialogues continue to be a mainstay of undergraduate philosophy curricula. It is also another way in which the genre of the Socratic dialogue is unlike Indian philosophical commentary, which seems designed to repel the casual reader through its refusal to clearly label who each speaker is, its frequent use of technical vocabulary, and its unwillingness to explore what is at stake in human terms in the winning or losing of a debate.

Socrates is not just a disembodied voice, as he would be were some Indian philosophical text discovered where his views functioned as a prima facie counterpoint (*pūrvapakṣa*) to the main position being argued. He does things, and in so doing has been understood for centuries as the physical embodiment of a virtuous human life. Unlike Parmenides, who derives authority for his philosophy by putting it in the mouth of a goddess, Plato shows how philosophy is a human endeavour, a comportment of a body speaking and acting in relation to other human bodies. Although Socrates is not a god, he stands at the centre of Plato's works, in an ambiguous relation to their author.

The 'disembodied' feature of philosophical commentary in India lent itself in the twentieth century to perennialist interpretations of these texts.[38] In spite of the attempt by systematic philosophers to suppress historical particularity and individual personality, there are nonetheless ample reminders that the views Vedāntins fought over were by and about human beings. For instance, after the Viśiṣṭādvaita Vedānta philosopher Rāmānuja summarizes at length the philosophy of his main opponent, the Advaita (Non-dual) Vedānta, he begins his comprehensive refutation of its views with an *ad hominem* attack:

> This entire theory rests on a fictitious foundation of altogether hollow and vicious arguments, incapable of being stated in definite logical alternatives, and devised by men who are destitute of those particular qualities which cause individuals to be chosen by the Supreme Person revealed in the Upaniṣads; whose intellects are darkened by the impression of beginningless evil; and who thus have no insight into the nature of words and sentences, into the real purport conveyed by them, and into the procedure of sound argumentation, with all its methods depending on perception and the other instruments of right knowledge.[39]

Unlike the Advaitins, who take original ignorance (*avidyā*) to be the source of human suffering, Rāmānuja pinpoints evil (*pāpa*) as the cause of his opponents' problems. They are wicked men who refuse to perform the rituals prescribed in the Vedas, and thus are incapable of correct understanding. Compare this portrayal of Rāmānuja's opponents' fallibility with Plato's expression of human ignorance at the end of Socrates' dialogue with the self-proclaimed religious expert Euthyphro on the nature of piety. Euthyphro fails repeatedly in his attempts to define a concept he claims to know so well. Yet Socrates offers

---

[37] One poignant moment, of course, is Arjuna's despair as he surveys his kinsmen and beloved teachers in the first chapter of the *Bhagavad Gītā*. Another is Bhiṣma's death on a bed of arrows at the conclusion of his philosophical teaching in the *Mokṣadharma Parvan* of the *Mahābhārata*.

[38] Among perennialist thinkers who interpreted Vedānta without concern for the human contexts of its thinkers were Aldous Huxley and Joseph Campbell. Ironically, another name for Vedānta is 'exegesis of the embodied' (śārīraka-mīmāṃsa), specifically, the investigation of the embodied self's relation to *Brahman*.

[39] Rāmānuja, *The Vedānta Sūtras with the Commentary by Rāmānuja*, trans. George Thibaut, Sacred Books of the East 48 (Delhi, 1989), p. 39.

no established doctrine (*siddhānta*), no definition of piety that readers can take away from the dialogue, merely the anticipation of a continued philosophical journey:[40]

> Socrates: And so we must go back again, and start from the beginning to find out what the holy is. As for me, I never will give up until I know .... So tell me, peerless Euthyphro, and do not hide from me what you judge it to be.
>
> Euthyphro: Another time, then, Socrates, for I am in a hurry, and must be off this minute.
>
> Socrates: What are you doing, my friend? Will you leave, and dash me down from the mighty expectation I had of learning from you what is holy and what is not, and so escaping from Meletus' indictment? I counted upon showing him that now I had gained wisdom about things divine from Euthyphro, and no longer out of ignorance made rash assertions and forged innovations with regard to them, but would lead a better life in the future.[41]

Doxography

The word 'doxography' was first coined in 1879 by the philologist Hermann Diels. He was primarily concerned with Greek and Roman texts, but his term has been adopted to refer to a group of texts produced in pre-modern India, usually but not always in Sanskrit. The majority of extant doxographies in Indian manuscript libraries, however, date from the fourteenth to the seventeenth centuries, suggesting that it was in the late medieval and early modern periods that doxography became a central concern of Indian philosophers. The most familiar of these to Western scholars is Mādhava's *Sarvadarśanasaṃgraha* (Compendium of all philosophical systems), but there were many, many others, often described in their titles as 'compendia' (*saṃgrahas*) or 'compilations' (*samuccayas*).[42] These medieval texts also frequently described themselves as cataloguing 'the six philosophical systems' (*ṣaḍdarśana*) or 'all philosophical systems' (*sarvadarśana*). Like the genres discussed previously, the 'Gītā' and 'polemic,' doxographies have received little attention outside a small coterie of Indological scholars. When these texts are discussed, it is almost always with an eye to the data that these texts might provide us for reconstructing the intellectual history of India at the time that they were written. However, one early example of doxography hints that the doxographical form in India may have evolved out of narratives recounting dialogues between a single spiritual seeker and his or her various teachers.[43]

---

40 This is not to say that Socrates never expresses positive philosophical views; middle dialogues such as the *Republic* argue quite forcefully for specific ideas of justice and political organization, for instance (see Kahn, *Plato and the Socratic Dialogue*, pp. 96–100).

41 Plato, *The Collected Dialogues of Plato*, p. 185.

42 Names of these texts include *Sarvasiddhāntasaṃgraha*, *Sarvamatasaṃgraha*, *Sarvadarśanakaumudī*, *Ṣaddarśanasamuccaya*, *Ṣaḍdarśananirṇaya*, *Ṣaḍdarśanīsiddhāntasaṃgraha* and *Sarvasiddhāntapraveśaka* (see Halbfass, *India and Europe*, pp. 350–1). For more on doxography in late medieval India, see Nicholson, *Unifying Hinduism*, pp. 9–14 and pp. 144–65.

43 See, for instance, Olle Qvarnström, 'Haribhadra and the Beginnings of Doxography in India', in N.K. Wagle and Olle Qvarnström (eds.), *Approaches to Jaina Studies: Philosophy, Logic, Rituals, and Symbols*, ed. (Toronto, 1999), pp. 169–210, and Halbfass, *India and Europe*, pp. 350ff.

The earliest extant Indian doxography is Cāttaṉār's sixth century CE Tamil Buddhist poem *Maṇimēkalai*.[44] *Maṇimēkalai* is the story of a South Indian temple dancer and courtesan who seeks to give up her profession in order to pursue the Buddhist virtues of charity and philosophical study and to eventually become a Buddhist nun. The text is extraordinary insofar as it is the only extant Buddhist narrative written in Tamil. For this reason, it was widely neglected and only rediscovered by scholars in the nineteenth century. It is also a text that defies easy genre classification. Although large parts of the text follow Tamil literary conventions, the last sections comprise a lengthy compendium of the teachings of the various philosophical systems, culminating with a discussion of Buddhist logic. Just as this text was overlooked by scholars of Tamil because of its Buddhist content, it has been overlooked by historians of Indian philosophy because it was written in Tamil, not Sanskrit. However, chapters 27–9 of the poem have numerous characteristics in common with later Sanskrit doxography. Therefore, *Maṇimēkalai* can be described as an Indian doxographical source that predates Haribhadra's eighth-century 'Compilation of the Six Systems' (*Ṣaḍdarśanasamuccaya*), previously described by most scholars as the earliest of the genre in India.[45]

In its chapters on the philosophical systems, *Maṇimēkalai* adheres to conventions that are also quite common in later Sanskrit doxographies. It begins its typology of the schools according to the number of means of valid knowledge (*pramāṇa*s) that each accepts. And, like many texts that followed it, it lists the schools of philosophy (*darśanas*) as being six. Also like later doxographies, this number seems purely conventional. Although Cāttaṉār lists six systems, he does so in the midst of a discussion of many systems and thinkers who do not find their way onto this official list. It seems that the notion of the 'six systems' predated both Cāttaṉār's sixth-century and Haribhadra's eighth-century text, and that both are working from an earlier template. The two doxographers are clearly aware that there are more than six schools in total, but also feel compelled to include this number.

The information presented in the doxographical chapters of *Maṇimēkalai* is in the form of encounters between the temple dancer Maṇimēkalai and the representatives of various philosophical schools. Cāttaṉār presents the basic information about the ten *pramāṇas* and the six schools in Maṇimēkalai's encounter with a logician (*pramāṇavādin*). After her introduction to a few logical categories, Maṇimēkalai encounters representatives of sects that are found nowhere in the logician's list of the six systems. In order, she meets a Śaiva (*śaivavādin*), Brahma-worshipper (*brahmavādin*) a follower of the Veda (*vedavādin*), an Ājīvika, a Digambara Jain (*nigaṇṭhavādin*), a Sāṃkhya, a Vaiśeṣika, a Materialist (*bhūtavādin*), and finally the Buddhist teacher Aravaṇa Aḍigal.[46] Maṇimēkalai expresses distaste at the doctrines of the Ājīvikas and Materialists, in particular. Other systems, such as the Jains and Sāṃkhyas, are depicted with some sympathy.[47] But the text represents

---

44 On the difficult question of *Maṇimēkalai's* dates, see Paula Richman, *Women, Branch Stories, and Religious Rhetoric in a Tamil Buddhist Text* (Syracuse, NY, 1988), pp. 160–1.

45 Also see Malcolm Eckel's discussion of *Maṇimēkalai* in the context of his work on Bhāviveka's *Madhyamakahṛdayakārikā* (Malcolm D. Eckel, *Bhāviveka and His Buddhist Opponents*, Harvard Oriental Series 70 [Cambridge, MA, 2009], pp. 15–17).

46 Based on the content of the teachings of the *brahmavādin*, it is clear that this epithet means 'worshipper of the God' rather than 'Vedāntin'. It is also further evidence that the Vedānta school, given a central place in the historiography of Indian philosophy, was not very well known in India before the tenth century CE (see Nicholson, *Unifying Hinduism*, pp. 24–38).

47 After the Sāṃkhya teaching Cāttaṉār says that 'Maṇimēkalai listened to this account with lively interest' (Alain Danielou [trans.], *Manimekhalaï: The Dancer with the Magic Bowl by Cāttaṉār*

Buddhism as the highest teaching, and other teachings are depicted as worthwhile only insofar as they point towards Buddhist truths.[48] In this way, the structure of chapters 27–9 of *Maṇimēkalai* anticipates later doxographies such as Mādhava's *Sarvadarśanasaṃgraha*, which also proceeds dialectically from lower doctrines to the highest truth. Only when Maṇimēkalai listens to the Buddhist doctrines presented by Aravaṇa Aḍigal does she find 'the truth … free from all inconsistency'.[49] Cāttaṉār's story culminates with Maṇimēkalai's full acceptance of Buddhist teachings and of 'the life of austerity … that is indispensable for attaining wisdom and being free of the burden of faults that bind us to the interminable cycle of rebirth'.[50]

The *Sarvadarśanasaṃgraha* (Compendium of All Philosophical Systems) is traditionally ascribed to the Advaita Vedānta philosopher Mādhava, who lived in the fourteenth century as a minister of the Vijayanagara empire, and eventually became the head of the Advaita monastery at Śṛṅgeri reputedly founded by Śaṅkara.[51] Mādhava's text is more than simply a complete and objective description of all of the philosophical schools. It is an idealized representation of the state of philosophical affairs according to the worldview of one of the most famous exponents of Advaita, the author of enormously popular Advaita texts such as the *Pañcadaśī* and *Śaṅkaradigvijaya*. Like other late medieval Vedānta doxographies, the *Sarvadarśanasaṃgraha* begins with lesser philosophical schools, progressing in order of their acceptability, until it finally culminates in the highest philosophy, Advaita Vedānta.[52] In a dialectical fashion that may remind modern readers of Hegel, Mādhava presents each philosophical school as a corrective to the one that came before it. So, for instance, the Cārvāka school presents the view in the first chapter that there is only one valid means of knowledge, perception. Immediately at the beginning of chapter two, the Buddhists challenge this view, offering arguments in support of an additional means of knowledge, rational inference. Mādhava continues with this conceit for approximately the first eight chapters of his work, but he uses it less and less as its artificiality becomes more and more apparent. How does Vaiśeṣika atomism function as the logical corrective to the Raseśvara Śaiva sect, for instance? Nonetheless, the overall impression of his text is that the schools function together in a dialectical process – although none of the central doctrines of the Buddhists can be accepted by the Advaita Vedānta, the Buddhists' refutation of Cārvāka views can be accepted without reservation. This process is sometimes problematic, since the grounds by which the Buddhist disproves some Cārvāka theories are not acceptable

[New Delhi, 1993], p. 135 and p. 139). Maṇimekalai's Buddhist teacher remarks that Buddhist logic is itself based on the teachings of the Jain teacher Jinendra, who was the first to establish that the two means of knowledge are perception (*pratyakṣa*) and deduction (*anumāna*) (Dainelou, *Manimekhalaï*, p. 152).

48 See Anne E. Monius, *Imagining a Place for Buddhism* (New York, 2001), p. 66.

49 This translation is from Danielou, *Manimekhalaï*, p. 172.

50 Ibid.

51 Some recent scholars dispute Mādhava's authorship of the *Sarvadarśanasaṃgraha*. The fourteenth-century date of the text, however, is not disputed. See preface to Klaus K. Klostermaier (trans.), *Sarvadarśanasaṃgraha, Chapter 16: Śaṅkaradarśanam* (Chennai, 1999), pp. v–vi. On the question of who founded the Śṛṅgeri *maṭha*, see Matthew Clark, *The Dasanami-Samnyasis: The Integration of Ascetic Lineages into an Order* (Leiden, 2006).

52 The *Sarvasiddhāntasaṃgraha*, ascribed to Śaṅkara, is very similar to Mādhava's *Sarvadarśanasaṃgraha* in its structure. However, it abandons any explicit claim that each later system refutes the former in its fifth chapter (out of twelve) (M. Rangācārya [trans. and ed.], *Sarvasiddhāntasaṃgraha of Śaṅkara* [New Delhi, 1983]).

to an Advaitin. A refutation of Cārvāka hedonism on the basis of the Buddhist doctrine of momentariness, for instance, is unacceptable, since Advaita does not accept that all entities in the world only exist for a moment before they pass out of existence. In other cases, however, Buddhist arguments are acceptable – such as the Buddhist arguments accepting the validity of rational inference (*anumāna*), a means of knowledge accepted by both the Buddhists and Vedāntins but rejected by the Cārvākas.

This hierarchical, dialectical format is the main point of contact between late medieval Vedānta doxographies such as the *Sarvadarśanasaṃgraha* and the narrative progression of the sixth century Buddhist poem *Maṇimēkalai*. Of course, there are no explicit characters or plot in the *Sarvadarśanasaṃgraha*, just a presentation of a series of doctrines, each superior to the last. But there is a drama here – it is the drama of the gradual accumulation of wisdom leading to enlightenment, the same story that we find at the end of the *Maṇimēkalai*. Instead of a Buddhist nun as the central character, the central character of the *Sarvadarśanasaṃgraha* is each of the text's readers, in dialogue with each of the systems presented chapter-by-chapter as we are led toward the ultimate truth of Advaita Vedānta.

Conclusion

At the beginning of this chapter I raised the question of whether texts such as Gītās, especially those Gītās in which a god addresses a mortal, can properly be considered as philosophy. By applying a definition such as Antony Flew's, the *Bhagavad Gītā*, along with many celebrated Greek texts, would be excluded from the philosophical canon. Besides Parmenides' *On Nature*, another group of texts that would have to be excluded are most works of the ancient Cynics. One influential historian of philosophy, Pierre Hadot, has described the Cynics as a 'limit case' for what can and cannot be considered philosophy. Although Cynicism was widely considered a school of philosophy by Diogenes Laertius and other doxographers, Hadot observes that Cynicism 'was a philosophy in which philosophical discourse was reduced to a minimum'.[53] So, for instance, when Zeno argues that motion is impossible, Diogenes the Cynic does not speak; he just stands up and begins to walk. When it is proved that human beings have horns, Diogenes merely touches his head. He does not deign to formulate a verbal refutation (*uttarapakṣa*) to Zeno's prima facie view (*pūrvapakṣa*). Here Diogenes himself is the text, the living embodiment of the Cynics' philosophy.

Among Indian philosophical schools, the group most often likened to the ancient Cynics are the Pāśupatas, a group of ash-smeared yogis who understood meditative union with the god Śiva as the highest goal of human life. The similarity is primarily in their behaviours, not their doctrines. Both groups teach that one should behave like animals: the Cynics, of course, were said to behave like dogs (hence the origin of their name, from the Greek word *kyōn*). *Pāśupata Sūtra* 5.18 recommends behaviour like a cow or deer, since those animals have great tolerance for physical discomfort.[54] Diogenes the Cynic was famous for living in a tub, and for engaging in behaviours out in the open usually only considered acceptable behind closed doors. During the second stage of the Pāśupata vow, aspirants were instructed to engage in shameless public behaviours such as snoring,

---

[53] Pierre Hadot, *What is Ancient Philosophy?* (Cambridge, 2002), p. 109.

[54] See Haripada Chakraborti (ed. and trans.), *Pāśupata Sūtram with Pañcārtha-Bhāṣya of Kauṇḍinya* (Calcutta, 1970), p. 165.

babbling incoherently, and making lewd gestures at young women, in order to invite abuse from passers-by. As the commentator Kauṇḍinya explains:

> A wise man should seek lack of honor like ambrosia;
>
> The good brahmin should hate honor like poison;
>
> For he who is despised lies happy, freed of all attachment.
>
> The monk should never think of the faults [or] the evil of another.[55]

In a classic 1962 article by Daniel Ingalls comparing the Pāśupatas and Cynics, Ingalls suggests that for both groups, philosophy was not the main concern. In Ingalls' view, the Pāśupata doctrines were little more than a half-hearted borrowing of Sāṃkhya-Yoga concepts.[56] These doctrines, he says, had little or nothing to do with the Pāśupatas' cultic behaviours. For both the Cynics and Pāśupatas, Ingalls says, practice came first. The details of their philosophical doctrines came later, and were not an essential feature of either group: 'in both traditions philosophy was something secondary in point of time and can furnish us with no evidence concerning the origin of the two cults.'[57]

The attitude expressed here by Ingalls that neither the Cynics nor the Pāśupatas were concerned primarily with philosophy, is typical among modern scholars writing about both groups. But what if the problem is that we mean something different by philosophy than the ancient Greeks did? And similarly, what if our idea of what should be properly considered a *darśana* has also been coloured by ideas about what constitutes a 'philosophical system', as this is the most common translation of the word *darśana*? Ancient Greek doxographers agree that Cynicism is one of the most noteworthy philosophies. Similarly, doxographies in medieval India like the *Sarvadarśanasaṃgraha* list the Pāśupatas among the *darśanas*. As early as the *Mahābhārata*, the Pāśupatas are listed as one of the four 'wisdoms' (*jñānas*) alongside followers of the Veda, Sāṃkhya-Yoga, and Pañcarātra.[58] Yet in spite of the predominance of the Pāśupatas on the lists of philosophies in pre-modern India, they rarely receive mention today in the works of scholars of Indian philosophy.

These facts point to an obvious conclusion. It is not that these pre-modern texts are unphilosophical. Rather, it is the professors in our modern philosophy departments who are often not doing philosophy in the traditional sense of the word. This conclusion is reinforced by a recent piece written by Colin McGinn for the *New York Times*. McGinn, formerly a professor in the philosophy department at the University of Miami, writes of repeated conversations with strangers on airplanes and at cocktail parties who, when they learn he is a 'philosopher', ask his practical advice about how they can overcome personal challenges and lead more fulfilling lives. He realized from such exchanges that

---

55 From Kauṇḍinya's commentary on *Pāśupata Sūtra* 3.3 (Daniel H.H. Ingalls, 'Cynics and Pāśupatas: The Seeking of Dishonor', *Harvard Theological Review* 55/4 [1962]: 286).

56 I disagree with Ingalls' characterization of Pāśupata doctrines. Sāṃkhya-Yoga has a dualistic metaphysics, but the Pāśupatas teach a theistic difference-in-identity that has closer affinities to the teachings of the *Bhagavad Gītā* and the Śvetāśvatara Upaniṣad.

57 Ingalls, 'Cynics and Pāśupatas', p. 294.

58 See Mark S.G. Dyczkowski, *The Canon of the Saivagama and the Kubjika Tantras of the Western Kaula Tradition* (Albany, 1988), p. 19.

his own articles and books have almost nothing to do with such common concerns. In other words, he remarks, what academic philosophers do today has so little connection to what was called philosophy in the ancient world that departments like his require a new name. On etymological grounds, he finds the name philosophy, the love of wisdom, rather presumptuous. It is also inappropriate, he notes, because most academic philosophers today are concerned with 'knowledge of abstract theoretical matters', not primarily with wisdom.[59] He therefore coins a new word. McGinn proposes that scholars like him change the name of their discipline to 'ontics' instead of philosophy, to preclude further misunderstandings. If McGinn is correct – and he certainly seems to be on to something – then we can say with some relief that texts like the *Bhagavad Gītā* and Parmenides' *On Nature* are probably philosophical after all. The Upaniṣadic and Buddhist dialogues described in this volume by Black, the Jain dialogues described by Esposito and Nichols, and the Buddhist dialogues described by Osto can also be added to this list. Perhaps by exploring new modes of expression and cultivating a philosophical orientation toward our daily lives, someday we may join Parmenides, Diogenes, and the authors of the *Bhagavad Gītā* in being able to call ourselves philosophers too.

References

Adluri, Vishwa, *Parmenides, Plato, and Mortal Philosophy: Return from Transcendence* (New York: Continuum, 2011).

Blondell, Ruby, *The Play of Character in Plato's Dialogues* (New York: Cambridge University Press, 2002).

Bronkhorst, Johannes, *Greater Magadha: Studies in the Culture of Early India* (Leiden: E.J. Brill, 2007).

Brown, C. Mackenzie, *The Triumph of the Goddess* (Albany: State University of New York Press, 1990).

Chakraborti, Haripada (ed. and trans.), *Pāśupata Sūtram with Pañcārtha-Bhāṣya of Kauṇḍinya* (Calcutta: Academic Publishers, 1970).

Chinmayananda, Swami (trans.), *Ashtavakra Geeta* (Madras: Chinmayananda Publications Trust, 1972).

Clark, Matthew, *The Dasanami-Samnyasis: The Integration of Ascetic Lineages into an Order* (Leiden: E.J. Brill, 2006).

Clooney, Francis X., *Theology After Vedānta: An Experiment in Comparative Theology* (Albany: State University of New York Press, 1993).

Danielou, Alain (trans.), *Manimekhalaï: The Dancer with the Magic Bowl by Cāttaṉār* (New Delhi: Penguin Books, 1993).

Dezso, Csaba (trans.), *Much Ado About Religion by Jayanta Bhaṭṭa* (New York: New York University Press, 2005).

Dreyfus, Georges B.J., *The Sound of Two Hands Clapping: The Education of a Tibetan Buddhist Monk* (Berkeley: University of California Press, 2003).

Dyczkowski, Mark S.G., *The Canon of the Saivagama and the Kubjika Tantras of the Western Kaula Tradition* (Albany: State University of New York Press, 1988).

Eckel, Malcolm D., *Bhāviveka and His Buddhist Opponents*, Harvard Oriental Series, 70 (Cambridge, MA: Harvard University Press, 2009).

[59] Colin McGinn, 'Philosophy by Another Name', *The Stone Blog* (1 April 2012).

Flew, Antony, *Introduction to Western Philosophy: Ideas and Argument from Plato to Popper* (London: Thames and Hudson, 1971).

Ganeri, Jonardon, 'The Hindu Syllogism: Nineteenth-Century Perceptions of Indian Logical Thought', *Philosophy East and West* 46/1 (1996): 1–16.

Garfield, Jay, *Empty Words: Buddhist Philosophy and Cross-Cultural Interpretation* (New York: Oxford University Press, 2003).

Hadot, Pierre, *What is Ancient Philosophy?* (Cambridge, MA: Harvard University Press, 2002).

Halbfass, Wilhelm, *India and Europe: An Essay in Understanding* (Albany: State University of New York Press, 1988).

Herring, Herbert (trans. and ed.), *On the Episode of the Mahabharata Known by the Name Bhagavad-Gita* (Delhi: Munshiram Manoharlal, 1995).

Ingalls, Daniel H.H., 'Cynics and Pāśupatas: The Seeking of Dishonor', *Harvard Theological Review* 55/4 (1962): 281–98.

Kahn, Charles H., *Plato and the Socratic Dialogue* (New York: Cambridge University Press, 1996).

Kalupahana, David J. (ed. and trans.), *Mulamadhyamakakarika of Nagarjuna: The Philosophy of the Middle Way* (Delhi: Motilal Banarsidass, 2006).

Kapstein, Matthew (trans.), *The Rise of Wisdom Moon by Kṛṣṇamiśra* (New York: New York University Press, 2009).

King, Richard, *Indian Philosophy: An Introduction to Hindu and Buddhist Thought* (Edinburgh: Edinburgh University Press, 1999).

Klostermaier, Klaus K. (trans.), *Sarvadarśanasaṃgraha, Chapter 16: Śaṅkaradarśanam* (Chennai: Adyar Library and Research Centre, 1999).

Matilal, Bimal K., *The Character of Logic in India* (Albany: State University of New York Press, 1998).

———, *Ethics and Epics: The Collected Essays of Bimal Krishna Matilal, volume 2* (New York: Oxford University Press, 2002).

Mayeda, Sengaku (ed. and trans.), *A Thousand Teachings: The Upadesasahasri of Sankara* (Albany: State University of New York Press, 1992).

McGinn, Colin, 'Philosophy by Another Name', *The Stone Blog* (1 April 2012) <http://blogs.nytimes.com/2012/03/04/philosophy-by-another-name/>.

Minkowski, C.Z., 'Janamejaya's *Satta* and Ritual Structure', *Journal of the American Oriental Society* 109/3 (1989): 401–20.

Monius, Anne E., *Imagining a Place for Buddhism* (New York: Oxford University Press, 2001).

Nehru, Jawaharlal, *The Discovery of India* (Delhi: Oxford University Press, 1981).

Nicholson, Andrew J., *Unifying Hinduism: Philosophy and Identity in Indian Intellectual History* (New York: Columbia University Press, 2010).

———, (ed. and trans.), *Lord Śiva's Song: The Īśvara Gītā* (Albany: State University of New York Press, 2014).

Palmer, John, *Parmenides and Presocratic Philosophy* (Oxford: Oxford University Press, 2009).

Plato, *The Collected Dialogues of Plato*, ed. Edith Hamilton and Huntington Cairns (Princeton: Princeton University Press, 1996).

Pollock, Sheldon, 'The Theory of Practice and the Practice of Theory in Indian Intellectual History', *Journal of the American Oriental Society* 105/3 (1985): 499–519.

Qvarnström, Olle, 'Haribhadra and the Beginnings of Doxography in India', in N.K. Wagle and Olle Qvarnström (eds.), *Approaches to Jaina Studies: Philosophy, Logic, Rituals, and Symbols* (Toronto: Center for South Asian Studies, 1999), pp. 169–210.

Rāmānuja, *The Vedānta Sūtras with the Commentary by Rāmānuja*, trans. George Thibaut, Sacred Books of the East 48 (Delhi: Motilal Banarsidass, 1989).

Ramanujan, A.K. 'Where Mirrors are Windows: Towards an Anthology of Reflections,' in Vinay Dharwadker (ed.), *The Collected Essays of A.K. Ramanujan* (New Delhi: Oxford University Press, 1999), pp. 6–33.

Rangācārya, M. (ed. and trans.), *Sarvasiddhāntasaṃgraha of Śaṅkara* (New Delhi: Ajay Book Service, 1983).

Richman, Paula, *Women, Branch Stories, and Religious Rhetoric in a Tamil Buddhist Text* (Syracuse, NY: Maxwell School of Citizenship and Public Affairs, 1988).

Sastri, N.S. Ananta Krishna, *The Bhāṭṭa Dīpikā of Khaṇḍadeva with Prabhāvalī, the Commentary of Śambhu Bhaṭṭa* (New Delhi: Sri Satguru Publications, 1987): vol. 1.

Sharma, Arvind, 'The Role of the Anugītā in the Understanding of the Bhagavadgītā', *Religious Studies* 14 (1978): 261–7.

Smiley, Timothy (ed.), *Philosophical Dialogues: Plato, Hume, Wittgenstein*, Proceedings of the British Academy 85 (Oxford: Oxford University Press, 1995).

Thoreau, Henry David, *A Week on the Concord and Merrimack Rivers* (New York: The Library of America, 1989).

Tieken, Herman, 'Kill and be Killed: The *Bhagavadgītā* and *Anugītā* in the *Mahābhārata*', *Journal of Hindu Studies* 2/2 (2009): 209–28.

Tubb, Gary and Emery Boose, *Scholastic Sanskrit: A Manual for Students* (New York: American Institute of Buddhist Studies, Treasures of the Indic Sciences Series, 2007).

Vogt, Katja, 'Ancient Skepticism', *Stanford Encyclopedia of Philosophy* (16 December 2010) <http://plato.stanford.edu/entries/skepticism-ancient/#AcaSke>.

PART III
Moving Between Traditions

Chapter 8
Bowing to the Buddha: The Relationship between Literary and Social Dialogue in the Nikāyas[1]

Michael Nichols

Introduction

Dialogue, understood as a conversation or debate between two or more individuals, is a prevalent feature of the collection of Pāli Buddhist *sutta*s (texts) known as 'Nikāyas'. This originally oral literature – dating from roughly the third century BCE and set down in writing around the beginning of the Common Era – represents some of the earliest evidence of Indian Buddhist thought to which scholars have access. As such, these texts provide valuable insights into the constitution, beliefs, and interactions of early Indian Buddhist communities. At the same time, we must keep in mind, as Richard Gombrich explains, that 'the *sutta*s are artifacts, not perfect records of actual conversations'.[2] The impulse to use the Buddhist Nikāyas as historical documents is thus complicated by the fact that the texts were primarily intended to reflect a Buddhist perspective and worldview, not accurately report history. By the same token, through analysis of these texts we can still learn a great deal about how early Buddhist communities perceived rival religious groups, the debates they undertook, and their views of what was at stake in those encounters. In the following, I examine how episodes of dialogue in the Nikāyas and the representation of the rival interlocutors might elucidate facets of Buddhist social perceptions and worldviews. Throughout, then, I will be discussing two interwoven senses of dialogue. The first, and primary focus of this piece, is the operation of *literary dialogue*, which simply refers to the story the Buddhists recorded within the Nikāya texts themselves. The second is *social dialogue*, which refers to the historical interactions and realities that existed outside the world of the texts. Other chapters in this volume focusing on Buddhist texts (Black, Crothers, Appleton) also address, if only implicitly, the question of these extra-textual referents within the literary dialogues. To a great degree, the exact nature of social dialogue has been lost to history and, as noted by Gombrich, we cannot take Buddhist literary dialogues as sure evidence for the tenor and conduct of historical social dialogue. Yet, as Brian Black has noted regarding formalized debate in the Upaniṣads (*brahmodya*), beyond simply providing narrative frames, literary dialogues provide insight about the texture of social interaction.[3] So, too, in this volume Patton argues that even some earlier Vedic hymns can be read as commentaries on social dialogue in their own right. Thus, in addition to discussing the literary nature of dialogue

---

[1] I would like to thank both Laurie Patton and Brian Black for their insightful and thorough reading of an earlier version of this chapter. While I was unable to incorporate all their suggestions, their advice was crucial for the final form of the piece.

[2] Richard Gombrich, *How Buddhism Began: the Conditioned Genesis of the Early Teachings* (Delhi, 1996), p. 29.

[3] Brian Black, *The Character of the Self in Ancient India* (Albany, 2007), p. 70.

in the Nikāyas, this piece will also investigate what literary dialogue – the world within the text – might suggest about Buddhist perspectives on social dialogue and interactions that are obtained outside the texts.

As both 'dialogue' and the 'Nikāyas' are expansive categories, I am necessarily selective in my treatment. First, I will be dealing with the *Dīgha*, *Majjhima*, and *Samyutta Nikāya*s, which are the collections in which dialogue as a literary form is most prevalent. Second, as the principal character in the Nikāyas, I will look primarily at dialogues involving the Buddha. Further, rather than deal with each kind of group or individual with whom the Buddha conversed, in the sections that follow I will focus in turn on three groups: Brahmins, Jainas, and Devas. My reason for doing so is twofold. On the one hand, these three groups represent the vast majority of dialogic partners for the Buddha throughout the Nikāyas, allowing us to discuss the largest proportion of the phenomenon of literary dialogue in the Nikāyas. On the other hand, together Brahmins, Jainas, and Devas represent three of the most powerful cultural forces with which the Buddhist traditions contended in the social dialogue outside the realm of the texts: the pervasive presence and influence of Brahmanism in ancient India, the existence of competing renouncer traditions, and the cultural prevalence of belief in supernatural deities.

Before proceeding with my analysis, I will give a brief survey of some of the general ideas and conclusions that will emerge. While some themes of literary dialogue in the Nikāyas carry over regardless of the dialogic partner, we will find that the Buddha varies tactics depending on the unique position and identity of his interlocutor. This is in keeping with Ralph Flores' general comment that, throughout the Nikāya *sutta*s, the Buddha consistently delivers the *dhamma* through means appropriate to each audience.[4] With the following, I would slightly modify Flores's observation: while the Buddha's message appears to have been honed to fit particular audiences, it was directed less toward individuals than groups. Though the Buddha's means of persuasion is different depending on whether the interlocutor is a Brahmin, Jaina, or Deva, the approach taken to members of the same group was common. This suggests that the Buddhist teaching was calibrated toward different audiences from a very early point in time, but at the level of social group.

At the same time, we find overarching concerns throughout these dialogues regardless of the audience. Each episode seeks to portray the Buddha as intellectually, morally, and even cosmologically superior to his dialogic partner. This superiority is achieved by several recurrent literary conventions. Most prominent are the use of stock phrases indicating conversion and deference to the Buddha, spatial 'lowering' (a process by which the Buddha's interlocutor inevitably ends up on a lower physical level relative to the Buddha), and the continual theme of the Buddha as a revealer of hidden truths, either about the nature of reality or the interlocutor's own personal character. The tailoring of each dialogue to its respective recipient, on the other hand, provides clues to how Buddhists may have attempted to calibrate their message differently to affect different prominent ancient Indian social groups or, in the case of Devas, cultural concepts. One could also regard the concern with these three groups as an interest in redefining certain practices, such as ritual and lineage, ascetic conduct, or honor due to the gods. Each of those themes surfaces in due time below. I have chosen to frame my discussion not around practices, but around characters, because literary dialogues do not take place between practices, but between characters.

---

[4] Ralph Flores, *Buddhist Scriptures as Literature: Sacred Rhetoric and the Uses of Theory* (Albany, 2008), p. 53.

On this premise, I have divided the following into four sections. The first three isolate literary dialogues between the Buddha and one of the particular groups mentioned: Brahmins, Jainas, and Devas. To provide some flavour of the dialogues in these different categories, in each section I will focus in detail on at least one text of the Buddha's dialogue with a member (or members) of the group in question.[5] In the rest of each section I will refer to other examples (though in lesser detail) and draw on the entire range of instances to characterize the techniques of literary dialogue particular to that group. After discussing the three groups in turn, in the conclusion I will compare the literary form of dialogue across these three categories, using the commonalities to reveal the general themes of Buddhist literary dialogue in the Nikāyas. By analysing the contrasts, we can appreciate the ways in which Buddhists regarded interactions with each group differently, and what those differences might mean for the social dialogue that occurred outside of the texts.

The Buddha and Brahmins

The Buddhist interaction with Brahmins has received the lion's share of scholarly attention to this point. This is not without reason, as any cursory survey of the corpus shows that interaction with Brahmins occupies a large portion of the Nikāya texts. In light of this proportion, by beginning with the Nikāya's portrayal of dialogue with Brahmins, we can gain a general sense of Nikāya literary dialogue at the outset. I will first summarize two key examples, starting with the *Ambattha Sutta* of the *Dīgha Nikāya* before proceeding on to the *Brahmāyu Sutta* of the *Majjhima Nikāya*. In the first story, the older Brahmin Pokkharasāti asks his young student Ambattha to see the Buddha and ascertain whether he is truly wise, as reports say, and has the thirty-two 'marks of a great man' (Pāli, *mahāpurisa-lakkhanam*). Ambattha takes this as instruction to challenge the Buddha and in this spirit, rather than salute Gotama and move to one side as other visitors do, Ambattha remains standing in front of the sage. He compounds this slight by then defaming the Buddha's heritage as a Shakyan, who he claims were a degenerate people inferior to Brahmins. Through his superior knowledge of lineages, however, the Buddha reveals that the young Brahmin himself is actually descended from a slave girl (of the Shakyans, no less). The audience initially asks Gotama not to embarrass the Brahmin, but after Ambattha admits the claim, the onlookers heckle and tease the young Brahmin. The Buddha then intervenes on Ambattha's behalf, recounting the positive aspects of the Brahmin's lineage and engaging him in a discussion on the merits of birth, versus the moral conduct of the *dhamma*. Ambattha admits he and his teacher are defective regarding this moral conduct and turns his attention to observing the Buddha's thirty-two marks. He confirms all but the long tongue and sheathed penis, which Gotama – psychically sensing Ambattha's intention – then displays. The young Brahmin takes his leave and goes to report to his teacher Pokkharasāti, who is horrified at his student's hostile behaviour. After sharply correcting Ambattha, Pokkharasāti sets out to visit the Buddha and also confirms the latter's thirty-two marks. The older Brahmin offers

[5] When referring to Nikāya texts I will provide both the Pāli Text Society notation as well as page citations from the available English translations. This will hopefully allow both specialists and non-specialists in Buddhist Pāli texts to locate the passages I discuss. Further, though at times I will give particular Pāli terms, the quotations I will use are from the English translations by Maurice Walshe, and Bhikkhus Ñānamoli, and Bodhi. These translations are generally quite reliable and I have seen no reason to duplicate them, except when clarifying certain terms.

Gotama a meal, at which we are told he 'sat down to one side on a low stool' near the Buddha.[6] The Buddha delivers a discourse on *dhamma*, emphasizing dependent origination, and Pokkharasāti achieves insight. The Brahmin then makes a declaration which is found verbatim in many other texts figuring in our discussion. I will refer to this statement hereafter as the 'declaration of conversion formula':

> It is as if someone were to set up what has been knocked down, or to point out the way to one who had got lost, or to bring an oil-lamp into a dark place, so that those with eyes could see what was there.[7]

With that, Pokkharasāti and his entire family become lay followers of the Buddha.

The *Brahmāyu Sutta* possesses many of the same themes of the preceding *sutta*. It tells the story of the elderly Brahmin Brahmāyu, said to be more than one hundred years old, and his interest in the teachings of the Buddha. Like Pokkharasāti, rather than see the Buddha himself, Brahmāyu sends a student (Uttara) to confirm Gotama's teaching and his possession of the thirty-two marks. Unlike Ambattha, though, Uttara does not challenge Gotama, but instead simply questions him and reports back to Brahmāyu. The elderly Brahmin himself visits the Buddha, but only after being introduced by yet another student, during the sage's visit to a large number of Brahmin householders. After greeting each other amiably, Brahmāyu asks about the thirty-two marks and the Buddha displays the two normally unapparent: the tongue and sheathed penis. Gotama then grants Brahmāyu permission to ask any question he wants, and the elderly Brahmin asks, 'How does one become a Brahmin?'[8] The Buddha answers that a Brahmin is one who knows former lives, abandons birth and death, and has a mind free from lust. In other words, he implies that a true Brahmin is a Buddha. Brahmāyu then prostrates with his head at the Buddha's feet, causing the Brahmin householders in the audience to marvel at the power Gotama must possess to elicit this reaction from an elder Brahmin. Finally, Brahmāyu gives the declaration of conversion formula, offers a meal to the Buddha, and becomes a follower.

As these two examples demonstrate, Nikāya dialogues with Brahmins contain certain salient themes: (1) Buddhist redefinition of the category 'Brahmin,' (2) ambivalence toward Brahmanism in general and a distinction between certain Brahmins in particular (i.e. the respectful Pokkharasāti versus the petulant Ambattha), and (3) the Brahmin's conversion and the acquisition of patronage. Other scholars have remarked extensively on the first aspect. As Bailey and Mabbett put it, 'Buddhism mapped itself on a structure supplied by the Brahmins, defining itself by reference to what it was not; a series of systematic oppositions identified its relationship to the preexisting hierarchy.'[9] Steven Collins has characterized this Buddhist redefinition as a shift from a social emphasis (purity of birth, ritual role, etc.) to an ethical emphasis (correct understanding and practice, etc).[10] Focusing on the *Ambattha Sutta*, Brian Black has observed that the text forms a triad with two following *suttas* in the

---

[6] *Dīgha Nikāya* (henceforth DN) I 109; Maurice Walshe (trans.), *The Long Discourses of the Buddha: a Translation of the Dīgha Nikāya* (Boston, 1995), p. 124.

[7] DN I 110; Walshe, *The Long Discourses of the Buddha,* p.. 124.

[8] MN II 144; Ñānamoli and Bodhi, *The Middle Length Discourses of the Buddha*, (Boston, 1995), p. 752.

[9] Greg Bailey and Ian Mabbett, *The Sociology of Early Buddhism* (Cambridge, 2006), p. 121.

[10] Steven Collins, *Selfless Persons: Imagery and Thought in Theravāda Buddhism* (Cambridge, 1982), p. 33.

Dīgha Nikāya, the *Kūtadanta* and *Sonadanda Sutta*s, with each renegotiating the category 'Brahmin' in a specific manner.[11] In the *Kūtadanta Sutta*, the Buddha instructs a Brahmin and king on sacrificial procedures, ultimately defining alms-giving as the optimal sacrifice rather than animal slaughter.[12] In the third of these texts, the *Sonadanda Sutta*, the Brahmin Sonadanda engages the Buddha in a discussion of the true qualities of a Brahmin. The end result is identical to the discussion in the *Ambattha Sutta*, with Gotama convincing the Brahmin that wisdom and virtue are the only necessary attributes of a Brahmin.[13]

In addition to these three texts, the *Assalāyana Sutta* targets Brahmanical ties to the god Brahmā, but within the larger context of another aspect of Brahmin identity: social hierarchy. In this text, Assalāyana receives five hundred Brahmin visitors who complain that the Buddha is offering his teaching to all *vanna*s. They ask Assalāyana to debate Gotama, but this young Brahmin is reluctant, saying it is very difficult to argue with one as accomplished as the Buddha. After three requests, Assalāyana visits the Buddha, greeting him amiably and sitting to his side. He begins the debate with the premise (most likely invoking the Vedic *Purushasukta*) that Brahmins are the highest *vanna*, 'born as sons of Brahmā, from his mouth and head', while others are thus lower born.[14] The Buddha, of course, disagrees with this assessment, and points out numerous inconsistencies between Assalāyana's claim and actual social reality. To the dismay of the assembled Brahmins, Assalāyana cannot help but be swayed by the Buddha's arguments and, after giving the declaration of conversion formula, becomes a lay follower.[15]

From this evidence, as past scholarship has argued, it is clear that Buddhist literary dialogues with Brahmins in the Nikāyas attempted to create a new definition of 'Brahmin'. However, we can also see that each dialogue is targeted toward a particular aspect of Brahminhood and employs different rhetorical techniques. The *Ambattha*, *Brahmāyu*, and *Sonadanda Sutta*s all work to cast true Brahminhood as mastery of ethics and wisdom rather than mastery of the Vedas. The *Kūtdanta* and *Assalāyana Sutta*s, on the other hand, reorient the concepts of ritual and *vanna*, respectively. Similarly, within the dialogues themselves we find the Buddha portrayed as using different techniques to debate or converse with his Brahmin interlocutors. In the *Assalāyana*, Gotama contends with the notion of Brahmanical social supremacy by drawing out logical inconsistencies with that claim. He argues, for example, that Brahmins are born from their mother's wombs, not the mouth of a god,[16] and asks Assalāyana whether it would make sense if an unvirtuous Brahmin achieved union with Brahmā simply through birth, while a virtuous *khattiya* does not attain union with Brahmā simply through birth as a *khattiya*. The variation in topic and rhetorical technique suggests a range in approaches and responses to Brahmins, perhaps calibrated to the concerns of particular Brahmin audiences who may have emphasized one aspect of Brahmin identity (lineage, ritual, etc.) more than another.

---

[11] Brian Black, 'Rivals and Benefactors: Encounters between Buddhists and Brahmins in the Nikāyas', *Religions of South Asia* 3/1 (2009) 31.

[12] DN I 127–49; Walshe, *The Long Discourses of the Buddha*, pp. 133–41.

[13] DN I 123; Walshe, *The Long Discourses of the Buddha*, p. 130.

[14] MN II 148; Ñānamoli and Bodhi, *The Middle Length Discourses of the Buddha*, p. 764.

[15] MN II 157; Ñānamoli and Bodhi, *The Middle Length Discourses of the Buddha*, p. 770.

[16] This is similar to a passage in the *Aggañña Sutta*, a lengthy satire on the Vedic view of creation put forth in the *Purushasukta*. See also Richard Gombrich, 'The Buddha's "Book of Genesis?"', *Indo-Iranian Journal* 35 (1992): 159–78.

The foregoing points to a second theme in these *sutta*s: a general atmosphere of ambivalence between Buddhists and Brahmins. As Ryūtaro Tsuchida has shown,[17] Nikāya *sutta*s recognize and respond to different kinds of Brahmins, which Tsuchida delineates as householder and ascetic. The preceding analysis, however, shows that the distinctions go even deeper. There are, for instance, the distinctions between elder and younger Brahmins (Brahmāyu and Uttara) as well as respectful and petulant (Pokkharasāti and Ambattha). Sometimes, as in the *Brāhmana Samyutta*, characters quickly move from scorn to respect for the Buddha.[18]

The feeling appears to be mutual, however, for in these texts the Buddha also is seemingly of two minds about his rivals. At times he is blunt in his criticism, for example telling Vāsettha and Bhāradvāja in the *Tevijja Sutta* that if one maintains belief in union with Brahmā without empirical evidence, 'does not the talk of that man turn out to be stupid?'[19] At other instances, though, the Buddha is shown as keenly sensitive and gracious to his Brahmin interlocutors, even when the same courtesy has not been shown to him. For instance, after Ambattha's true ancestry is revealed and the crowd begins to turn on him, the Buddha quickly lessens the Brahmin's humiliation by expounding his good qualities.[20] Additionally, both Sonadanda and Brahmāyu are described as being nearly paralysed with anxiety in the Buddha's presence, fearing that they will say something to embarrass themselves. Sensing this dismay, in both cases, the Buddha opens the discussion himself to ease the Brahmins' worry. Thus, the overall portrayal of Brahmin–Buddha dialogue in this literature shows a mixture of tension, reorientation, and consideration, on both parts.

Going further, there is the theme of conversion and patronage, which is often accompanied by two significant literary conventions. The first is prominent reference to the thirty-two marks of the Buddha's body. These marks are a concern for Pokkharasāti and Ambattha in the *Ambattha Sutta*, Brahmāyu in the *Brahmāyu Sutta*, and Sonadanda in the *Sonadanda Sutta*. The prospect that Gotama possesses these marks not only inspires the Brahmins' visits to the Buddha, but also confirms the truth of the *dhamma*. In the last example, Sonadanda must first convince fellow Brahmins of the propriety of his visit to the ascetic Gotama. As justification, he recites Gotama's virtues, noting especially his possession of the thirty-two marks.[21] The thirty-two marks are thus portrayed in these texts as playing a central motivating factor for Brahmins to participate in dialogue with the Buddha.

Last, these conversions are usually accompanied by the stock phrase I have termed the 'declaration of conversion formula'. This phrase is also accompanied in the texts by an emphasis on the spatial proximity and position of the particular Brahmin to the Buddha. In cases where the interlocutor is initially belligerent (Ambattha, Bhāradvāja), we are told the Brahmin approaches and remains standing in front of the Buddha, while friendly visitors (Brahmāyu, Sonadanda) sit to one side. In either case, during the course of the conversation, as the *Ambattha* and *Brahmāyu Sutta*s show, as the Brahmin is swayed by the Buddha's words, they kneel before him, even putting their head to his feet, whether

---

17 Tsuchida Ryūtaro, 'Two Categories of Brahmins in the Early Buddhist Period', *Memoirs of the Research Department of the Toyo Bunko*, No. 49 (1991).

18 *Samyutta Nikāya* (henceforth SNI 160–64; Bhikkhu Bodhi (trans.), *The Connected Discourses of the Buddha: a Translation of the Samyutta Nikāya* (Boston, 2000), pp. 254–8.

19 DN I 243; Walshe, *The Long Discourses of the Buddha*, p. 190.

20 DN I 95; Walshe, *The Long Discourses of the Buddha*, p. 116.

21 DN I 116; Walshe, *The Long Discourses of the Buddha* , p. 127.

they were originally affable or not. In the case of Sonadanda's initial meeting with the Buddha, he sits to one side; but when he hosts Gotama for a meal, he takes a 'low stool'. After the Buddha's *dhamma* talk, the Brahmin ultimately declares that due to his position he cannot always publicly show proper esteem to Gotama, but if he takes off his turban or raises his goad from his carriage, this should be taken as equivalent to bowing his head to the Buddha's feet.[22] In other *sutta*s, this phenomenon sometimes occurs on a larger scale, as in the *Sāleyyaka, Verañjaka* and *Nagaravindeyya Sutta*s, where we are told that the Brahmin populations of entire villages convert, give the formulaic phrase, and bow at the Buddha's feet.

The Buddha and Jainas

The themes of the body and conversion/submission to the Buddha recur in other dialogues throughout the Nikāyas and I will revisit them in the conclusion. First, though, besides contending with the pre-existing authority of the Brahmins, Buddhist traditions in early India also dealt with competition from fellow ascetic groups. These other renouncer groups similarly challenged Brahmanical ideology and privilege while competing with Buddhists for patronage. Dealing with these rival groups thus presented its own unique challenges, which are also enshrined within the Nikāyas. Several texts, such as the *Kosalasamyutta*, *Abyākatasamyutta*, and *Sāmaññaphala Sutta*, contain lists of the leaders of competing renouncer groups. Those mentioned invariably include Makkhali Gosāla, leader of the Ājīvakas, and an individual referred to as 'Nigantha Nātaputta'. Other sources call this latter individual 'Mahāvīra', and the group he led, though called 'Niganthas' (Pāli, 'unfettered') throughout the Nikāyas, is known otherwise as the Jainas. While A.L. Basham has argued that Gosāla's Ājīvakas were the primary opponents of the Buddhists among these rival ascetic groups,[23] the Jainas in fact are quite prominent debate opponents for Buddhists in the Nikāyas. The dialogic encounter between Buddhists and Jainas has been relatively understudied, especially in comparison to the encounter between Brahmins and Buddhists. One notable exception can be found in Uma Chakravarti's work, *The Social Dimensions of Early Buddhism*. In that book, Chakravarti helpfully discusses the prevailing layers of distinctions between Brahmins and renouncers, as well as the ways in which renouncers differentiated among themselves.[24] By analysing the literary representation of dialogues with Jainas in the Nikāyas, this section will not only add another dimension to the notion of dialogue in these Buddhist texts, but also contribute to the nascent understanding of Buddhist–Jaina discourse.

One of the primary texts I will focus on is the *Upāli Sutta* of the *Majjhima Nikāya*. In this text, Dīgha Tapassasī, described as a disciple of Nātaputta, encounters the Buddha after an alms round. They engage in discussion on whether 'evil' (*pāpam*) is rooted in the body (the position of Dīgha Tapassasī and Nātaputta) or the mind (the Buddha's perspective). Though each is shown as pressing the other, asking three times whether the other truly holds his respective view, the debate is shown as respectful and amiable.[25] Later, Dīgha Tapassasī reports this encounter to Nātaputta, who praises the disciple for holding to his

[22] DN I 126; Walshe, *The Long Discourses of the Buddha*, p. 132.

[23] A.L. Basham, *History and Doctrines of the Ājīvikas* (Delhi, 1951), p. 55.

[24] Uma Chakravarti, *The Social Dimensions of Early Buddhism* (Delhi, 2008), pp. 49–55.

[25] MN I 372–3; Bodhi and Ñānamoli, *The Middle Length Discourses of the Buddha*, pp. 478–9.

position. The householder Upāli, a Jaina patron, then declares that if he had his chance, he would debate the Buddha and 'drag the recluse Gotama to and drag him fro and drag him round about'.[26] Nātaputta fully endorses this desire, but Dīgha Tapassasī warns that 'the recluse Gotama is a magician and knows a converting magic by which he converts disciples of other sectarians'.[27] The disciple gives this warning three times and Nātaputta disregards it three times in turn, sending Upāli to debate the Buddha. When the householder meets Gotama, they debate the same topic – whether 'evil' (*pāpam*) ultimately arises from the body or mind – and the Buddha leads Upāli into a series of contradictions that clearly show the mind's fundamental pre-eminence over the body. Upāli becomes a lay follower, giving the declaration of conversion formula, and the Buddha proceeds to further impress the householder by graciously asking that Upāli continue his family's tradition of patronizing the Jainas as well. Word of the conversion spreads, though when Dīgha Tapassasī tells Nātaputta, the Jaina leader refuses to believe it, again despite three repetitions. Finally, Nātaputta decides to ask Upāli, and we are told that the householder receives his guest, 'in the highest, best, chief, most excellent seat', whereas in the past he would have ceded that position to the Jaina.[28] Upāli confirms that he is now a lay patron of the Buddha, causing Nātaputta to go on a tirade: 'it is as if a man went to castrate someone and came back castrated himself, just as if a man went to put out someone's eyes and came back with his own eyes put out'.[29] Upāli then recites a series of verses extolling the virtues of the Buddha, to which Nātaputta has a violent reaction: 'hot blood then and there gushed from his mouth'.[30]

This *sutta* displays the prominent themes of literary dialogue involving Jainas: 1) emphasis on views and treatment of the body, particularly in terms of ascetic practice, and their connection to violence, 2) indirect confrontation, and 3) contest for patronage. In terms of the first point, as we saw, the key doctrinal issue in the *Upāli Sutta* was whether the body or mind is to blame for 'evil' (*pāpam*) impulses. The Jainas in the text set out a dim view of the body, while the Buddha identifies the mind as the source of moral and immoral behaviour. Due to this divide, Jainas historically have recommended rigorous ascetic practices to purge the body, whereas Buddhist doctrine emphasizes the so-called 'middle way' between extreme self-mortification and hedonism. This distinction comes across explicitly in some texts, such as the *Mahāsīhanāda Sutta*, in which the Buddha argues, against the rival ascetics Kassapa and Nigrodha, that self-mortification is effective only when combined with right understanding.[31] In general, the Nikāya literary dialogues with Jainas tend to connect their practice of self-mortification with violence expressed toward others. The *Upāli Sutta* has Nātaputta react to the householder's conversion with violent metaphors directed toward Upāli, i.e., blinding and castration. Soon after, he exhibits a violent reaction himself by vomiting blood. In the *Abhāyarājakumāra Sutta*, as Nātaputta suggests a conundrum he believes will confound the Buddha, he declares in similarly violent imagery that when Gotama wrestles with the problem, it will be like 'an iron spike put in a man's throat – he cannot vomit it or swallow it'.[32]

---

26 MN I 374; Bodhi and Ñānamoli, *The Middle Length Discourses of the Buddha*, p. 480.

27 MN I 375; Bodhi and Ñānamoli, *The Middle Length Discourses of the Buddha*, p. 480.

28 MN I 383; Bodhi and Ñānamoli, *The Middle Length Discourses of the Buddha*, p. 487.

29 MN I 383; Bodhi and Ñānamoli, *The Middle Length Discourses of the Buddha*, p. 488.

30 MN I 387; Bodhi and Ñānamoli, *The Middle Length Discourses of the Buddha*, p. 492.

31 DN I 167; Walshe, *The Long Discourses of the Buddha*, pp. 153–4.

32 MN I 393; Bodhi and Ñānamoli, *The Middle Length Discourses of the Buddha*, p. 498.

Taken together, in each case the Buddhist text portrays Nātaputta defending rigorous self-mortification, i.e. violence against his own body, while verbally expressing violence against the bodies of others. While a Jaina patron, Upāli also expresses violent sentiments, initially bragging he would 'drag Gotama to and fro'. Elsewhere, other Nikāya texts similarly show that when Jainas are challenged, violent tendencies emerge. In the *Mahāsaccaka Sutta*, the Nigantha Saccaka converses with Gotama over doctrine, commenting at the end that he is impressed with the Buddha's calm and amiable demeanor in the face of debate and criticism. In contrast, he notes that when challenged other renouncer leaders, of whom he names Makkhali Gosāla and Nātaputta in particular, 'prevaricated, led the talk aside, and showed anger, hate, and bitterness'.[33] Nātaputta is the sole focus of this description in the *Cūlasakuludāyi Sutta*. Here the renouncer Sakuludāyi tells the Buddha that Nātaputta claims the power of omniscience, but when pressed 'prevaricated, led the talk aside, and showed anger, hate, and bitterness'.[34] These texts seem designed to give the impression of Jainas as self-righteous, claimants of powers they do not actually possess, and simmering with anger and violence just below a façade of meditative calm. The Buddha, on the other hand, is portrayed as authentic in all these areas.

Two other *sutta*s make an explicit connection between the self-directed violence of severe Jaina asceticism and their irascible nature. In the *Cūladukkhakkhanda Sutta* the Buddha talks with the householder Mahānāma and relates a past dispute about the propriety of severe asceticism with a group of Jainas. As his final remark in that debate, the Buddha points out that if current experiences are the result of past actions, as both Jainas and Buddhists hold, then the severe austerity Jainas propose would only be appropriate if each and every one had been a notorious murderer in a past existence: 'those who are murderers, bloody-handed evil-doers in the world, when they are reborn among human beings, go forth into homelessness as Niganthas [Jainas]'.[35] This story convinces Mahānāma that the Buddhist position on asceticism is correct and he becomes a lay follower. Similarly, in the *Devadaha Sutta* the Buddha recounts a debate with Jainas to a congregation of bhikkhus. Commenting on the Jaina practice of severe asceticism, the Buddha recounts arguing that, 'if the pleasure and pain that beings feel are caused by what was done in the past, then the Niganthas surely must have done bad deeds in the past, since they now feel such painful, racking, piercing feelings'.[36]

Taken with the other *sutta*s describing the Jainas' violent sentiments and angry dispositions, the implication of these Nikāya texts is not merely that Jainas once committed aggressive acts in past lives, but that they currently possess the same fierce temperament. The intention of this portrayal seems very clearly to cast doubt on the worthiness of Jainas to receive patronage, and the consequent strengthening of the case for Buddhism. In support of this interpretation, careful observation reveals that the encounter between Buddhists and Jainas occurs not between the Buddha and a Jaina, but rather through a 'middle man' representative of the householder sphere of life. In this way, while the texts find ways of putting Buddhist and Jaina positions in dialogue, generally it is dialogue via an intermediary, or dialogue *in absentia*.

This is the case with the householders Upāli and Mahānāma in the previously discussed *Upāli* and *Cūladukkhakkhanda Sutta*s. The same structure occurs in the *Cūlasāropama*

---

33 MN I 250–51; Bodhi and Ñānamoli, *The Middle Length Discourses of the Buddha*, , p. 343.

34 MN II 30–31; Bodhi and Ñānamoli, *The Middle Length Discourses of the Buddha*, p. 655.

35 MN I 93; Bodhi and Ñānamoli, *The Middle Length Discourses of the Buddha*, p. 188.

36 MN II 222; Bodhi and Ñānamoli, *The Middle Length Discourses of the Buddha*, p. 832.

Sutta, in which the Buddha's interlocutor is the Brahmin Pingalakoccha, who becomes a lay follower once Gotama reveals the deficiencies of rival ascetic schools, especially the Niganthas.[37] In the *Gāmanisamyutta*, the Buddha similarly converts a householder, Asibandhakaputta, by revealing the intemperate and inconsistent views of Jainas. In this case, Asibandhakaputta was once a Jaina patron, but decides to switch allegiance after listening to the Buddha's reasoning.[38] The *Cittasamyutta* gives another advantage, as the Buddhist lay follower Citta confronts Nātaputta himself. The Jaina leader attempts to trap Citta, asking the householder if he has faith in the Buddha's teaching. When Citta responds negatively, Nātaputta initially praises him as honest and straightforward. However, when Citta further explains that he has no need for faith, as experience has borne out the Buddha's teaching, Nātaputta angrily exclaims, 'How crooked is this Citta the householder! How fraudulent and deceptive!'[39] By this time, though, Citta has thoroughly outmanoeuvred Nātaputta, and the Jaina is once again revealed as bellicose and erratic.

Predominantly, in these texts, the point of contact occurs between a potentially patronizing householder and either the Buddha or a Jaina. Due to the pervasive presence of a 'middle man' in these Nikāya dialogues with Jainas, I would contend that the *sutta*s were less about the Jainas themselves than gathering potential donors and patrons. This raises the third theme of these texts: conversion and patronage. Significantly, whereas we saw in the preceding section that literary dialogues with Brahmins almost always resulted in their conversion to the *dhamma*, this is not the case with Jainas. Rather, the Buddha's dialogic partners and subsequent converts in these *sutta*s are householders, some of whom (like Upāli and Asibandhakaputta) were previously Jaina patrons. This leads to the conclusion that literary dialogues between the Buddha and Jainas were meant to gain patronage of important householders at the expense of Jaina rivals, which is the sense we find in Dīgha Tapassasī's warning of the Buddha's 'magic conversion power'. The differing portrayals of the Buddha and Nātaputta certainly contribute to this impression, as Gotama, similar to the texts involving Brahmins, comes across as gracious and magnanimous, even suggesting Upāli continue support for Jainas out of consideration for his past obligations. Nātaputta, on the other hand, is arrogant and obdurate, refusing to heed repeated warnings, disregarding reports that his patron had deserted him, and reacting with verbal abuse when the truth is finally made apparent. These portrayals, in short, paint a picture of competition between groups for patrons, and the Buddhist texts put forward a vision of their camp as gracious, moderate towards ascetic practice, and therefore more worthy of donors.

The Buddha and Devas

Besides humans of different sectarian affiliations, the Nikāyas contain numerous stories of the Buddha's dialogues with divine and supernatural figures. Many, such as the gods Brahmā and Indra (called 'Sakka' in Buddhist texts) are also prominent in other Indian religions, while others, such as Māra – god of death and desire who rules over and represents the realm of *samsāra* – are more specific to Buddhist traditions. A particularly good example of the distinctive aspects of these dialogues comes in the *Brahmanimantanika Sutta*. In

37 MN I 198–205; Bodhi and Ñānamoli, *The Middle Length Discourses of the Buddha*, pp. 291–7.

38 SN IV 317–23; Bodhi, *The Connected Discourses of the Buddha*, pp. 1340–44.

39 SN IV 298–300; Bodhi, *The Connected Discourses of the Buddha*, pp. 1327–8.

that text, the Buddha relates to a group of bhikkhus that he once sensed Baka the Brahmā[40] had developed the 'pernicious view' (*pāpakam ditthigatam*) that 'this is permanent, this is everlasting, this is eternal', contradicting the truth of *anicca* (impermanence).[41] He immediately travelled to Baka's heavenly realm, where the god amiably greeted the Buddha and reiterated his wrong view. The Buddha countered with an espousal of *anicca*, at which point Māra intervened, taking possession of a member of Baka's assembly to espouse support of the Brahmā's view. Through this assembly member, Māra declared the god's power: 'This Brahmā is the Great Brahmā, the overlord, the untranscended',[42] and so forth – as opposed to the Buddha's relative unimportance, arguing that there have been innumerable Brahmins and *samana*s like Gotama in the past and Baka has seen them all come and go. Given Gotama's supposed inferiority, Māra warned the Buddha (through his assembly-man puppet) not to contradict the words of a Brahmā. Gotama, however, was unimpressed and stated, 'I know you, evil Māra. Do not think, "he does not know me." You are evil Māra, and the Brahmā and the members of Brahmā's assembly have all fallen into your hands, they have all fallen into your power.'[43]

In response to this exchange, Baka the Brahmā reiterated his claim to permanence, adding an aspect of Māra's argument:

> Before your time, bhikkhu, there were recluses and Brahmins
> in the world whose asceticism lasted as long as your whole life.
> They knew when there is another escape beyond, that there is
> another escape beyond, and when there is no other escape beyond,
> that there is no other escape beyond. So, bhikkhu, I tell you this:
> you will find no other escape beyond and eventually you will reap
> only weariness and disappointment. If you will hold to the earth,
> you will be close to me, within my domain for me to work my will
> upon and punish.[44]

In other words, while Baka initially greeted the Buddha amiably, he has now adopted Māra's antagonism and goes so far as to threaten Gotama. In the *Brahmanimantanika Sutta*, the Buddha reacts to Baka by allowing the *deva* to make this estimation of his powers, then declaring, 'now, good sir, how far do you understand my reach and sway to extend?'[45] Gotama then delineates his powers, explaining that they extend into realms of being and understanding far outside Brahmā's sphere of control. He concludes by saying, 'Thus,

[40] As the use of an identifying proper name suggests, there are multiple Brahmās in Buddhist cosmology.

[41] MN I 326; Bodhi and Ñānamoli, *The Middle Length Discourses of the Buddha*, p. 424.

[42] MN I 327; Bodhi and Ñānamoli, *The Middle Length Discourses of the Buddha*, p. 425.

[43] MN I 327; Bodhi and Ñānamoli, *The Middle Length Discourses of the Buddha*, pp. 425–6. I have made one amendment to this, and following, translations involving Māra. The Pāli phrase 'Māra Pāpimā' is often translated as 'Māra, the Evil One', which I believe connotes a sense of eternality and personification of supreme evil that is lacking in Buddhist and Indian religious traditions. As a result, I translate this and other instances of the phrase as 'evil Māra' (with a lowercase 'e', omitting the personifying 'One') to escape this connotation while preserving a sense of Māra's power and animosity. For a fuller discussion of these issues, see Michael Nichols, 'Scholarly Approaches to "Evil" and the Figure of Māra in South Asia', *Religion Compass* 4 (2010): 1–8.

[44] MN I 328; Bodhi and Ñānamoli, *The Middle Length Discourses of the Buddha*, p. 426.

[45] MN I 328; Bodhi and Ñānamoli, *The Middle Length Discourses of the Buddha*, p. 426.

Brahmā, in regard to direct knowledge, I do not stand merely at the same level as you. How then could I know less? Rather, I know more than you.'[46] To support these words, the Buddha then gives a display of power, rendering himself invisible to the Brahmā and his assembly. He invites the Brahmā to attempt the same, and when the god is unable to do so, the assembly declares, 'we have never before seen or heard of any other *samana* or Brahmin who had such great power and such great might as this *samana* Gotama'.[47] Unwilling to give up yet, Māra again possesses a member of the assembly to say, 'before your time, bhikkhu, there were also *samanas* and Brahmins who claimed to be accomplished and awakened'.[48] Recognizing that this is Māra again, the Buddha replies, 'those *samanas* and Brahmins, evil Māra, who claimed to be fully awakened were not fully awakened. But I who claim to be fully awakened, am fully awakened'.[49] At this point, Māra disappears and Baka renounces his pernicious view.

This text reveals that the primary theme of literary Nikāya dialogues with Devas is the demonstration of the superior knowledge and power of the Buddha, whether the Deva(s) involved are deluded by false perceptions (Baka the Brahmā), overtly aggressive (Māra), or obsequious allies and students of the Buddha. In all these cases, the Buddha displays his superior understanding and the Deva either flees (as in the case of Māra) or affirms the Buddha's pre-eminence. In the *Brahmanimantanika Sutta*, the Buddha employs both sober discourse on the *dhamma* as well as displays of supernatural power to reveal his higher authority.

As with the dialogues surveyed in the previous sections, whether the Devas involved are obsequious or hostile, spatial imagery plays a large role in demonstrating the particular *deva*'s intent as well as the revelation of the Buddha's inherent supremacy. Starting with allies of the Buddha, in contrast to Baka in the *Brahmanimantanika Sutta*, other Nikāya texts feature a Brahmā named Sahampati who is extremely reverent toward Gotama, frequently soliciting *dhamma* instruction from him. In fact, according to the *Brahmasamyutta*, Sahampati is instrumental in the Buddha's initial decision to teach.[50] On that occasion, we are told that after awakening the Buddha experienced doubt as to whether other beings could comprehend his doctrine. Sahampati sensed Gotama's hesitation and, fearing for the world without the benefit of the *dhamma*, descended to earth from his Brahmā realm to kneel before the Buddha, give *añjalī*, and implore the awakened one to teach.[51] Sakka likewise is shown descending from his celestial palace on numerous occasions to kneel before the Buddha and seek advice. On one occasion he asks, 'having slain what does one sleep soundly? Having slain what does one not sorrow? What is the one thing, Gotama, whose killing you approve?' The Buddha proceeds to reinterpret the premise of the question, responding, 'the killing of anger, Vāsava [Sakka], with its poisoned root and honeyed tip: this is the killing the *arhats* praise'.[52] On both occasions, then, the *deva* comes

46 MN I 329, Bodhi and Ñānamoli, *The Middle Length Discourses of the Buddha*, p. 427.

47 MN I 330; Bodhi and Ñānamoli, *The Middle Length Discourses of the Buddha*, p. 428.

48 MN I 330; Bodhi and Ñānamoli, *The Middle Length Discourses of the Buddha*, p. 428.

49 MN I 331; Bodhi and Ñānamoli, *The Middle Length Discourses of the Buddha*, p. 429.

50 SN I 136–8; Bodhi, *The Connected Discourses of the Buddha*, pp. 231–3. This occurs also in the *Mahāpadāna Sutta*, though with an unnamed Brahmā, and *Anguttara Nikāya* II 20. For more discussion of this invitation, see Dhivan Jones, 'Why Did Brahmā Ask the Buddha to Teach?', *Buddhist Studies Review* 26/1 (2009): 85–102.

51 SN I 137, Bodhi *The Connected Discourses of the Buddha*, p. 232.

52 SN I 237; Bodhi, *The Connected Discourses of the Buddha*, p. 337.

to the Buddha as a supplicant student, asking for assistance in carrying out aspects vital to the identity and duty of each. As a Brahmā, according to Brahmanical traditions, Sahampati would be considered a creator and sustainer of the cosmos. It is thus an obvious irony that Sahampati beseeches the Buddha to teach the *dhamma* that will be the salvation of the world. Similarly ironic is Sakka, the archetypal Deva of the *khattiya* class, asking Gotama if and how one can perform violence. I will revisit the potential import of these exchanges for understanding social dialogue, but for now it is significant to remark that in both cases, through his teaching, the dialogues display that even the gods seek out the Buddha for his teaching.

Besides friendly Devas like Sakka and the Brahmā Sahampati, we have also seen the antagonistic example of Māra. In addition to Māra, the Buddha also encounters other hostile gods whose animosity, similar to Ambattha's, is partially articulated by their physical demeanor. Sūciloma, a *yakkha* (i.e., natural 'spirit deity'),[53] wondering if Gotama is a 'contemptible *samana*' (*samanaka*), approaches the Buddha and looms threateningly over him, warning that if the sage cannot answer a question about the source of lust and hatred, the *yakkha* will drive him insane, split his heart, or hurl him across the Ganges. The Buddha calmly gives a stock phrase, answering that he sees no one in all the world, with its Māra, Brahmās, ascetics, or Brahmins – in other words, anyone among either humans *or* gods – capable of performing such acts, and then calmly answers the question.[54] Similarly, in the *Devatāsamyutta*, a group of minor gods calling themselves *ujjhānasaññino* ('fault-finders') appear before the Buddha, hover over him, and charge that he is not as wise as he claims to be. Gotama simply explains that he is unattached to the world, and 'the wise do not pretend'. These 'fault-finding' Devas are humbled by his words, landing on the ground to put their heads at Gotama's feet.[55] In another case, somewhat similar to the *Brahmanimantanika Sutta* involving Baka, a 'certain Brahmā' develops the notion that his realm is unattainable by any human, whether ascetic or Brahmin. Rather than reduce this Brahmā to prostration, in this instance the Buddha instead uses his power to appear in that Brahmā's world and hover above the Deva's head.[56] Through these displays of wisdom and supernatural power, the texts consistently portray the Buddha as superior even to the Devas.

I have argued elsewhere[57] that another aspect of literary dialogue with Devas in the Nikāyas is their use as 'mirrors and models' for particular sectarian groups. We have already seen that the representation of Devas in these texts ranges from subservient to aggressive. On the one hand, Sahampati the Brahmā and Sakka, both Buddhist literary adaptations of Brahmanical deities, recognize the Buddha as their ultimate authority, not only regarding the *dhamma*, but also their social roles, as Sakka does regarding proper *khattiya* conduct. An obvious subtext of this trope is that human Brahmins and *khattiya*s ought to model these deities and recognize the Buddha's teachings regarding proper social rules, as well as the teacher's moral pre-eminence. On the other hand, examples of antagonistic gods, of which Māra is the most prominent, might mirror negative exchanges. Indeed, on certain occasions, Māra is clearly shown espousing ideas and beliefs indicative of Buddhist rivals, both Brahmanical and ascetic, implying that Devas or humans who do not recognize the

[53] This is Robert DeCaroli's term. See Robert DeCaroli, *Haunting the Buddha* (Oxford, 2004).

[54] SN I 207; Bodhi, *The Connected Discourses of the Buddha*, p. 306.

[55] SN I 23–4; Bodhi, *The Connected Discourses of the Buddha*, pp. 112–13.

[56] SN I 144–6; Bodhi, *The Connected Discourses of the Buddha*, pp. 239–41.

[57] See Michael Nichols, 'The Two Faces of Deva: the Māra/Brahmā Tandem', *Religions of South Asia* 3/1 (2009): 45–60.

Buddha's authority are under Māra's control.[58] As we saw in the *Brahmanimantanika Sutta*, Baka the Brahmā's delusional view and antagonism is largely attributed to Māra's malignant influence. Additionally, in the *Devaputtasamyutta*, several minor gods praise sectarian rivals of the Buddha, such as Makkhali Gosāla and Nātaputta, and at the end we are told that this is due to possession by Māra.[59] Other times, Māra himself espouses the doctrinal points or objections of Jainas and Brahmins during disputes with the Buddha. In the *Mārasamyutta* he accuses the Buddha of ascetic laxity since he follows the middle way, a prominent objection on the part of Jainas.[60] Elsewhere, he even assumes the physical form of a Brahmin to criticize a group of bhikkhus for not adhering to *varnāśramadharma*.[61] By disarticulating the literary dialogue with Devas into these dual representations, we can thus appreciate how these texts mirrored sectarian debates by placing the words of rivals into the mouths of gods. At the same time, by showing that Devas either accept or (in the case of Māra) flee before the Buddha's authority, the stories also model the ideal resolution of these debates.

Conclusions: Principal Characteristics of Dialogue in the Nikāyas

We can now compare the literary aspects and strategies of these dialogues, with a concern for how these literary dialogues were calibrated according to the group involved, are concerned with patronage, and thus potentially reflect aspects of social dialogue. First, depending on the Buddha's interlocutor, a different topic is at stake and thus a different rhetorical strategy is employed. As we saw with Buddha–Brahmin dialogues, a recurrent strategy in those *sutta*s was reference to the Buddha's thirty-two marks. These marks, however, play no part in the Buddha's dialogues with Jainas or Devas. The basis for this discrepancy might be the foundation of the thirty-two marks in royal symbolism: besides indicating a world-redeeming *dhamma* king, narratives of Siddhattha Gotama's life usually indicate that the marks also signal potential for political leadership and dominance. Given the special symbiotic, cross-legitimizing relationship between Brahmins and kings, the emphasis on the thirty-two marks in *sutta*s dealing with Brahmins may be a targeted rhetoric to cast the Buddha as a new king to whom priests could (and should) subordinate themselves.[62] In this light, the Buddhist texts seem to suggest that the Buddha is not just a Kshatriya spiritual

---

58 Māra's appearances in the Nikāyas are far greater in number than I have space to cover. The most extensive appearance of Māra in the Nikāyas occurs in the *Mārasamyutta*, where the Deva is also frequently employed as a strawman, making assertions regarding the permanence of phenomena or the goodness of desire that the Buddha quickly rebuts with an aspect of the *dhamma*. For just a few examples, see SN I 103–6; Bodhi, *The Connected Discourses of the Buddha*, pp. 195–8.

59 SN I 65–7; Bodhi, *The Connected Discourses of the Buddha*, pp. 161–3.

60 SN I 103; Bodhi, *The Connected Discourses of the Buddha*, p. 195.

61 SN I 117; Bodhi, *The Connected Discourses of the Buddha*, p. 209.

62 At the same time, we should be aware, as John Powers points out, that these marks, at least as a complete list of thirty-two, do not have a definitive Brahmanical antecedent, even though the Buddhist texts themselves insist otherwise. Instead, Powers argues, they are suggestive of a symbolic rhetoric meant to portray the Buddha as an extraordinary being with a correspondingly extraordinary physical form. See John Powers, *A Bull of a Man*, (Cambridge, MA, 2009), pp. 227–8. For related issues, also see Susanne Mrozik, *Virtuous Bodies: The Physical Dimensions of Morality in Buddhist Ethics* (Oxford, 2007) and Reiko Ohnuma, *Head, Eyes, Flesh, and Blood: Giving Away the Body in Indian Buddhist Literature* (New York, 2007).

leader, but a ruler. However, as Brian Black notes, 'while these scenes present the Buddha as superior to Brahmins in observable ways, they also, to a certain extent, render the Buddha's status as a "great man" dependent upon the verification of educated Brahmins'.[63] Elsewhere, Black observes in the specific case of the character of Ambattha in the *Ambattha Sutta*, who was almost certainly based on the Upaniṣadic character Shvetaketu, that the Buddhist–Brahmin relationship was composed of intricate layers of mutual deference and rejection.[64] The usage of the thirty-two marks is thus exemplary of the complicated dynamic of affirmation and negation that characterizes Buddhist–Brahmin literary dialogue in the Nikāyas, and quite possibly marked the social dialogue that occurred between those two groups in ancient India.

In light of their negative view of the body, Jainas would be far less likely to appreciate a rhetorical move such as the thirty-two marks and thus it is unsurprising that these marks are not mentioned in those dialogues. Rather, we saw that the main thread of the Jainas' dialogues involved the propriety of asceticism and its severity. Likewise, it is not an aura of royal prestige which the Buddha draws upon in discussion or contest with Devas, but wisdom and, just as often, supernatural power. This serves to reinforce the Buddha as the cosmological superior of even the gods. In each case, then, the literary dialogue is crafted around an issue central to the particular persona of the Buddha's interlocutor. Against Brahmins, the Buddha displays superior knowledge of Vedic ritual and texts, against Jainas he reveals superior understanding of asceticism, and when contending with gods, he displays supernatural power beyond even their abilities. By besting his interlocutors in whichever realm they are normally considered dominant, the literary dialogues aggrandize the Buddha as supreme in all fields. Elsewhere in this volume we notice the same triumphalist tendency in Jaina dialogues (Esposito, Geen) and later Brahminical ones (Rohlman).

The foregoing also brings to light the importance of the symbolism of the body in the particular relationship expressed between the Buddha and each of these three groups. In short, the relative comportment of the body in each case is used to communicate the superiority of the Buddha. For Brahmins, as we saw, this is done through the thirty-two marks. In terms of Jainas, their negative view and punishment of the body reveals the deficiency and extremity of their teaching, as well as the latent violence and aggression of their temperaments. Finally, throughout stories of the Devas, who cosmologically are supposed to exist above humans, the Buddha locates his body at a higher spatial level.

Second, patronage is another consistent theme which, though prominent in each category, also reveals crucial differences. We observed that dialogues with Brahmins almost always conclude with the Brahmin, whether originally amiable or not, converting to the *dhamma* and becoming a patron. Jainas are not similarly targeted and Devas, while the Buddha shows concern to instruct them and correct their wrong views, are also not especially sought after as converts. This difference may shed light on the connection between literary and social dialogue. Since the terms of debate with Brahmins center heavily on aspects of Brahmanical ideology and emphasize conversion, this suggests that these texts may have been directed toward Brahmins with the express purpose of gaining their support. The narrative structure of Nikāya *sutta*s involving Jainas, however, is such that the Buddha engages Jainas themselves only indirectly and instead converts householder patrons, like Upāli and Mahānāma, who either previously supported the Jainas or were on the fence between the two groups. Similarly, through the process of 'mirroring and modeling',

---

[63] Black, *Rivals and Benefactors*, p. 34.

[64] Brian Black, *The Character of the Self in Ancient India* (Albany, 2011), pp. 136–61.

literary dialogues with Devas indirectly reflect debates with rival sects. In terms of how the literary dialogues might have aligned with a social audience, it seems that while *sutta*s about Brahmins or *deva*s may well have been directed toward Brahmins, the structure of Jaina *sutta*s suggests an intended audience of potential householder patrons.

Finally, three literary conventions common to these texts seem particularly revealing of the potential atmosphere of social dialogue. First, the Buddha is consistently shown as one who reveals what is otherwise hidden, both in terms of the true nature of reality, but also, via the act of dialogue, the true qualities of the individuals or gods with whom he converses. To give just one example from each category, in the *Ambattha Sutta*, Gotama reveals Ambattha's true, and by contemporary social conventions, questionable line of descent. In the *Upāli Sutta*, the inherent violence of extreme self-mortification manifests itself in Nātaputta's outburst of verbal abuse and bloody vomit; and in the *Brahmanimantanika Sutta*, he reveals the power of Māra behind Baka the Brahmā's wrong views. Second, what I have termed the 'declaration of conversion' formula is found throughout these texts: 'It is as if someone were to set up what has been knocked down, or to point out the way to one who had got lost, or to bring an oil-lamp into a dark place, so that those with eyes could see what was there.' Third, we have also observed that interlocutors are almost always brought to a state of spatial subordination to the Buddha. Whether it is friendly or hostile Brahmins, householders once sympathetic to Jainas, or Devas descending from the heavens, the Nikāyas consistently emphasize the gradual lowering in physical stature of the Buddha's interlocutors relative to the awakened one. In succession, as they often are in the texts, these three interrelated literary conventions operate in the following manner: the Buddha reveals the hidden truth, the interlocutor acknowledges this revelation through the declaration of conversion formula, and then the declaration is enacted physically by spatial subordination to the Buddha. In its own way, each of these conventions overturns the current status quo: what was hidden becomes apparent, the ignorant become knowledgeable, and the socially or cosmologically high become low. When read together and related to social dialogue, these symbolic conventions clearly imply the desire to upend the beliefs of rivals and reinterpret or reject common ideas in a manner favourable to Buddhist principles. This strengthens the interpretation of some, such as Oliver Freiberger, that the Pāli Canon partly served the purposes of propaganda for Buddhists 'to attract followers, and to reinforce their own religious identity'.[65] From the foregoing analysis of literary dialogue in the Nikāyas, one of the most expansive parts of the Pāli Canon, it would seem this interpretation has some weight.

Indeed, these literary dialogues in general, though in some ways calibrated toward different audiences and/or characters, consistently draw upon aspects of the Indian cultural milieu only to paint these ideas and figures as fundamentally lacking. At the same time, the fact that these points are made through literary dialogue, representing exchange and give and take between individuals, as opposed to philosophical diatribe or invective, indicates complex Buddhist engagement with their rivals rather than simple dismissal. Still, the sense comes through quite plainly that, from the Buddhist perspective, in order for these social groups to capture what they have missed or lost, they must – both figuratively and literally – bow to the Buddha.

---

[65] Oliver Freiberger, 'Negative Campaigning', *Religions of South Asia* 3/1 (2009): 61–2.

Abbreviations

DN *Dīgha Nikāya*
MN *Majjhima Nikāya*
SN *Samyutta Nikāya*

References

Bailey, Greg and Ian Mabbett, *The Sociology of Early Buddhism* (Cambridge: Cambridge University Press, 2003).

Basham, A.L., *History and Doctrines of the Ājīvikas* (Delhi: Motilal Banarsidass, 1951, 1981 reprint).

Black, Brian, *The Character of the Self in Ancient India* (Albany: State University of New York Press, 2007).

———, 'Rivals and Benefactors: Encounters between Buddhists and Brahmins in the Nikāyas', *Religions of South Asia* 3.1 (2009): 24–43.

———, 'Ambattha and Shvetaketu: Literary Connections between the Upanishads and Early Buddhist Narratives', *Journal of the American Academy of Religion* 79.1 (2011): 136–61.

Bodhi, Bhikkhu (trans.), *The Connected Discourses of the Buddha: a Translation of the Samyutta Nikāya* (Boston: Wisdom Publications, 2000).

Chakravarti, Uma, *The Social Dimensions of Early Buddhism* (Delhi: Munshiram Manoharlal, 1987, 2008 reprint).

Collins, Steven, *Selfless Persons: Imagery and Thought in Theravāda Buddhism* (Cambridge: Cambridge University Press, 1987).

DeCaroli, Robert, *Haunting the Buddha* (Oxford: Oxford University Press, 2004).

Flores, Ralph, *Buddhist Scriptures as Literature: Sacred Rhetoric and the Uses of Theory* (Albany: State University of New York Press, 2008).

Freiberger, Oliver 'Negative Campaigning', *Religions of South Asia* 3/1 (2009): 61–76.

Gombrich, Richard, 'The Buddha's Book of Genesis?', *Indo-Iranian Journal* 35 (1992): 159–78.

———, *How Buddhism Began: the Conditioned Genesis of the Early Teachings* (Delhi : Munshiram Manoharlal, 1996; 2010 reprint).

Jones, Dhivan Thomas, 'Why Did Brahmā Ask the Buddha to Teach?' *Buddhist Studies Review* 26/1 (2009): 85–102.

Mrozik, Susanne, *Virtuous Bodies: the Physical Dimensions of Morality in Buddhist Ethics* (Oxford: Oxford University Press, 2007).

Ñānamoli, Bikkhu and Bhikkhu Bodhi (trans.), *The Middle Length Discourses of the Buddha: a Translation of the Majjhima Nikāya* (Boston: Wisdom Publications, 1995).

Nichols, Michael, 'The Two Faces of Deva: the Māra/Brahmā Tandem', *Religions of South Asia* 3/1 (2009): 45–60.

———, 'Scholarly Approaches to "Evil" and the Figure of Māra in South Asia', *Religion Compass* 4 (2010): 1–8.

Ohnuma, Reiko. *Head, Eyes, Flesh and Blood: Giving Away the Body in Indian Buddhist Literature* (New York: Columbia University Press, 2007).

Powers, John, *A Bull of a Man: Images of Masculinity, Sex, and the Body in Indian Buddhism* (Cambridge, MA: Harvard University Press, 2009).

Tsuchida, Ryūtaro, 'Two Categories of Brahmins in the Early Buddhist Period', *Memoirs of the Research Department of the Toyo Bunko*, No. 49 (Tokyo: the Toyo Bunko, 1991).
Walshe, Maurice (trans.), *The Long Discourses of the Buddha: a Translation of the Dīgha Nikāya* (Boston: Wisdom Publications, 1995).

Chapter 9
The Power of Persuasion: The Use of Dialogues to Justify and Promote 'Early' Renunciation in the Jaina and Hindu Traditions

Jonathan Geen

According to an early Jaina text, King Śreṇika, the powerful ruler of Magadha during the time of the Jaina savior Mahāvīra, once took a pleasure excursion to a grove where he happened to spy a young Jaina ascetic. Impressed by the ascetic's youthful appearance, Śreṇika approached him and said: 'Though you are a young man of good family, O ascetic, you have renounced the world; at a time for the enjoyment of pleasures, you have entered into asceticism – I would like to hear the reason for this.'[1] Obliging the king, the ascetic explained what had prompted his decision to renounce, and, as a result of their dialogue, the king was converted to Jainism.[2]

King Śreṇika's desire to understand what would drive a young man in the prime of life to renounce the world is, I believe, a very natural one. In the Jaina tradition, renunciation involves turning one's back on the everyday social world, cutting all family ties, and practising harsh and often solitary asceticism; it is a seemingly radical decision for anyone to make, particularly for one who is still in the prime of life. Such a profoundly life-altering decision, causing potentially painful and irreparable rifts within families, cries out for an explanation, and in the early Jaina tradition, such explanations were often presented as dialogues. Elsewhere in this volume, Esposito gives compelling illustrations of the Jaina use of dialogue for complex doctrinal purposes. Here, I shall examine the uniquely persuasive use of the dialogical literary form to both justify and promote 'early'[3] renunciation in the Jaina tradition. Specifically, I will address two Jaina dialogues in which young men[4] who wished to renounce were compelled to justify their decision to their parent(s),[5] who at first offered up alternatives or objections, but were later persuaded to grant their permission. By way of comparison, I will then examine two similar dialogues from the brāhmanical Hindu tradition.[6] As Black, Crothers, and Nichols also show in this Part, comparative study of the dialogical across traditions in early India can yield quite fruitful results.

---

[1] *Uttarajjhayaṇa-sutta* 20.8; all translations are my own.

[2] Cf. Buddhist *Sāmaññaphala-sutta*.

[3] That is, in youth, prior to marriage, or early middle age, prior to seeing one's offspring grow up.

[4] Although young women also renounced to become nuns in the Jaina tradition, here we will focus exclusively upon men.

[5] Similar dialogues are also found between husband and wife, such as the dialogue between Jambūsvāmin and his eight new wives as well as with a thief (*Sthavirāvalīcarita* 2–3); for a variant of this dialogue, see *Dharmābhyudaya* 8.

[6] It is not possible to accurately date the dialogues discussed here, though they all come from texts that date from the fifth century CE or earlier.

Jaina Attitudes towards 'Early' Renunciation

The centrality of renunciation and asceticism in Jaina doctrine is so well known that it requires few words here.[7] From the earliest extant Jaina sources,[8] which most often take the form of sermons or discourses, the following points regarding renunciation can be clearly established: there is no spiritual liberation without the practice of perfect non-violence, and perfect non-violence necessitates renunciation;[9] the ownership of property and the entanglements of familial relationships inherent in householder life make perfect non-violence, and thus liberation, impossible,[10] though pious householders may attain heaven;[11] renunciation for the sake of liberation should be undertaken as soon as possible, while one is still in the prime of life, for the opportunity to be born as a human who hears the Jaina doctrines is rare and one's lifespan is uncertain;[12] in the process of attaining liberation, no one, including one's family and friends, can be of any assistance;[13] on the contrary, one's family and friends may even try to dissuade one from renouncing, or may try to lure one back into worldly life through guilt-provoking pleading or worldly temptations;[14] notwithstanding the urgency to renounce, not everyone, at every moment, is suited to renunciation, and thus some may be destined to failure in ascetic life if they unwisely adopt it at the wrong time.[15] These attitudes regarding renunciation, though often illustrated and analysed in greater depth, are to be found reiterated in Jaina literature extending from early medieval times up to the present day.

Although the ultimate motive for renouncing the world was the attainment of spiritual liberation, the Jainas catalogued[16] ten specific precipitating events which might provoke renunciation: one's own inclination; anger; poverty; a dream; a promise; past-life memories;[17] sickness;[18] being disrespected; being informed by a god;[19] and affection for a

---

7 For a discussion of renunciation in the Jaina tradition, see, e.g., P.S. Jaini, *The Jaina Path of Purification* (Delhi, 1979), pp. 241–71; Paul Dundas, *The Jains* (New York, 1992), pp. 129–60.

8 It is generally agreed by scholars that *Āyāraṃga-sutta* (*Ācārāṅga-sūtra*) Book 1, *Sūyagaḍaṃga* (*Sūtrakṛtāṅga*) Book 1, and sections 1–8, 10–11, 14–17, 25, 27, and 35, of the *Uttarajjhayaṇa-sutta* (*Uttarādhyayana-sūtra*) represent the earliest extant layer of the Śvetāmbara Jaina Canon; see S. Ohira, *A Study of the Bhagavatīsūtra: A Chronological Analysis* (Ahmedabad, 1994), p. 5.

9 *Āyāraṃga-sutta* 1.1.1.5–6.

10 *Āyāraṃga-sutta* 1.2.1.1; 1.2.2.2; *Sūyagaḍaṃga* 1.1.1.2; 1.1.1.4; 1.1.4.3.

11 *Sūyagaḍaṃga* 1.2.3.13; *Uttarajjhayaṇa-sutta* 5.22–24.

12 *Āyāraṃga-sutta* 1.2.1.5; *Sūyagaḍaṃga* 1.2.1.1–2; 1.7.10–11; *Uttarajjhayaṇa-sutta* 4.1; 4.8–9; 10.28–30.

13 *Āyāraṃga-sutta* 1.2.1.3; *Sūyagaḍaṃga* 1.2.1.4; 1.9.4–5.

14 *Āyāraṃga-sutta* 1.6.1.5–6; *Sūyagaḍaṃga* 1.2.1.16–22; 1.3.2.1–22.

15 *Āyāraṃga-sutta* 1.6.4.1. The consequences of failure in ascetic life may include: returning to worldly life, e.g. the story of Ārdra(ka)kumāra, friend of King Śreṇika's son Abhaya (*Triṣaṣṭiśalākāpuruṣacarita* 10.7.177–305; Phyllis Granoff, *The Forest of Thieves and the Magic Garden: An Anthology of Medieval Jain Stories* [New Delhi, 1998], pp. 21–37); creating a heretical ascetic tradition, e.g. Marīci's heresy (*Triṣaṣṭiśalākāpuruṣacarita* 1.6.1–52); or dying as an ascetic with a sinful desire (*nidāna*) that causes problematic rebirth, e.g. the past-life story of Kṛṣṇa's rival Kaṅsa (*Triṣaṣṭiśalākāpuruṣacarita* 8.2.52–61). As an example of those wholly unsuitable for renunciation, see the story of Kṛṣṇa (*Antagaḍadasāo* 5.1; *Triṣaṣṭiśalākāpuruṣacarita* 8.11.49–50ab).

16 *Ṭhāṇaṃga-sutta* (*Sthānāṅga-sūtra*) 712.

17 As is the case in our two Jaina dialogues below.

18 As was the case in the dialogue between King Śreṇika and the Jaina ascetic above.

19 As is the case with every Jina.

child (who is renouncing). More generally, however, renunciation was justified by a state of 'dispassion' (*vi*+√*rañj*, e.g. *virakta*; *vairāgya*), often translated as 'disgust with worldly existence', experienced by the would-be renunciate, though the events that inspire this dispassion are varied.[20]

Renunciation as an Individual's Choice

Despite the strong doctrinal emphasis upon the necessity of renunciation for attaining liberation, the Jainas also cultivated a large lay community, who quickly out-numbered ascetics, and who followed a lay-path (*śrāvaka-dharma*)[21] rather than an ascetic-path (*yati-dharma*). But the lay-path was nevertheless said to be designed only for those unable (*akṣama*; *asakta*)[22] for any reason to pursue the ascetic-path. Furthermore, Jainas tended to view the path of a lay follower as ideally ending in renunciation, defining a specific series of stepping-stones leading from layperson to renunciate,[23] such that a pious Jaina layperson who felt 'early' renunciation was not an option could pursue a slower path to renunciation. Thus, the Jaina faithful, as well as new converts to Jainism, were given a choice between lay and ascetic status, and the decision to renounce was left up to the individual.[24]

Requirement for Parental Consent

When 'early' renunciation was desired by a young man, for whatever reason, it was customary among Jainas[25] that he first obtain parental permission before taking the vow.[26] The fact that parents might be deeply pained by, and therefore strenuously resist, a child's desire for 'early' renunciation was openly acknowledged in the biography of Mahāvīra himself. According to the Śvetāmbara tradition, Mahāvīra, while still in the womb, took a vow not to renounce the world until his parents had died, in order to spare them the pain of

---

20 A classic example is Bāhubali, son of Ṛṣabha (the first Jina of the current epoch), who renounced out of disgust at his own thirst for kingship, in which he almost killed his own brother Bharata (*Triṣaṣṭiśalākāpuruṣacarita* 1.5.519–798).

21 For a discussion of medieval manuals (*śrāvakācāras*) outlining the duties of Jaina lay folk, see R. Williams, *Jaina Yoga: A Survey of the Medieval Śrāvakācāras* (Oxford, 1963).

22 *Triṣaṣṭiśalākāpuruṣacarita* 6.7.190; 7.11.68.

23 In the case of Śvetāmbara Jainism, these are known as the eleven *paḍimā* or stages a layperson takes towards renunciation; see, e.g. *Uvāsagadasāo* 1.71; Dundas, *The Jains*, pp. 161–2. In another formulation of the path to liberation, represented by the so-called 14 *guṇasthānas*, or stages ranging from perfect ignorance to perfect enlightenment as reflected by decreasing karmic obstruction (Helmuth von Glasenapp, *Jainism: An Indian Religion of Salvation* [Delhi, 1999], pp. 221ff.), Jaina lay-status represents only the fifth of 14 stages (Williams, *Jaina Yoga*, p. 34).

24 Narratives and/or dialogues are rarely found in which young or middle-aged people are persuaded to renounce against their will. The Jaina story of Bhavadatta and Bhavadeva (e.g. *Sthavirāvalīcarita* 1.288–389), apparently inspired by the Buddhist story of the Buddha's half-brother Nanda (e.g. Aśvaghoṣa's *Saundarananda*), is a notable exception.

25 Dundas, *The Jains*, p. 133.

26 The requirement to obtain parental consent may have been designed, in part, to avoid the charge of 'stealing' young people away from their families.

separation,[27] which might have constituted an act of violence towards them.[28] The necessity of gaining parental consent prior to renouncing must have routinely led to the sorts of dialogues discussed below.

Objections to 'Early' Renunciation

The objections to 'early' renunciation offered up by the parents in our Jaina dialogues below relate to their own religious affiliation: in the first dialogue, the parents are brāhmanical Hindu, whereas in the second, they are lay-Jainas. Brāhmanical Hindu doctrine, in contrast to that of the Jainas, tended to resist 'early' renunciation and prescribed renunciation only after a full life of active participation in society (as student and married householder).[29] This delay was justified, in part, by the Vedic requirement to repay three debts before renouncing: to the seers (through Vedic study), the ancestors (through offspring), and the gods (through sacrifices).[30] In the first dialogue, the brāhmanical Hindu father, initially at least, relied upon this ready-made and authoritative objection to 'early' renunciation. The lay-Jaina parents in our second dialogue, who had no convenient doctrinal objection to 'early' renunciation at their disposal, nevertheless counseled their son to delay renunciation until old age, in order to forestall the numerous hardships of monkhood while enjoying the sensuous pleasures suited for a person in the prime of life. As noted above, the delaying of complete renunciation until old age had gained some currency amongst the early Jaina lay-community.

Two Jaina Dialogues on 'Early' Renunciation

In order to observe how such objections were answered, let us now examine our two Jaina dialogues. Both are drawn from the Śvetāmbara Jaina Canonical *Uttarajjhayaṇa-sutta*.[31]

---

[27] *Kalpa-Sūtra* 91, *Triṣaṣṭiśalākāpuruṣacarita* 10.2.46–8.

[28] He is also said to have agreed to get married so as not to disappoint his mother (*Triṣaṣṭiśalākāpuruṣacarita* 10.2.147–9), and after the death of his parents, he is said to have obtained the permission of his elders prior to renouncing (*Kalpa-Sūtra* 110), and that he demonstrated compassion towards his grieving brother by delaying his renunciation for yet a further year (*Triṣaṣṭiśalākāpuruṣacarita* 10.2.166–8). In the Digambara tradition, however, Mahāvīra is described as remaining unmarried and renouncing while his parents were still alive, though he first obtained their consent (*Uttarapurāṇa* 74.298).

[29] For the development of this position, see Patrick Olivelle, *Saṃnyāsa Upaniṣads: Hindu Scriptures on Asceticism and Renunciation* (New York, 1992), pp. 46–57, and *The Āśrama System* (New York, 1993).

[30] *Mānavadharmaśāstra* 4.257–8; for the Vedic authority on these three debts, see *Taittirīya-Saṃhitā* 6.3.10.5. For alternative Hindu interpretations of renunciation, in which physical withdrawal from society was deemed unnecessary, see, e.g., *Mahābhārata* 6.23–40 (*Bhagavad Gītā*); the story of Cūḍālā from the *Yoga-Vāsiṣṭha*.

[31] The *Uttarajjhayaṇa-sutta*, one of four so-called *mūlasūtras* of the Śvetāmbara Jaina Canon (which, as a whole, is typically assigned to the fifth century CE), has been described as 'probably the best-known Jaina anthology' (Jaini, *The Jaina Path of Purification*, p. 66) and 'a complete, though concise, exposition of Jainism' (K.C. Lalwani, *Uttarādhyayana Sutra: The Last Testament of Bhagavān Mahāvīra* [Calcutta, 1977], p. v). According to tradition (e.g. *Kalpa Sūtra* 147), the *Uttarajjhayaṇa-sutta* comprises the final statement of Mahāvīra prior to his death, though in fact the text appears

The first dialogue (14.1–28) takes place between a father, who was a 'brāhmanical *purohita* intent on Vedic rites' (14.5) and his two sons who wished to renounce the world as Jaina monks, in part due to their remembrance of their past lives in which they had performed 'austerities and self-restraint' (14.5). Approaching their father, the sons declared: 'As this so-called life is seen to be ephemeral, filled with much uncertainty, and not long-lasting, we take no pleasure in householder life; having come to inform you, we will at once adopt asceticism' (14.7). Interestingly, the sons do not explicitly ask their father for permission to renounce, though it is clear from the dialogue that they seek to convert him. In an effort to change their minds, the father said: 'those who know the Vedas' have declared that 'there will be no [higher] world for those without sons' (14.8). He thus counselled them to first study the Vedas, offer food to priests, have sons, and enjoy domestic life; only when their own sons were ready to take over the household would it be time to depart to the forest. The sons replied that such worldly pursuits had no power to provide any protection or shelter (*tāṇaṃ*) for a person, and thus were unacceptable.

When the father tried to tempt them with wealth, women, and family, the sons replied: 'How can wealth, or kin, or sense pleasures aid in the practice of the *dharma*? We will become ascetics (*samaṇas*), bearing many good virtues, and roaming about freely, begging our food' (14.17). Next, the father suggested that the soul was merely a product of the body, arising with the body and perishing with it, implying that any activities directed at securing afterlife-states or avoiding reincarnation were misguided. But his sons insisted that the soul was eternal, though bound by fetters that were the 'cause of worldly existence' (14.19), and that the world was harassed, penned in, and subject to the passing of the 'unfailing ones'. Their father, alarmed, was anxious to know what these threatening forces were; at this point, the father appears to have accepted the role of student.

His sons asserted that 'the world is harassed by Death and penned in by Old Age; the [passing] nights are known as the unfailing ones' (14.23). Though somewhat convinced, the father still suggested that they should continue living together for awhile, after which they could all go forth as ascetics together. The sons, refusing to trust that Death would remain at bay while they delayed their renunciation, insisted that they renounce at once: 'We shall this very moment adopt that *dharma* by which, once obtained, we shall not be born again' (14.28). With this, the sons departed, and the father, now devoid of sons and being convinced by their arguments, likewise renounced.

Our second dialogue (19.1–98) features King Balabhadda, Queen Miyā, and their son Balasirī, commonly known as Miyāputta.[32] As a young man, Miyāputta lived in a beautiful palace with his wives, and was designated heir to the throne. One day, through his palace window, he spied a passing ascetic (*samaṇa*), and suddenly had the thought: 'I believe that

---

to be an ancient primer compiled for the instruction of new monks (W. Schubring, *The Doctrine of the Jainas, Described after the Old Sources* [Delhi, 2000], p. 115). The enduring popularity of the *Uttarajjhayaṇa-sutta* is testified by the extant illustrated manuscripts which artistically depict events described in the text itself, including the *Miyāputtijjaṃ* (our second dialogue); for an example from the sixteenth century, see W.N. Brown, *Manuscript Illustrations of the Uttarādhyayana Sūtra* (New Haven, CT, 1941).

[32] A similar though condensed version of this dialogue was incorporated into Śvetāmbara versions of the Universal History, by ascribing it to a man known as Puruṣasiṃha/Purisasīha, a past-life of the fifth Jina of the current epoch, Sumati (e.g. *Caüpannamahāpurisacariyaṃ* 7; *Triṣaṣṭiśalākāpuruṣacarita* 3.3.1–120). Digambara versions of Sumati's past-life, however, do not include such a dialogue (see, e.g. *Uttarapurāṇa* 51.1–14; *Mahāpurāṇa of Puṣpadanta* 42.3).

I have seen him before in a previous life' (19.6). Upon this realization, Miyāputta's mind was cleansed and memory of his past lives (*jāīsaraṇa*) arose.

He recalled being 'an ascetic in his previous life' (19.8), and, experiencing an immediate disgust for worldly things, he went straight to his parents, declared his intention to become a Jaina monk, and asked for their blessing:

> The five great vows [taken by Jaina monks] are known to me, as is the sufferings in hells and rebirth in sub-human species. I am disgusted with the pleasures of the world: O mother and father, you must allow me to go forth [as an ascetic]! (19.10)

He then elaborated upon his disgust with worldly existence, stating that 'the cycle of rebirth is nothing but misery', and concluding with: 'Thus, in this world ablaze with Old Age and Death, I shall carry my soul beyond it all, if only you agree' (19.23).

Interestingly, his parents freely acknowledged this low assessment of worldly life, but proceeded to point out the many difficulties of a monk's life, as well as the thousands of requisite qualities a monk requires. They catalogued the difficulties in maintaining the five great vows and many other hardships,[33] including hunger, thirst, heat, and cold. They declared: 'O son, being so tender and clean-scrubbed, you are fit for pleasure! You are simply not able to keep to the life of an ascetic, son!' (19.34). Finally, they suggested that Miyāputta first enjoy the world of the senses, and that 'you may practice the *dharma* afterwards' (19.43).

Miyāputta did not dispute the hardships of a monk's life, but rather suggested that such trials and tribulations paled in comparison to the endless sufferings of life in *saṃsāra*:

> I have endured frightful agonies of body and mind an endless number of times, miseries and dangers again and again. In this wasteland of Old Age and Death, which is a storehouse of dangers, I have endured many frightful births and deaths. (19.45–6)

Miyāputta then enumerated a ghastly list of bone-chilling horrors he had suffered in past lives, either in one of the many Jaina hells or as various earthly plants and animals. He concluded by stating: 'My dear father, the agonies and miseries experienced in the hells are incalculably worse than the agonies witnessed in this world of men' (19.73).

Undaunted, his parents reminded him that when a monk gets sick, no remedy is permitted. But Miyāputta pointed out that animals in the wilderness likewise have no doctors or medicine, and that he, Miyāputta, would roam about the wilderness like an animal: 'having adopted the behavior of animals, [a monk] treads the upward path' (19.82).[34] At last his parents relented, saying, 'Go, O Son, as you please' (19.85). Diligently following the life of a monk, Miyāputta eventually 'achieved the incomparable perfection' (19.95). By way of conclusion, the narrator of the dialogue suggested that anyone who hears this story of Miyāputta ought to follow his path of renunciation and perfection.

Clearly, these two dialogues have a number of points in common: the motive for renunciation in both is said to be remembrance of past-lives, and as a result, the young men are admirably steadfast and undaunted by their parents' objections, demonstrating that their desire to renounce was not merely a passing fancy; the unsatisfactoriness of life

[33] Cf. *Uttarajjhayaṇa-sutta* 2.

[34] Cf. *Baudhāyanadharmasūtra* 3.2.19; 3.3.22. For a discussion of similar 'animal-like' practices in the Hindu tradition, see Olivelle, *Saṃnyāsa Upaniṣads*, pp. 107–12.

in *saṃsāra* is emphasized, as is the ever-present threat of Old Age, Death, and rebirth, thereby rendering ridiculous the notion of delaying renunciation; and the objections raised by the parents in both dialogues was not that renunciation was bad in itself, but that 'early' renunciation was either inappropriate or too difficult. The main difference between the two dialogues relates to the religious affiliation of the parents: in the first, the father is a Hindu Brahmin, who is converted by his sons and joins them in renunciation (representing a victory for the Jaina tradition), whereas in the second, the parents were already lay-Jainas, and thus no conversion was required.

Dialogues and the Power of Persuasion

In addition to promoting 'early' renunciation in sermons and dialogues, Jainas also produced many third-person narrative accounts[35] of the renunciation of both men and women, young and old. In such accounts, we are typically informed as to the precipitating 'event' which provoked the renunciation, though oftentimes such events seem rather generic in nature, and little detail is provided on why, exactly, such a provoking event resulted in the renunciation of one person but not others,[36] how the person's family reacted, or, in cases of 'early' renunciation, how the person managed to obtain parental permission.

There are, however, certain narrative accounts, most of which date from the medieval period, which are directly focused on the decision to renounce and, in some cases, the familial fall-out resulting from that decision. Phyllis Granoff has collected, translated and discussed a number of such stories, and has suggested:

> Stories are sometimes the only genre of literature that provides answers to this fundamental and to us very natural question: why did men and women leave behind their loved ones and renounce the world to become monks and nuns? (Granoff, *Forest of Thieves*, p. 9)

Such narratives have the virtue of providing an in-depth examination of specific trials and tribulations of life in *saṃsāra* that seem to adequately explain why a given individual chose to abandon worldly life and renounce.[37] Given this consistent promotion of 'early' renunciation in Jaina sermons, narratives and dialogues, it is worth exploring what the dialogical form offers the issue of 'early' renunciation that is not found in other literary forms.[38]

The adoption of 'early' renunciation is a two-step process: first, a young man must decide to renounce, and second, he must persuade his parents to grant their permission. A monological literary form, such as a sermon, is ideal for presenting a series of sound reasons for 'early' renunciation (particularly to an already-sympathetic audience), and may

---

35 Narrative literature comprised a significant portion of the (Śvetāmbara) Canon and became especially vast during the medieval period.

36 For example, following a sermon delivered by a Jina, some members of the audience always renounce, while others do not.

37 In some cases, these narratives contain first-person dialogues embedded within them, and thus constitute a mixed narrative/dialogical form.

38 I assume that such dialogues are conscious creations, chosen by an author as the literary form best suited to the content being presented. Although the dialogical form may be recruited for a wide variety of distinct purposes, here I will focus on the utility of dialogue in persuasively resolving competing points of view regarding 'early' renunciation.

even warn would-be renunciates that their decision to renounce might meet with parental resistance. Third-person narrative accounts, at times, provide convincing explanations for a young person's choice to renounce, but often do not explain how parental consent was obtained. Both of these literary forms may prove persuasive with regard to the merits and even urgency of 'early' renunciation, but they do not typically confront the sorts of realistic objections and doubts likely to be raised by one's family, nor how such objections were to be met.[39] There is something suspiciously unrealistic or pat about accounts of young people who renounce the world without a struggle and with little or no acknowledgement that there are obvious forces weighing against it, including the orthodox brāhmanical Hindu tradition and parental affection and possessiveness. In the context of two such staunchly disparate positions regarding 'early' renunciation (i.e. pro and con), genuine persuasion requires dialogue.

Unlike monological sermons or strictly third-person narrative accounts, dialogues between would-be renunciates and their parents permit questions, objections and doubts to be repeatedly raised and answered. And a carefully constructed dialogue, which allows a debate on 'early' renunciation to be controlled and directed as the author sees fit, demonstrates, or at least gives the appearance, that 'early' renunciation has successfully withstood a variety of realistic objections, and that the young people concerned have won both the respect of their parents and the hard-fought permission to renounce. Such dialogical depictions of persuasion are, I suggest, themselves inherently compelling and uniquely persuasive.

In the free-market religious economy that arose in India beginning in the sixth–fifth centuries BCE, in which new upaniṣadic doctrines were being promulgated and the renunciatory śramaṇic traditions such as Jainism and Buddhism were taking root, religious affiliation became, perhaps for the first time on a large scale, a strictly voluntary affair[40]; and in the competition for converts, the power to persuade was crucial. By this time, the Vedic tradition had accrued a significant weight of ancient authority, and in order to compete with brāhmanical orthodoxy, teachers such as the Mahāvīra and the Buddha had to develop an authority of their own, based largely upon what they taught and how persuasive they were.

Thus, Jaina and Buddhist scriptures frequently depict Mahāvīra (and his *gaṇadharas*), and the Buddha (and his chief disciples), engaging in back-and-forth conversations or dialogues with various people, in which mildly curious or even initially hostile people are gradually persuaded by the teachings. As a result of this scriptural tendency, the dialogical form itself, quite apart from any specific content, came to be associated with authoritative and persuasive teachings, and the repeated use of such dialogues may have trained audiences to pay as close attention to what was being said as to who was saying it.

This phenomenon seems to be important in the Jaina dialogues presented above. In these dialogues, and others like them, there are, at least in the background, competing authorities: on the one hand, there is the authority of pro-renunciation teachers such as Mahāvīra, and on the other hand, the natural, god-given authority of the parents, bolstered by an orthodox brāhmanical (or even lay-Jaina) tradition that did not support or promote 'early' renunciation. As competing authorities tend to cancel one another out and produce a stalemate, the young men were not able to merely rest upon the personal authority of a

---

39 Where such objections are dealt with in narrative accounts, they usually take the form of dialogues embedded within the narrative.

40 Olivelle, *Saṃnyāsa Upaniṣads*, p. 33.

teacher; none of the young men, for example, justified their 'early' renunciation by citing the authority of Mahāvīra or some other omniscient Jaina sage, nor did they counter their parents appeal to Vedic authority with some predetermined authority of their own. Rather, the young men engaged in a dialogue that clearly provided their reasons for desiring 'early' renunciation and that persuasively answered all objections. The one source of 'authority' all of the young men drew upon was their own memories of past-lives, which imbued them with an unshakable confidence that 'early' renunciation was both reasonable and desirable.

Interestingly, in the course of their dialogues with their parents, the young men took on the role of teacher. This results in an interesting inversion[41] of the typical scenario where elder teaches younger; in our dialogues, the young person becomes the teacher of his elders, perhaps mirroring the historical fact that representatives of the 'younger' śramaṇic/renunciatory traditions needed to teach, and ultimately persuade, representatives of the elder brāhmanical tradition if they ever expected to gain converts or, at the very least, gain parental permission for 'early' renunciation.

There is insufficient evidence to allow us to know for certain how such dialogues were used in practice, or who their target audiences were, but one may speculate that such dialogues may have served not only to justify and inspire 'early' renunciation, but also to serve as rehearsal-transcripts for any young man wishing to renounce and who sought the permission of his parents. Moreover, such dialogues may have served to promote parental acceptance, or at least tolerance, of a child's decision to take on 'early' renunciation.

Hindu Dialogues on 'Early' Renunciation

Despite the common brāhmanical injunction to delay renunciation until old age, the Hindu tradition does contain some literature,[42] including dialogues, that mitigates this injunction, and which supports and justifies 'early' renunciation; and similar to the Jainas, it was customary among Hindus[43] to first obtain parental permission prior to renouncing. Included in this literature is what Winternitz[44] dubbed 'ascetic-poetry', which contained the doctrines of ascetics who competed with the Brahmins and 'in which they preached their doctrines of abstinence and contempt of the world'.[45] This 'ascetic-poetry', which was shared by Hindus, Buddhists and Jainas, includes many of the epic-dialogues (*itihāsa-saṃvāda*) of

---

41 This inversion is reminiscent of that found in several *vedānta upaniṣad*s, in which Brahmins are taught new religious doctrines by kings.

42 e.g. the *Saṃnyāsa-Upaniṣads*, the eleventh-century *Yatidharmasamuccaya*. *Jābāla-Upaniṣad* 4, for example, states: 'Now, whether a man has taken the vow of Vedic initiation or not, has graduated from Vedic study or not, has taken up his fire or not, he should renounce on the very day in which he becomes dispassionate', an assertion reiterated in *Nāradaparivrājaka-Upaniṣad* 3;6, *Paramahaṃsavrājaka-Upaniṣad* 2, and *Maitreya-Upaniṣad* 2.3.10. Such dispassion is said (*Nāradaparivrājaka-Upaniṣad* 5; *Bṛhatsaṃnyāsa-Upaniṣad* 2) to arise as a result of previous good acts (*prākpuṇyakarmavaśāt*) in past lives. Moreover, *Yatidharmasamuccaya* 2.46 states that the Vedic injunction to repay the 'three debts' applied only to those who were not dispassionate (Olivelle, *Saṃnyāsa Upaniṣads*, p. 45).

43 The requirement to obtain permission to renounce from one's family is, in the Hindu tradition, explicitly referred to in *Kaṭhaśruti Upaniṣad* 1; 2.3.

44 M. Winternitz, *A History of Indian Literature*, vol. 1, trans. V. Srinivasa Sarma (Delhi, 1981), p. 300.

45 For *Saṃnyāsa*-upaniṣadic passages similarly expressing contempt for worldly life, see *Maitreya-Upaniṣad* 1.2–3; 2.2.1–4; *Nāradaparivrājaka-Upaniṣad* 4; *Yājñavalkya-Upaniṣad* 4.

the *Mahābhārata*, as well as certain dialogues found in the Hindu Purāṇas.[46] Our two Hindu dialogues below appear to come from this latter genre.[47]

The first Hindu dialogue, 'an ancient epic-dialogue between father and son' (12.169.2), is from the *Mahābhārata*'s *Śāntiparvan* (12.169),[48] and shares so many features with our first Jaina dialogue as to appear to be a variant of the same basic dialogue. The father is described as a Brahmin 'devoted to the study of the Vedas' (12.169.3), while his intelligent son, called Medhāvī, was 'conversant with the path to liberation (*mokṣa*)' (12.169.4). In answer to the son's question about the best path to pursue given the fleeting nature of life, the father suggested the traditional step-wise brāhmanical path, relegating renunciation to old age: 'Having mastered the Vedas as a celibate student, O son, he should desire sons for the sake of sanctifying the ancestors, and, having established his sacred fires, perform the prescribed offerings and sacrifices. Then, having entered the forest, he should become a contemplative sage' (12.169.6).

The son's objection to this step-wise progression was that Death was ever stalking, and there was no guarantee that one would ever reach the 'traditional' age for retreating to the forest. In what is almost a verbatim repetition from our first Jaina dialogue above,[49] the son declares that Death, Old Age, and the passing nights encompass the world, which, as above, had an alarming impact on the father. The son concluded: 'Thus, even a young man ought to be devoted to righteous virtue, for the span of life is certainly uncertain' (12.169.15). Quoting Holy Scripture (*śruti*), the son suggested that one ought to retreat from the village to the forest (12.169.23). In the forest, he suggested, one may discover the 'truth', which was the only worthwhile pursuit in life: 'From confusion one arrives at death, whereas through truth, one achieves immortality' (12.169.28). Given the fact that the son was able to quote scripture, and that his arguments appear to be based, in part, upon the teachings of the *vedānta upaniṣads*, it appears he had already studied the Veda (absolving him of his first 'debt'). As for the other debts, producing offspring and conducting sacrifices, the boy declared: 'Out of the Self, I was born by the Self, and though childless, I, intent upon the Self, will return to the Self – no child need rescue me' (12.169.34), and 'How can a wise man such as me sacrifice by means of the cruel animal-sacrifices, or by sacrifices for gaining power (such as the demons do), whose effects are impermanent?' (12.169.31).[50] At the conclusion of the dialogue, both father and son renounced.

Our second Hindu dialogue, from *Mārkaṇḍeya-Purāṇa* 10–41,[51] displays a marked similarity to our second Jaina dialogue in its lengthy recounting of the horrors of life in *saṃsāra*. This dialogue is between a Brahmin father and his son Sumati/Jaḍa, who we are

46 Winternitz, *A History of Indian Literature*, vol.1, p. 391.

47 For a discussion of such shared ascetic-poetry in the Jaina tradition, see Charpentier's introduction to the *Uttarādhyayana-Sūtra* (pp. 43–8). The Buddhist Pāli-Canon also contains a great deal of this pro-renunciation ascetic-poetry.

48 In the Bengali Vulgate edition of the *Mahābhārata*, this story appears twice, almost verbatim, at 12.175 and 12.277; the version in the critical edition (12.169), which is used here, contains variants from both. The *terminus ante quem* for the critical edition is generally assigned to about 400 CE.

49 Cf. *Uttarajjhayaṇa-sutta* 14.21–3 and *Mahābhārata* 12.169.7–9.

50 On non-violence, see also 12.169.25; 29.

51 With the exception of the *Devīmāhātmya*, the *Mārkaṇḍeya-Purāṇa* is one of the oldest Purāṇas, and may be as early as the third century CE (see W.D. O'Flaherty, *Hindu Myths* [New York, 1975], p. 18).

told was rather apathetic or stupefied in appearance (*jaḍa-rūpin*), in marked contrast to Medhāvī above. As expected, the father spoke to his son as follows:

> O Sumati, [first] you must learn by heart the Vedas, from the beginning and in proper order, intent upon service to your teacher and eating begged food only. Then, taking up the life of a householder, and having offered the best of sacrifices, you must have children, who are to be wished for. After that, you must resort to the forest. Finally, my son, while living in the forest, you must become a mendicant, free of worldly ties. In this way, will you attain to that *brahman* where, once achieved, you shall suffer no longer. (10.11–13)

Getting no response from his stupefied son, the father repeated his advice over and over. At last, Sumati replied with a laugh:

> My dear father, many times over have I learned these texts which you now advise me to study, as well as various other manuals on art and architecture. Myriad lifetimes and more have arisen in my memory. (10.16–17ab)

Sumati then proceeded to summarize for his father these countless lifetimes,[52] in which he: was repeatedly forced to abandon his beloved family members; suffered from sicknesses a thousand times over; suffered in the womb, as a child, in youth, and in old age; had been born as a Brahmin, Kṣatriya, Vaiśya, and Śūdra, as well as among the birds, beasts, and insects of the earth;[53] had been, by turns, both rich and poor, master and slave, powerful and powerless, the giver and receiver of blows, and the reveller and the mourner. And as a result of remembering these myriad lifetimes, he attained the knowledge that leads to liberation. He said to his father:

> While thus wandering in this perilous circle of *saṃsāra*, I attained the knowledge leading to final release. Where this is known, the entire collection of texts dealing with religious action, known as the Rig, Sāma and Yajur [Vedas], are without merit and do not appear to be relevant to me … Therefore, my dear father, having abandoned this world of non-stop sorrows, I shall depart; does not this triple *dharma* [of the Vedas], so full of *adharma*, appear like the fruits of sin? (10.27–8; 32)

Astonished, his father asked how this grand wisdom had suddenly arisen in one who, until this time, had appeared so stupefied. Sumati related a prior birth in which this knowledge had arisen: he had been a Brahmin who had achieved a high state of knowledge through the practice of *yoga* and had become a famous teacher. But through his own carelessness, his good character was drawn towards ignorance and he was ruined. Remembering the knowledge attained in that previous lifetime, Sumati no longer had use for the orthodox brāhmanical path:

> This, my memory of past lives (*jātismaraṇa*), is indeed the fruit of knowledge and charity, my dear father, and it is not achieved by men who resort to the triple *dharma*. I am one

---

52 Cf. *Mahābhārata* 14.16.28–43.

53 Here, Sumati does not explicitly state that he had been previously reborn in hell, but beginning in *Mārkaṇḍeya-Purāṇa* 13, he relates an incident he witnessed while in hell.

> who resorts to the *dharma* familiar from a previous existence; having focused my mind on the absolute, I shall strive for the liberation of my soul. (10.43–4)

Sumati then offered to answer any questions his father might have.[54] The dialogue that ensues is made up of a series of questions and answers between father and son, in which the terrors of *saṃsāra* are made plain. This begins with a discussion of what happens to a person as he dies, and what may await him, including both heaven and hell. As in the second Jaina dialogue, the terrors of hell are examined in great detail. This is followed by a discussion of how a person is reborn, beginning with the fetal stage:

> There [in the womb], any number of conditions in *saṃsāra* come to its mind; and thus, being afflicted no matter where it turns, it arrives at a disgust with worldly existence (*nirveda*). 'As soon as I am free of this belly here, never again will I act thusly; I shall strive hard to ensure I will not arrive again in a womb.' Thus it thinks, having remembered hundreds of sorrows of past lives, which were experienced previously and which arose from fate. (11.13–15)

Such noble intentions notwithstanding, reminiscent of the vow taken by Mahāvīra while still in the womb, the memory of such past miseries is, we are told, wiped clean by Viṣṇu's *māyā* as soon as the child leaves the womb, and thus the soul 'is made to revolve in this circle of *saṃsāra* like a water jug attached to a rope in a well' (11.21). By way of summary, Sumati declared to his father: 'There is not, my dear father, so much as a single pleasure in this world filled with hundreds of sorrows. Thus, how can I, who strive for liberation, attend to the triple *dharma*?' (11.32) When the father asked Sumati what should be done to escape *saṃsāra*, Sumati replied:

> If, my dear father, you unhesitatingly place your faith in my words, then having abandoned your householder status, you must devote yourself to the life of a forest-dweller ... Then, you will obtain that *yoga* which is the remedy for one's connection to suffering, the cause of liberation (*mukti*), incomparable, indescribable, and unnameable. (16.3; 6)

After further protracted discussion, Sumati once again advised his father to renounce the world and seek his own liberation, and asked for (and obtained) his father's permission to do the same. Both men then departed for the forest and achieved final liberation.

As noted above, these two Hindu dialogues justifying and promoting 'early' renunciation are remarkably similar to, if not bona fide variants of, our Jaina dialogues. While it is true that, in the first dialogue, the young man in part justifies his wish to take 'early' renunciation by appealing to the authority of *śruti*, that is not his only argument. And in the second dialogue, the only 'authority' appealed to is the young man's personal remembrance of past lives. In other words, once again, the young men, who adopt the role of teacher, sway their initially-reluctant parents largely through persuasive dialogue rather than appeals to authority.

---

[54] It is worth noting, in the context of the 'three debts' owed by a Brahmin prior to renouncing, that Sumati here suggests that answering his father's questions will make him debt-free (*an-ṛṇya*; 10.45).

Conclusions

The reason for the marked similarity of our Jaina and Hindu dialogues poses little mystery, and is not entirely to be explained by inter-tradition borrowing. From a parent's perspective, whether Jaina or Hindu, the primary objection to 'early' renunciation is much the same: renunciation is acceptable, but should be delayed until old age. Where the desires are similar (i.e. 'early' renunciation) and the objections are similar (i.e. renunciation should be delayed), it is not surprising that, regardless of doctrinal tradition, the solution would be similar. Were space to allow it, a similar (though somewhat distinct) dynamic could have been demonstrated from early Buddhist texts as well.[55] The fact that 'early' renunciation was justified in dialogues in multiple traditions speaks to the effectiveness and persuasiveness of this literary form.

The persuasiveness of these dialogues does not rely upon any preconceived doctrinal authority, nor are the young men in the dialogues invested with any special authority of their own, beyond their unshakable conviction that 'early' renunciation is the only viable path for them. Rather, the persuasiveness arises out of the dialogue itself. In a world of competing authorities, where the brāhmanical (and perhaps even lay-Jaina) tradition represented a potential bulwark against the tradition of 'early' renunciation, a young man desiring to renounce was forced to persuasively argue for it all on his own, with absolute certainty and steadfast conviction. Such conviction appears to be a practical necessity for any young man desiring 'early' renunciation, and it is largely this independent and individual conviction that makes these dialogues so compellingly persuasive. (Similarly compelling, even moving, relational dimensions are evident in the Hindu and Buddhist dialogues discussed elsewhere in this volume by Crothers and Black.) In three of our four dialogues, the parents were brāhmanical Hindus, and in all three of these cases, the parents not only granted their sons permission to renounce, but were persuaded to renounce themselves. Thus, these dialogues represent not only the victory of the young men involved, but also of the renunciatory traditions as a whole.

References

Primary Sources and Translations

Antagaḍadasāo, trans. L.D. Barnett (London: Royal Asiatic Society, 1907).
Āyāraṃga-sutta, ed. H. Jacobi (London: Pali Text Society, 1882).
Caüppaṇṇamahāpurisacariam of Ācārya Śrī Śīlāṅka, ed. Pt. Amritlal Mohanlal Bhojak (Ahmedabad: Prakrit Text Society, 2006).
Dharmābhyudaya of Udayaprabhasūri, ed. Ācārya Jinavijayasūri, Siṅghī Jaina Series 4 (Mumbai: Siṅghī Jainaśāstra Śikṣāpīṭha, 1949).
Dharmasūtras of Āpastamba, Gautama, Baudhāyana, and Vasiṣṭha, ed. and trans. P. Olivelle (Delhi: Motilal Banarsidass, 2000).
Kalpa-Sūtra, ed. and trans. K.C. Lalwani (Delhi: Motilal Banarsidass, 1979).
Mahāpurāṇa of Mahākavi Puṣpadanta, 3rd edition, ed. P.L. Vaidya (New Delhi: Bharatiya Jnanpith, 2006).

---

55 Cf. Buddhist *Raṭṭhapāla-sutta*.

Mahābhārata, ed. V.S. Sukthankar et al. (Poona: Bhandarkar Oriental Research Institute, 1933–41).
Mānavadharmaśāstra (Manu's Law Code), ed. and trans. P. Olivelle (New York: Oxford University Press, 2005).
Minor Upaniṣads, ed. F.O. Schrader (Madras: The Adyar Library, 1912).
Pāli Tipiṭaka and Commentaries <www.tipitaka.org>.
Sthavirāvalīcarita or Pariśiṣṭaparvan of Hemacandra, 2nd edition, ed. H. Jacobi (Calcutta: Asiatic Society of Bengal, 1932).
Sthānāṅgasūtram, with the Commentary of Abhayadevasūri, ed. Muni Jambūvijaya (Mumbai: Śrī Mahāvīra Jaina Vidyālaya, 2003).
Sūyagaḍaṃga, trans. H. Jacobi in Jaina Sūtras, Part II, Sacred Books of the East, vol. XLV (Oxford: Oxford University Press, 1895).
Taittirīya Saṃhitā, trans. A.B. Keith, Harvard Oriental Series 18–19 (Cambridge, MA: Harvard University Press, 1914).
Triṣaṣṭiśalākāpuruṣacaritamahākāvyam, Vol. 1 (Parvan 1), ed. Munirāja Śrīcaraṇavijayajī Mahārāja; Vol. 2 (Parvans 2–4), ed. Munirāja Śrīpuṇyavijayajī Mahārāja; Vol. 3 (Parvans 5–7) and Vol. 4 (Parvans 8–9), ed. Śrīramaṇīkavijayajī Gaṇi and Vijayaśīlacandrasūri; (Ahmedabad: Kalikālasarvajña Śrīhemacandrācārya Navama Janmaśābdī Smṛti Śikṣaṇa-Saṃskāranidhi, 2001); Vol. 5 (Parvan 10), ed. Vijayaśīlacandrasūri (Ahmedabad: Kalikālasarvajña Śrīhemacandrācārya Navama Janmaśābdī Smṛti Śikṣaṇa-Saṃskāranidhi, 2012).
Uttarādhyayanasūtra, Being the First Mūlasūtra of the Śvetāmbara Jains, ed. Jarl Charpentier (Uppsala: Archives D'Etudes Orientales, 1922).
Uttarapurāṇa of Ācārya Guṇabhadra, ed. and Hindi trans. Pannalal Jain (New Delhi: Bharatiya Jnanpith, 2007).
Uvāsagadasāo, the Seventh Aṅga of the Śvetāmbara Jainas, trans. A.F.R. Hoernle (Calcutta: The Asiatic Society, [1885–90] Reprinted 1989).
Yogavāsiṣṭha, ed. and trans. V.L. Mitra and R.P. Arya, Parimal Sanskrit Series 49 (Delhi: Parimal Publications, 1998).

Secondary Sources

Brown, W.N., *Manuscript Illustrations of the Uttarādhyayana Sūtra* (New Haven, CT: American Oriental Society, 1941).
Dundas, Paul, *The Jains* (New York: Routledge, 1992).
Glasenapp, Helmuth von, *Jainism: An Indian Religion of Salvation*, trans. of *Der Jainismus: Eine Indische Erlösungsreligion* (1925) by Shridhar B. Shrotri (Delhi: Motilal Banarsidass Publishers, 1999).
Granoff, Phyllis, 'Jain Stories Inspiring Renunciation', in D.S. Lopez Jr. (ed.), *Religions of India in Practice* (Princeton, NJ: Princeton University Press, 1995).
———, *The Forest of Thieves and the Magic Garden: An Anthology of Medieval Jain Stories* (New Delhi: Penguin Books, 1998).
Jaini, P.S., *The Jaina Path of Purification* (Delhi: Motilal Banarsidass, 1979).
Lalwani, K.C., *Uttarādhyayana Sutra: The Last Testament of Bhagavān Mahāvīra* (Calcutta: Prajñānam, 1977).
O'Flaherty, W.D., *Hindu Myths* (New York: Penguin, 1975).
Ohira, S., *A Study of the Bhagavatīsūtra: A Chronological Analysis* (Ahmedabad: Prakrit Text Society, 1994).

Olivelle, Patrick, *Saṃnyāsa Upaniṣads: Hindu Scriptures on Asceticism and Renunciation* (New York: Oxford University Press, 1992).
———, *The Āśrama System* (New York: Oxford University Press, 1993).
———, *Rules and Regulations of Brahminical Asceticism* (Albany: State University of New York Press, 1995).
Schubring, W., *The Doctrine of the Jainas, Described after the Old Sources*, 2nd revised edition, trans. Wolfgang Beurlen (Delhi: Motilal Banarsidass, 2000).
Williams, R., *Jaina Yoga: A Survey of the Medieval Śrāvakācāras* (Oxford: Oxford University Press, 1963).
Winternitz, M., *A History of Indian Literature*, vol. 1, trans. V. Srinivasa Sarma (Delhi: Motilal Banarsidass, 1981).

Chapter 10
Trusted Deceivers: Illusion-Making Ascetics, Paṇḍitas, Brahmins, and Bodhisattas and the Conditions for the Dialogic in *Arthaśāstra* and *Jātaka* Scenarios of Rule[1]

Lisa Wessman Crothers

There is a unique dialogic moment in the court of the king of Videha, as depicted in the *Mahā Ummagga Jātaka*, the Buddhist 'Birth Story of the Great Tunnel'. In a riddling contest, the Brahmin *paṇḍita* Senaka and Bodhisatta Mahosadha, both royal sages to the king, exchange knowing glances, and are thus able to read each other's minds and intentions.[2] The scene provides a narrative window into the dimensions of dialogue that go unexamined; namely, the complex nonverbal and verbal factors that contribute to dialogue. One might imagine such factors merely to be a question of grammar, since the scene uses familiar 'modes of expression halfway between direct and indirect speech', to convey the interlocutors' own thoughts or words.[3] I refer to another kind of 'grammar' at work in this communication – the grammar that underlies royal discourses and dialogues between kings and advisors in Buddhist and Brahmanical texts. This grammar is comprised of factors of relationality and trust that provide some of the conditions for dialogue to occur in the first place – knowing looks cast between sagely advisors, facial expressions, tacit appeals to social and religious authority and nonverbal performance of authoritative knowledge. Such factors all operate in and through a grammar of trust (and distrust) that make face to face communication possible and/or necessary.

We rarely ask ourselves about the factors that lead us to pursue a particular line of dialogue, as we engage in dialogue. Are these factors comprised only of the words of our interlocutor? Or are the factors those which we actually see in the person before us? Or do we choose our words – if we are indeed *sammukkham*, speaking face to face – due to things we know are true or should be true in the person before us? Trust and its potential antitheses are the non-apparent dimensions of dialogue, which include nonverbal and verbal relational dynamics.

I use two related approaches to 'reading' for the dialogic in South Asian narratives. The first involves reading for that which is not apparently dialogic (as in Rohlman's consideration in this volume of how 'metaphorical dialogue' between texts is facilitated

---

[1] I dedicate this work to my students, Sam Easterday and Sally Kendrick, whose exemplary *guṇas* exceed those even a Bhīṣma might envision; and to my loyal *Sherpa* who helped me carry this to fruition.

[2] *Jā* 6, p. 351, ln 14–30; and p. 352, ln 1–2.

[3] Steven Collins on the uses of 'indirect speech clauses' in Pāli language texts. *A Pali Grammar for Students* (Chiang Mai, 2006), p. 166.

by 'dialogues within texts'). The second approach involves reading for the non-apparent dimensions of obviously and paradigmatically dialogical narratives, as in the exchanges around kings at court depicted between the sages above. This second way of reading reveals the communications in dialogue that involve more than words. In what follows, I read for the non-apparent dimensions of dialogue in order to show the dynamics of trust and its antitheses in the personal dialogues among kings and trusted members of court. I also consider the non-apparent dimensions of dialogue at the macro level (among and across traditions) in order to demonstrate how Buddhist and Brahmanical texts participate in a shared imagination of royal trust, deception and espionage in royal settings. This shared imaginary of trust and deceit in turn directs us back to the first way of reading for the dialogic – to reading for the ways that the creators of a Buddhist text use their ideas of the Brahmanical *paṇḍita* 'sage' counselor's and *khattiya* 'warrior' king's respective expertise and knowledge at court.

The Bodhisatta as Mahosadha in the *Mahā Ummagga Jātaka* (henceforth *MUJā*) enters a royal imaginary of deception shaped by royal śāstric – treatise-construed expertise, as in *Arthaśāstra* – ideologies and shows how Buddhist expertise and knowledge operates in royal contexts. The Bodhisatta's expertise encompasses the subtlety of nonverbal and social predicates. In making its own use of the pervasive royal imaginary of trust and deception, the *MUJā* provides a narrative demonstration that a Buddha-to-be is more adept than any other trusted 'sage' (*paṇḍita* in the *MUJā*) in tricky tactics required of rule and in the nonverbal and verbal skills associated with royal communications and relationships.

I begin these considerations with a brief discussion of the non-apparent dimensions of dialogue that Kauṭilya's *Arthaśāstra* suggests aspiring courtiers should master in order to communicate effectively in royal settings. These dimensions are key nonverbal predicates and markers of communication that make possible royal dialogue and the relationships that dialogue founds or sustains. Next, I bring forth the strategic models for royal action – the *upāya* and *ṣaḍguṇa*, relational tactics and deceptions – in the *Arthaśāstra* to provide context for the narrative ideas about such royal tactics in the *MUJā*. The models of action in *Arthaśāstra* show that the success of such models relies not only on skill and wisdom, but depends as well upon certain levels of trustworthiness. This is an understanding of the link between wisdom and trustworthiness that the *MUJā* shares. Thus, I discuss the *Arthaśāstra*'s conception of deceptive relational scenarios (*upadhā*) designed to discern the extent of a man's trustworthiness. The tactics and relational responses envisioned in such *upadhā* point to a dialectical relationship between trust and deception (i.e., trust relies on deception and successful deception is predicated on certain markers of trust). This relationship between trust and deception, in turn, provides points of entry for dialogue and provisional predicates for relationship.

But how do dialogue, trust and deception work together to provide advisors and spies the power to carry out royal plans? This mechanism becomes evident if one considers the repertoires of action of the *Arthaśāstra*'s 'trusted deceivers, at large'. 'Trusted deceivers' in this case are the ascetics and mendicants who hold sway or roam in espionage on behalf of the king and his closest advisors. Here I focus on the nonverbal and verbal predicates of dialogue and trust that occur in the *Arthaśāstra*'s hypothetical designs for turning sages and religious wanderers toward deceptions in the service of royal reconnaissance and espionage. I end with a consideration of the nonverbal and verbal predicates of dialogue and trust at work in analogous tricks and tactics that occur in royal relationships depicted in the *MUJā*. Ultimately, the Bodhisatta Mahosadha's use of tricks and tactics raises (and answers) questions about the true ally on which to rely within a royal imaginary constituted through the dialogical and intersubjective realms of trusts and deceptions.

Nonverbal Predicates of Dialogue in Kauṭilya's *Arthaśāstra*

The *Arthaśāstra* recommends tactics for regulating one's image with the king and court, many of which include observation of physical markers or signs that nonverbally communicate. Two associated chapters in Book Five concerning the proper behaviour for a royal 'dependent' or 'courtier', the *anujīvin*, at court (*Aś* 5.4–5) discuss the bodily gestures, sounds and movements that are part of the lexicon of communication with kings. The instructions also contain implicit and explicit warnings about the dangers that might befall one for missing nonverbal cues in dialogue. These chapters provide context for nonverbal dimensions and predicates of dialogue, which those aspiring to serve kings should be familiar with in order to succeed.

The *anujīvin* is a common denomination for a 'courtier' used in Brahmanical and Buddhist textual culture. (The advice in these chapters seems addressed to *anujīvins* who have already obtained this position).[4] The nature of the instructions – the rhetoric of words and actions to which the text directs the *anujīvins* – envisions persons (males) aspiring to the importance and power that can be had through closer relationship to the king and the service of other royals at court.[5] He is '[a]n expert in worldly matters [who] should seek service with a king through people who are dear to and intimate with him …' (5.4.1).[6]

If the *anujīvin* succeeds in obtaining a position with a self-possessed king, the *wise* aspirant to a close advising relationship with a king guards himself by managing his own affect and gestures: 'He should scrutinize his gestures and bearing' (5.5.5).[7] Moreover, he communicates with the king by these same means: 'I [the *anujīvin*] should be allowed through the use of signs to prevent you [the king] from imposing punishment out of lust or anger' (5.4.7).[8] The text addresses also the most basic of this conduct: how the new *anujīvin* should enter and take his seat near the king: 'Once he is appointed, he should enter the designated place with permission. And he should sit on one side if placed close by and on a farther seat if placed at a distance' (5.4.8).[9] The position of and the manner in which he takes his seat communicates his respect for the power differences that are expressed through physical structures. The *anujīvin* learns that he should neither talk nor laugh too loud, but also guard the perception of what he does say by assuring that he does not speak to a topic without having experience with it, nor converse in an uncultured or unreliable

---

[4] The term that fits the role of 'courtier' in the *MUJā* is *amacca*, the most basic designation for a person who acts in some official role for kings in their realm. Although the term *anujīvin* does not occur in the *MUJā*, it does in the *Vidhura Paṇḍita Jātaka* (No. 545), which immediately precedes the *MUJā* in the *Mahā Nipāta* collection of Jātaka tales.

[5] Ganapati Sastri suggests that the *anujīvin* is positioning to be a counselor (*mantry-ādayaḥ*). *Arthasastra of Kautalya*, tr. N. P. Unni, with the Śrīmūlam Commentary of Mahamahopadhyaya T. Ganapati Sastri (3 vols, Trivandrum Sanskrit Series, 1984).

[6] *King, Governance, and Law in India: Kauṭilya's Arthaśāstra, A New Annotated Translation by Patrick Olivelle* (Oxford, 2013), p. 264.

[7] Ibid., p. 266.

[8] Ibid., p. 264.

[9] Ibid.

way, nor with mendacity: 'He should not do the following: combative speech; statements that are impolite, indistinct, incredible, or untrue...' (5.4.9). Moreover, '[he] should refrain from doing the following: speaking secretly with another man; ... contracting one eye or lip, knitting the eyebrows' (5.4.10).[10] When verbal and nonverbal come together as terms of action, they form a rhetoric of proper comportment that is instrumental to demonstrating one's success in negotiating royal dialogue.

Such advice to the *anujīvin* indicates concern to cultivate (and to protect) by normalizing conduct 'from the ground up'; at these most foundational points of access to communication and dialogue. It is apparent that mismanaged personal comportment would detract from the image of one's intelligence. An inability to understand various gestures or inability to discern a king's mood from how he or others move about or use glances would belie any mastery in sensitivity to and command of royal contexts a close confidant of a king would claim to possess. I assert that the text's attention here to nonverbal minutiae of communicating (even instructing the *anujīvin*'s proper entry into a king's presence) reflect the elementary dimensions of dialogue deemed suitable to idealized relationship cultures at court.

Kauṭilya gives concrete advice to those aspiring to be close associates at court and to be successful in these roles. One must attend to bodily communication, because of the respect (or disrespect) that gestures and postures convey. Theoretically, any courtier must be able to interpret the signs of favour or disfavour in the faces of the king. For instance there are instructions that range from how to gauge a king's mood and relative satisfaction or dissatisfaction (5.5. 7–8) from his attitude, gestures and facial expressions (5.5.5–9), to how to interpret non-human signs that might augur danger for any courtly advisor: 'He should, moreover, pay attention to a change in behavior of even nonhuman beings' (5.5.10).[11] All the instructions seem designed to anticipate the king's needs during communications and to attend to one's status in one's relationship with the king and his court. The threat of failure or danger resides in discerning the verbal and nonverbal lexicon of royal satisfaction and dissatisfaction.

When exercised in royal cultures, these behaviours are also the building blocks of royally construed – through *brāhmaṇa*, *kṣatriya* (or other *varṇa*) and general royal (*rājanya*) ideals and actions – sophistication, reliability and truthfulness.[12]

Risks Inherent in Nonverbal Communication

In addition, concerns about unwitting betrayals of confidences in counsels point to the challenges of conveying what is intended to be conveyed in royal dialogues. 'Now, counsel

[10] Ibid.

[11] Ibid., p. 266.

[12] I emphasize the *rājanya* experience in order to imagine a context beyond the typical *kṣatriya brāhmaṇa* dichotomy/dialectic. *Rājanya* as a category functionally includes not only *kṣatriya* kings and princes, but the other 'royal' persons closely associated with kings – princes of lesser caste or caste-less, royals tied to kings either through loyalty, devotion and role, family, teaching lineage or affinal relationships. This category would include royal figures like Karṇa, Vidura, or Kuntī in *MBh* traditions. *Rājanya* also could include the expansive roles across and within this category, that Śākyamuni embodies as the Bodhisatta in *jātaka* tales (and that monks and nuns embody in these tales). Reading for the *rājanya* experience in this way provides a literary stop with which to pause and consider the negotiations of social excellence and *dharma* in royal contexts beyond what one might expect of them.

is divulged (*mantrabhedaḥ*) by the gestures and bearing (*iṅgitākārābhyām*) of envoys, ministers and the [king]. Gesture is acting in a non-normal way (*iṅgitam anyathāvṛttiḥ*). Bearing is putting on an expression' (1.15.7–9).[13] There is a two-fold expectation about the communicative force of nonverbal factors of dialogue: First, there is the expectation that royal agents should be able to communicate (*saṃjñālipibhiḥ*) 'through signs and written messages' (1.12.11).[14] Second, there is the expectation that secret communications would be divulged through the same means. As for the first expectation, note the distinctions among the agents, and the directions their communications are envisioned to take: 'The apprentices of clandestine establishments should communicate the secret information gathered by spies through signs and written messages. Neither they nor the clandestine should know each other' (1.12.12).

The caution that these agents not know each other speaks to a dimension of the second expectation – that royal communication can be divulged unwittingly (putting any clandestine operation at risk). The wrong person could either receive or misperceive the nature of these communications. For instance, the text warns 'certainly royal counsel is given away' (*mantrabhedaḥ*, literally, 'counsel is broken') if the wrong person were to observe the 'gestures' and 'bearing' (*iṅgitākārābhyām*) of the king and his envoys and ministers (*dūtāmātyasvāminām*). Our outside expert is cautioning even the one who directs the activities, the king (*svāmin*).

Upāya in *Arthaśāstra*: Rudimentary Tactics for Relationships and Strategic Alliances

The nonverbal signs and signals exchanged between kings and his close servants are part of the dialogic repertoire that make possible the social bonds and efficacy of the advisor–king relationship. The four *upāya* and six *guṇa* form the foundational structure of these relational modes of mutual influence. The four *upāya* are important modes of counsel and rule – conciliation (or diplomacy), bribery (or financial influence), discord, and force (military deterrence and war).[15] These are the four strategic means – *upāyacaturvarga*, as Kauṭilya formulates them in the *Arthaśāstra* – that kings, advisors and close ministers are exhorted and presumed to know, in addition to knowing the 'features of the six strategies' (*ṣāḍguṇya*): dual-policy, peace-making, war, mobilizing forces, lying in wait, and seeking asylum.[16] While a detailed exposition of these strategic terms is beyond the scope of consideration here, a brief sketch of their use and function in royal conduct provides some basis for thinking about how these strategies may have refracted into other genres, particularly the dialogic scenarios in the *Mahā Ummagga Jātaka* (*MUJā*).

These royal strategies – the four *upāya* and the six *guṇa* – involve expansive repertoires of behaviour directed at managing the networked relationships in which advisors and kings operate in the course of counsel and rule. Manu's *Dharmaśāstra* (*MDh*) describes the four *upāya* as the

---

13 *King, Governance, and Law in India*, p. 84.

14 Ibid., p. 79.

15 Book I.134; *The Pañcatantra*, tr. Patrick Olivelle (Oxford, 1997), p. 56.

16 *Aś*, Book 7. The Sanskrit *ṣaḍguṇa* is strengthened to *ṣāḍguṇya* by the editor so to reflect its discussion as an abstract category of six qualities associated with rule. To be consistent with most other texts, hereafter I will use *ṣaḍguṇa*. *MBh* 12.57.16 or 12.116.22 the concepts appear as *ṣaḍvargam* and *MDh* 7.160 as *ṣaḍguṇa*. For an alternate view of *ṣāḍguṇya*, see Ludo Rocher, 'A Note on to *Ṣāḍguṇya*', in Ācārya-Vandanā, ed. Samaresh Bandyopadhyay (Calcutta, 1982), pp. 319–25.

means to 'bring under his [the king's or advisor's] control all the adversaries he encounters' (*MDh*, 7.107).[17] Queen Kuntī in the *Mahābhārata* demonstrates a similar understanding of *upāya*, when she incites her recalcitrant *kṣatriya* son, Yudhiṣṭhira, to fight for his ancestral power and the land associated with it (*MBh*, 5.130.30): 'Unearth your ancestral share that lies buried, strong-armed son! Do it with persuasion, bribery, subversion, punishment or policy.'[18] Associated with these *upāya* are the six sets of tactics (*ṣaḍguṇā*) that allow a king to progress from an unstable position to a stable one; and to progress from a stable position to advancing his expansionary interests, according to Kauṭilya (*Aś*, 7.1.38). All resources, material and human, are imagined to be manageable under the aegis of these sets of tactics. Speaking to their efficacy, the senior minister, Ciraṃjīvin, in Book III of the *Pañcatantra* states – 'When a man is anchored [in these *ṣaḍguṇā*] is there any doubt that he will succeed?'[19]

The most common group of royal strategic means – the four *upāya* of conciliation, bribery, discord and force – are organizing principles of strategies and actions designed to influence and control a royal opponent or object of alliance. There are multiple varieties of *upāya* theorized for diverse contexts. As one example, *Arthaśāstra* 9.7.68–72 suggests coordinating particular *upāya* to meet the dangers which a ruler might meet from particular kinds of persons, ranging from intimate associates, allies or seditious ministers to 'those who possess [significant] power' (*śaktimatsu*). Collectively, all the *upāya* are directed at royal relationships and those who participate in them in some way. Individually, each *upāya* denotes a particular action principle, a common aim or trajectory of action around which other strategies are centered. In terms of application, conciliation (*sāma*) is preferred over any other *upāya*, while the use of force (*daṇḍa*) is considered a means of last resort, since force is conceived as heaviest in its consequences (9.5.56–61). All the *upāya* but *daṇḍa*, force, begin with dialogue and the relationships that are created, extended and broken through dialogue.

The *Arthaśāstra* makes some suggestions about the basis and modes of approach to dialogue for those that would follow its instructions. For instance, the text's preferred mode of conciliation (*sāma*) is usually predicated on some kind of friendship. The *sāma* discussion stipulates multiple predicates for friendly alliance: for the person who comes forward with his own integrity (*śaucena*) as the basis for a new friendship, or for the person of good intentions who values making alliance (*maitrīpradhānaṃ*) (9.6.22). Even so, underlying such amicable auspices in conciliation tactics is the pervasive impetus in *Arthaśāstra* to manipulate relationships. At the behest of advisor or king, a royal secret agent can be 'posing as a friend' (*mitravyañjanaḥ*) to learn one's true feelings, so as to use them to the king's advantage (9.5.27). The possibility and threat that a close associate may be merely posing as a friend may be just the reality shaping the continual scrutiny of royal associates for suitability to be in relationship with kings (and his closest confidants) in the first place.

Whether real or not, the possibility of friendship is the object of royal dialogues such as these. Royal 'friendships' require appealing to some common basis for dialogue, and thus cultivating some initial common ground for trust. The *Arthaśāstra* suggests its would-be tactical master (king or close advisor) find some common ground or problem with which to begin a dialogue and initiate a relationship.[20] The feelings that one king might have about

---

17 *Manu's Code of Law*, tr. Patrick Olivelle (Delhi, 2005), p. 160.

18 *Mahābhārata* 3 The Book of Virāṭa and the Book of the Effort, tr. J.A.B. Van Buitenen (Chicago, 1978), p. 430.

19 *Pañcatantra*, tr. Olivelle, p. 110.

20 Senaka and the Bodhisatta unite as such around the royal question, *pañha* with which I began this chapter.

his own virtuous conduct (his exercise of *dharma*) is one such source of commonality. In order to capitalize on this self-regard, the *Arthaśāstra* presents a repertoire of conciliatory means (*sāma upāya*) to be used against the one who is 'dharmic' (*dhārmikaṃ*). The text suggests one might forge the basis for common ground in these ways: 'he should appease by appealing to assistance rendered by them in the past, present or future over a shared injury, or to a former connection through ancestors (*sambandhena pūrveṣāṃ*) or by praising his conduct, learning, family and birth' (9.6.21).[21] Thus, in the context of *sāma upāya* recommended against a virtuous or dharmic man, his birth, learning, and shared history of relationship become expedient means, artful devices that a king and his close advisors use to facilitate a relationship that might also increase royal power and control.

The *Arthaśāstra*'s theoretical tactics about causing dissension, *bheda upāya*, demonstrate that one can also increase or leverage power and control to one's advantage by provoking rifts in relationships (*bheda*). The *upāya* principle of *bheda* uses dialogues of nefarious sorts to alienate persons from one another (9.5.28). Also highly intersubjective in nature, a skilful tactician of *bheda* lays dialogic traps to discern one's inner thoughts (9.5.27), or whispers secretly to sow distrust (9.5.28).[22] I discuss in detail instigating whispers such as as these in the next section. For now, to summarize, it is evident from the *sāma* and *bheda* examples alone that the exercise of the *upāya*s involves manipulating the bonds of royal relationships, but around different strategic aims. The *upāya* of enticing into beneficial alliance through gifts (*dāna*) can be in the service of either *sāma* or *bheda* tactics (or both). Finally, when applications of these three more intersubjective *upāya* have not succeeded, the text recommends a concerted use of coercion or force (*daṇḍa*).

Functionally related to these *upāya*s, the six *guṇa*s (*ṣaḍguṇa*) also are important means for creating and managing relationships, but of relationships with external and more formidable foes and allies.[23] These six are: dual-policy, peace-making, war, mobilizing forces, lying in wait, and seeking asylum. Together, the six *guṇa*s and *upāya* are the foundational structure of the *Arthaśāstra*'s conception of royal advisory means and strategies. Like the four *upāya*, each of the six *guṇa* consists of a dynamic repertoire of behaviours that can involve political and economic ploys, as well as psychological, familial and other social levers to achieve the particular aim (peace-making, war, asylum, etc.). The means and conditions for using these strategies are complex, and thus beyond the scope of this study. Nevertheless, the narrative impress of them is compelling: the *Arthaśāstra* dedicates all of Book 7 to them; the *Dharmaśāstra* of Manu redacts the same expedients (*MDh*, 7.160–80) into a précis of recommended tactics for kings. The *Pañcatantra* dedicates entire books to discussion of the *upāya* and contains dialogues where would be masters of these tactics discuss the benefits and risks of employing them (of which only three open the door to wisdom, as in *Pañcatantra* I.134).[24] Each text shares a foundational element – reliance on deceptive tactics in relational settings.

Its sheer ubiquity may be the reason for the inclusion of deception as a 'fifth type of strategy' in the *Pañcatantra* (III.56–57), even though 'not mentioned by the authors of

---

21 *Aś* 9.6.21, Sanskrit from GRETIL, accessed 13 August 2012.

22 The *bheda upāya* also figures prominently in the *MUJā*, as we shall see below.

23 The six *guṇa* according to Hartmut Scharfe's study of Kauṭilya's use of the *guṇa* are particularly to manage the 'circle of kings'. Hartmut Scharfe, *Investigations in Kauṭalya's Manual of Political Science*, 2nd ed. (Wiesbaden, 1993), pp. 107–8.

24 See Olivelle's translation of *Pañcatantra* for this use of the three, which excludes the fourth, force (*daṇḍa*).

authoritative texts'.[25] Considering the *Pañcatantra*'s use of deceits outside of 'authoritative texts', and the deceptions inherent in *upāya* tactics in the *Arthaśāstra* as well as the inclusion of them within Manu's text together, all suggest that royal reliance on deceptive tactics were necessary. Perhaps this necessity explains the inclusion of the *upāyas* within the constraints of Manu's *Dharmaśāstra* – an inclusion that gives Manu a narrative say in how the *upāyas* and *guṇas* should be used. Encompassing royal tactics into its fold also gives Manu its say in how the relationship between the king and *brāhmaṇa* should proceed and the varieties of 'cultured' *brāhmaṇa*, the śiṣṭa as the proper *brāhmaṇa*, on whom a king should rely.[26]

The *Arthaśāstra* addresses the risk of reliance posed to the king (primarily) by means of contrived relational settings. An examination of these testing contrivances, the *upadhās*, will bring to light the relationship between deception and trust, which affects dialogues between a king and his trusted deceivers. Moreover, since these examples show other kinds of uses of the nonverbal predicates of dialogue, they provide an additional basis for understanding the testing dialogues and innerlogues around wisdom (and its use with integrity) in the *Mahā Ummagga Jātaka*.

Upadhā Modes of Discerning Integrity: Contrived Dialogic Tests and Deceptive Tactics

As I suggested earlier, in moments involving counsel especially, kings and royal associates are at risk while engaged in dialogues, in spite of the cooperative nature of their relationships at court. We saw that communications can go awry among king and courtiers and secret counsel can be exposed nonverbally. Relying on nonverbal predicates of dialogue seems to heighten the potential for risk; for checking the meaning of nonverbal signs does not appear as straightforward as in verbal dimensions of dialogue. The risks involved in royal dialogue makes evident the need for caution and control; but the risks do not explain the extent of suspicion inherent in the king's test question with which I opened this chapter.

This suspicion is heightened by the paradox of a king's need to trust members of court to carry out his commands and aims and his knowledge that he can be deceived at the hands of the men in whom he places this trust. For instance, in the *Mahābhārata*, the elder Bhīṣma states: 'Trusting anyone absolutely leads to the complete annihilation of one's dharma and success, while never trusting anyone is no different than death' (*MBh*, 12.81.10).[27] Nevertheless, three chapters later, after having explained to king Yudhiṣṭhira the basic truth and meaning of royal teachings, Bhīṣma relates that he has also 'declared this highest secret – kings' never trusting anyone'.[28]

Embracing the vagaries of royal trust, the *Arthaśāstra* attempts to provide some basis through which to prove trustworthiness. Paradoxically, the earliest instances of deceptive tactics in the *Arthaśāstra* occur in the tests designed to investigate the extent of a man's trustworthiness. These are structured test scenarios (*upadhā*) enacted through appeals to

---

[25] *Pañcatantra*, tr. Olivelle, p. 122. Olivelle also suggests the 'central' argument of the *Pañcatantra* is that 'craft and deception' are foundational to the science of rule (ibid., p. xxxv).

[26] Manu stratifies *brāhmaṇa* attainments for kings to consult. See *MDh*, 7.57–8 (*viśiṣṭa*) and 12.109 (*śiṣṭa*) for some examples.

[27] Bhīṣma speaking to Yudhiṣṭhira; *Mahābhārata: Book 11 The Book of the Women, Book 12 The Book of Peace, Part I*, vol. 7, tr. James L. Fitzgerald (Chicago and London, 2004), p. 372.

[28] *Mahabharata*, tr. Fitzgerald, p. 387.

reputation, affection, and power within seditious dialogues designed to prove – in certain circumscribed areas at least – a man could be trusted not to deceive the king. Moreover, these *upadhā* are meant to determine not just that the one being tested can be trusted not to deceive the king, but also that he could/can be trusted to be able to deceive effectively on behalf of the king. These dynamics of tests of trust (and the directions deception should take) are well illustrated by the Bodhisatta Mahosadha's actions in the *MUJā*, as we shall see.

Of course, elements of the nonverbal predicates of dialogue that I have discussed are at play in more complex ways in these *upadhā*. Thus, the *Arthaśāstra* devotes an entire chapter of its first book (*Aś*, 1.10) to the tests of the 'integrity' (*śuciḥ*) of royal associates. These tests are carried out 'by means of dissimulations' or 'by testing schemes' (*upadhābhiḥ*), of which there are four contextual scenarios: the test of *dharma* (religious or ritual propriety); the test of *artha* (wealth); the test of *kāma* (desire); the test of *bhaya* (fear).[29] While a detailed examination of these tests is beyond our scope here, a brief discussion of the scheme designed to test *dharma* should bring the trust and deception dynamic into view.[30] In addition to the *dharma* scheme, the *artha* scheme (enacted through the king's advisor in charge of war activities or 'commander of army', the *senāpati*) should provide some context for the machinations of Senaka to protect his relationship to and power gained through Vedeha, the king who trusts him as his *paṇḍita*, his wise sage, in *MUJā*. Although there are many thematic corollaries between *Arthaśāstra* testing schemes (*upadhā*) and deceptions and those carried out by trusted persons in the *MUJā*, the *dharma* and *artha* schemes resonate most with the theme of 'trusted deceiver'.

The *dharmopadhā* scheme (*Aś*, 1.10.2–4) is designed to prove how a minister (*amātya*, *amacca* in Pāli) will behave in contexts involving *dharma*. The aim of this *upadhā* is to flush out men who would violate their obligations to the king in order to protect their sense of obligations to *dharma* in this context and the priest. Even though this testing scheme invokes dharmic obligations and boundaries, the man being tested must demonstrate that he would put his loyalty to the king *before* dharmic concerns. This conception of the order of dharmic obligation stands in stark relief to the hierarchy of priorities that the *Arthaśāstra* accords them earlier in the text. Nevertheless, the test of integrity in the *dharmopadhā* above presumes that the king is capable of disregarding these very ideals.

This conception of loyalty to king versus *dharma* echoes the suspicion that the *Śāntiparvan* conveys (in its royal śāstric mode as teacher of *rājadharma*) about royal friendships (*MBh*, 12.81.4–5): The friend who would put *dharma* first is not fully to be trusted.

The *Arthaśāstra* also contrives a testing scheme with respect to the allure of wealth or material gain (*arthopadhā*). The scheme offers significant gains for aligning with the commander of the army (*senāpati*) against the king. Importantly, the *upadhā* uses the subject's trust in the commander as a basis for the deception. In this test, the king dismisses the commander for having supported someone unfit (*asat-pragraheṇa*) for duty (*Aś*, 1.10.5). The commander then proceeds to instigate through the whispers of his expert agents – ministers who might be turned to traitors against the king over the *senāpati*'s

---

[29] *dharmopadhā* (Aś 1.10 vv. 2–4), *arthopadhā* (vv. 5–6), *kāmopadhā* (vv. 7–8) and *bhayopadhā* (vv. 9–12) respectively.

[30] I discuss these tests, the conditions of trust necessary for successfully deceiving, and the dangers of using deception (*Aś* 1.10.17–19) – all elements of the dialectic of trust and deception – in my PhD dissertation, 'The Eyes of Power and Dharma: Conceptions of the Advisor in Early India', Emory University, 2013.

dismissal. In general, this ruse presumes to entrap a dishonest minister on two fronts: the first, by drawing on his relationship with the commander (*senāpati*) and testing his loyalty to the king over the general.

The nonverbal predicates of trust at play in the testing scenarios above include social position (knowledge of intimacy with the king, trust and reliance on the status and power the *senāpati* might have had with the test subject) and intersubjective realities (human understanding of the emotions that a dismissed powerful man might have and the actions these might provoke). In the discussion of nonverbal predicates that follow, trust necessarily takes the lead in initiating dialogic encounters, since contact occurs between religious figures and the subjects of a king's realm that come to these figures for help. This point of intersection between a religious field of merit like a wandering sage and the person who acknowledges and relies on his power is another important fulcrum of royal deceptive tactics. I refer to the dimensions of trust that persons grant to the authority on which a religious specialist relies as he whispers words of rebellion into the ears of recalcitrant monks, or appeals to the friendly connection he may have with the king or other royal agent to make himself credible enough – trusted enough to deceive.

Trusted Deceivers in a Royal Realm 'At Large'

In this section, I discuss the deceptive communications and uses of trust at the macro-level – the royal machinations set to extend throughout and to the borders of a king's realm – as suggested in the *Arthaśāstra.* These examples implicate accomplished religious figures known in Indic culture, such as wandering ascetics and students gathered around renunciant teachers. Moreover, these examples point to some specifics of the royal imaginary of deception (especially regarding renunciants) with which the rhetoric of the *MUJā* indicates it must contend.

The deceptions in these scenarios are complex moments of verbal (direct and indirect) and nonverbal dialogic encounter. Their purpose throughout is to authenticate as veritable and trustworthy persons posing as religious figures, even as they are acting deceptively on behalf of the king's power. The means by which this aim of preserving and enhancing the king's power include the following repertoire of dialogic expression, including not only explicit moments of dialogic encounter (both direct speech and indirect 'whispers', as the *Arthaśāstra* states) but more importantly, a repertoire of nonverbal dialogic predicates (e.g., the wearing of ascetic garb and the bodily – gestural expressions expected of persons of religious power and position) that confirm the trust that makes effective the explicit dialogic expressions in which these deceivers engage. The tactics of these deceivers (as theorized in the *Arthaśāstra*) and their narrative depictions (which we will see in the *MUJā*) illustrate how social trust and deception contribute to each other.

The tactics rely on an integrated system of local, at large agents and pathways of communications between them that lead up to those who are manipulating tactics at the macro level (those that comprise the trusted royal circle around the king). Thus, the *Arthaśāstra* hypothesizes in painstaking detail a net of royal associates that are imperative to creating and maintaining the king's power and authority. The creation of this web or net involves manipulation and display of royal power gained through royal consecration, intertwined with power articulated through the espionage of the illusion-making of religious specialists, or those who wear the disguise of religious specialists and mendicants.

Royal power is thus predicated on powers associated with religious roles, which in turn are empowered by and through bonds with other social roles. The king and his closest advisors orchestrate these activities – publically and secretly – to substantiate the king's power and the perception of the king as ultimate master of his realm. There are stationary spies and those who rove about the kingdom (1.12.1–5), those who are traders (1.11.11–12, 15), shaven or matted haired ascetics (1.11.13), apostate recluses (1.11.4–7), female wanderers and female shaven haired ascetics (1.12.4–5), female mendicants (1.12.13–14), students and householders (1.11.2), and farmers (1.11.9); these are the most familiar of many.[31]

The king and his agents cast a wide net of informants, each in their kind possessing just as expansive a collection of expertise that relies on the nonverbal predicates of trust and the dialogues various trusts cultivate. Since the text suggests that no region or person is to be left unobserved (even the king's closest advisors), no social role is to be devoid of its spies.

The Marks of Authority

Spies are hypothesized to engage in the structured life activities (*āśramas*) or social groups (*varṇas*) that comprise the normal constituency of persons in the kingdoms described in the *Arthaśāstra*. The normalcy of these roles only better enables the spies to help the king create a broad presence and web of observation. Once in place, the spies – directed by the king and his ministers and advisors – are set to play on the expectations that royal subjects have about the roles the spies assume.

The religious roles of the renunciant (*pravrajita*) and the wandering mendicant (*parivrājika*) in addition to the social expectations that accompany them create and substantiate the credibility and efficacy of royal spies more than any other social role. These figures must have been perceived as carrying more advantages to royal deception in their functions than others, for they appear most frequently in the *Arthaśāstra* as agents of espionage and divisive subterfuge. As we shall see, the *MUJā* demonstrates its dialogic engagement with the *Arthaśāstra* by its narrative focus on these sorts of figures and their work. It takes artifice to create the illusion of being veritable religious figures, but it also requires the inherent socio-religious constraints (or credible freedom from restraint) on such persons in their roles as well.

For the ways in which his role leaves him unconstrained by obligations of place and family, the wandering religious mendicant is in a special position to perform reconnaissance for the king. For the one who has left behind the renunciant life, the marks and function of his lifestyle become powerful tools for ensnaring other mendicants to the king's service. The complex predicates and dimensions of dialogue – nonverbal and verbal – will become clear as we proceed through the recommendations of the *Arthaśāstra*:

> One who has renounced renunciant life, and endowed with intelligence and integrity is the apostate monk (*udāsthitaḥ*). Equipped with plenty of money and assistants, he should get work done in a place assigned for the practice of some occupation. (1.11.4–5)[32]

---

[31] Olivelle also provides a taxonomy of these roles in his annotated translation of the *Aś*, pp. xv–xvi.

[32] Adapted from *Kauṭilīya Arthaśāstra*, ed. R.P. Kangle, Part 1, A Critical Edition with a Glossary (Delhi, 1988). Part 2, Translation and Introduction, 2nd ed. (Bombay, 1972). Part 3 (Delhi: Motilal Banarsidass, 1988).

These are nonverbal predicates that communicate the authenticity of this spy (and basis for trust) to the subjects of the deception. Reading further into this section:

> From the profits of this work, he should provide all wanderers with food, clothing and residence. And to those among them who seek such a livelihood, he should secretly propose (*upajapet*): 'In this very garb, you should work in the interest of the king and present yourself here at the time of meals and payment'. And all wandering monks should make similar secret proposals in their respective orders. (1.11.6 – 8)[33]

The obviously dialogic dimensions are directed at creating the authenticity of these spies by having them engage in work that would be expected of persons in the roles they are playing. However, since the trusted deceivers' work is in the service of the royal web or reconnaissance and espionage, dialogue is instigative by means of the role they play. Kings and their closest agents approve of this kind of deception on the part of their trusted deceivers. Regarding specifically the 'garb' they use to authenticate themselves as we shall see, is the element of disguise the Bodhisatta Mahosadha uses, but to a different end in the *MUJā.*

This position of the stationary mendicant spy (*udāsthitaḥ*) is to be filled by one who is has left behind the renunciant life. As the *Arthaśāstra* goes on to construct the role above, this spy's primary usefulness to the king is to enlist other mendicants to act in the same way. In the passage above, this former renunciant spy is to provide food, clothing and shelter to all mendicants (*sarva-pravrajitānām*). In this way he acts as a householder, serving mendicants by feeding them as they make their begging rounds. However, even as he feeds them, the mendicant spy is surveying the other wandering renunciants (*pravrajitā*) to serve as possible secret agents.

Communications conveyed through whispers (indirect speech) are as powerful as direct dialogic speech. The surreptitious recruitment of future spies involves dialogue, albeit secretive and instigative in nature. The *Arthaśāstra* uses the Sanskrit verb, *upajap* 'to whisper (into someone's ear)', which stresses the sneaky, dangerously intimate, sideways dialogue through which royal instigators communicate. The text suggests the mendicant should secretly propose (*upajapet*): 'In this very garb, you should work in the interest of the king and present yourself here at the time of meals and payment' (1.11.7). All wandering monks (*sarva-pravrajitāś*) should make secret proposals (*upajapeyuḥ*) in the same way to respective orders (*svaṃ vargam*) (v. 8). This term occurs in the sense of 'whispering to instigate rebellion or sedition' in the *Śāntiparvan* of the *Mahābhārata*, Manu, and the *Kāthāsaritsāgara* (MW 198A). Given that the former wandering mendicant is doing this to lure other renunciants into the king's service, it is appropriate to understand 'whispering to rebellion' as the sense conveyed in the *Arthaśāstra* as well. Presumably, this spy only engages in such destructive whispering to those he judges to be like him, those 'desiring subsistence' (*vṛttikāmān*).

Nonverbal cues are as important to these deceptions as are mendicant whisperings. Wandering monks are to retain their mendicant garb, even though they are no longer really mendicants, and by means of these marks, act as spies. The text suggests that these spies should work to bring about the king's aims (*rājārthaś caritavyo*) 'by means of this same garment' (*etenaiva veṣeṇa*). In other words, the garment that they had worn as an ascetic devoted to the renunciant lifestyle would be the garb that they retain. *Veṣa* can mean

---

[33] Adapted from ibid.

merely, 'dress, apparel, ornament, artificial exterior, or assumed appearance' (*MW* 1019B). In the context of a garment used to signal a role which these renunciants no longer live, the stress should be placed on the assumed appearance. Therefore, the individuals that the mendicant spy has turned from religious renunciation to espionage retain their appearance of wandering mendicants, although now they wear their robes in order to deceive. Their cloaks communicate to those who understand their significance that these mendicants are moving about from dwelling to dwelling to receive offerings. Unknown, however, is that these mendicants are at the same time performing reconnaissance for royals.

The wandering ascetics' authenticity is predicated on more than ascetic robes. Because of the power and authority of the role, the wearing of the robes and the *bearing* of the person in them, is a form of nonverbal dialogic expression. Authority and marks of role, robe and bearing – all these communicate that the ascetic is to be trusted. An enemy's trust in the powers that mendicants are perceived to possess is also crucial. Thus, conventional perceptions that a person can cultivate merit by feeding wandering ascetics substantiate their efficacy as 'trusted deceivers'. The religious illusions the *Arthaśāstra* suggests mendicant spies orchestrate can only be effective if the enemy of the king has trust in the veracity of *nāgas* (snake deities), omens, sacred trees, astrologers, all-knowing sages and divine image. The text assumes that this kind of trust can be utilized to an enemy's disadvantage. A mendicant's social position gives his or her robes the power to instigate and gather information in innocence, banking on social trust in their role.

Hermits and wandering ascetics are conceived as having considerable connections of influence with the public, royal officers and rival kings. The power of the matted-haired ascetic to serve the king derives as much from his religious functions as from the secrecy kept over his relationship to the court. The spread of the net of espionage did not know the bounds of gender: even wandering female mendicants could be in collusion with kings, queens and their mutual rivals. The extent of religious specialist involvement in the system of surveillance as the *Arthaśāstra* imagines them is remarkable. The mechanisms of trust and deceit that the *Arthaśāstra* imagines for mendicant spies provide a basis from which to consider uses of trust and deception, as well as the valence of trusted persons and trusted deceivers in the *Mahā Ummagga Jātaka*. This is of utmost importance to the *MUJā*, because the ultimate trusted deceiver turns out to be the Bodhisatta Mahosadha.

Following the advice of the *Arthaśāstra*, royal advisors and agents that understand and know how to use the various strategies of *artha* could infiltrate royal courts of traitors and enemies (*Aś*, 9.6.34–41) in order to sow dissension from within (*Aś*, 9.6.50–51). If we bring the narrative machinations of the *MUJā* into consideration, close advisors like the *paṇḍita* Senaka use deceptive tactics against personal enemies at court. A deceiver can use the disguises of another social role to communicate and augment trustworthiness in the service of deceit. Nonverbal signs such as smiles, emotional connection and familiarity also communicate one's aims in dialogues with kings and courtiers – these communications can deceive as well as aid kings.

Upāya and Its Hierarchical Limits

A final word about the use of tricky tactics by trusted servants and trusted deceivers is necessary before proceeding to the comparative analysis of the *MUJā*. With every royal tactic or *upāya* – however expertly executed – Brahmanical and Buddhist texts devoted to royal concerns, narratively at least, attest to the riskiness of applying the *upāya*. For instance, concomitant to the *Arthaśāstra*'s discussion of tactics designed to serve the manipulation of relationships of advantage or disadvantage, is the text's revelation that certain risk situations (*āpadaḥ*) can arise from the use of royal relationships: 'Such are the risks; here is how to overcome them'(*ity āpadaḥ; tāsāṃ siddhiḥ;* Aś, 9.7.67). The text demonstrates uncanny confidence in the repertoires associated with the four *upāya* 'tactics' to overcome them before moving to the particular methods of which it discusses (*Aś*, 9.7.67–75).

The hierarchy of application associated with the four *upāya*, with which we are now more familiar, is worth noting. While the discussion in the *Arthaśāstra* of these methods of mitigating these dangers is beyond the scope of our discussion, briefly noting the text's concern with these dangers provides some necessary context for going forward into considering the various strategies (*upāya* in general, and *upāya* used as *upadhā*) of trusted servants and trusted deceivers in the *Mahā-Ummagga-Jātaka* (*MUJā*). The *Arthaśāstra* suggests that one assesses and orchestrates *upāya* through the degree of intimacy one may possess in relation to a king.

As we shall see below in the *MUJā*, the Bodhisatta Mahosadha, as the son of a powerful merchant (*seṭṭhi*, Pāli in the *jātaka*), resides at this level of remove from the king. The links between the hierarchy of use of the *upāya* and the extent of relationality with the king are clear. This example also demonstrates that risks were presumed to exist, from relationships of closest intimacy with a king, outward to the leaders in the closest of circles of social positions around a king, to the various leaders working with and through him in his realm.

Going forward into analysis of the *MUJā*, the *Arthaśāstra*'s situational and hierarchical links of *upāya* to the degree of royal relationship in particular give us a conceptual index for the sense of risk exhibited in the narrative dialogues of the *MUJā*. At the apparently dialogic level, these are the king's concerns with the trustworthiness of the Bodhisatta, Mahosadha, the newest wise man (*paṇḍita*) to enter the royal fold (*rājakula* in the text) as well as the king's unrelenting concern to test and prove the wisdom of his courtly sages. The indications of a presumed atmosphere of royal deception or 'royal imaginary of deceit or deception' – as I will call this habitus of trust, deception and the recursive nature of dialogues in creating this trust/deception dialectic – will become clear. My discussion of the nonverbal predicates of dialogue in the *Arthaśāstra* above should help us understand the various non-apparent dimensions of dialogue depicted among sages, kings and the Bodhisatta, the Buddha-to-be, in the *MUJā*. In the end, we will see that this royal imaginary of deception shapes the manner in which this Buddhist text imagines dialogic moments and relationships at court and drives the *MUJā*'s particular arguments about being a wise person and the very exercise of such wisdom. The text is concerned not just to demonstrate the perfection of the Buddha's wisdom in the *jātaka*, but to go beyond royal and Brahmanical arguments about the nature of wisdom, to set important limits on the ways in which a sage uses wisdom within the royal imaginary of deception.

Jātaka Dialogic Predicates of Trust and Deception and their Inversions

The rhetoric and scenarios of rule in Buddhist texts portray the deceit inherent in royal relationships and the pragmatics of rule enacted through them. Overall, advisors and ministers in Buddhist *Nikāyas* are imagined as either dissimulating sycophants in service of a king, or thieving drains on frontier Buddhist communities and royal treasuries. If these agents happen to be *brāhmaṇa* they possess little of the exemplary qualities typical of them in Brahmanical texts. Thus, according to *Jātaka* conceptions of them, a king's advisors, ministers and their minions typically are a negative force; either leading kings astray or using deception to bring kings to power.[34]

The *Mahā Ummagga Jātaka* (*MUJā*) enters the royal imaginary of deceit and uses iconic royal arts of rule (*nīti* or *kṣatravidyā*) to transform artful or deceitful stratagems to reflect the Bodhisatta's mastery over Brahmanical and / or *rājanya* ideals of action. The *upāya* of Mahosadha within the royal imaginary of the *MUJā* stands in dharmic contrast to powerful *brāhmaṇas'* predilections to *upāya* that use deception and tricks of wisdom to serve their own ends, not just the aims of their king. At least, such is the argument of *jātaka* that seek to prove the supremacy of the Buddha *dharma*, like the *MUJā*. In order to prove this supremacy, such narratives must inhabit the deceptive culture of influence presented above, and yet its exercise of idealized actions must keep some kind of remove from the ways in which advisors like Senaka use tricks and illusions.

As will unfold in the discussion below, the *MUJā* anticipates and engages Brahmanically idealized actions rooted in śāstric methods of mediating royal power. The text's narrative aim is evident in its frame-story – to demonstrate the supremacy of the Bodhisatta in crushing 'heretical doctrines', and converting *brāhmaṇas*, śramaṇas and *devas* with his superior wisdom.[35] His superior wisdom is agonistic – demonstrated and construed through the royal idiom of wisdom tests and taunts from king and his Brahmanical advisors. Through the course of this *jātaka*, the Bodhisatta Mahosadha, the son of a wealthy merchant (*seṭṭhi*) and householder (*gahapati*), becomes a close advisor to two intimately connected kings, Vedeha, king of Mithilā, and Cūḷani Brahmadatta, king of Pañcāla. Mahosadha acts like other clever advisors in the tale (four referred to as *paṇḍita*, one as *brāhmaṇa*) – who use the means of *sāma upāya* – to create encounters and connections between these kings; first through enmity, then through marriage alliance. The narrative turns to contra relationship tactics, *bheda upāya*, machinations of these kings' trusted advisors that encompass an extensive narrative trajectory in the *MUJā*. Within this trajectory, the *MUJā* renders a Bodhisatta Mahosadha with the skills of a Kauṭilyan expert in *artha*, who uses means that stop just short of success for success' sake and harm to others.

Therefore, the focus is on examples that illuminate the shared imagination of espionage and trickery that imbue multiple types of relationship in narratives construed for and through the royal idiom. The markers of this shared imagination are nonverbal communication (gestures), innerlogue, cloaked or deceptive speech and like measures that are instrumental to the dialogues that make and break connections among royals and other strategic relationships of rule, and the continual wisdom and integrity tests necessary to having continued relationship with kings.

Upāya in the *MUJā*

Buddhist narratives demonstrate some facility, if not intimacy, with all dimensions of the four *upāya* and six *guṇa*, deceptive and otherwise. However, it must be stressed that the sense of *upāya* wielded by the Bodhisatta/Buddha Śākyamuni in these *jātaka* tales is very different than the concept of *upāya* that becomes so important to *Mahāyāna*

---

[34] See *Mahāsīlava-Jātaka* (No. 51), as only one of many examples.

[35] *Jā* 6, p. 156. Parenthetical references in the body of the text are to Cowell and Childers' translation of the Pāli text, unless otherwise indicated. Fausbøll's edition of the Pāli text page numbers are enclosed in square brackets [...] in the notes.

textual production.[36] It may surprise some readers to see *upāya* involving skilful tricks or deceptions in textual *Nikāyas* not usually associated with *Mahāyāna* Buddhist traditions. In the *MUJā*, *upāya* occurs in its generic sense of 'tactic' or 'strategy', in addition to compound references as 'constructive tactic' (*upāyakusalo*), wielded by royal advising sages (*paṇḍitas* and *brāhmaṇas*) in positions of trust with kings at courtly scenarios. For instance, a *brāhmaṇa* advisor named Kevaṭṭa in another court declares the city of Mithilā as unassailable 'because of Mahosadha's wisdom, since he is a skilled tactician' (*evaṁ paññāya sampanno upāyakusalo*).[37] Kevaṭṭa himself is 'adept' in *upāya*.[38]

Pāli *Jātaka* such as the *MUJā* that depict advising scenarios have yet other *upāya* in mind – those that *khattiyas*, *brāhmaṇas* and *seṭṭhis* in the *MUJā*, kings, priests and leading merchants deploy for influence and power. An example from the *Taccha Sūkara Jātaka* (No. 492) claims that an elder forest-dwelling monk, Dhanuggaha-tissa, was 'an expert in strategy' in both the birth story (*atītavatthu*) and the narrative historical present of Buddha (*paccuppannavatthu*) in the frame story. The monk suggests an 'arrow' battle array and digging of trenches that echo the *guṇas* of mobilizing forces and going to war.[39] These Buddhist texts presume that advisors and kings know and use these pragmatic systems of influence and power. Non-Buddhist strategies of influence and royal success, the *upāyas* and *guṇas*, are referred to as *nīti* or *kṣatravidyā* and *rājaśāstra* or *arthaśāstra*. These terms are Buddhist *Nikāya* tropes for strategic means that are harmful and in need of transformation by Buddhist teachings or *dharma*.

Proof Tests of the Presaged: Dialogue and Innerlogue around Mahosadha

The tests of character in the *Arthaśāstra* give us some framework in which to consider other narratives that test for deceivers and trusted close advisors who may be likely to deceive, as they appear in the *MUJā*. When we enter the *MUJā*, the trustworthiness of Senaka and his fellow *paṇḍita* associates is presumed. That the king has bestowed trust and the regular access to dialogue with him that follows on trust is indicated in the opening sequence of the text. Senaka, the most revered of four *paṇḍitas* to the king, is shown with the others coming to the king's inner chambers as part of daily conversations with him (*MUJā*, 156–7). Then the king Vedeha tells of his portentous dream of four pillars of fire, which are exceeded by a larger fifth pillar of fire. The king calls on Senaka to interpret the dream, which he does by the 'power of his supernatural attainments', *sippabalena*.[40] With his divine eye (*dibbacakkhunā*), Senaka interprets the dream that presages the replacement of Senaka and his fellow sages by a fifth sage (a yet unborn Bodhisatta Mahosadha).

Nevertheless, in spite of this prediction the Bodhisatta must prove that he is trustworthy to the king. King Vedeha's belief in Mahosadha's trustworthiness is mercurial. This indicates, as shown in the *Arthaśāstra* examples, concern over incipient or inevitable deception. King Vedeha's trust attachments to his other *paṇḍita* advisers at this point are not as tenuous

[36] For a discussion of how *upāya* functions in particular Mahāyāna contexts see Michael Pye, *Skilful Means: A Concept in Mahayana Buddhism* (London, 2003).

[37] *Jātaka*, ed. Fausbøll [393.22].

[38] Ibid. [393.24].

[39] *Jātaka or Stories of the Buddha's Former Births*, ed. E.B. Cowell (6 vols, Oxford, Reprint, 1995), vol. 5, p. 219–20.

[40] *Jātaka*, ed. Fausbøll [330.26].

as his trust in the newcomer, Mahosadha. Rather, King Vedeha's attachment to his wise advisers is firm when we enter the narrative – until Mahosadha arrives, the fifth flame from the prophecy that will exceed all the royal wise men. This prophecy of a future *paṇḍita* that will exceed the wisdom (and the exercise of it in royal tactics) of Senaka and the rest of the royal *paṇḍitas* provides the interpretive frame for Senaka and his machinations to maintain his intimacy and influence with the king that make him as a trusted deceiver.

At the beginning of his service to King Vedeha, the Bodhisatta Mahosadha must contend with deceptive sages (directed against him, as newcomer) in King Vedeha's court. Recalling what we know of trust / deception problems in the *Arthaśāstra*, these sages are threatened by Mahosadha's wisdom and the primary place of relationship with the king that this wisdom may gain. Senaka – the wisest and also the most intimate of the king's four *paṇḍitās* ('sages') – tests Mahosadha's wisdom and right to be called a sage'.[41] On the surface of things, Senaka is testing the Bodhisatta's fitness to serve as advisor to his king. But, as suggested above, secretly, the *paṇḍita* Senaka is using these tests to prevent Mahosadha's coming to court because he fears being replaced as close advisor, as he states to himself: 'From the time of his coming I shall lose all my glory and the king will forget my existence' (*MUJā*, 160).

The king questions Senaka regarding Mahosadha. At the end of the questions (all designed to prove whether Mahosadha is a *paṇḍita*), since the king was pleased by the demonstrations of Mahosadha's wisdom, he asked:

> 'Well, Senaka, shall we send for the sage?' But Senaka, grudging [Mahosadha's] prosperity, said, 'That is not all that makes a sage; wait'. On hearing this, the king thought: 'The sage Mahosadha was wise even as a child, and took my fancy. In all these mysterious tests and counter-quips he has given answers like a Buddha. Yet such a wise man as this Senaka will not let me summon him to my side. What care I for Senaka? I will bring the man here.' (*MUJā*, 169)

The innerlogue of the king shows that he is now becoming suspicious of Senaka, or at least willing to go around Senaka's advice in order to bring a wiser sage to his court. More important for our reading of the dialogic here, the text uses both the dialogue between Senaka and the king, and their 'innerlogue' to show their changing relationship of trust (leading to deception).

The king having taken this course of action, Senaka entered the presence of the king and said:

> 'Sire, did you go to the East Market-town to bring the sage back?' 'Yes, sir,' said the king. 'Sire', said Senaka, 'you make me as one of no account. I begged you to wait awhile; but off you went in a hurry, and at the outset your royal horse broke his leg'. The king had nothing to say to this. (*MUJā*, 169)

Here, Senaka appears to be interpreting the broken leg of the horse as an omen, which he connects to the king having gone against his advice: 'You make me as one of no account.'

---

[41] This subtext (of many) provides an opportunity for the Bodhisatta to prove his superior wisdom, as he cleverly resolves eighteen challenges to his wisdom (*MUJā*, 160–69), most of which involve adjudicating community disputes over theft of property (such as the god Sakka's theft of a chariot), and family (as in the case of two men claiming the same wife).

The king's silence reads like an assent to Senaka's assertion. The rhetorical action in the dialogue is one of rebuke, which invokes Senaka's idea of the normal predicates of relationship between a *paṇḍita* and king: Senaka's status and the king's taking of his advice. Scheming, Senaka delays the king calling Mahosadha a bit longer, and allows him to use the accident and delay as a means to construct yet another deceptive test of Mahosadha.

Nonverbal Predicates of Dialogue and Trustworthiness in the *MUJā*

> On another day [the king] asked Senaka, 'Shall we send for the sage, Senaka?' 'If so, your majesty don't go yourself but send a messenger, saying "O sage! As I was on my way to fetch you my horse broke his leg: send us a better horse and a more excellent one." If he takes the first alternative he will come himself, if the second he will send his father. Then will be a problem to test him.' (*MUJā*, 169)

In the quotation above, we see Senaka intends to trap Mahosadha into responding to the king's summons of him through actions to show father/son respect or to show respect and honor to the king who summoned Mahosadha. As Senaka contrives it, 'the problem to test him' is designed to elicit more than one moral obligation at the same time, as a trap. This is a similar synchronic convergence of more than one dharmic obligation observed in the *Arthaśāstra*'s test of *dharmopadhā*. As Senaka seems to envision it, either option will expose a flaw in Mahosadha's wisdom and judgment: He will either favour the king (but not his father) or his father (but not the king).

> The sage on hearing the summons recognized that the king wished to see himself and his father. So, he went to his father, and said greeting him, 'Father, the king wishes to see you and me. You go first … The king will speak kindly to you, and offer you a householder's seat; take it and sit down. When you are seated, I will come; the king will speak kindly to me and offer me such another seat. Then I will look at you; take the cue and say, rising from your seat, Son Mahosadha the wise, take this seat. Then the question will be ripe for solution.' (*MUJā* 169–70)

In this dialogue with his father, the Bodhisatta Mahosadha shows he has understood and anticipated the mechanism of the test as Senaka constructed it. Mahosadha's directions to his father demonstrate that he is one step ahead (at least) of Senaka – another dimension of the *MUJā*'s argument about the superiority of his wisdom and his mastery of royal tactics and the expert use of both.

Mahosadha's restatement of 'the question' (posed by Senaka) stresses the counter tactic inherent in his instruction to his father: 'the question will be ripe for solution'. The tactic is multifaceted. It evokes the dialogic nature of bodily position with respect to powerful figures; of gestures of affection, honor or respect. Mahosadha is rising to meet the challenge of Senaka's test, which involves an instrumental use of honor and affection, in order to prove one's grasp of (or flush out ignorance about) the importance of these particular intersubjective dimensions of relationships. He does so using the courtly lexicon of honour and respect we observed above in the *Arthaśāstra*'s instructions to the new courtier (*anujīvin*) (5.4–5). This testing exchange – and the behaviour of those depicted in the dialogues in response to this test – is a key proof of the communicative power of the nonverbal predicates of dialogue. By this deceptive change in the seating, Mahosadha has demonstrated his knowledge of courtly protocol and tactics, and he has begun to demonstrate his superiority to Senaka's knowledge (and his selfish motives). At the same time he has demonstrated proper respect both to his father and the king, thus escaping the entrapment of Senaka's test of moral obligations and social loyalties.

Return to the Question: King Vedeha's Tests of His Sages

For all the tactical challenges and concerns that revolve around royal dialogue, trust and deception examined thus far, the *MUJā* plays with all these in King Vedeha's riddling question about the unlikely relationship he observed between the goat and the dog that provoked the king's test question (with which I began this chapter). The *MUJā* narratively employs tactics observed in *Arthaśāstra* to demonstrate the Bodhisatta's unfolding mastery in this realm. More areas of integrity than the four indicated in the *Arthaśāstra* tests are desired at court, if we consider the test question of Vedeha. The *Mahā-Ummagga-jātaka* engages in similar tests as in the *Arthaśāstra*, although the *jātaka* includes extensive tests of wisdom as essential to being in relationship with the king. Tests of wisdom or displays of wisdom provide the basis of relational power at court – because it is the power of wisdom that is the axial way to dialogue with the king. As such, the power of wisdom is also the power of continued relationship and influence with the king.

This scenario begins not with one advisor testing another, as we have seen so far, but rather with the king testing all of his advisors. If we recall from the beginning of this chapter, the king was determined to banish those who could not answer the question, since he had no need of ignorant men (*duppaññajātikehi*). Here is the basis of the king's question, which involves *upāya* – in the Pāli, a cooperative *upāya* that brings together (*upāyena samaggā*) two unlikely allies:

> The dog ate the meat and the goat ate the grass; and so by this *device* (*upāyena*) they lived together in harmony by the great wall. When the king saw their friendship (*mittadhammaṁ*) he thought – 'Never have I seen such a thing before. Here are two natural enemies living in friendship together. I will put this in the form of a question to my wise men; those who cannot understand it I will banish from the realm, and if anyone guesses it I will declare him the sage incomparable.' (*MUJā*, 176)[42]

Recall that in response to the king's question, after interpreting Mahosadha's nonverbal behaviour, Senaka arranges for a delay to consider and answer the question. Knowing the risks to their positions, Senaka instructs the sages each to consider carefully (*upadhārethā*).[43] As the sages are away at their respective homes, Mahosadha consults with Queen Udumbarā and retraces the king's steps to see for himself the event that provoked the king's question/riddle (*MUJā*, 177). As Mahosadha observed the cooperative tactics between the 'goat and the dog', he knew he had solved the question. But only Mahosadha passes the test of wisdom, for although the other sages considered the question (note the root similarity of the Pāli *upadhārethā* to the *Arthaśāstra*'s Sanskrit, *upadhā*) the four wise men could not answer it for themselves.

So they went to Mahosadha because they knew he would have the answer:

---

42 *Jātaka*, ed. Fausbøll [351].

43 Ibid. [352:17].

> [They] sent to announce their coming, and entering spoke politely to him; then standing on one side they asked [Mahosadha]: 'Well, sir, have you thought out the question?' 'If I have not, who will? Of course I have.' 'Then tell us too.' He thought to himself, 'If I do not tell them, the king will banish them, and will honour me with the seven precious things. But let not these fools perish – I will tell them.' So he made them sit down on low seats, and to uplift their hands in salutation, and without telling them what the king had really seen, he composed four stanzas, and taught them one each in the Pali language, to recite when the king should ask them, and sent them away. (*MUJā*, 177)

This is an intriguing use of dialogue and its predicates between Mahosadha and the other four paṇḍitās within the narrative. Note the nonverbal body language conveying respect of the wisdom Mahosadha possesses and that they seek ('spoke politely...standing on one side'). These verbal and nonverbal rhetorical actions must precede the bestowing of knowledge, which is the answer that only the Bodhisatta knows. The nonverbal predicates of this moment of bestowal of knowledge include the following displays of respect for the teacher. The four wise men sit below the Bodhisatta, and further show respect in gesture, as indicated by the Anjali, thus acknowledging and submitting to his superior status. In doing so, the four ask for Mahosadha's help. In response, he composes verses in Pāli, which he gives to them.

Mahosadha 'composed a verse and once he had made each one learn it in Pāli, he dismissed [them]' (*gāthā bandhitvā Pāliṁ eva uggaṇhāpetvā uyyojesi*).[44] The Pāli use of the causative here stresses the incisive nature of the nonverbal predicates of dialogue. Such predicates comprise the dialogic rhetoric of action – the unspoken gestures of communication, causing to sit, making them hold postures of supplication, making them learn – all highlight the superior possession of knowledge and power of the Bodhisatta.

Mahosadha's innerlogue has even more to tell us about the superiority of his wisdom and how he uses it. We learn through Mahosadha's innerlogue – where he internally deliberates whether to withhold what he knows from the other sages or not – that he knows he would receive great reward (the seven precious things) but at the expense of the sages. This inner display of Mahosadha's wisdom shows that he uses the power of his wisdom for the benefit of others, and to avoid harm – even as he is doing so deceptively (by withholding the source and full nature of what he understands).

After bestowing the answers in Pāli, the next day they all went to wait on the king. The four wise men and Mahosadha sat where they were told to sit, and the king first asked Senaka: 'Have you solved the question, Senaka?' Here begins another round of deception in royal dialogue. Senaka's response is the first dissimulation in this exchange. He withholds that his answer comes from Mahosadha: "Sire, if I do not know it who can?' 'Tell me, then.' 'Listen, my lord', and he recited a stanza as he had been taught: 'Young beggars and young princes like and delight in ram's flesh; dog's flesh they do not eat. Yet there might be friendship betwixt ram and dog' (*MUJā*, 177). Although Senaka recited the stanza he did not know its meaning (*gāthaṁ vatvāpi Senako atthaṁ na jānāti*; 353:22). The king did understand because he had seen the thing (... *rājā pana attano pākaṭatthatāya jānāti*). 'Senaka has found it out (... *Senakena tāva ñāto* ... 353:23), he thought ...'. After finishing with Senaka, the king proceeds to query the remaining three wise men. The deceptive

44 Ibid. [353:11–12].

exchange continues (albeit with different verses) as it did with Senaka. Each withholds the source of his knowledge, and each recites without knowing the meaning of his verse. And, in each case, the king ends as he did with Senaka, thinking to himself that each of these wise men had also found out the answer to his question.

Senaka's verse (along with the other three) marks the distinction between the wisdom of these four and the wisdom of the Bodhisatta: the other sages are able only to recite what they had been taught. This attainment distinguishes the Bodhisatta/Buddha from every other brilliant *brāhmaṇa* who learns and recites the Vedas from tradition. Having original wisdom (and ultimately perfect wisdom) is the base-line social distinction in what many consider early Indian ideas about the nature of the Bodhisatta/Buddha: A 'Buddha' teaches others the highest knowledge that he earns and possesses, first.

> Next the king questioned the sage: 'My son, do you understand this question?' 'Sire, who else can understand it from Avīci to Bhavagga, from lowest hell to highest heaven?' 'Tell me, then.' 'Listen, sire'; and he made clear his knowledge of the fact by reciting these two stanzas:
>
> 'The ram, with eight half-feet on his four feet, and eight hooves, unobserved, brings meat for the other, and he brings grass for him. The chief of Videha, the lord of men, on his terrace beheld with his own eyes the interchange of food given by each to the other, between bow-wow and full-mouth.' (*MUJā*, 178)

After hearing the response of Mahosadha, the text makes clear that the king does not know that the others had received their knowledge from Mahosadha, and so he is pleased to think that each of the five had found the answer to the riddle by his own wisdom.

A review of the tactical manipulations of Senaka, the other sages, and Mahosadha is in order. Deception at the most basic level occurs where the king comes to believe all knew the answer to his question through the evocative *gāthā* Mahosadha had taught each of the four sages. With respect to the 'trusted deceivers': first, the four *paṇḍitās* each deceived the king by reciting a verse answer as if it were his own, based in his own knowledge. Second, the Bodhisatta deceived the king by creating verse answers for the sages to use to prove their wisdom and withholding the fact that ultimately, he was the only one who knew the answer and source of the questions. Moreover, Mahosadha deceived the sages by saving for himself the direct answer to the king's query, which would reveal the distinctiveness of his answer, and thus his true understanding.

Regarding the effect of this on the king, he is made to believe that he understood through each verse the Bodhisatta taught the sage to recite. Each Pāli *gāthā* recited by the individual sages would evoke in the king's mind a semblance of the answer – providing the illusion that each sage knew the answer. This is verse recitation as deceptive tactic.

There is deep texture to this misperception, considering the king is made to think he understands, because he has seen the real thing, the goat and the dog. Nevertheless, only the Bodhisatta really sees things, and understands them. As we can see, in the eyes of the king, each of the sages in the testing dialogues demonstrates knowledge; the subtlety of which the king claims for his own wisdom, as he is the creator of the question for the sages to solve. However, the king's wisdom is as limited as the knowledge of the other sages here. The king did not realize that the most subtle display might involve no display.

The ultimately wise communication exchanged in this dialogue is the insinuated and unspoken. While all the *paṇḍitās* had kept to themselves exactly who had resolved the question and had composed the evocative riddling verse, only one sage held the answer. The rhetorical actions of the withholding and the use of knowledge were those of the Bodhisatta's: Mahosadha secreted himself as the resolver of the king's question out of compassion for the other sages. He upheld the reputation for wisdom that the sages already had by composing evocative verses that would make the king think that each sage had discerned the answer on his own. This is royal *upāya* of the highest form, which is central to the argument of the jātaka. Composing the verses in Pāli for the sages to recite, which in the recitation communicates to the king that they are like any *subhāṣita*, is actually showing the distinctiveness of Mahosadha's wisdom.

At the outermost level, the 'Goat and Ram Question' in the *MUJā* functions as an allegory of cooperation between unlikely allies – like Senaka and the other *paṇḍitās* and Mahosadha – to achieve an aim through some clever tactic (*upāya*). The deception begins with the agreement made between the *paṇḍitās* and the Bodhisatta: They cooperated (out of need) like the goat and the dog who attained what each needed, by means of the other's realm of access.

Querying the Basis of the Accomplished Man's Means of Action

What are we to make of all this royal deception? The dialogue between the king and queen below indicate that they both approve of Mahosadha's deception:

> Queen Udumbarā knew that the others had got their knowledge of the question through the sage; and thought she, 'The king has given the same reward to all five, like a man who makes no difference between peas and beans. Surely my brother should have had a special reward.' So she went and asked the king, 'Who discovered the riddle for you, sir?' The five wise men, madam.' 'But my lord, through whom did the four get their knowledge?' 'I do not know, madam.' 'Sire, what do those men know? It was the sage [Mahosadha] – who wished that these fools should not be ruined through him, and taught them the problem. Then you give the same reward to them all. That is not right; you should make a distinction for the sage.' The king was pleased that the sage had not revealed that they had their knowledge through him, and being desirous of giving him an exceeding great reward, he thought, 'Never mind: I will ask my son another question, and when he replies, I will give him a great reward.' (*MUJā*, 179)

The queen's wish for a more distinctive reward for Mahosadha is tacit approval of Mahosadha's deception. She informed the king that Mahosadha had kept his ultimate knowledge a secret, because he did not want the sages to be banished because of him.[45] The king was pleased with the reasons for Mahosadha's deception. Nevertheless, the tests of wisdom and trust continue. Although the *MUJā* has demonstrated Mahosadha's wisdom, it remains to prove through competitive dialogue that his wisdom is tempered by care.

In the continuing test, Mahosadha and Senaka engage in lengthy *saṃvādana* about the comparative merits of wealth (Senaka's position) versus wisdom (Mahosadha's position) as the means to power and influence. The text sets the stage for the extent of expertise Mahosadha must face in the debate at outset, specifically the authority of family tradition. The question 'had been handed down from generation to generation in Senaka's family',

45 Synopsis based both on ibid. [VI: 355.27–356] and Cowell's translation of *Jā* 6, pp. 179–80.

and so he was able to give the first response immediately. This dialogic argument proceeds with several metaphors for wisdom and wealth and the perceived limits and strengths of each. In the interest of brevity I will highlight portions of the *saṃvādana* that show Mahosadha's retorts are designed to establish the supremacy of Buddhist wisdom over any wisdom a Senaka might possess.

Once the wise men come to the king's court, he poses to Senaka the first stanza in the 'Question of Poor and Rich':

> Endowed with wisdom and bereft of wealth, or wealthy and without wisdom – I ask you this question Senaka: Which of these does the accomplished man (*seyyo*, Skt. *śreya*) declare skilful (*kusalā vadanti*)? (*MUJā*, 179)[46]

Senaka replies at once because of the familiarity he has from his family tradition. This familiarity is a nonverbal predicate that serves as the basis for trust in authenticity of Senaka's answer.

> Verily, O king, wise men and fools, men educated or uneducated, do service to the wealthy, although they be high-born and he be base-born. Beholding this I say: The wise is mean, and the wealthy is better. (*MUJā*, 179)

The king takes control of the dialogue in order to narrow the test to a competition only between Senaka and Mahosadha. Note that in his address to Mahosadha, the king identifies him as 'exceedingly wise' (*anomapaññaṁ*) and as one who knows *dhamma* and repeats the question: 'fool with wealth or a wise man with small store, which of the two do clever men call the better?' To which Mahosadha replied:

> 'The fool commits sinful [*pāpāni*] acts, thinking "In this world I am the better"; he looks at this world and not at the next, and gets the worst of it in both. Beholding this I say: The wise is better than the wealthy fool.' (*MUJā*, 179)

'Well, you see Mahosadha says the wise man is the best.' In giving this reply, the king looks squarely at Senaka (*evaṁ vutte rājā Senakaṁ oloketvā*) and delivers Mahosadha's answer – making the contrary assertion, at the same time as looking at him is enticing Senaka further into debate.[47] The nonverbal dimension of this dialogic exchange is perhaps more important than the verbal because it shows the king's management of the debate. He decides how it will proceed and ultimately who will win. At this moment the king is challenging Senaka to continue. And continue it does, until Senaka adds powerful nonverbal predicates of dialogue – inherited prestige and gestures of respect to the king – thinking this dialogic maneuver will win the debate. Senaka recited this stanza, thinking that he would silence Mahosadha:

> We are five wise men (*pañca paṇḍitā mayaṁ bhadante*], venerable sir all waiting upon you with gestures of respect (*sabbe pañjalikā upaṭṭhitā*); and you are our lord and master,

---

46 Adapted from *Jātaka*, tr. Fausbøll [356.9–12].

47 Ibid. [357:14].

> like Sakka, lord of all creatures, king of the gods. Beholding this I say: The wise is mean, the rich is better. (*MUJā*, 181)[48]

As Senaka interprets these nonverbal predicates of dialogue that communicate or demonstrate that they are trusted enough to be in the king's close company – such 'gestures of respect' conveyed to this kind of person (around the king) communicate the power of wealth over wisdom.

Senaka thinks he will finally silence the sage and win the argument by letting his own prestige and presence at court speak for the superiority of wealth over wisdom. Thus, he brings into the dialogue the king's status markers of the sages being at his court, and the presence of himself and his fellows as dialogic indicators that wealth trumps the wise. The king himself thought this a good response on Senaka's part– considering as it did his own prestige, and the conception that wise men at his court speak to the power of the relationship between king and *paṇḍitās*.

> When the king heard this he thought, … I wonder whether my son will be able to refute it and to say something else.' So he asked him, 'Well, wise sir, what now?' But this argument of Senaka's there was none able to refute except the Bodhisatta, [who] refuted it by saying, 'Sire, what does this fool know? He only looks at himself and knows not the excellence of wisdom.' (*MUJā*, 181)

Mahosadha proves his point by reciting this winning verse:

> 'The wealthy fool is but the slave of a wise man, when questions of this kind arise; when the sage solves it cleverly, then the fool falls into confusion. Beholding this I say: The wise is better than the wealthy fool.' (*MUJā*, 182)

The king declares Mahosadha the victor, describing him as the 'most accomplished teacher of dhamma' (*kevaladhammadassi*).

Mahosadha's winning stanza argues that Senaka's presence at court as indicative of the supremacy of wealth is false because it relies only on Senaka's presence, status and reliance on the king's reputation and power as evidence. By contrast, Mahosadha's wisdom is superior because he is aware that happiness and discomfiture touch humans (*sukhadukkhena puṭṭho*) in ways that belie the opposition of wealth and wisdom contrived in the king's test of the two sages. This dialogue is significant as well for its nonverbal dimensions, which I have highlighted above. Those nonverbal moments (such as the king's look at Senaka) and the appeals to the nonverbal predicates of dialogic relations (as in Senaka's final appeal in the debate) both advance and help decide the outcome of the dialogue. In short, they help determine who is wisest, and thus who can be trusted. Finally, in the overall narrative of the *MUJā*, after this proof of his wisdom comes Mahosadha's marriage to Amarā. Following upon the marriage, the *paṇḍitās* engage in 'breaking' or *bheda upāya* to eliminate the threat of Mahosadha to their position of supremacy in relation to the king. This episode needs to be examined, to complete our analysis of the *MUJā*'s engagement with śāstric wisdom.

---

[48] Ibid. [362.5].

Trusted Deceivers in the *Mahā Ummagga Jātaka*

The king's waning 'care' for Senaka, plays into Senaka's anxiety at losing the status that attends a primary intimate connection with the king. Yet, the risk at losing the primacy of this connection – primacy meaning that Senaka is the wisest and first choice – was only the first impetus to Senaka's deceptions of his king to save his position by attempting undermining tests of Mahosadha's right to be called a sage, *paṇḍita*. Our focus now turns to the manipulations (by all sides) of the terms of royal relationship through dialogic encounters both verbal and nonverbal, specifically regarding *bheda upāya*.

At this point, following the hierarchy of *upāya* as shown in the *Arthaśāstra*, Senaka engages in *bheda upāya* to break this relationship between the king and Bodhisatta Mahosadha (*MUJā*, 185–6). The details of Senaka's fractious *upāya* scenarios involve theft from the king, the use of female servants to plant the king's belongings in Mahosadha's house, to take advantage of Mahosadha's wife Amarā, and lying to deceive the king into thinking Mahosadha is a thief and therefore his enemy (*MUJā*, 185–6).

This move toward a more aggressive *bheda* tactic follows on the acknowledgment of the wisdom of Mahosadha's by means of multiple tests we have seen in the (*MUJā*). Now the politically perspicacious advisor Senaka gathers his fellow advising *paṇḍitās* to 'find a means to make a breach between the Bodhisatta sage, Mahosadha and the king'.[49] Senaka proposes a *bheda* strategy: Senaka and his *paṇḍita* associates each steal an item belonging to the king and use their servant girls to plant the stolen items in the Bodhisatta's home to make the Bodhisatta appear a thief. Senaka and his fellow advisors target the Bodhisatta's household, thinking their servants can deceive his wife (Amarā) into receiving stolen goods.

This misperception of Amarā's wisdom on the part of the *brāhmaṇa* sages' forms their impetus to deceptive action to destroy the connection between their king and Mahosadha (*MUJā* 185): 'Friends, we are not enough for this common man's son Mahosadha; and now he is gotten in the wife cleverer than himself. Can we find a means to make a breach between him and the king?'[50] They decide on a ruse of planting stolen items in Mahosadha's home to discredit him and make the king distrust him.

Amarā's *Upāya*: Nonverbal Predicates of Trust and Deception

Both Amarā and Senaka's spies (*paṇḍitas*' servants) use the unspoken and spoken dimensions of dialogue to their advantage, in this case, trust. They are also using unspoken assumptions about trust and what it achieves in dialogue. Coming to Mahosadha's house to plant the stolen items, the *paṇḍitas*' servants are banking on Amarā's trust in incidental exchanges that typically occur between servants and the wife of the house. In turn, each servant-spy delivers the incriminating stolen items within jars of fruit, in flower garlands and other domestically construed ruses (*MUJā*, 186).[51]

Senaka and his fellow advisors target the Bodhisatta's household, thinking their servants can deceive Amarā into receiving stolen goods. Previously however, the text has established

---

[49] Senaka aims to discredit the Bodhisatta – who had replaced Senaka in his counseling intimacy with his king – by making the king (Vedeha of Mithilā) think him a thief, grounds for breaking the relationship.

[50] Adapted from *Jātaka*, tr. Fausbøll [368].

[51] Ibid.

Amarā's intelligence (*MUJā*, 182–3) and ability to meet any challenge. Just as a close advisor would do of any servant to a king, Mahosadha had put Amarā through Kauṭilyan-like tests of her wisdom and integrity before he married her.[52] Mahosadha's test topics paralleled the *Arthaśāstra*'s *upadhā*, although tailored to meet Amarā's scope of action – the social customs incumbent on women, money, lust and fear (*MUJā*, 184–5). Thus, in the examples from the *MUJā* that follow, Amarā enters the royal imaginary of deception as the tried and trusted wife of the Bodhisatta, ready to use the nonverbal predicates of dialogue, trust, dialogic dissimulation and gesture, and even writing to reveal the espionage and tricks (the *bheda* strategies) of Mahosadha's adversaries at court. Even though this part of the *MUJā* narrative foregrounds Amarā, it nevertheless continues to show Mahosadha's superiority in wisdom and specifically his mastery of śāstric tactics, because Amarā, having been tested by and then married to Mahosadha, is acting as he would.

In the following episode, we see Amarā's repertoire of responses to Senaka's *bheda* strategies that he executes through his female servants. It is worth quoting this passage at length, in order to observe the verbal and nonverbal dimensions of these exchanges as the servants attempt to slander Mahosadha by planting the king's stolen items in his house:

> Senaka put the jewel in a pot of dates and sent it by a slave-girl, saying, 'If anyone else wants to have this pot of dates, refuse, but give them pot and all to the people in Mahosadha's house.' She took it and went to the Mahosadha's house, and walked up and down [offering her dates for sale]. But the lady Amarā standing by the door saw this: she noticed that the girl went nowhere else, [thinking] there must be something behind it; she cried herself to the girl, 'Come here, girl, I will take the dates.' When she came, the mistress called for her servants, but none answered, so she sent the girl to fetch them.
>
> While she was gone Amarā put her hand into the pot and found the jewel. When the girl returned Amarā asked her, 'Whose servant are you, girl?' 'Paṇḍita Senaka's maid.' Then she enquired her name and her mother's name and said, 'Well, give me some dates.' 'If you want it, mother, take it pot and all – I want no payment.' 'You may go, then,' said Amarā, and sent her away. Then she wrote down on a leaf, 'On such a day of such a month the teacher Senaka sent a jewel from the king's crest for a present by the hand of such and such a girl. Pukkusa sent the golden necklet hidden in a casket of jasmine flowers; Kāvinda sent the robe in a basket of vegetables; Devinda sent the golden slipper in a bundle of straw. She received them all and put down names and all on a leaf, which she put away, telling the Great Being about it.' (*MUJā*, 186)

Here we see Amarā uses her own ruses in what she does and does not say to the spies that come to her door. Her words to the spies seem to communicate that she does not know what is going on; through verbal niceties she accepts the plants of the king's stolen objects into her home. Amarā's actions, however, speak otherwise. She does not trust the women/spies coming to her door because she observed in their behaviour – 'by discerning from movement or gesture', *iṅgitasaññāya* – that they were attempting a deception, for instance by observing them going nowhere else to sell their dates.[53] Amarā's ability to interpret gestures as warning signs, echoes *Arthaśāstra* warnings that clandestine operations could

[52] The tests of Amarā's purity in the *MUJā*, 184–5 (ibid. [367–8]) bring to mind the four *upadhā* testing scenarios in Kauṭilya (*Aś*, 1.10.7–20). Namely, the Bodhisatta orchestrates the tests of his future wife's integrity just as close advisors to kings test the integrity of new royal ministers.

[53] Adapted from *Jātaka*, tr. Fausbøll [368.29].

be betrayed by gesture or bearing. Thus, Amarā shows here that she too is a master of discerning the meaning in nonverbal predicates of behaviour.

Amarā cleverly records in writing each planted item on a palm leaf – along with the name of each servant and the name of the king's 'trusted' *paṇḍita* that sent the servant and the date – as if she were recording any domestic delivery. Amarā's written record of the deliveries eventually proves the guilt of the Senaka and his fellows.[54] The tricks of the *paṇḍita* sages to the king are no match for a wife of the Bodhisatta, who knows how to read deceitful body language, and uses to her advantage both the spoken word and written word in the quotidian dialogues that occur at her door.

That the narrative depicts the wife of the Bodhisatta wise enough to spot espionage and to deflect traps suggests, first, that one must be wise in order to be in proximity and relationship to a Buddha (his wife in this case). Second, it suggests that this wisdom involves the ability to read nonverbal dialogue and deflect tricks through counter-response to her opponent's ruse. The servants of the *paṇḍitās* come to her under false pretenses, she sees through their pretences, and responds in kind; that is, she deceives them in order to take advantage of their attempted deception of her. Here we see the intersection between the verbal and the nonverbal in the dialogic moment. Third, this moment in the text demonstrates that the royal imaginary of deceptive tactics is so pervasive that all members of a king's court – wives to advisors – would be aware of suspicious behaviour and be ready with counter-tactics to tricks and deceits.

Bodhisatta Mahosadha and the Nonverbal Predicates of Dialogue and Trust

Turning back to Mahosadha's responses to Senaka's *bheda* strategies, Mahosadha must flee the court and take up a disguise to avoid Senaka's actions. Successfully deceived by his trusted *paṇḍitas*, the king is angered beyond reason and denies Mahosadha's request for an audience, and orders Mahosadha's arrest. Warned off by his own spies, Mahosadha flees the king's wrath and takes up the life of a potter, working at this lowly craft in disguise (*MUJā*, 186). In doing so Mahosadha engages in his own *upāya* responses to *bheda*, just as Amarā did. In this deceptive encounter, we see Mahosadha in his disguise:

> the Great Being ... after fetching clay and turning his master's wheel, sat all clay-besmeared on a bundle of straw eating balls of rice dipped in a little soup. Now the reason why he did so was this: he thought that the king might suspect him of desiring to grasp the sovereign power, but if he hear that he was living by the craft of a potter this suspicion would be put away. (*MUJā*, 188)

One of the king's courtiers finds Mahosadha, and reports to the king of Mahosadha's new occupation and place of residence. The king, pleased, sends for Mahosadha:

> with the mud stains yet upon him [Mahosadha] mounted in the chariot and went to town. The courtier told the king of his arrival. 'Where did you find the sage, my son?' 'My lord, he was earning his livelihood as a potter in the South Town; but as soon as he heard that you had sent for him, without bathing, the mud yet staining his body, he came.' The king

---

[54] Ibid. [370].

> thought, 'If he were my enemy he would have come with pomp and retinue; he is not my enemy.' (*MUJā*, 189)

As the *MUJā* depicts Mahosadha's tactical response, it is important that he dispel distrust through the nonverbal rhetoric of action – which speaks to the king of his character. To do so he uses disguise; assuming the bearing and marks of social position in order to counter the dissension Senaka was sowing with the king. He is prevented from communicating with the king directly, so Mahosadha communicates with him nonverbally – through the social position that he assumes when he flees the king. This deception works, especially in its details: Mahosadha's mud-stained appearance speaks to his humility, a signal the king understands, and which helps re-establish trust with the king.

The Bodhisatta's use of the potter's social position is an important nonverbal moment of communication, so singular that the text interprets it for us within the *jātaka*: 'he [Mahosadha] thought that the king might suspect him of desiring to grasp the sovereign power, but if he heard that he was living by the craft of a potter this suspicion would be put away' (*MUJā*, 188). As the text imagines the communicative power of the potter disguise, this step down in status nonverbally signals Mahosadha's real intentions – service not sedition – and trustworthiness to the king. Mahosadha well knows the ability of nonverbal social cues to communicate. Mahosadha knows that the impurity associated with the potter life will serve to show the king that assuages his king's suspicions that was manipulating events to serve his own designs for attaining royal power. Moreover, by lying in wait as a potter, Mahosadha counters the ploys of the *brāhmaṇa* sages, using social position as disguise; one of the tools any 'crooked,' *kauṭilya*, advisor might use. Paradoxically, Mahosadha is using a false social position – working as a potter – to communicate his true nature to the king. This is an ironic or paradoxical form of deception and *upāya.* The disguise paradoxically reinforces trust between the king and Mahosadha, and shows both Mahosadha's true intentions (service to the king) and Senaka's false intentions (self-protection).

When the king's agent finds Mahosadha seated in his potter's disguise, he derides Mahosadha that his famous wisdom has not brought him prosperity but led him to this lowly position: 'Is it true, as they say that you are one of profound wisdom? So great prosperity, cleverness, and intelligence [do] not serve you, thus brought to insignificance, while you eat a little soup like that' (*MUJā*, 188). Mahosadha's retort intones a sense of command over more than a mere potter's wheel (which is all the king's agent can see):

> Blind fool! By the power of my wisdom when I want to restore that prosperity I will do it … I make weal ripen by woe, I discriminate between seasonable and unseasonable time, hiding at my own will; I unlock the doors of profit; therefore I am content with boiled rice. When I perceive the time for an effort, maturing my profit by my designs, I will bear myself valiantly like a lion, and by that mighty power you shall see me again. (*MUJā*, 188)[55]

According to tradition, this particular *jātaka* demonstrates the Bodhisatta's perfection of wisdom. But here, this wisdom is couched in śāstric ideals for advisors – knowing the right time and place to act, bringing plans to fruition by his own *upāya*, the tactics and means (both verbal and nonverbal) he deploys to demonstrate wisdom, create trust, and expose those who are untrustworthy. Mahosadha is not pretending to the king's power here as the

---

55 Ibid.

bheda tactics of Senaka aimed to establish; rather he is pointing to his own mastery over a kind of wisdom that entails hiding under disguise of lower birth station, the ability to bring about success, *artha*, by his own *upāya*. He is the wielder of a better *dharma*, in a context made inimical to *dharma* by unscrupulous advisors.

Conclusion

These examples of dialogic engagements shed light on my argument that the dialogues of this study are shaped by a royal imaginary of deception. Reading the *Mahā Ummagga Jātaka* as a 'treatise' or śāstra in light of a practical and tactical royal treatise such as the *Arthaśāstra* indicates that the communities around these texts were taking part in a larger dialogue with each other, across tradition (and genre), regarding the role of trust and deception in making royal power efficacious.

Mahosadha represents a Buddhist conception of deceptive practice for royal contexts that aims beyond the attainments of mere *artha* or success for kings and beyond the exercise of skills possessed by typical wise men (*paṇḍitās*) in the service of royal success. Mahosadha exhibited his understanding of the complex predicates of dialogue – including his grasp of their role and function in sustaining or breaking royal relationships. His superior wisdom provided him the skill to engage in deceptions and to establish himself as trustworthy in a way that incorporates but transcends śāstric wisdom. As Mahosadha participates in deceptive tactics, the *MUJā* interrogates the exercise of wisdom with respect to its rhetorical power to express, inculcate or undermine loyalties in royal relationships. As the text engages the rhetoric of words and action, the *MUJā* does what we have come to expect in narrative competitive dialogues such as these.[56] The *MUJā* interrogates, challenges and displays: using dialogic competition to let the power of wisdom wielded by a bodhisatta be seen for what is. Mahosadha exhibits (*paññāya ānubhāvaṁ*) an extraordinary state of experience-based wisdom, which exceeds that of any wise man or *paṇḍita* with superior attainments like Senaka. All *paṇḍitās* deserving of the name (desserts which King Vedeha, Senaka and Mahosadha heartily tested throughout the *MUJā*) have certain powers of wisdom that they exercise through various royal repertoires of *upāya*. Mahosadha's only supereminence to the wisdom of the other wise men may only be in the dharmic basis of their respective *upāyas* – whether the deceptions emerge out of Brahmanical or Buddhist *dharmas*.

We have seen the *Arthaśāstra*'s web of ascetics and other religious personae turned to deceptive strategies designed to cultivate, execute and especially display royal power. Intrinsic to the creation of this web are shared assumptions about the power such religious persons possess as well as the forms that communicate – the signs, clothing, gestures, and ways of talking to adepts and believers – such persons possess such power. Thus, the general social trust in a 'trusted deceiver's' power and efficacy is what makes these positions effective tools of deception.

The *Mahā Ummagga Jātaka* is one Buddhist narrative response to a cultural logic that anticipates deceitful stratagems executed through ascetics and wandering religious

[56] For wisdom demonstrations in royal courts see Brian Black, *The Character of the Self in Ancient India: Priests, Kings, and Women in the Early Upaniṣads* (Albany, 2007), pp. 71–2. Black has also identified an aspect of the shared courtly rhetorical context with which I have been concerned here. See his 'Ambaṭṭha and Śvetaketu: Literary Connections between the Upaniṣads and Early Buddhist Narratives', *Journal of the American Academy of Religion* 79/1 (2011): 136–61.

practitioners. Considered in light of the *Arthaśāstra* examples above, the *MUJā's* ideas about royal use of *upāya* and their associated repertoires seem a narrative refraction of trust and deception through royal intellectual cultures sufficiently pervasive as to be inescapable. Narratively inescapable that is. For what does a *jātaka* like the *MUJā* at least – of the *Mahā Nipāta* collection of *jātaka* that engage royal *rājanya* concerns and metaphors of action – invite us to do as readers?

I have read the *Mahā Ummagga Jātaka* as a 'treatise' as much as a 'birth story', due to its engagement with topics that occur in royal treatises such as Kauṭilya's *Arthaśāstra*. I assert that reading the *MUJā* as a treatise – even though it is not generically called such – allows one to see that the *jātaka* does more than employ strategies of 'trusted deceivers' and kings in order to demonstrate the Bodhisatta's 'perfect wisdom' in these settings.[57] They invite us narratively to consider the fissure zones of competing doctrines. In other words, *jātaka* such as the *MUJā* read as incisive, technical literature that is also a religious narrative provide one of many narrative proving grounds for ideals of practices and doctrines.

This is evident in the narrative depiction of Mahosadha's ability to meet counsel with counsel, to best a tricky 'sage', a *paṇḍita* advisor such as Senaka and his colleagues. Thus, if deceptive *brāhmaṇas* and śramaṇas are not to be a source of consternation for dharmic communities – like the ones that created the *MUJā* – wishing to influence those at court, they must deceive in order to gain the trust of kings. In other words, it takes reliance on the inter-subjective dimensions of dialogue and reliance on ideas of the varieties of intimacy that can be had with kings, to play successfully into this cultural dialogic of deceptively created religious efficacy.

Trusted deceivers employ their association with such kings to prove their own religious merit and create and make effective their religious power. Brahmanical and Buddhist interlocutors want their communities to have primary influence over kings, and enter the royal imaginary of trust based deceptions as a means to gain it. Advisors and their secret agents narratively succeed or are thwarted as they work to lay the illusory and deceptive foundations of a king's power. Successes or failures in tricky pragmatics are normative arguments for royal relationship as much as they are ideological arguments for the benefit of either Brahmanical or Buddhist influence in *rājanya* courts. This recursive logic of influence – inter-subjective and collaborative in its agencies – fuels the narrative pragmatics of deception. And, this recursive influence is accomplished through the logic of trust and deception, all of which is expressed dialogically, verbally or not.

Relative to the Brahmanical examples used here, the Buddhist *Mahā Ummagga Jātaka* uses modes of deception in ways it considers beyond typical destructive royal strategies (*nīti*); this is the text's religious or dharmic argument. Nevertheless, the Bodhisatta uses these modes of deception as well. What does it mean for the Bodhisatta to enter the royal imaginary of deception, thinking with and beyond deceptive sages and kings, using his own tricks and spies to carry them out?[58]

---

[57] Many have asserted that *jātaka* tales aim to convey particular morals or exemplars of Buddhist morality. In her description of the *MUJā* at least, Naomi Appleton follows in this tradition about the function of *jātaka* tales, stating that Mahosadha 'solves various riddles and outwits his competitors, demonstrating his perfection of wisdom'. See her *Jātaka Stories in Theravāda Buddhism: Narrating the Bodhisatta Path* (Farnham, 2010), 72.

[58] Scholars are now examining the subject of religious deceptions more broadly. Liz Wilson, in *Charming Cadavers* (Chicago, 1996), has pointed out some of these engagements in deception in her work on representations of females. Sara McClintock has recently argued, across a wider range of examples, that the Buddha Śākyamuni can be seen as a trickster figure, that is, 'a narrative expression

Given that some Brahmanically construed texts (such as Kauṭilya's *Arthaśāstra*) engage in deception by manipulating the roles of various renunciants, it should not surprise us to see Buddhist literature at pains to establish the Buddha and his representatives as a clear alternative to the pragmatics (deceptive or otherwise) of Brahmanical influence. It would be incumbent on competing Buddhist communities to argue for the superiority of Buddhist dharmic influence, especially when royal pragmatics in śāstric texts like the *Arthaśāstra* suggest manipulation of idealized actions of religious mendicants.

However, even as it may be incumbent on competing communities to create agonistic narratives to demonstrate their superiority, it is more interesting to see what this influence looks like. More can be said about the nature of this dharmic influence if we follow the *MUJā* argument – in both its story of the present and past – that the Bodhisatta is cultivating and/or demonstrating his 'perfect wisdom' in settings where *brāhmaṇa* and *rājanya* wisdom traditions hold sway. Though critical of how *brāhmaṇa* or *rājanya* sages use tactics to prove wisdom and solve problems, the Bodhisatta and his spouse Amarā use tricks and veiled deceits as well. Why then, would such a lengthy *jātaka* narrative depict a trusted person like Mahosadha or Senaka engaged in some ruse in highly intersubjective settings such as royal dialogues? Is there some answer in the aim to which the deception is directed? Senaka, though trusted by Vedeha from the beginning of the text, withholds information, and engages in deceptive practices to protect his own power and influence with the king. The Bodhisatta withholds information and deceives in order to serve and protect the king and others in the text, as well as demonstrate that royal strategy can be exercised without physical harm and breaking of trust.

In the dialogic contexts of these *MUJā* narratives – where analogous deceptive tactics would only be evidence of the fifth *upāya* if it were enacted in analogous narrative royal scenarios as occur in the *Pañcatantra* – what are we to make of Mahosadha's deceits that do not seem to break trusts? Do small deceptions break trust? Or is the trust that Mahosadha preserves in his exercise of tactics with King Vedeha point to a more foundational trust?

The text shows that 'trust' is not simply broken and that the constitution of trust is not simple either. The trusts these 'trusted deceivers' are shown as breaking are specific to social-relational context; and they are meant to preserve the primary relationship and responsibility of relationship that a sage to the king holds. Trusts may be continually tried, as in Mahosadha's experience, and the experience of the royals around him, as they occur in complex dialogical contexts. Two Pāli verbs are used throughout the *MUJā* as Mahosadha, Senaka and King Vedeha teasingly, tauntingly, test in these ways: *upadhāreti* (to engage something, consider something, causatively, so to bring the object being examined into view); and *vīmaṁsati* (to consider, deliberatively, to question in a manner that might result in trust). Vedeha recited his rhetorical query into Mahosadha's tactics, 'testing him' (*vīmaṁsanto*) wondering why Mahosadha did not harm him.[59]

What are we to make of these proof tactics of discernment – tricks, small deceits that, if used prudently, invoke the predicates of trust in relationship inducing ways? Recall the scenario where the King of Videha (through his Queen) came to know and approved how Mahosadha had tricked him into thinking Senaka and the other sages knew the answer to the

of a paradox', here being the paradox of an absolutely unconditioned figure appearing and acting in the world as a part of conditioned experience. Sara L. McClintock,. 'Compassionate Trickster: The Buddha as a Literary Character in the Narratives of Early Indian Buddhism', *Journal of the American Academy of Religion* 79/1 (2011): 109.

59 See *Jā* 6, tr. Fausbøll [374.19–24].

'Goat and Ram' question. To Vedeha, Mahosadha's use of deceit against him in this instance was a sign of prudent wisdom. The king wanted to reward him, but decided to question him and prove his wisdom yet again. The inexorable 'test, so to trust' logic is instructive. Perhaps the *MUJā* is aiming at some bedrock kind of trust in its interrogation and use of deceptions and trusted deceivers. Moreover, given the dynamism of the dialogues of test, I argue that deceits are necessary to create or preserve deeper trusts (or responsibilities to relationships of trust).

Could the *MUJā* reflect a royal imaginary of deception so compelling as to shape the discourse of how perfect wisdom is to be demonstrated? *Upāya* exercised through the Bodhisatta's hands gains new meaning in his role as 'trusted deceiver'. The Bodhisatta's wisdom – and by extension other Buddhists, such as Amarā the Bodhisatta's spouse, exceed kings and other sages in their use and mastery of the predicates of dialogue – encompasses nonverbal dimensions of communication, uses the markers of social function to communicate his trustworthiness when denied access to direct speech with the king. Mahosadha's mastery of the nonverbal and social predicates of dialogue demonstrates superior wisdom through a rhetoric of action as well as the rhetoric of discourse to let Buddhist dharmic actions speak for themselves. Reading for such non-apparent dimensions of dialogue, the *MUJā* expands the wealth of signs for us to interpret within dialogic encounters.

The *MUJā* demonstrates a keen sense of the currency of dialogue and relationship. Thus, the text's complex field of rhetoric resonates with the powerful exchanges of prestige and knowledge that Brian Black demonstrated in the dialogic forms and rhetoric of the Upaniṣads.[60] Particular to the narrative culture of the *MUJā*, is a concern to inculcate distinctions in the kind of wisdom exchanged in the relationships with kings as represented in the figure of the Bodhisatta Mahosadha. Mahosadha is tried for trustworthiness continually. In turn, he employs similar and more subtle tactics – nonverbal and verbal – to prove his trustworthiness and superior wisdom. Royal *upāya* as Mahosadha wields it undermines the harmful results of *upāya* enacted by *brāhmaṇa* sages in the service of aggressive kings. It takes Mahosadha's kind of wisdom to bring his *upāya* to success. Though it is helpful to see that there are distinctions in how *jātaka* tales as a genre work diachronically with and through conceptions of the Buddha's *pāramī*-s or 'perfections'[61] my analysis of Mahosadha's exercise of *upāya*, royal tactics and tricks, shows that it is important to consider generic distinctions in a perfection like *pañña* or wisdom, as well as continue to rethink the genre itself.

As we have seen, the creator(s) of the *MUJā* narratively cross genres and use or *re*appropriate śāstric and royal (*rājanya*) conceptions of the highest mediating roles (*paṇḍita*, *brāhmaṇa paṇḍita* and queens) at court in order to make a place for themselves in the rhetoric of influence. My language here – of crossing and using genres – may not be the ideal way to articulate what I am reading in this *jātaka*, but it is a good way to raise my questions about such texts. By embracing the culture of trusted servants that manipulate royal relationships and power, a Buddhist narrative use of royal *upāya* tactics like these can show Buddhist attainments in the nonverbal and social predicates of dialogue, savvy in the competitive debates between kings and their courtiers which these predicates cue and sustain, as well as capability in the intrasubjective elements of trust and deception that make royal dialogue possible.

---

[60] Black, *The Character of the Self in Ancient India*.

[61] See Appleton, *Jātaka Stories in Theravāda Buddhism*.

What are we to think of such a narrative embrace? It is evident from the way that the *MUJā* enters and uses the royal imaginary of deception (as the examples from Kauṭilya's *Arthaśāstra* suggest) that it is familiar with this narrative culture of tricks and deceits. Moreover, the use, or proper use as the *MUJā* argues, of tricks and deception are important dimensions of idealized wisdom and perfected action encompassed in Mahosadha's 'majestic wisdom' (*pañña ānubhāvaṁ*) one of the common superlatives for his wisdom in the *MUJā*. As these dimensions are played with in the *MUJā*, the skill of its playfulness emerges in at least two levels. On one level, it appears that relationships with kings are a tactical means to showing (testing?) the supremacy of Buddhist conceptions of idealized action in these relationships. On another level, as the narrative tries these ideals out the *Mahā Ummagga Jātaka* points to and retains the paradoxical power and necessity to step into, and out of, the role of 'trusted deceiver' to meet particular aims through a variety of skilful tactics.

Abbreviations

Aś	*Arthaśāstra* of Kauṭilya
GRETIL	Göttingen Register of Electronic Texts in Indian Languages
Jā	Jātaka
Jm	*Jātakamālā*
ln	line
MBh	*Mahābhārata*
MDh	Manu's *Dharmaśāstra* (*Mānava - Dharmaśāstra*)
MUJā	*Mahā Ummagga Jātaka*, No. 548
MW	Monier Williams's *Sanskrit English Dictionary*
Skt.	Sanskrit
tr	translation or translator
v(v)	verse(s)

References

Primary Sources

Aśvaghoṣa's Buddhacarita or Acts of the Buddha, tr. E.H. Johnston (New Delhi: Munshiram Manoharlal Reprint, 1995 [Orig. pub, Lahore, 1936]).

Jātaka or Stories of the Buddha's Former Births, ed. E.B. Cowell (6 vols, Oxford: Pali Text Society, Reprint, 1995).

Jātaka, together with its commentary, ed. V. Fausbøll (London: Luzac and Company, Pali Text Society Reprint, 1963 [Orig. pub. 1877]).

Jātakamālā of Ārya Śūra, GRETIL access, based on the edition by P.L. Vaidya, Buddhist Sanskrit Texts, 21 (Darbhanga: The Mithila Institute, 1959).

Kauṭilīya Arthaśāstra, ed. R.P. Kangle, Part 1, A Critical Edition with a Glossary (Delhi: Motilal Banarsidass, 1988). Part 2, Translation and Introduction, 2nd ed. (Bombay: University of Bombay, 1972). Part 3 (Delhi: Motilal Banarsidass, 1988).

King, Governance, and Law in India: Kauṭilya's Arthaśāstra, A New Annotated Translation by Patrick Olivelle (Oxford: Oxford University Press, 2013).

Life of the Buddha, by Aśvaghoṣa, tr. Patrick Olivelle. Eds Isabelle Onians and Somadeva Vasudeva. In *The Clay Sanskrit Library*, eds Richard Gombrich and Sheldon Pollock (New York: New York University Press and JJC Foundation, 2008).

Long Discourses of the Buddha: A Translation of the Dīgha-Nikāya, tr. Maurice Walshe (Boston: Wisdom Publications, 1995).

Mahābhārata, GRETIL, Kyoto archive of Sanskrit E-texts, Unicode (UTF-8), input by Muneo Tokunaga, revised by John Smith (Cambridge).

Mahābhārata 3 The Book of Virāṭa and *the Book of the Effort*, tr. J.A.B. Van Buitenen (Chicago and London: University of Chicago Press, 1978).

Mahābhārata: Book 11 The Book of the Women, Book 12 The Book of Peace, Part I, vol. 7, tr. James L. Fitzgerald (Chicago and London: University of Chicago Press, 2004).

Manu's Code of Law: A Critical Edition and Translation of the Mānava-Dharmaśāstra, tr. and ed. Patrick Olivelle, South Asia Research Series (New York: Oxford University Press, 2005).

The Majjhima-Nikāya 2, ed. Robert Chalmers (London: Pali Text Society, 1898).

Middle Length Discourses of the Buddha: A Translation of the Majjhima Nikāya, 3rd ed, tr. Bhikkhu Ñāṇamoli, revised by Bhikkhu Bodhi (Boston: Wisdom Publications, 2005).

Pañcatantra Reconstructed, ed. and tr. Franklin Edgerton, *Vol. 1: Text and Critical Apparatus*, American Oriental Series 2, Introduction and translation (New Haven: American Oriental Society, 1924).

Pañcatantra: The Book of India's Folk Wisdom, tr. Patrick Olivelle, World's Classics (Oxford and New York: Oxford University Press, 1997).

Upaniṣads, tr. Patrick Olivelle (Oxford and New York: Oxford University Press, 1996).

Secondary Sources

Appleton, Naomi, *Jātaka Stories in Theravāda Buddhism: Narrating the Bodhisatta Path* (Farnham: Ashgate, 2010).

Black, Brian, *The Character of the Self in Ancient India: Priests, Kings, and Women in the Early Upaniṣads* (Albany: State University of New York Press, 2007).

________, 'Rivals and Benefactors: Encounters between Buddhists and Brahmins in the Nikāyas', *Religions of South Asia* 3/1 (2009): 25–43.

________, 'Ambaṭṭha and Śvetaketu: Literary Connections between the Upaniṣads and Early Buddhist Narratives', *Journal of the American Academy of Religion* 79/1 (2011): 136–61.

Bowles, Adam, *Dharma, Disorder, and the Political in Ancient India: the Āpaddharmaparvan of the Mahābhārata* (Leiden and Boston: Brill, 2007).

Jamison, Stephanie, 'Women "Between Empires" and "Between the Lines"', in Patrick Olivelle (ed.), *Between the Empires: Society in India 300 BCE to 400 CE*, South Asia Research Series (Oxford and New York: Oxford University Press, 2006), pp. 191–214.

Lubin, Timothy, Donald R. Davis, Jr., and Jayanth K. Krishnan (eds), *Hinduism and Law: An Introduction* (New York: Cambridge University Press, 2010).

McClintock, Sara L., 'Compassionate Trickster: The Buddha as a Literary Character in the Narratives of Early Indian Buddhism', *Journal of the American Academy of Religion* 79/1 (2011): 90–112.

McClish, Mark, 'Political Brahmanism and the State: A Compositional History of the *Arthaśāstra*,' Ph.D. Dissertation, University of Texas at Austin, 2009.

Pye, Michael, *Skilful Means: A Concept in Mahayana Buddhism* (London: Routledge, 2003).
Rocher, Ludo, 'A Note on to *Ṣāḍ-guṇya*', in Samaresh Bandyopadhyay (ed.), Ācārya-Vandanā: D.R. Bhandarkar Birth Centenary Volume (Calcutta: University of Calcutta, 1982), pp. 319–25.
Scharfe, Hartmut, *Investigations in Kauṭalya's Manual of Political Science*, English tr., 2nd rev. ed. (Wiesbaden: Harrassowitz, 1993).
Strong, John S., *The Legend of King Aśoka: A Study and Translation of the* Aśokāvadāna, Buddhist Tradition Series 6, ed. Alex Wayman (Delhi: Motilal Banarsidass Publishers, 2002 [1989]).
Wilson, Liz, *Charming Cadavers: Horrific Figurations of the Feminine in Indian Buddhist Hagiographic Literature* (Chicago: University of Chicago Press, 1996).

Chapter 11
Dialogue and Difference: Encountering the Other in Indian Religious and Philosophical Sources[1]

Brian Black

Introduction

In his book *The Argumentative Indian*, Amartya Sen has brought attention to India's long tradition of accommodating diversity through public discourse and debate. This toleration of diversity, according to Sen, has been 'explicitly defended by strong arguments in favour of the richness of variation, including fulsome praise of the need to interact with each other, in mutual respect, through dialogue'.[2] In this chapter I would like to explore Sen's claim by focusing on three dialogues from traditional sources: the Ajātaśatru–Gārgya dialogue in the *Bṛhadāraṇyaka Upaniṣad*, the *Soṇadaṇḍa Sutta* of the *Dīgha Nikāya*, and the Janaka–Sulabhā dialogue in the *Mahābhārata*. First, I will bring attention to how each dialogue depicts an encounter between disputants who are defined by their differences, whether these differences are along the lines of caste, religious tradition, or gender. Then, I will explore how each dialogue confronts the differences between the two characters and their viewpoints both by offering a perspective that transcends the differences between the characters and by leaving the outcome of the debate to some extent open-ended, thereby accommodating both perspectives. As we consider each dialogue within its larger textual context, I will suggest that these encounters with difference can be seen as a crucial and recurring aspect of Indian religious and philosophical literature. These three dialogues, along with many of the other dialogues considered in this book – particularly those discussed by Geen and Nichols – have interesting implications regarding current attempts, by Amartya Sen and others, to recover an ancient Indian tradition of argumentation and toleration.

Dialogue One: Ajātaśatru and Gārgya

Our first dialogue, which appears in the *Bṛhadāraṇyaka Upaniṣad* (BU), begins when Dṛpta-Bālāki Gārgya, a 'learned' (*anūcāna*) Brahmin, proposes to deliver a teaching to Ajātaśatru, King of Kāśi. Ajātaśatru replies enthusiastically, offering to give Gārgya a thousand cows and commenting upon how receiving such a teaching will likely enhance his reputation.[3] The

---

[1] I would like to thank the following conversation partners with whom I have discussed many of the themes of this chapter: Simon Brodbeck, Gavin Hyman, Laurie Patton, Chakravarthi Ram-Prasad, Benedict Smith, and Lynn Thomas.

[2] Amartya Sen, *The Argumentative Indian: Writings on Indian Culture, History and Identity* (London, 2005), p. 17.

[3] Ajātaśatru's comment – 'People will run crying "A Janaka, a Janaka"' (BU 1.2.1) – suggests he thinks that by hosting philosophical debates he might be compared to Janaka, the famous philosopher-

Brahmin begins: 'It is the person (*puruṣa*) up there in the sun that I worship as *brahman*' (BU 2.1.2).[4] The King replies: 'Do not talk to me about him. I worship him as the highest, as the head and king of all beings. Whoever worships him this way becomes the highest, the head and king of all beings' (BU 2.1.2). A similar exchange appears eleven more times, with Gārgya equating *brahman* with the *puruṣa* in the moon (*candra*), lightning (*vidyut*), space (*ākāśa*), wind (*vāyu*), fire (*agni*), water (*apsu*), a mirror (*ādarśa*), sound (*śabda*), the quarters (*dikṣa*), a shadow (*chāyāmaya*), and the body (*ātman*) (BU 2.1.2–13).

Finally, the King asks him: 'Is that all?' (BU 2.1.14). When the Brahmin confirms that this is everything he has to teach, the King replies: 'It is not known by this' (BU 2.1.14). This prompts Gārgya to ask Ajātaśatru to be his teacher, at which point the King comments that taking on a Brahmin as a student is a reversal of their prescribed social roles: 'It is against the natural order (*pratiloma*) for a Brahmin to be taught about *brahman* by a *Kṣatriya*' (BU 2.1.15).

Assuming the role of the teacher, Ajātaśatru takes Gārgya by the hand to observe a sleeping man. Using the same terminology as Gārgya had used throughout his teaching, Ajātaśatru addresses the question: when this man was asleep, where was the '*puruṣa* made of knowledge' (*vijñānamaya puruṣa*). He then explains that the *puruṣa* was in the heart, having gathered the vital energies (*prāṇa*s). Subsequently, all the senses (speech, sight, hearing, and mind) are grasped by the *puruṣa*. In deep sleep, Ajātaśatru explains, the *puruṣa* rests in the citadel of the heart. At the end of this teaching, Ajātaśatru equates *puruṣa* with *ātman*, explaining that the self is the reality behind everything else: 'the truth of the truth' (*satyasya satyam*; BU 2.1.20).

As we can see, this dialogue features a confrontation between two interlocutors who offer different religio-philosophical perspectives and who are distinguished from each other along the lines of *varṇa*. The *Bṛhadāraṇyaka Upaniṣad* – in its concise, non-descriptive style – does not explicitly portray Gārgya negatively, but there are hints even before he begins his instruction that his teaching is in some sense limited or incomplete. At the beginning, he is called *dṛpta*, which means proud. He is also described as *anūcāna*, which can have the connotation of reciting or repeating, and which we might interpret as part of setting up a contrast between the Brahmin who merely memorizes and restates traditional learning and the King who understands and is able to explain a teaching of the self. Furthermore, as opposed to most other teachers in the Upaniṣads, who are often reluctant to share their knowledge, Gārgya offers to teach.[5]

The distinction between Gārgya and Ajātaśatru is not merely about who knows more, but is equally about what type of knowledge each one of them has mastered. Gārgya's teaching is based on knowing the connections between the Vedic sacrifice and the cosmos. This type of knowledge, which seeks to identify the underlying connections (*bandhus* –

king, who also appears in the *Bṛhadāraṇyaka Upaniṣad* (see books three and four). For the relationship between the Janaka in the *Bṛhadāraṇyaka Upaniṣad* and the one in the dialogue with Sulabhā from the *Mahābhārata*, see footnote 10.

4 Translations of the Upaniṣads, sometimes slightly modified, are from Valerie Roebuck's *The Upaniṣads* (London, 2003).

5 The reluctant teacher is a recurring trope in the Upaniṣads. See Brian Black, 'The Rhetoric of Secrecy in the Upaniṣads', in Steven Lindquist (ed.), *Religion and Identity in South Asia and Beyond: Essays in Honor of Patrick Olivelle* (New York: Anthem Press, 2011), pp. 106–7 and Jonardon Ganeri, *The Concealed Art of the Soul: Theories of Self and Practices of Truth in Indian Ethics and Epistemology* (Oxford, 2007), pp. 16–20; see also Brian Black, *The Character of the Self in Ancient India: Priests, Kings, and Women in the Early Upaniṣads* (Albany, 2007), pp. 29–58.

literally meaning 'bonded' or 'related') that exist among different orders of reality, is typical of Vedic ritual texts.

In comparison, Ajātaśatru's discourse is more naturalistic and experiential, discussing the vital energies of the body (*prāṇa*s), sleep, and the processes of life and death. Also, in contrast to the interactive exchanges in the first part of the dialogue, the King's teaching is uninterrupted.[6] There are also a number of aspects of Ajātaśatru's discourse that are similar to the teachings of other Upanishadic figures, such as Uddālaka Āruṇi and Yājñavalkya. First, there is the hint of empirical observation, as the King begins his teaching when observing the sleeping man;[7] then there is the focus on bodily processes and the attempt to explain what keeps the body alive. Also, the King uses a metaphor of a spider, which is similar to a number of natural metaphors used by other teachers in the Upaniṣads.[8] Through juxtaposition, this dialogue contrasts the Brahmin's ritual symbolism with the King's discourse on the mental and physiological processes of sleep and underlying reality of the self.

Crucial to the contrast between the teachings is the *varṇa* difference between the two characters. This is highlighted when the King comments on the reversal of the natural order when he takes on the role of the teacher in place of the Brahmin. It is interesting that Ajātaśatru notes the exceptional circumstances of a King teaching a Brahmin, despite the fact that the *Bṛhadāraṇyaka Upaniṣad* contains other episodes where a King instructs a Brahmin.[9] As we will return to below, this dialogue can be seen as part of a wider concern throughout the Upaniṣads with negotiating the relationship between Brahmins and Kṣatriyas.

As is typical of dialogues in the Upaniṣads, the encounter between Gārgya and Ajātaśatru ends with a lack of closure. What I am referring to here is the absence of any explicit outcome of their discussion. We do not learn, for example, whether or not Gārgya really learns from or is transformed by Ajataśatru's teaching. Nonetheless, Ajātaśatru's repeated challenges to Gārgya's discourse and the Brahmin's capitulation to these challenges when asking to be the King's student, characterize this discussion as in some sense competitive. Seen in this way, then the fact that Ajātaśatru's teaching finishes the dialogue without being interrupted, combined with the fact that the King's views align with other Upaniṣadic teachers such as Uddālaka Āruṇi and Yājñavalkya, indicates that Ajātaśatru offers the superior teaching.

Dialogue Two: the Buddha and Soṇadaṇḍa

Our next dialogue, which is also discussed in Nichols' chapter, is from the *Soṇadaṇḍa Sutta* of the *Dīgha Nikāya* (DN). It features a discussion between the Buddha and the well known and wealthy Brahmin Soṇadaṇḍa. After hearing reports that the Buddha is

---

[6] Indeed, when the King invites the Brahmin to participate by asking him what happens to the *puruṣa* when the man is asleep, Gārgya remains silent, not knowing the answer (2.1.16).

[7] Similarly Uddālaka Āruṇi relies on a number of observations of the natural world in his teaching to his son Śvetaketu in the *Chāndogya Upaniṣad* (6.8–16).

[8] See, for example, Yajñavalkya's use of metaphors in his teachings to King Janaka (BU 4.4.3–4) and his wife Maitreyī (BU 4.5.8–13).

[9] The *Kauṣītaki Upaniṣad* (KsU) also contains a version of this dialogue. Like the BU version, the KsU version also remarks on the unusual circumstance of a king teaching a Brahmin, yet has other episodes in which a king teaches a Brahmin.

a fully enlightened being, Soṇadaṇḍa decides to go and see for himself. However, on his way Soṇadaṇḍa begins to have concerns that he will not be able to answer the Buddha's questions and will consequently lose his reputation. His doubts recur when he is in the presence of the Buddha, who, reading his mind, questions him 'from his own field as a teacher of the three Vedas' (DN 4.11),[10] asking him about the qualities of a Brahmin. At first Soṇadaṇḍa lists five qualities: (1) well-born on both mother's and father's side; of pure descent for seven generations; (2) a scholar versed in mantras; (3) handsome and pleasing; (4) moral; and (5) wise. However, the Buddha challenges Soṇadaṇḍa by asking if all five qualities are essential, or if, perhaps, some could be left out. Soṇadaṇḍa agrees that not all five are equally necessary and the discussion carries on until only two qualities remain: (4) morality (*sīla*) and (5) wisdom (*pañña*). At this point Soṇadaṇḍa's own followers begin to question him, accusing him of adopting the words of the Buddha. Finally, Soṇadaṇḍa is not able to define either quality, so he asks the Buddha to define them for him: 'We only know this much, Gotama. It would be well if the Reverend Gotama were to explain the meaning of this' (DN 4.23).

The Buddha responds by announcing his own qualities as a Buddha and then gives a long discourse on the moral practices (*sīla*s) and how to be in control of the senses. The *Soṇadaṇḍa Sutta* is one of several *sutta*s in the Nikāyas to include this list of 'moral practices' (*sīlakkhandhavagga*), a thorough register of actions that monks and nuns should avoid in order to be 'perfected in morality'.[11] The Buddha goes on to explain how one should control the senses: 'develop restraint' of the eye-faculty, the ear-faculty, the nose-faculty, the taste-faculty, and the mind-faculty (see DN 2.41–63). At this point the Buddha proclaims: 'That, Brahmin, is morality (*sīla*)'. Then the Buddha discusses the psychological consequences of practising such physical and mental disciplines: gladness arises, then delight, then tranquility, then joy, then a concentrated mind, then the four *jhāna*s (see DN 2.75–81). Subsequently, the Buddha describes various insights and the cessation of the corruption (see DN 2.83–97), at which point he proclaims: 'That, Brahmin, is wisdom (*pañña*)'. Implicit in the Buddha's teaching is that the states of consciousness one needs to develop to reach *nirvāṇa* can only be achieved if they are preceded by following the Buddha's moral instructions. In other words, the repeated practice of the Buddha's moral injunctions will produce a psychological transformation. While these teachings appear in several *sutta*s, in the *Soṇadaṇḍa Sutta* the Buddha explicitly links these teachings to the qualities of a Brahmin by equating the *sīlakkhandhavagga* with morality and by equating the different mental states achieved through meditation with wisdom. In other words, the Buddha defines the two qualities that make up a Brahmin in terms of Buddhist teachings and practices.

Soṇadaṇḍa responds to the Buddha's discourse by asking to become a lay supporter and offering a meal to the Buddha. After their meal, Soṇadaṇḍa sits on a stool beside the Buddha and expresses his concerns about his reputation: 'If when I have gone into the assembly I were to rise and salute the Lord, the company would despise me. In that case my reputation would suffer, and if a man's reputation suffers, his income suffers' (DN 4.26). He then explains that, although he acknowledges the Buddha's superiority in private, he

---

[10] All translations of and references to the *Dīgha Nikāya* are from Maurice Walshe, *The Long Discourses of the Buddha: A Translation of the Dīgha Nikāya* (Boston, 1995).

[11] As Damien Keown points out, there is considerable overlap between this list of moral practices and other moral lists in the Pāli Canon, such as the five precepts, the eight precepts, the ten precepts, and the ten paths of good action (Damien Keown, *The Nature of Buddhist Ethics* [London, 2001], p. 31).

will not rise to greet the Buddha in an assembly, nor will he bow at his feet, but that when he instead joins his palms or takes off his turban, the Buddha should take it as if Soṇadaṇḍa had shown his full respect. The *Soṇadaṇḍa Sutta* concludes after relating that the Buddha delivered a talk on *Dhamma*, which inspired and delighted Soṇadaṇḍa.

There are a number of similarities between this dialogue and the previous one. Again we have a confrontation between two interlocutors who espouse different religio-philosophical ideas and who are designated as different from each other, this time along the lines of religious affiliation, as well as *varṇa*. Similar to Gārgya, Soṇadaṇḍa speaks first about his own area of expertise, but is systematically challenged by his interlocutor until his lack of knowledge is exposed and he literally runs out of things to say. At this point, the Buddha, similar to Ajātaśatru, assumes the role of the teacher and offers a superior instruction. In addition to sharing the two-part structure and a similar dynamic between the two characters, the *Soṇadaṇḍa Sutta* juxtaposes two very different types of discourse: in this case the Brahmanical concern with maintaining an elite status for Brahmins is contrasted with the Buddha's teaching on morality and wisdom. As with Ajātaśatru, the Buddha delivers a strong challenge to his interlocutor's teaching, in this case demonstrating that he knows the characteristics of Brahminhood better than Soṇadaṇḍa himself. Perhaps similar to Gārgya being described as *anūcāna*, Soṇadaṇḍa can recite the qualities of a true Brahmin, but he cannot define them.

In contrast to the concise style of the Upanishadic dialogues, the Nikāyas are more explicit in characterizing the Brahmin negatively: he is insecure before meeting the Buddha, he is not able to answer questions from his own field of expertise, and – even when privately acknowledging the Buddha's superiority – he will not agree to salute the Buddha with the proper reverence, instead insisting that if he were to do this, he might lose the respect of his own followers. Also, in contrast with how the Buddha interacts with other Brahmin interlocutors who feature in the Nikāyas, he does not teach Soṇadaṇḍa the four noble truths, nor does he proclaim that the Brahmin has attained the 'pure and spotless Dhamma-eye' at the end of the *sutta*.

The *Soṇadaṇḍa Sutta* is also much more explicit about the outcome of the debate. While we never learn what happens to Gārgya after he receives Ajātaśatru's instruction, Soṇadaṇḍa praises the Buddha's teaching. He then pledges to be a lay supporter for the remainder of his life, before inviting the Buddha for a meal. As I have discussed elsewhere,[12] there are reasons to be cautious about characterizing this *sutta* as a debate, not least of which is the fact that Soṇadaṇḍa seems to concede the superiority of the Buddha even before their encounter. Nonetheless, similar to Ajātaśatru, the Buddha clearly emerges as having the superior teaching.

[12] Brian Black, 'Rivals and Benefactors: Encounters between Buddhists and Brahmins in the Nikāyas', *Religions of South Asia* 3/1 (2009): 36.

Dialogue Three: Sulabhā and King Janaka

Our third dialogue, from the *Mokṣadharma* section of the *Mahābhārata* (12.308), features King Janaka[13] and the female sage Sulabhā.[14] In this scene, Sulabhā is depicted as adept at yoga and as one who has attained *mokṣa* – characteristics that are quite rare for a female character in Brahmanical literature. An intriguing aspect of this scene is that Sulabhā, using her yogic powers, enters into Janaka and conducts her entire argument from inside the King's body.[15]

At the beginning of this episode, Sulabhā is a wandering ascetic who hears reports from other renouncers that King Janaka has achieved *mokṣa* without giving up his kingdom. Doubtful of these claims, she uses her yogic powers to put on an immaculately beautiful body and travel to the court in the wink of an eye, to find out for herself about Janaka's claims to be enlightened. When she arrives, after accepting the King's hospitality, she challenges him to an argument in front of the assembly. At this point she uses her 'knowledge of yoga and enters into [the King's] being with her being' (12.308.16).[16] This marks the beginning of their debate.

Janaka speaks first, posing a series of questions to Sulabhā about who she is:

> Where have your homeless wanderings taken you, blessed woman and where will you go? Whose are you? And where are you from? I cannot get a clear sense of your learning, of your age, or of the ethnic group you were born in, so please convey answers to these matters in this assembly of pious people. (12.308.20–1)

Janaka returns to these questions throughout his argument, challenging Sulabhā's claims of achieving *mokṣa* by questioning her social identity in terms of class, family, and gender. At one point he specifically questions how she can be an ascetic when she is so young and beautiful (12.308.54)

After these initial questions, Janaka begins his philosophical argument. In what is basically a defence of *karmayoga*, he argues that one can achieve enlightenment without renouncing the world. He says he is beyond karma, because his knowledge keeps his actions from producing results, like a seed that has been roasted and can no longer germinate (12.308.33). *Mokṣa*, the King argues, does not come from not having any possessions, but

---

[13] It is unclear whether this is the same Janaka as the philosopher-king of the Upaniṣads. Arti Dhand ('Paradigms of the Good in the *Mahābhārata*: Śuka and Sulabhā in Quagmires of Ethics', in Simon Brodbeck and Brian Black [eds], *Gender and Narrative in the* Mahābhārata [London, 2007], p. 261) points out ways in which the Janaka in this dialogue is depicted differently from the King Janaka who appears in another dialogue in the *Mahābhārata.* Following Patton ('Traces of Śaunaka: A Literary Assessment', *Journal of the American Academy of Religion* 79/1 [2011]: 113–35), who discusses Śaunaka as a literary character, we might take the many appearances of the name Janaka as representing different personae, but nonetheless sharing set of literary characteristics. See also Brian Black and Jonathan Geen, 'The Character of "Character" in Early South Asian Religious Traditions', *Journal of the American Academy of Religion* 79/1 (2011): 6–32.

[14] For discussions of this dialogue, see also Dhand and Ruth Vanita, 'The Self Is Not Gendered: Sulabha's Debate with King Janaka', *National Women's Studies Association Journal* 15/2 (2003) 76–93.

[15] The ability to enter into another's body is mentioned in the *Yoga Sūtra* (3.21).

[16] Translations of this dialogue, sometimes slightly modified, are from James Fitzgerald, 'Nun Befuddles King, Shows *Karmayoga* Does Not Work: Sulabhā's Refutation of King Janaka at MBh 12.308', *Journal of Indian Philosophy* 30/6 (2002): 641–77.

rather it is knowledge that releases one's bonds with the world. Such arguments are similar to the arguments of Kṛṣṇa in the *Bhagavad Gītā*. It is interesting here, though, that Sulabhā rejects these arguments in favour of the view that one must live the life of a renouncer in order to achieve enlightenment.

Sulabhā responds to Janaka's discourse by outlining the characteristics of a proper argument and then addressing Janaka's question of who she is from a completely different perspective. Rather than speak of herself in terms of her social identity, Sulabhā talks about her selfhood in more abstract terms. Using proto-Sāṃkhyan terminology, she discusses twenty components that are responsible for the origination and passing away of beings, explaining that there is an unmanifest nature (*prakṛti*) that becomes manifest in these twenty components. During the course of her argument she goes from the general to the specific, arguing that if the King were a truly enlightened being he would not have been concerned with her social identity: that his question of who she is – from the point of view of an enlightened person – can only be discussed in terms of the combination of the twenty components and cannot be answered in terms of one's social identity. From this perspective, she poses the question to Janaka: 'Since you see yourself within yourself by means of yourself, why do you not, in exactly the same way, by means of yourself, see yourself in someone else?' (12.308.126). In other words, Sulabhā argues that if Janaka is enlightened enough to see his own true nature, then he should be able to see the true nature of others as well – if he were truly enlightened he would see no distinction between himself and Sulabhā.

Similar to the first two dialogues, this encounter features two interlocutors who offer conflicting teachings and whose personal identities are distinguished from one another, this time along the lines of gender. As with Gārgya and Soṇadaṇḍa, Janaka presents his argument first, only for his views to be challenged and then supplanted by Sulabhā. In addition to being challenged, and again similar to Gārgya and Soṇadaṇḍa, Janaka is portrayed negatively. At the beginning of the dialogue, for example, he is referred to as *dharmadhvaja*, which can mean 'hypocrite' or 'impostor' (12.308.4). Also, Janaka is the one who offers to speak first, which, as we saw with Gārgya, can be an indicator that one is proud and/or one's knowledge is incomplete. Furthermore, during his argument Janaka repeatedly insults Sulabhā, calling her a wicked woman and accusing her of using her yogic powers as a poison (12.308.65, 68). Indeed, after Janaka's argument, Bhīṣma, the narrator of this episode, relates that the King's statements were 'unpleasant' (*asukha*) and 'inappropriate' (*ayukta*) (12.308.76). In contrast, Sulabhā is described as 'lovely' and her argument 'even lovelier' (12.308.77). Also similar to our dialogues from the Upaniṣads and Nikāyas is the contrast between the type of discourse offered by the two interlocutors, with Janaka espousing the view of *karmayoga*, while Sulabhā delivers a teaching more characteristic of the renunciate traditions.

Throughout, a major theme in this dialogue is the gender difference between Janaka and Sulabhā, particularly in relation to the curious circumstances of both characters inhabiting the same body during their discussion. Janaka accuses Sulabhā of joining herself inappropriately with a man from a different social order, claiming that she has broken a number of social taboos by entering his body. According to Janaka, she has crossed distinctions of both caste and clan. Furthermore, Janaka argues that one who is unenlightened should not be joined with one who is enlightened, and that Sulabhā should not give herself to another man if she already has a husband (12.308.62). Here Janaka suggests that there is a physical dimension to her inhabiting his body. Further on, he alludes to a sexual dynamic of their interaction, arguing that one who is a renouncer should not still love and comparing their encounter to a man and a woman who desire each other (12.308.69).

In her rebuttal Sulabhā maintains that because of her yogic powers she can dwell inside him without touching him, and, consequently, that there is no actual mixing or merging going on. Furthermore, she challenges Janaka's arguments about her social identity: she claims she is not a Brahmin, but a *Kṣatriya*; she is not unfaithful because she has no husband; she is the one who is enlightened and if he were enlightened she would not be able to inhabit his body; and finally, if Janaka were truly enlightened these class distinctions would not matter anyway.

At the end of her argument the narrative recounts: 'After he heard these reasoned and significant statements, the King did not say anything further' (12.308.191). Similar to our dialogue from the Upaniṣads, this narrative does not offer any details about whether or not Janaka is transformed by Sulabhā's teaching. However, the fact that the narrative criticizes his words during the debate and that he is silenced at the end suggest that Sulabhā wins the argument.

Dialogue as Encounter with the Other

As we have seen, each of these dialogues includes interlocutors who are defined by their differences, whether they be different castes, different religious traditions, or different genders. In each case, the differences between the interlocutors are both embodied by the characters and overtly addressed during their discussion: Ajātaśatru comments on the *varṇa* difference between himself and Gārgya when pointing out that Kings do not normally teach Brahmins; the Buddha contrasts the Brahmanical with the Buddhist way of defining a true Brahmin; and both Janaka and Sulabhā address the gender dynamic of their encounter. A crucial component of each dialogue is encountering and negotiating the differences between the characters.

What I would like to suggest when looking at these dialogues together is that there is an ongoing commitment to confronting difference in Indian religious and philosophical sources. In this way, we might see these episodes as instances of Sen's claim that Indian traditions address the need to interact with each other through dialogue. In making this suggestion, I am not arguing that dialogue is essentially or naturally inclusive, nor am I claiming that all dialogues in ancient Indian sources do what the ones we have examined here do – as the different chapters in this book demonstrate, the dialogue form can be used in a variety of ways. Moreover, it is important to keep in mind that these dialogues are idealized and stylized literary constructions. We cannot naively assume that these are accurate accounts of real conversations or that the views of each party are represented in their best possible light. These dialogues are all presented from a particular perspective and would come across quite differently if recounted from the opposite point of view. If, for example, the initial interlocutor had been offered a counter-argument, then perhaps Gārgya would have questioned Ajātaśatru's means of knowing the '*puruṣa* made of knowledge'; Soṇadaṇḍa might have taken the opportunity to define the qualities of a Brahmin differently, pointing out that the Upaniṣads had already made the important distinction between those who achieve the status of Brahmin by birth and those who achieve it through knowledge; or perhaps Janaka – even if agreeing with her points about gender – could have questioned if Sulabhā's argument necessarily leads to the conclusion that *karmayoga* does not work. Keeping in mind that the dialogue form can be employed to contain, distort, sanitize, or silence opposing views, we might wonder to what degree these episodes are 'real' dialogues.

Clearly, these dialogues are asymmetrical in the sense that one point of view is favoured over another – even though, as we will see, these encounters are perhaps not as lopsided as they first appear to be. Yet even if these dialogues do not attempt a neutral or objective vantage point, they nevertheless are 'real' in the sense that within each dialogue's larger textual context, each is part of a broader concern with exploring and negotiating relationships with others. The dialogue between Gārgya and Ajātaśatru, for example, is part of an ongoing consideration of interactions between Brahmins and Kings in the Upaniṣads.[17] Similarly, the relationship between Buddhists and Brahmins is a recurring topic of reflection in the Nikāyas,[18] while gender identities are examined on multiple occasions throughout the *Mahābhārata*.[19] In each textual context, dialogue is a central, but not the only, means of exploring such encounters with difference. In other words, I would like to suggest that while these dialogues might not depict actual conversations between individuals, they do reflect real examinations of tolerance and plurality. Moreover, these dialogues do not merely 'represent' other voices, but could be seen as instances of an active engagement with others, a reaching out to other social groups, other religious communities, other gendered bodies.

Dialogue as Transcending Difference

In addition to setting up an initial encounter with difference, each dialogue explores methods of argumentation and disputation, while finally offering a perspective from which to overcome the differences between the characters. As we have seen, all three dialogues follow a similar structure, featuring two interlocutors and two distinct sections, with the arguments of the first interlocutor in the first section and of the second interlocutor in the second section. In each case the views of the first interlocutor are challenged and then supplanted by the second interlocutor. The dialogues from the Upaniṣads and the Nikāyas have further similarities, as in both cases the first part of the dialogue is interactive, where the Brahmin character is repeatedly challenged when offering his view, and where the second part of the dialogue is an uninterrupted discourse by the non-Brahmin character. The interactive aspect of these dialogues allows the second interlocutor to demonstrate knowledge of his opponent's argument. Ajātaśatru's responses to Gārgya, for example, indicate that he knows the Brahmin's teaching, while the Buddha clearly shows that he knows the qualities of a Brahmin better than Soṇadaṇḍa. The dialogue between Janaka and Sulabhā is different from the first two, as both of their arguments are non-interactive; instead of challenging Janaka as he builds his case, Sulabhā offers a point by point rebuttal after his argument.

In addition to juxtaposing two arguments and establishing a hierarchy between them, each dialogue presents a perspective that transcends the differences between the two conflicting views. As we have seen in our first dialogue, there is a clear distinction between the type of knowledge presented by each interlocutor. Yet despite adopting a

---

[17] See Black, *The Character of the Self in Ancient India*, pp. 103–31.

[18] See Black, 'Rivals and Benefactors', and Joy Manné, 'The Dīgha Nikāya Debates: Debating Practices at the Time of the Buddha', *Buddhist Studies Review* 9/2 (1992): 117–36.

[19] See Nancy Falk, 'Draupadī and the Dharma', in Rita M. Gross (ed.), *Beyond Androcentrism: New Essays on Women and Religion* (Missoula, Montana, 1977); Simon Brodbeck and Brian Black, *Gender and Narrative in the* Mahābhārata (London, 2007); and Arti Dhand, *Woman as Fire, Woman as Sage: Sexual Ideology in the* Mahābhārata (Albany, 2008).

radically different style of discourse and philosophical orientation, Ajātaśatru repeatedly uses the term *puruṣa*, thereby redeploying the terminology of his interlocutor, rather than completely rejecting Gārgya's argument. Moreover, unlike Gārgya's teaching, which is restricted to the ritual arena, the preserve of Brahmins, Ajātaśatru focuses on the human body, states of consciousness, and physiological processes – topics that we might see as less esoteric, less likely to be confined to the expertise of a particular social group. In other words, in comparison with Gārgya's teaching, which is in some sense limited to Brahmins, Ajātaśatru's teaching is available to both Kings and Brahmins. In this way, we might see Gārgya's teaching as reinforcing the *varṇa* distinctions between the King and himself, and Ajātaśatru's teaching as transcending the *varṇa* distinction between them.

There is a similar relationship between the two teachings presented in the *Soṇadaṇḍa Sutta*. As we have seen, Soṇadaṇḍa's discourse emphasizes the distinctions between Brahmanism and Buddhism, with the narrative suggesting that knowledge of the qualities of a true Brahmin would be typical of a discourse from the 'field of a teacher of the three Vedas' (DN 4.1). In other words, the Brahmin's knowledge is depicted as consisting of knowing the qualities that distinguish Brahmins from everyone else. The Buddha, however, redefines the qualities of a Brahmin in terms of Buddhist ethical and meditative practices, thereby redefining the status of Brahmin in terms of actions that are available to everyone, rather than in terms of the lineages of a select few. As such, the Buddha defines the qualities of a Brahmin in such a way that they transcend distinctions between Buddhists and Brahmins.

Similar to Ajātaśatru and the Buddha, Sulabhā offers a perspective that goes beyond the differences between her interlocutor and herself. At the beginning of his discourse, Janaka claims that he no longer sees things as pairs of opposites (12.308.31), yet much of his argument rests upon setting up binary oppositions between himself and Sulabhā, including Brahmin/*Kṣatriya* and householder/renunciate. In particular, Janaka focuses on the gender differences between Sulabhā and himself, raising doubts about her ability to attain *mokṣa*. If we were to take Janaka's view to its logical conclusion, not only is Sulabhā not enlightened, but she could not possibly be enlightened because she is a woman. In her response, Sulabhā directly asks Janaka: how does someone who is freed from the pairs of opposites ask 'who are you, whose are you, and where do you come from'? In challenging Janaka's position, though, there is nothing in her views that prohibits Janaka from achieving *mokṣa*, as long as he renounces his role as King. Again we see that while the interlocutors take different philosophical positions, they also embody their differences; in this case Sulabhā not only argues that one who is liberated transcends gender distinctions, but her inhabitation of Janaka's body demonstrates her philosophical point – despite physical appearances and social constructs, there is no ontological distinction between them. Through both her arguments and her actions, then, Sulabhā represents a model for enlightenment that is beyond the dualities of gender distinction, and therefore is as available for women as it is for men.

In looking at our three dialogues together, in each case the first interlocutor presents a teaching that reinforces the differences between the two characters, while the second character presents a discourse that transcends their differences. Each dialogue follows a certain progression, involving questions and answers, and moving from discord to harmony. In the first two dialogues we have noted that Ajātaśatru and the Buddha challenge their interlocutors in similar ways: Ajātaśatru repeatedly asks Gārgya to give him a deeper understanding of *puruṣa*; the Buddha challenges Soṇadaṇḍa to define the most foundational characteristics of a Brahmin. This type of challenge employed by Ajātaśatru and the Buddha does not lead their interlocutor to a contradiction in their arguments, but rather forces them to admit to a lack of depth to their knowledge. Subsequently, both Ajātaśatru and the Buddha expand upon the arguments of their opponents by redeploying their terminology, yet neither of them explicitly addresses their interlocutor's arguments when they deliver their own teachings. In other words, rather than the type of dialectical arguments we often see in Plato's dialogues, in these cases we see more of a juxtaposition of almost two completely disconnected types of arguments, where the second argument uses some of the same terms, but in a different conceptual context.

The dialogue between Janaka and Sulabhā unfolds differently. As mentioned above, Janaka – unlike Gārgya and Soṇadaṇḍa – speaks without Sulabhā interrupting him. In this way, this dialogue does not have the exchange of questions and answers, nor does it explore the same methods of refutation. But even more than the other two, this dialogue lays out a method for conducting an argument, with Sulabhā outlining five aspects of speech: subtlety (*saukṣmya*), deliberation (*saṁkhyā*), clear order (*krama*), a conclusion (*nirṇaya*), and purpose (*saprayojana*), in each case giving an example to illustrate what she means. She then explains how she will articulate her speech, promising not to say too much or too little, not to say anything off topic or untrue, adding that she will not be affected by emotions such as love, anger, fear, or greed. She then talks about the interaction between speaker and hearer, explaining that when they agree, meaning arises; but when a speaker disrespects the hearer, then the speaker only speaks for his own sake, or the speech is simply useless for the other. She concludes: 'Only he who declares meaning that is not opposed to either of the two is a true speaker, no one else is' (12.308.94). This declaration, that her speech will have 'this kind of meaning', resonates with the inclusive conclusion she makes at the end of her argument. Yet despite following her own guidelines for proper disputation, the agreement between the speakers – which she claims constitutes meaning – never happens. Nonetheless, despite not living up to Sulabhā's own standards of reaching a meaningful conclusion, this dialogue – similar to the other two – offers a unifying perspective in response to views placed in opposition to one another.

Dialogue as Accommodation

While each dialogue can be seen as culminating in a point of view that transcends difference, each encounter also offers a possible reading in which the debate could be seen as unfinished or unresolved. In our first dialogue, Ajātaśatru appears to win the argument, yet – as we noted above – the dialogue ends with a lack of closure. Moreover, similar dialogues in the Upaniṣads often balance out the King's superior teaching with an emphasis on accommodation and compromise. Between the *Bṛhadāraṇyaka* and the *Chāndogya Upaniṣads* there are four distinct dialogues which include an encounter between Brahmins and Kṣatriyas. While these do not all follow the same pattern, in each case there is a negotiation of status between the characters, with the trope of a King teaching a Brahmin appearing in three of them. Even when Kings deliver teachings to Brahmins or defeat a Brahmin in a debate, they make concessions. As I have argued elsewhere, Brahmins get paid by Kings even if they do not offer a teaching or even if their teaching is superseded by a King's.[20] (2007: 105–110). Despite depicting Kings as more knowledgeable than Brahmins, these dialogues nevertheless portray the Kings as respectful, hospitable and magnanimous towards Brahmins. While the Gārgya–Ajātaśatru dialogue does this less than

[20] Black, *The Character of the Self*, pp. 105–10.

other dialogues in the Upaniṣads, it is important to see this episode as embedded within a textual context that represents the relationship between the Brahmin and the King as mutually dependent and continually in the process of negotiation.[21]

The relationship between Buddhists and Brahmins in the Nikāyas is similarly complex. In the *Dīgha Nikāya*, nine of the thirty-four *sutta*s feature a verbal exchange between the Buddha and a prominent Brahmin,[22] while the *Majjhima Nikāya* devotes an entire section of ten *sutta*s to dialogues between Buddhists and Brahmins. As I have explored elsewhere, these encounters between Buddhists and Brahmins reveal conflicting attitudes.[23] Clearly, these scenes criticize Brahmanism, including specific challenges to the status of Brahmins, the Vedas, and Vedic rituals. Also, these scenes portray Brahmins as recognizing the superiority of the Buddha, prostrating themselves in front of him, and asking to be his lay disciples. However, they also tend to include compromise and concession as integral aspects of the Buddha's dealings with Brahmins. As we have seen, the Buddha, despite exposing the Brahmin's ignorance, does not humiliate Soṇadaṇḍa in public, but defends him in front of his followers. This accommodative stance towards the Brahmin is further emphasized at the end of the dialogue when the Buddha allows Soṇadaṇḍa to choose his own method of salutation. Implicitly, Soṇadaṇḍa can claim to be a lay supporter despite not changing any of his behaviour as a Brahmin. The *sutta* thus ends with a compromise, with Soṇadaṇḍa neither renouncing his views, nor changing his practices. If we were to take this episode as competitive, then we might see Soṇadaṇḍa as coming out ahead at the end of the encounter: despite being exposed as less knowledgeable, the Brahmin gets to dictate the terms of their relationship.

Perhaps even more than the other two, the dialogue between Janaka and Sulabhā leaves us with contradictory resolutions. Sulabhā is one of several strong female characters – along with Draupadī, Śakuntalā, and Sāvitrī, as well as others – who challenge authoritative male figures in verbal disputes in the *Mahābhārata*. One of the ways in which these scenes are different from the encounters between Brahmins and Kings in the Upaniṣads and between Brahmins and Buddhists in the Nikāyas is that the female characters in the *Mahābhārata* do not have a common worldview; in other words, unlike the Brahmins of the Upaniṣads and Nikāyas, the women of the *Mahābhārata* do not share a particular doctrinal position. Nonetheless, these scenes are similar to the others we have examined in the sense that that the gender dynamic of the encounter is explored by the characters in comparable ways as the caste or religious differences in other contexts.

Some of the recurring issues involve whether women have the right to speak and, if they do, whether their views can be as authoritative as those of men. While Sulabhā seemingly emerges victorious in her debate with Janaka, other female characters often have their authority to speak questioned and are only able to have their arguments considered seriously when men speak on their behalf.[24] Similarly, the fact that Sulabhā only wins her argument while inside Janaka's body might suggest that, despite her reasoned arguments, her views are only accepted in the court when the King is the mouthpiece for her discourse.

---

21 Black, *The Character of the Self*, pp. 110–19.

22 Manné, 'The Dīgha Nikāya Debates': 136.

23 Black, 'Rivals and Benefactors'.

24 For further discussion about the issue of authority for female speakers, see Black, *The Character of the Self in Ancient India*, pp. 133–68; and Brian Black, 'Eavesdropping on the Epic: Female Listeners in the *Mahābhārata*', in Simon Brodbeck and Brian Black (eds), *Gender and Narrative in the* Mahābhārata (London, 2007).

However, unlike cases of female ventriloquism which occur in the *Bṛhadāraṇyaka Upaniṣad*, Sulabhā's identity is not masked nor is her agency denied; rather her ability to enter the King's body in the first place is an indication of her yogic powers.

As we have seen, there are details in the dialogue clearly suggesting that Sulabhā wins the argument, such as the fact that she gets the last word – which is often a marker of superiority in these episodes – as well as Bhīṣma's favourable portrayal of Sulabhā's view when he is narrating the story to Yudhiṣṭhira. However, even though he is silenced at the end, there are indications that Janaka's claims to have achieved *mokṣa* are indeed accepted as true, with Bhīṣma describing the dialogue as 'a conversation between a man who had attained *mokṣa* and a woman who had attained *mokṣa*' (12.308.19).

Janaka's lineage and philosophical perspective also align him with a number of authoritative figures in the *Mahābhārata*. At the beginning of his argument, for example, Janaka claims that his teacher is Pañcaśikha, from the same *gotra* as Parāśara. Interestingly, this would connect him to Vyāsa, the reputed author of the *Mahābhārata*, who is the son of Parāśara. Also, as we noted above, Janaka's views echo Kṛṣṇa's teaching in the *Bhagavad Gītā*. In other words, despite her apparent victory within this episode, Sulabhā's argument runs counter to one of the central philosophical claims of the *Mahābhārata* – that one can reach the highest religious goals while continuing to engage in this world. Furthermore, Janaka's views are similar to those expressed by Bhīṣma, whose own stance throughout his post-war instruction to Yudhiṣṭhira – despite his apparent endorsement of Sulabhā's view when narrating this story – is more in line with the doctrine of *karmayoga*. Taking all this into consideration, the text seems to endorse both arguments: within the context of the dialogue itself, Sulabhā appears to be the clear winner of the argument; yet within the context of Bhīṣma's instruction to Yudhiṣṭhira, Janaka's view seems to be preferred.

Reading the three dialogues together, we see that in each case there is some degree of ambiguity regarding the outcome. As we have seen in Nicholson's chapter, the philosophical genre of polemic contains formal requirements that each section ends with a final decision. Nicholson contrasts this with Platonic dialogues, which often end without an established conclusion. Although I am proposing that the dialogues considered here also portray a degree of uncertainty, it is important to distinguish the ambiguity in these encounters from the notion of *aporia*, as seen in Plato's dialogues. Whereas the *aporia* in Plato tends to be explicit, with the discussion 'postponed to another occasion' or Socrates 'confessing his own ignorance',[25] the unresolved character of the dialogues discussed here is more oblique. Ajātaśatru, the Buddha, and Sulabhā all appear to win their arguments. It is only when we read these dialogues in their wider textual contexts that we see that the outcome might not be so straightforward. Moreover, in the Greek context *aporia* can refer to the unsolvable contradictions of a particular argument. As Dmitri Nikulin explains: 'Socratic refutation discloses a perplexing difficulty, an *aporia*, that seems incapable of resolution because of the contradiction that results from the dialogical exchange.'[26] While both Ajātaśatru and the Buddha expose the limitations of their interlocutor's knowledge, neither of them demonstrate a logical contraction in their opponent's arguments. Sulabhā goes further in showing that Janaka's non-dualism should also apply to gender, but she herself offers a solution to Janaka's contradiction, rather than presenting his views as inherently insolvable. In other words, the lack of resolution in these encounters is not

[25] Diskin Clay, *Platonic Questions: Dialogues with the Silent Philosopher* (University Park, Pennsylvania, 2000), p. 166.

[26] Dmitri Nikulin, *Dialectic and Dialogue* (Stanford, 2010), p. 14.

presented as a philosophical conundrum, but rather as an ambivalence concerning the social hierarchy of the two characters. Seen in this way, the inconclusive character of the dialogues suggests an accommodative approach to social interactions, with the lack of closure allowing interlocutors to save face and opening spaces within the text to tolerate potentially subversive positions.

Conclusion

We began this chapter by noting Amartya Sen's recent claims that India has had a long tradition of accommodation and toleration through dialogue. In this chapter I have explored this claim by focusing on three specific dialogues from traditional sources. As I have argued, traditional Indian religious and philosophical texts show a recurring commitment to exploring difference through dialogue. But rather than insisting on either finding a common ground or on accepting plurality, they often maintain a delicate balance between these two strategies. If – along with Sen – we are looking for examples of where Indian religious and philosophical traditions explore issues related to modern debates about pluralism and diversity, then it seems to me that these dialogues, as well as others, from the Upaniṣads, Nikāyas, and *Mahābhārata*, are an excellent place to start.

References

Black, Brian, *The Character of the Self in Ancient India: Priests, Kings, and Women in the Early Upaniṣads* (Albany: State University of New York Press, 2007).

———, 'Eavesdropping on the Epic: Female Listeners in the *Mahābhārata*', in Simon Brodbeck and Brian Black (eds), *Gender and Narrative in the* Mahābhārata (London: Routledge, 2007).

———, 'Rivals and Benefactors: Encounters between Buddhists and Brahmins in the Nikāyas', *Religions of South Asia* 3/1 (2009): 25–43.

———, 'The Rhetoric of Secrecy in the Upaniṣads', in Steven Lindquist (ed.), *Religion and Identity in South Asia and Beyond: Essays in Honor of Patrick Olivelle* (New York: Anthem Press, 2011), pp. 101–25.

Black, Brian and Jonathan Geen, 'The Character of "Character" in Early South Asian Religious Traditions', *Journal of the American Academy of Religion* 79/1 (2011): 6–32.

Brodbeck, Simon and Brian Black, *Gender and Narrative in the* Mahābhārata (London: Routledge, 2007).

Clay, Diskin, *Platonic Questions: Dialogues with the Silent Philosopher* (University Park, Pennsylvania: Pennsylvania State University Press, 2000).

Dhand, Arti, 'Paradigms of the Good in the *Mahābhārata*: Śuka and Sulabhā in Quagmires of Ethics', in Simon Brodbeck and Brian Black (eds), *Gender and Narrative in the* Mahābhārata (London: Routledge, 2007).

———, *Woman as Fire, Woman as Sage: Sexual Ideology in the* Mahābhārata (Albany: State University of New York Press, 2008).

Falk, Nancy, 'Draupadī and the Dharma', in Rita M. Gross (ed.), *Beyond Androcentrism: New Essays on Women and Religion* (Missoula, Montana: Scholars Press, 1977).

Fitzgerald, James, 'Nun Befuddles King, Shows *Karmayoga* Does Not Work: Sulabhā's Refutation of King Janaka at MBh 12.308', *Journal of Indian Philosophy* 30/6 (2002): 641–77.

Ganeri, Jonardon, *The Concealed Art of the Soul: Theories of Self and Practices of Truth in Indian Ethics and Epistemology* (Oxford: Oxford University Press, 2007).

Keown, Damien, *The Nature of Buddhist Ethics* (London: Palgrave Macmillan, 2001).

Manné, Joy, 'The *Dīgha Nikāya* Debates: Debating Practices at the Time of the Buddha', *Buddhist Studies Review* 9/2 (1992): 117–36.

Nikulin, Dmitri, *Dialectic and Dialogue* (Stanford: Stanford University Press, 2010).

Olivelle, Patrick (trans. and ed.), *The Early Upaniṣads: Annotated Text and Translation* (New York: Oxford University Press, 1998).

Patton, Laurie, 'Traces of Śaunaka: A Literary Assessment', *Journal of the American Academy of Religion* 79/1 (2011): 113–35.

Roebuck, Valerie (trans.), *The Upaniṣads* (London: Penguin Books, 2003).

Sen, Amartya, *The Argumentative Indian: Writings on Indian Culture, History and Identity* (London: Penguin Books, 2005).

Vanita, Ruth, 'The Self Is Not Gendered: Sulabha's Debate with King Janaka', *National Women's Studies Association Journal* 15/2 (2003): 76–93.

Walshe, Maurice (trans.), *The Long Discourses of the Buddha: A Translation of the Dīgha Nikāya* (Boston: Wisdom Publications, 1995).

Index